CONTENTS

Preface v

January 1
February 33
March 65
April 97
May 129
June 161
July 193
August 227
September 259
October 293
November 327
December 361

Index 399

PREFACE

When was the dollar sign invented? When was the first check written? How were industrial giants—like the Medici, Microsoft, Maytag, and MGM—created? How were some of them killed off? Who created the first Wall Street panic? Who said, "A stockbroker is someone who takes all your money and invests it until it's gone," or "A mine is a hole in the ground with a liar standing next to it"? These are just a few of the thousands of milestones, quotes, and stories to be found in *This Day in Business History*, all organized by day of the year.

The first book of its kind, *This Day in Business History* was written for the layman, for the professional, for the student or teacher, for the public speaker, and for anyone else who enjoys rich history, tales of human nature in the marketplace, or pithy insights into commercial adventures. Triumphant lives, hard-driving executives, outrageous scandals, heartbreaking failures, jaw-dropping blunders—these are the meat of business history, from the ancients to Enron, to be found in this book.

Collection of the material essentially began one afternoon about 15 years ago, when I came across a story about Marie Curie, who in 1911 had one Nobel Prize and would soon be awarded another, yet her nomination to the French Academy of Sciences was turned down by its all-male membership. This little-known tale of naked prejudice in the face of outstanding achievement sparked the idea of creating a volume of historic events arranged by day of the year. After publishing writings on various topics in this format, the search for material relating specifically to business, management, and economics began in earnest in 1997. Newspapers, professional journals, biographies, and histories of specific companies or commerce in general have been among the most useful sources.

The hunt for great dates, great quotes, and great stories has been a highly enjoyable experience. I can only hope that the fun and excitement of this project seeps through to the reader.

There were a number of indispensable contributions to this book by others: the support of my family; the hours of skilled, dedicated work of editors Holly McGuire, Charlie Fisher, and Karen Steib; the wisdom and talent of agent Michael Snell; and the world-class performance of the McGraw-Hill organization as a whole. I am indebted to them all.

JANUARY

JANUARY 1

1449   Lorenzo "the Magnificent" de Medici is born in Florence, heir and eventual undertaker to the fabulous Medici banking empire. At its height, under his grandfather Cosimo and his father, Piero "the Gouty," the empire had branches throughout Europe; controlled wars and governments through loans; managed the pope's finances; and had interests in mining, insurance, textiles, real estate, and agriculture. Its demise was a function of its size and of the greatness of Lorenzo in other areas. He devoted too much attention and capital to statesmanship and the arts to be able to oversee commercial interests properly. Poor communication and inadequate supervision of the independent branch managers produced corruption and bankruptcies. The empire had fizzled out by the time of his premature death in 1492.

1895   In Battle Creek, Michigan, C. W. Post creates his first usable batch of Monks Brew, a cereal-based substitute for caffeinated beverages. Later called Postum, it was the foundation of his cereal empire.

1900   "If you're going to make money, you must look money" was a favorite saying of "Diamond" Jim Brady, who on this day records $16,596,863 in advance orders for his employer, Pressed Car Steel Company of New Jersey.

1919   Edsel Ford, 25, becomes the second president of Ford Motor Company; employees are given a 20 percent pay raise.

1939   Bill Hewlett, 25, and Dave Packard, 26, sign the informal agreement that creates the HP partnership, based in a one-car garage on Addison Avenue in Palo Alto, California. This building is now designated "the birthplace of Silicon Valley." A coin toss decided the order of names.

JANUARY 2

1882   The revolutionary Standard Oil Trust agreement is completed and dated. Conceived by Samuel C. T. Dodd and drafted by him and Henry Morrison Flagler, the document transferred the stock and property of more than 40 companies into the hands of nine trustees, headed by John D. Rockefeller. The new entity efficiently controlled 90 percent of America's oil refineries and pipelines. Dodd called his creation a "corporation of corporations"; it was the first example of what is now called a holding company and was the model for trust formation in many other industries. It also led to passage of the Sherman Anti-Trust Act in 1890.

1949   Jack Benny's television show first airs on CBS, stolen from NBC by network founder William S. Paley in one of his many "checkbook raids" on NBC talent.

1992   "We're enjoying sluggish times, and not enjoying them very much." —President George H.W. Bush

JANUARY 3

1800   As refugees from the French Revolution, the du Pont family walks ashore at Newport, Rhode Island. The key figures were Pierre Samuel du Pont de Nemours (60, an economist of international stature) and his two sons, Victor (32, destined for a series of business failures) and Eleuthere Irenee (28, later to establish a Delaware gunpowder factory in 1802 that gave birth to the behemoth DuPont chemical corporation). Thomas Jefferson wrote his friend Pierre a letter of welcome and warning: "The present agonizing state of commerce, and the swarms of speculators in money and in land, would induce me to beseech you to trust no-body."

1871   Margarine is patented by Henry W. Bradley.

1899   The word *automobile* is used for the first time, in a *New York Times* editorial.

1921   Studebaker announces that it is leaving the horse-drawn carriage business. It had been the world's largest carriage maker in the late 1800s. It would now focus on making horseless carriages, the last of which appeared in 1966 in Canada.

1960   Ada Everleigh, ex-madam, dies at 83 in Virginia. Ada and her sister Minna had flourished as entrepreneurs in prostitution. They introduced advertising, illustrated brochures, and deluxe facilities in Chicago's Everleigh Club, America's most famous bordello. They opened a second building in 1902. Ada was responsible for hiring and managing the talent; Minna managed the finances. The backlash against the success and nature of Ada's business had run her out of several cities by the time of her death.

1979   Conrad Nicholson Hilton dies at 91 in Santa Monica, California. Shrewdness, caution, and financial acumen allowed him to build one of the world's most prestigious hotel chains; he started in 1918 with a $5,000 investment in the 40-room Mobley Hotel in Cisco, Texas (he had gone there to buy part interest in a bank, but the slow pace of the negotiations caused him to lose patience and put the money into the hotel). In 1949 Hilton Hotel Corp. gained control of the famed Waldorf-Astoria and in 1954 of the Statler Hotel chain. He started the Carte Blanche credit card company and founded Hilton International, which operated 75 hotels in 45 countries when it was purchased by TWA in 1967. When corporate control passed to son Barron, Conrad's autobiography *Be My Guest* was found next to Gideon's Bible in each of the company's 64,000 rooms.

JANUARY 4

1813   Sir Isaac Pitman, inventor of the modern shorthand system that bears his name, is born in Trowbridge, England. Although an expert and reformer in spelling, Pitman's system was the first based on sound rather than conventional spelling. A huge hit that was adapted to many languages, the system was taken to America by Pitman's brother Benn in 1852. By 1889, 97 percent of U.S. shorthand writers used his system. Queen Victoria knighted Pitman for his contributions to shorthand and commerce.

1896 America's first actors' union is chartered by the American Federation of Labor in New York City. The Actors' National Protective Union later joined with the White Rats and the Actors' Equity Association to form the Associated Actors and Artists of America, which held its first strike in the month it was formed (August 1919).

1926 Nomura Securities opens its doors for business in Osaka and branches in Tokyo, Nagoya, Kobe, and Kyoto, with a total of 84 employees. The first Japanese securities firm with a research department and direct sale of stock to the masses, it became Japan's largest stockbroker by the early 1960s and has long been the crown jewel in the Nomura financial empire. Its first president was Otogo Kataoka, a Christian who detested stock salesmen. But the real force behind Nomura Securities was the Buddhist Tokushichi Nomura II, who kept 98,800 of the 100,000 issued shares for himself and granted Kataoka just 200. Each of the five directors, including his own brother, Motogoro, got the same. Each 200-share stake was worth more than $100 million in 1987.

1996 "Many of the essentials of a fertile, creative environment are anathema to an orderly, well-run organization. In fact, the concept of 'managing research' is an oxymoron." —Nicholas Negroponte, cofounder and director, MIT Media Laboratory, in *Wired*

JANUARY 5

1720 The regent Philippe II, duc d'Orleans, appoints the colorful Scot John Law comptroller general of France. Since 1716 Law's advice and actions had reversed the downward economic spiral wrought by the Sun King, Louis XIV. Law was a national hero. "I myself," Voltaire recalled, "saw him pass through the galleries of the Palais-Royal followed by dukes and peers, marshals of France, bishops of the Church." But the recent prosperity partly rested on confidence in the anticipated riches from the New World that were controlled by Law's Mississippi Company. The bursting of the "Mississippi Bubble" was violent and fast, and by year's end Law and his family had to flee for their lives (see December 14).

1855   "If I had been technically trained, I would have quit," said the inventor of the safety razor, King Camp Gillette, who is born on this day into a family of tinkerers in Fond du Lac, Wisconsin. The Chicago fire of 1871 wiped out the family possessions, forcing King to take to the road as a traveling salesman. One of his employers not only encouraged his inventing, but also planted the idea of producing something disposable (hence creating renewable demand). Gillette had the basic razor design in 1895 but spent the next six years perfecting the blade. His first year in business (1903), his company produced 51 razors and 168 blades. The following year saw something of an increase: 90,000 razors, 12.4 million blades.

1913   Kemmons Wilson, creator of the Holiday Inn motel chain, is born in Osceola, Arkansas. The inspiration for his innovation came during a 1951 family trip from Memphis to Washington, when the price gouging and poor accommodations he encountered made him miserable: "I was seized by an idea: I could build a chain of affordable hotels, stretching from coast to coast. Families could travel cross-country and stay at one of my hotels every night." Kemmons's own career as a builder had gotten off to a rocky start years before, when he put up his first house on the wrong lot.

1914   James Couzens, general manager of the Ford Motor Company, announces a shocking $5.00 minimum daily wage for employees (far better than its competitors). Workers would now be paid $5.00 for eight hours instead of $2.40 for nine. The measures were intimately linked with another recent Ford revolution in manufacturing: the continually moving assembly line, which increased profits so that higher wages could be paid. This innovation also created a need for higher compensation due to the "dehumanizing" effects of the system, which were producing dissatisfaction and higher turnover in the workforce.

1981   The Dow Jones Industrial Average bursts through 1,000, spurred by the "buy aggressively" advice of Joseph Granville in his daily forecast letter. The self-professed guru had a bad feeling about other indicators, however, and the following day caused a stampede in the opposite direction with his assertion, "Sell everything. Market top has been reached." The Dow promptly fell 31 points on a record volume of 92.9 million shares traded.

JANUARY 6

1794   Rebecca Lukens, the first female manager in the steel industry (and possibly in any heavy industry), is born into a liberal and hardworking Quaker family in Coatesville, Pennsylvania. Established by her father and then taken over by her husband, the Brandywine Rolling Mill was nearly bankrupt when it came into Rebecca's hands after her husband died. Leaving the shop supervision to her brother-in-law, her talents in marketing and financial management reestablished solvency and a firm reputation for the company. Renamed the Lukens Steel Company in her honor, it is the oldest U.S. steel manufacturing firm still operating. She died December 10, 1854.

1838   Samuel F. B. Morse publicly demonstrates his electric telegraph for the first time, over three miles of wire strung around the Speedwell Iron Works in Morristown, New Jersey.

1872   The Wall Street buccaneer "Jubilee" Jim Fisk, 37, is fatally shot on the stairway of the Grand Central Hotel in New York City by Edward S. Stokes, a rival in business and romance. Stokes had been indicted that morning for attempting to blackmail Fisk. Fisk's career was as ugly as his end. His most memorable exploits were nearly destroying the Erie Railroad through embezzlement, bribery, and the issuance of fraudulent stock, and causing the nationwide panic of 1869 following his efforts with Jay Gould and others to corner the gold market by inflating its price.

1961   "Polishing the client's apple is no way to improve his advertising. Polishing a good idea is. And polishing. And polishing. And polishing. Until good becomes better. And better becomes best." —Advertisement for the advertising firm Young and Rubicam Inc., in *Printers' Ink*

1980   President Jimmy Carter signs a bill authorizing the largest federal bailout in history, granting $1.2 billion in loans to the Chrysler Corporation. It is a great victory for Lee Iacocca, who lobbied hard for the unprecedented action and then led the company's return to profitability in the coming decade.

2000   The disastrous AOL Time Warner merger is decided over a sumptuous dinner at the northern Virginia home of AOL boss Steve Case. Sometime between the 1990 Chateau Leoville–Las Cases wine and the chocolate mousse, Case and Time Warner CEO Gerald Levin broadly agreed to the deal. By 9:15 the next morning, following discussions at each of the two headquarters, history's largest merger was under way. "At some point," observed one of the assistants, "they had to swallow hard and jump off the cliff together."

2002   AOL Time Warner Inc. announces a one-time accounting write-off of $40 billion to $60 billion to adjust for overall market declines since the merger.

JANUARY 7

1782   Just three months after British general Charles Cornwallis's surrender at Yorktown, the first bank chartered by the U.S. Congress, the Bank of North America, opens its doors for business. Capitalized at $400,000, the bank was the vision of Robert Morris, "the financier of the American Revolution." The seed money came from three main sources: the government, a loan from the French, and Morris's own pockets.

1830   A passenger pays for a railroad ticket for the first time in American history. The cost was 9¢ to ride in a horse-drawn carriage on tracks between Pratt Street and Carrollton Viaduct in Baltimore, Maryland. This was essentially the birth of the Baltimore and Ohio Railroad Company (the B&O).

1872   Shot the previous day, "the Barnum of Wall Street," Jim Fisk, dies at 37. Despite the facts that his career was essentially one long crime spree and that the final shooting was caused in part by a fight over a mistress, Fisk's wife, Lucy, kissed him on his deathbed, murmuring, "He was a good boy."

1927   Transatlantic telephone service begins: Walter Sherman Gifford, president of AT&T in New York City, talks with Sir George Evelyn Murray, secretary of the British General Post Office in London. A three-minute call on the new service cost $75. The day was also the 93rd anniversary (**1834**) of the birth of Philipp Reis, German inventor of the first telephone-like devices. Reis, a teacher, did not see the commercial potential in his models, calling them "philosophical tools" to illustrate the nature of sound.

1996   "In large organizations, middle managers serve the purpose of relaying information up and down—orders down, numbers up. But with the new information technologies and more efficient forms of work, their purpose dwindles." —James Champy, U.S. business executive, in the *New York Times*

2000   A record for the biggest daily trading volume in one company is set when 136,846,600 shares of Lucent Technologies are traded on the New York Stock Exchange.

JANUARY 8

1675   The first commercial corporation in America—the New York Fishing Company—is chartered on this day by the governor and council of New York on behalf of the king of England's brother James, Duke of York, "for settleing a fishery in these parts." Shares in the company sold for £10.

1680   A trust is busted for the first time in America. On December 17, 21 coopers signed a pricing agreement in New York City. The 21 were brought to trial in the colonial council chamber on January 8. Their pact was annulled and the following verdict issued: "They are adjudged guilty, all that have signed the Contract, and are To pay each 50s, & either of them in publick employ to be dismist. The paym't to be to the Church or pious uses."

1825   Inventor of the cotton gin, Eli Whitney dies at 59 in New Haven, Connecticut. Whitney never profited from his seminal invention; rather than manufacture the machines, he and his partner, Phineas

Miller, unwisely decided to set up gins at strategic points and gin the cotton for a royalty. Farmers thought the royalty exorbitant, and the gins were easily duplicated. Whitney concluded, "An invention can be so valuable as to be worthless to the inventor." He went out of the cotton business in 1797 and soon developed his other great commercial contribution: manufacturing with interchangeable parts. He developed this system while fulfilling a government contract to produce muskets from 1797 to 1807.

1835 The United States pays off its national debt for the first time. The country zoomed into a period of prosperity, prices rose, and paper money flowed. Land speculation and wildcat banking flourished. It was the prelude to the panic of 1837, which sent the country into years of economic depression.

1889 Herman Hollerith patents the first electric machine that effectively tabulates numbers from punch cards. It was an important precursor of the modern computer, and through growth and merger, Hollerith's company eventually became the computer superpower IBM.

1914 Thomas J. Watson, Jr., is born in Dayton, Ohio, the same year that his father, Thomas J. Watson, Sr., joined C-T-R, the forerunner of IBM. Both Watsons would rise to lead that firm. Watson Jr. ardently pushed the company to go beyond tabulating machines into the nascent computer industry. Aggressive tactics and heavy outlays for research boosted IBM to dominance in computers; under Watson Jr.'s chairmanship (1956–1971), its stock increased in value by more than $36 billion. He once said, "I look for those sharp, scratchy, harsh, almost unpleasant guys who see and tell you about things as they really are."

1954 "Anybody who has any doubt about the ingenuity or the resourcefulness of a plumber never got a bill from one." —George Meany, president, American Federation of Labor, himself a former plumber

1987 The Dow Jones Industrial Average closes above 2,000 for the first time.

JANUARY 9

1324   Perhaps the single most influential figure in the globalization of world trade, Marco Polo, dies at 70 in the town of his birth, Venice. On his deathbed, he was allegedly asked to retract the "fables" he had told in his famous travelogue, *Il Milione*; his answer was that he barely told half of what he had actually seen.

1837   Robert Augustus Chesebrough is born in London to American parents. At 22 (1859), he was running a small chemical refining business in Brooklyn, New York, when he heard of Drake's discovery of oil in Titusville, Pennsylvania. He visited the site and became intrigued by "rod wax," an unused residue that accumulated on the rods of oil pumps and that workers claimed could heal cuts and burns. Chesebrough refined it in his lab and then used himself as a guinea pig by inflicting scores of cuts, scratches, and burns on his own body to test the efficacy of the salve. He had discovered Vaseline (he took the name from the German *wasser*—"water"—and the Greek *elaion*—"olive oil"). The conglomerate Chesebrough-Ponds Inc. was formed in a 1955 merger with a company founded by another 19th-century chemist, Theron T. Pond. Chesebrough died September 8, 1935.

1958   "Perseverance is the most overrated of traits, if it is unaccompanied by talent; beating your head against a wall is more likely to produce a concussion in the head than a hole in the wall." —Sydney J. Harris, in the *Chicago Daily News*

JANUARY 10

1860   History's first major factory accident occurs: 77 perish when a textile factory collapses in Lawrence, Massachusetts.

1901   At 10:30 A.M., on a small hill several miles south of Beaumont, Texas, three drillers scatter for safety as mud comes gushing out of their 700-foot well. Six tons of piping came shooting out of the hole, then there was calm. "What the hell are we going to do with the damn thing now?" asked one, just as another enormous roar preceded more mud, gas, and then oil. It was the Spindletop oil strike, the first major petroleum discovery in America. Texas became an oil wonderland, oil prices fell, and gasoline became an extremely attractive fuel.

1961   "No one can possibly achieve any real and lasting success or 'get rich' in business by being a conformist." —J. Paul Getty, in the *International Herald Tribune*

JANUARY 11

1759   The first life insurance company in America is incorporated in Philadelphia. The Corporation for the Relief of Poor and Distressed Presbyterian Ministers and of the Poor and Distressed Widows and Children of Presbyterian Ministers issued its first policy on May 22, 1761, to Francis Alison, secretary of the company.

1813   Pineapples are first planted in Hawaii. In the early 19th century, the islands were adopted by the American whaling fleet as its wintering grounds, which led to increasing visitation by merchants, explorers, settlers, and missionaries.

1864   Founder of England's famous Selfridge's department store, Harry Gordon Selfridge is born the son of a small storekeeper in Ripon, Wisconsin. "The customer is always right" was coined by Selfridge, who at 17 began working for the forerunner of the Marshall Field's store in Chicago. After 25 years there, he had accumulated a fortune, which he used to create his own large store on Oxford Street in London. Ingenious promotion and unique interior arrangements made his store an enormous success; personal extravagance spoiled it, eventually forcing the banks to replace him as head of the organization. "The famous store needs no name on the door," he said in happier times.

1937   Violence erupts on the twelfth day of a sit-down strike at the General Motors plant in Flint, Michigan, when police and GM security personnel move in to evict the strikers. At least 24 were injured and buildings were flooded with tear gas, but the workers held the buildings. This first major labor dispute in the U.S. auto industry ended after 44 days (see February 11).

JANUARY 12

1873   Daniel Frank Gerber, Sr., is born in Detroit, Michigan. In 1901, he helped found the Fremont Canning Company (first capitalized at $10,000) to provide a market for local farmers by canning their peas and later their beans and small fruits. The modern baby foods industry began in this modest facility in 1927, after a complaint by Gerber's daughter-in-law about the difficulty she had in straining peas for her newborn daughter. Soon strained peas were the company's biggest seller. At a time when existing baby foods were sold through pharmacies by prescription, with a price of about 35¢ a can, the Gerbers offered their products at 15¢ a can in grocery stores.

1906   The Dow Jones Industrial Average closes above 100 for the first time, in the run-up to the panic of 1907.

1964   Founder of the world's biggest bookstore, Amazon.com, Jeff Bezos is born to a 17-year-old mother and soon-to-be-absent father. At 30, after several corporate positions (including being the youngest vice president at Bankers Trust in New York), he decided to leap out on his own. "I tried to imagine being eighty years old, looking back on my life. I knew that I would hardly regret having missed the 1994 Wall Street bonus. But having missed being part of the Internet boom—that would have really hurt."

1999   William Whyte, the author who defined corporate conformity and warned against its growth in his 1956 classic *The Organization Man*, dies at age 81 in New York City. "He understands that the work-and-thrift ethic of success has grievously declined—except in the rhetoric of top executives," wrote C. Wright Mills in his review of Whyte's seminal bestseller. "[He understands] that the entrepreneurial scramble to success has been largely replaced by the organizational crawl." Explaining organization men, Whyte wrote, "They are the ones of our middle class who have left home, spiritually as well as physically, to take the vows of organizational life, and it is they who are the mind and soul of our great self-perpetuating institutions."

2003   Steve Case announces his resignation from AOL, in the wake of its disastrous merger with Time Warner in 2000. AOL stock closed at $15.03 the next day, down from $73.75 on the day before the merger was announced.

JANUARY 13

1404   The English parliament passes the Act of Multipliers, which prohibits alchemy (turning base metals into gold)—despite the fact that no one ever succeeded at it.

1840   "When tillage begins, other arts follow. The farmers therefore are the founders of human civilization." —Daniel Webster, in *Remarks on Agriculture*

1885   Alfred Carl Fuller is born in Wellsford, Nova Scotia. In 1906, after several jobs, Fuller organized the Capital Brush Company in Hartford, Connecticut, in a shed he rented for $11 a month. He employed one assistant. By 1910, he had 25 door-to-door salesmen and six factory workers; at this point he changed the firm's name to the Fuller Brush Company, which eventually spread nationwide and offered various products, with sales exceeding $130 million. His door-to-door salesmen became such a part of American folklore that in Walt Disney's *Three Little Pigs*, the wolf disguised himself as a Fuller Brush Man. Fuller died December 4, 1973.

2000   "We're a me-me-me generation. We're borrowing the savings of every nation in the world. We're . . . piling up a big tab. Now, I may think we're too big to have a run on us. You may think that. But it's possible that God does not." —Paul Samuelson, U.S. economist and winner of the 1970 Nobel Prize in Economics, on *Online NewsHour*

2001   Jack Grubman (the highest paid stock analyst in history, who earned over $20 million annually with Salomon Smith Barney) spends this Saturday in chatty, intimate e-mail correspondence with Carol Cutler, an analyst with the Government of Singapore Investment Corporation, which had invested heavily in telecommunications stock recommended by Salomon Smith Barney. At 5:18 P.M. Grubman blatantly admitted upgrading his recommendation of AT&T stock in November 1999 not because of improved value, but because Citigroup chairman Sandy Weill had asked him to. (Elevation in AT&T would help Weill in a boardroom power struggle he was waging.) Grubman's profit for his chicanery? "I used Sandy to get my kids in 92nd Street Y preschool . . ."

JANUARY 14

1826 The distinguished but short-sighted communications executive William Orton is born on a farm near Cuba, New York. He was commissioner of the Internal Revenue Service and president of Western Union, where in 1876 he was approached by Gardiner Hubbard of the Bell Telephone company and offered all of Alexander Graham Bell's telephone patents for $100,000. Orton refused with the snide question, "What use could this company make of an electrical toy?"

1845 Hawaii's Kamehameha III grants a small parcel of land at the Mauna Kea volcano to the Massachusetts-born kamaaini ("long-term resident") John Palmer Parker, who had jumped ship and settled in the islands at age 19. Parker married a granddaughter of Kamehameha 17 years later and served the royal family by managing its cattle. He parlayed his stake into the Parker Ranch, 227,000 acres and more than 50,000 head of Herefords—the largest privately owned ranch in the world.

1896 At 14, Carlo Ponzi emigrates from Italy to the United States. By 1920 he was declared a "financial wizard," offering 50 percent return on investment in 45 days and 100 percent in 90 days through international trade in postal coupons. His Securities and Exchange Co. at 27 School Street in Boston took in an estimated $15 million ($200,000 a day at its peak) before he was stopped and deported back to Italy. In Italy he was given a high position in the financial sector, but he embezzled funds and fled to Brazil. He died in 1949. His plan of paying investors with other investors' money instead of profits is now generically called a Ponzi scheme.

1949 The Justice Department files an antitrust suit against AT&T, seeking divestiture of its manufacturing subsidiary Western Electric. As *Fortune* described the presuit situation, AT&T "existed in a state possibly best described in terms of Zen: it was its own supplier and its own market to a degree almost unique." The suit was finally settled in 1956; AT&T was allowed to keep Western Electric in exchange for a promise to confine new business development to regulated markets.

1949 The first African American to head a Fortune 500 company, Franklin D. Raines, is born in Seattle, one of seven children born to parents who did not finish high school. His father, Delno, a city custodian, dug the foundation for the family home by hand; he paid $1,000 for a house that was about to be demolished and built a new home with the lumber. Franklin made history in 1999 when he became CEO of Fannie Mae.

2000 The Dow Jones Industrial Average hits its all-time peak: 11,722.98.

JANUARY 15

1609 History's first regular newspaper, *Aviso Relation oder Zeitung*, begins publication at Wolfenbuttel in Lower Saxony under the leadership of Julius Adolph von Sohne.

1794 "The laws of probability, so true in general, so fallacious in particular," said Edward Gibbon, in *Autobiography*. On this day Gibbon announces that he thinks himself "good for ten, twelve, or perhaps twenty years" more of life, falls ill that night, and dies the next day at 56.

1870 The great executive Pierre Samuel du Pont—who was a key designer of the reorganization and fantastic growth of both the explosives/chemical company DuPont and the automobile company General Motors—is born in New Castle County, Delaware, great-grandson of the founder of the family in America for whom he was named.

1943   The world's largest office building, the Pentagon, is completed at Arlington, Virginia. Designed by George Edwin Bergstrom of Los Angeles, the $83 million, five-story, five-sided structure has 6.5 million square feet of floor space, 17 miles of corridors, and 7,748 windows. It covers 34 acres and has a different color scheme on each floor.

1953   The nominee for secretary of defense, Charles E. Wilson (president of General Motors), says he sees no reason to sell his GM stock upon taking the cabinet post. He then uttered this famous—and frequently misquoted—explanation during closed Senate hearings: "I cannot conceive [of a conflict of interest] because for years I thought that what was good for our country was good for General Motors, and vice versa. The difference did not exist. Our company is too big. It goes with the welfare of the country."

1992   Tim Berners-Lee launches the first web browser on the Internet. Two years earlier he had invented the World Wide Web. "The search button on the browser no longer provides an objective search, but a commercial one," he observed in 1999.

JANUARY 16

1853   Andre Michelin is born in Paris, six years before brother Edouard. The Michelins established their bicycle tire company in 1888, then went on to become the first to use demountable pneumatic tires on automobiles and the first to market them successfully. The company also introduced the world's first radial tires in 1948; by then it was Europe's largest tire firm.

1908   Inventor R. L. Lynch reports to Washington newspapers his experimental demonstration of wrapping bread when it is taken from the oven, thus preventing contamination during distribution to customers. Local bread makers still adamantly opposed wrapping, insisting that it degraded taste and digestibility. A government chemist then tested Lynch's method extensively using various papers and found the bread as good or even better after 24 hours than the unwrapped bread and equal in condition to a freshly baked loaf. Bakers still opposed wrapping.

1951   As postwar industry and stock markets are really beginning to heat up, the Federal Reserve Board raises stock-purchase margin requirements from 50 percent to 75 percent (the percent of a purchase that must be paid for immediately without borrowing from the broker). The aim was to limit credit expansion.

1961   "Creativity is our single product. And heaven help the agency management that does not recognize that fact of life. They may wind up as unemployed as Zeppelin pilots." —Ernest A. Jones, president, MacManus, John & Adams, Inc., in *Advertising Age*

2002   The board of Tyco International Ltd. meets for the first time in the luxurious office building that CEO Dennis Kozlowski has built with company money in Boca Raton, Florida. Other board members had neither seen nor directly approved the facilities. There was a fitness center, executive dining facilities, and a palm-lined driveway. "It was ridiculous," said one upset director. "It didn't look like an office. It looked like a luxury hotel." When Lord Ashcroft greeted Kozlowski, he said, "Dennis, you've been a naughty boy."

JANUARY 17

1465   Johannes Gensfleisch zur Laden Gutenberg is granted a civil pension for services to Mainz, Germany, largely because of the printing industry that had sprung up around his invention of printing presses there. The grant consisted of a tax-free annual allowance of cloth, grain, and wine. Gutenberg was in his 70s, partially or totally blind, and financially ruined. He died three years later.

1867   "Take no more freight from the New York Central," Cornelius Vanderbilt orders the managers of his Hudson River Railroad. After months of unsatisfactory negotiations to gain either outright control of the Central or at least assured access to the freight and passengers that it brought to Albany from the west, Vanderbilt decided to beat down the Central. His order causes the railroad's freight to pile up in Albany, great discomfort in the middle of winter for its passengers wanting to get to New York City, and a sharp drop in the value of its stock. Within days, the Central agrees to a settlement, and by December Vanderbilt controlled the entire company. Legislators were troubled by Vanderbilt's tactics and power; at a hearing he was asked why he did not continue to negotiate. He replied, "I did not have the time. I went home. Life is not a bit too short for me, and I like to play whist. I will not permit any business to come in and interfere with that."

1925   "The chief business of the American people is business," says President Calvin Coolidge in a speech in Washington, D.C., to the Society of American Newspaper Editors. This sentence is often cited as the sum of Coolidge's philosophy. However, in the same speech he also said, "It is only those who do not understand our people who believe that our national life is entirely absorbed by material motives. . . . The chief ideal of the American people is idealism. I cannot repeat too often that America is a nation of idealists."

1934   Self-educated engineer Ferdinand Porsche sends his design for the Volkswagen ("people's car") to Adolf Hitler. The two met secretly in May in Berlin's Kaiserhof Hotel, where automobile history was made in about 15 minutes. Hitler directed that the car be air cooled; have four seats; and for the sake of streamlining, "should look like a beetle."

1936   A famous phrase in economics—"guns or butter"—is coined when propaganda minister Joseph Goebbels tells the German nation during a speech in Berlin, "We can do without butter, but despite all our love of peace, not without arms. One cannot shoot with butter but with guns . . ."

1949   The first Volkswagen Beetle arrives in the United States from Germany.

1961   A famous phrase in economics—"military-industrial complex"—is coined. President Dwight D. Eisenhower, in his farewell address, warned, "In the councils of government we must guard against the acquisition of unwarranted influence, whether sought or unsought, by the military-industrial complex. The potential for the disastrous rise of misplaced power exists and will persist."

JANUARY 18

1293   The most famous constitutional act of the Republic of Florence, the Ordinances of Justice, formally establishes the dominance of the guilds and merchants (the *popolo*) in government, placing strict regulations on the behavior and rights of the previously dominant nobles (magnates). True power in Florence resided in the hands of the wealthiest guilds until the advent of the Medici in 1434.

1841   "What the banker sighs for, the meanest clown may have—leisure and a quiet mind." —Henry David Thoreau

1854   The first person ever to receive a telephone call—Thomas A. Watson, who was Alexander Graham Bell's assistant and later became an important shipbuilder—is born in Salem, Massachusetts.

1861   Pioneering inventor of lace-making machinery John Heathcoat dies at 77 in Tiverton, England. Heathcoat patented the most expensive, complex textile machine in existence in 1809 and built a mill at Loughborough with partner Charles Lacy. Luddites (organized bands of English craftsmen who rioted against the machinery that was replacing them) invaded the plant in 1816 and destroyed 55 lace frames. Heathcoat then established a new mill with improved machines at Tiverton, where he continued to work on other inventions, including ribbon makers and methods to wind raw silk from cocoons.

1978   The anthem of frustrated workers, "Take This Job and Shove It" by Johnny Paycheck, hits number 1 on the Billboard charts.

JANUARY 19

1736   One of the founders of the Industrial Revolution, James Watt, is born in Greenock, Scotland. He made steam engines much more efficient and powerful, and thus finally practical for transportation and manufacturing. He also invented the pressure gauge; coined the term *horsepower*, and created the "centrifugal governor," the first feedback device in which the output of a machine controlled its operation ("the germ of automation," according to Isaac Asimov).

1791   "Those who have been once intoxicated with power and have derived any kind of emolument from it, even though but for one year, never can willingly abandon it. They may be distressed in the midst of all their power; but they will never look to anything but power for their relief." —Edmund Burke, in a letter to a member of the British National Assembly

1918   John H. Johnson, black publisher and entrepreneur, is born in Arkansas City, Arkansas, into the family of a sawmill worker (see November 1).

1971   "Power is the ultimate aphrodisiac." —Henry Kissinger, in the *New York Times*

1976   The New York Stock Exchange finally replaces the stock ticker and printer system with a computerized system. The speed of reporting trades immediately jumps from about 900 characters per minute to 36,000.

JANUARY 20

1503   An office is established in Seville, Spain, to supervise trade with the New World and, in particular, to oversee the expenses of Columbus, who on this day is in the area of Panama on his fourth and final voyage. Slaves, rather than the gold that the Spaniards craved, were the main source of immediate return on investment in the expeditions.

1870   Woodhull, Claflin & Co. opens its doors on Wall Street. It was the first stock brokerage in the United States (and probably in the world) run solely by women. It proved highly successful, due partly to the shrewdness of its proprietors, sisters Victoria Claflin Woodhull, 31, and Tennessee Celeste Claflin, 24; partly to their showmanship background (the family ran a traveling medicine and fortune-telling show); and partly to the sponsorship of Cornelius Vanderbilt. The ladies used their profits to establish a woman's rights and reform magazine, *Woodhull and Claflin's Weekly*.

1905   The Supreme Court orders dissolution of the Beef Trust in *Swift v. United States.* The verdict only caused a reorganization of the collusion between the Swift, Armour, Wilson, and Cudahy meatpacking companies. Public hatred of entrenched wealth and the development of monopolistic trusts in various industries was strong at this time. In 1900 Eddie Cudahy, heir to one of the Beef Trust families, was kidnapped by Pat Crowe, who ransomed him for $25,000. Crowe's guilt was clear. "I want to start right by confessing in plain English that I was guilty of the kidnapping," he wrote. Yet a jury found him innocent, apparently thinking his crime no worse than that of his victim.

1937   "We have always known that heedless self-interest was bad morals; we know now that it is bad economics." —Franklin D. Roosevelt, in his second inaugural address

1975   "Our banking system grew by accident; and whenever something happens by accident, it becomes a religion." —Walter B. Wriston, renowned CEO of Citibank, in *BusinessWeek*

JANUARY 21

1720   Air is first blown into the famous South Sea Bubble. Chancellor of the Exchequer Sir John Aislabie announces to the British parliament a new proposal whereby most of the enormous, war-inflated national debt would be assumed by the South Sea Company (founded largely on speculation in South American slave trade). In return, South Sea would be granted various trade monopolies, would be paid some interest on the debt, and would be allowed to pay off the debt with its own stock. South Sea would essentially be permitted to issue as much stock as it wanted and would be able to set its issuing value. The higher the market price rose, the richer the directors and their cronies would become. Aislabie did not mention the bribes paid to him and other ministers. The scheme was accepted (see April 7), and the stock price rose steadily from £128 in January, to £187 in February, to a criminally manipulated high of £1,050 in August. Then the bubble burst; the market collapsed in September, with prices scraping £100 in December. Investors, lenders, and public careers also collapsed.

1853   The first successful envelope-folding machine is patented. Dr. Russell L. Hawes of Worcester, Massachusetts, received U.S. Patent 9812 for the device, which allowed three workers to produce over 2,000 envelopes in an hour.

1905   Christian Dior—the couturier who not only changed the look of women's clothes, but also moved the center of the fashion industry from New York back to Paris—is born in Montecatini, Italy. Dior first trained to be a diplomat, but travel exposed him to his own penchant for the arts. The Great Depression forced him to begin illustrating fashions for the weekly French magazine *Figaro Illustre*. His rise as a designer went stratospheric in 1947 when he began a partnership with the French cotton/textile magnate Marcel Boussac.

JANUARY 22

1719   William Paterson, founder of the Bank of England in 1694, dies at 60 in Dumfries, Scotland. The Bank of England was the first central bank in modern history; its initial subscribers agreed to finance the war of King William III against France's Louis XIV in return for the right to make loans to others with newly issued notes backed by the king's promise to pay. Paterson quit within a year over a policy disagreement and began organizing a rival bank in London. When this fell through, he organized a colonizing expedition to the Isthmus of Panama, which he correctly saw as a strategic location (and would "thus hold the key of the commerce of the world"). He lost his fortune, his wife, and his child on the trip; he barely escaped with his own life.

1895   The nation's first union of manufacturers from diversified industries, the National Association of Manufacturers of the United States, is organized at a convention in Cincinnati, Ohio. The colorful, controversial Thomas P. Dolan was elected its first president.

1903   The United States gains "the key of the commerce of the world" (see above) with the signing of the Hay-Herran Treaty with Colombia for exclusive rights to build and operate a canal across the Isthmus of Panama. When the government of Colombia reconsidered the treaty terms in August, the Americans used their military to enforce a declaration of independence, with whom the United States immediately signed a new treaty.

1910   Harold S. Geneen is born in Bournemouth, England, son of a Russian-born concert manager who moved his family to the United States the following year. Geneen had some orchestrations of his own in his future. He was famous for tight, aggressive management; for working 19 hours a day; and for creating the world's largest conglomerate out of ITT, which was a loosely controlled, stagnating telecommunications network when he accepted its presidency in 1959. He acquired some 200 companies scattered throughout the world in a rainbow of industries, boosting ITT revenues from $765 million to over $8.5 billion in a decade. In *The Synergy Myth*, published the year of his death (1997), he wrote about management consulting concepts: "Like mushrooms, they look enticing, but their nutritional value can be suspect. Some are even poisonous."

2002   A dramatic demonstration of the changing nature of retail shopping occurs: once-great superstore Kmart declares bankruptcy, while newcomer e-tailer Amazon.com announces its first-ever quarterly profit.

JANUARY 23

1766   Typefounder and book developer William Caslon dies at 74 in London. His ability to design and cut exquisite typefaces led to an international reputation, commissions, and financial backing while he was still a young man. His name lives on in the typeface that bears his name, and his work helped to modernize the book, making it a separate creation rather than a printed imitation of the old hand-produced manuscript.

1914   "The chain system you have is a *slave driver*!" writes the wife of one worker to Henry Ford about his now-revered innovation to manufacturing, the moving assembly line. "*My God!* My husband has come home & thrown himself down & won't eat his supper—so done out!

Can't it be remedied? . . . That $5 a day is a blessing—a bigger one than you know but *oh* they earn it."

2003   IBM's new CEO Samuel J. Palmisano e-mails 300 senior managers, announcing the end of the company's 92-year-old executive management committee (an elite body that used to meet once a month to decide strategy). Palmisano felt it was too slow and too detached and was replacing its function with three teams from all parts of the organization. Five days later Palmisano (who had one year on the job) asked the board to cut his 2003 bonus and set the money aside in a pool to be shared by some 20 top executives based on their performance as a team.

JANUARY 24

1833   Investment banker Joseph William Drexel is born in Philadelphia. Both he and younger brother, Anthony Joseph Drexel, entered their father's successful banking business. Their father's death in 1863 coincided with a major turning point in the national banking system and in the American economy, bringing forth a flood of investment securities in public debt, railroads, mining, large factories, and urban real estate. The brothers went with the flood, transforming their firm into one of the country's largest investment banking houses and establishing a solid funding network between New York, Philadelphia, and Europe.

1860   French inventor Etienne Lenoir patents the first commercially successful internal combustion engine (the forerunner of the one found in virtually every automobile today). By 1865, 400 of his engines were in use in France and another 1,000 in Britain, mainly used in pumping and printing. In 1862 Lenoir built the first car with an internal combustion engine, which covered a six-mile course in two to three hours.

1899   "The man who makes no mistakes does not usually make anything." —Edward John Phelps, in a speech at Mansion House, London

1948   The "first true computer," the IBM SSEC (selective sequence electronic calculator) is introduced. This machine held 13,500 vacuum tubes and 21,000 electronic relays and was the first device capable of handling both data and instructions.

1984   The first Macintosh personal computer is introduced by Apple, on the 36th anniversary of the SSEC's introduction.

1996   Alcohol and firearms make a potent marketing combination. *ITAR-Tass* reports on this day that Kalashnikov Vodka will soon hit the shelves in various European cities. Mikhail Kalashnikov, whose AK-47 is the world's most deadly and most popular assault rifle, approved the use of his name on vodka produced by a Siberian distillery.

JANUARY 25

1787   Some 1,200 small farmers led by Revolutionary War veteran Daniel Shays storm the federal arsenal at Springfield, Massachusetts, seeking weapons. They were easily repulsed, and Shays's Rebellion dissolved completely the following month, but state laws were soon passed to ease the condition of the debt-ridden farmers who were being squeezed mercilessly on three sides—by a depressed economy; by a legislature anxious to pay off its war debt quickly with sharp taxes that mostly hit those of moderate income (it was estimated that farmers were paying a third of their income in taxes); and by aggressive, wealthy, out-of-town creditors who demanded foreclosures and imprisonment.

1890   In Columbus, Ohio, the United Mine Workers of America is organized as an affiliate of the four-year-old American Federation of Labor.

1940   "A conference is a gathering of important people who, singly, can do nothing but together can decide that nothing can be done." —Fred Allen, in a letter to William McChesney Martin, president of the New York Stock Exchange

1958   Robert R. Young, 60, famous for winning history's first widely publicized shareholder proxy battle in 1954 that gave him control of the New York Central Railroad (see June 14), turns a shotgun on himself in the billiard room of his Palm Beach mansion. Depression in the economy and in his spirit were apparently to blame.

1993   Sears Roebuck announces that it is discontinuing its famous catalog, first published in 1896. It sold everything from groceries to houses to tombstones, and the previous year went out to 14 million customers. Sears also announces closure of 115 "unprofitable" stores at a loss of 50,000 jobs.

JANUARY 26

1695   America's first workmen's compensation agreement is drawn up—by a pirate. Captain William Kidd, with legitimate business headquarters in both London and New York, sets forth the following terms of employment on the *Adventure Galley* of 787 tons burden: one fourth of the booty captured will be divided among the crew. Further, "If any man should Loose a Leg or Arm in ye said service, he should have six hundred pieces of Eight, or six able slaves; if any man should loose a joynt on ye said service, he should have a hundred pieces of eight."

1799   "Banking establishments are more dangerous than standing armies." — President Thomas Jefferson, in a letter to U.S. politician Elbridge Gerry

1921   The cofounder of Sony Corporation, Akio Morita, is born in Nagoya, Japan, into a family that made its fortune in the soy and sake industries. "The Japanese constantly pare down and reduce the complexity of products and ideas to the barest minimum," he wrote. "The influence of Zen and Haiku poetry are often evident in the simplicity and utility of Japanese designs."

1932   "Tell 'em quick and tell 'em often" was the promotional dictum of the colorful William Wrigley, Jr., who dies this day at 70. In 1891, at 30, he was selling soap and baking soda when he got the idea to give away chewing gum as a premium for buying the baking soda. He soon realized he was taking money for the wrong items, and by 1910 Wrigley's Spearmint was the nation's biggest selling gum. Advertising and other promotions were always a big part of William's business strategy; at one point his advertising budget was the largest in the world, and Wrigley's Gum was advertised in 30 languages.

1953   "You can't set a hen in one morning and have chicken salad for lunch." —George Humphrey, secretary of the treasury, on the impossibility of quick economic change, in *Time*

JANUARY 27

1686   Edmond Halley, 29, is elected clerk of London's Royal Society. As the society's first clerk and its first salaried official, one of his duties was to provide interesting observations on a regular basis. A genius at discerning patterns in mountains of numbers, he produced history's first meteorological chart and calculated the orbit of the comet that bears his name. Searching for another topic to investigate, Halley found it in meticulous population records for the city of Breslau, Germany, which were in the archives of the society. From these Halley produced the first true actuarial tables, allowing him to calculate survivorship probabilities and the price of insuring lives at different ages. His publication of the material in 1693 is a milestone in the insurance industry.

1855   Founder of the Quaker Oats Company, Henry P. Crowell is born in Cleveland. He purchased the Quaker Mill at Ravenna, Ohio, in 1881 and was a major innovator in the cereal business. In production, his was the first mill in history "to maintain under one roof operations to grade, clean, hull, cut, package, and ship oatmeal to interstate markets in a continuous process." In marketing, while his older and larger competitors continued the tradition of selling in bulk to wholesalers, Crowell packaged and advertised his brand, Quaker Oats, nationally as a breakfast cereal, a product class that was new to American tastes. He had to overcome an age-old prejudice against the oat (Samuel Johnson had defined oats as "a grain, which in England is generally given to horses, but in Scotland supports the people").

1880   Thomas Edison receives U.S. Patent 223,898 for his electric lightbulb. The effect was profound in human activity patterns in leisure and labor that will no longer be controlled by the sun.

1926   Flickering, indistinct pictures of two ventriloquist dummies move on a screen. Before an audience at London's Royal Institution, a self-employed Scottish engineer named John Logie Baird first demonstrated the wireless transmission of moving visual images, a process he called "television."

JANUARY 28

814   Gifted and enlightened administrator (as well as fierce warrior, who occasionally slaughtered hundreds of prisoners) Charlemagne dies of pleurisy at 70 in Aachen. It is said that his towering figure was buried sitting bolt upright on a throne. Once he had subdued most of Europe, he sought to reform it economically. His programs included standardization of the currency; minimization of taxes; simplification of the weights and measures; and encouragement of trade, education, new technologies, industry, and advanced forms of agriculture.

1957   "I don't think you can spend yourself rich." —George Humphrey, secretary of the treasury, on compensatory spending during business declines

2000   The Human Resources Administration of New York City announces that it will no longer funnel welfare recipients into jobs with the Psychic Network, a 900-number telephone service that offers clairvoyance at $4.99 a minute. To date, the company had hired 15 welfare enrollees, teaching them how to read tarot cards and predict the future.

2003   Kuwait opens the first stock-trading hall for women in the Persian Gulf, providing female traders with their own exchange room on a mezzanine overlooking the main trading floor in Kuwait City. The environment had previously been "extremely uncomfortable" for women, effectively barring them from participation.

JANUARY 29

1834   Workers on the unfinished, underfinanced Chesapeake and Ohio Canal stage a riot after a planned strike is brutally suppressed. President Andrew Jackson ordered Secretary of War Lewis Cass to send in the army, the first time federal troops were used in a U.S. labor conflict.

1840   Henry Huttleston Rogers is born in Mattapoisett, Massachusetts. "We are not in business for our health, but are out for the dollars," he once famously testified at a government investigation of Standard Oil. Rogers made great contributions to Standard Oil and to the industry as a whole. His first big splash was devising the machinery by which naphtha was successfully separated from crude oil, an invention of fundamental importance. Rogers became one of John D. Rockefeller's key lieutenants, conceiving and building the first major oil pipeline. Indeed, he was a key player in all the repressive business practices that made Standard Oil so dominant, earning him the nickname "Hell Hound Rogers." But there was another side to Rogers. Handsome, distinguished, and charming, he saved Mark Twain from financial ruin; financed the education of Helen Keller ("the best friend I ever had . . . the best man I have known," she said), and even charmed Ida Tarbell, renowned for the investigations that toppled Standard, who called him fondly, "as fine a pirate as ever flew his flag in Wall Street." He died May 19, 1907.

1954   "It takes two to make love and two partners to make trade agreements work. Unrequited trade or unrequited exports pay no better than unrequited love." —R. A. Butler, chancellor of the exchequer, comparing affairs of international commerce to affairs of the heart

1958   "Get A Job" by The Silhouettes hits the top of the record charts. On the same day in **1981** Dolly Parton reached that spot with "9 to 5." The former is about the woes of not having a job, the latter is about the woes of having one.

2001   John Hoffmann, head of Salomon Smith Barney's unit on global equity research management, delivers a shocking, damning internal presentation to his colleagues. Of the nearly 1,200 stocks that Salomon researched and rated for its clients, just one was judged "underperform" and not a single one was rated as "sell" at a time when many technology and Internet stocks were plummeting.

JANUARY 30

1882   Sosthenes Behn (president and founder, with his brother Hernand, of the International Telephone and Telegraph Corporation [ITT])

is born in St. Thomas, Virgin Islands. The Behn brothers began largely in extending credit on sugar crops; as a consequence of a crop failure in 1914, they acquired control of the Puerto Rican Telephone Company. Through careful management and vigorous expansion, in a decade their enterprise maintained a presence in 30 countries with assets of $535 million. ITT was organized in 1920 to raise cash for laying cable throughout the Caribbean and other projects; Behn chose the name purposely so that investors would confuse it with Alexander Graham Bell's well-established American Telephone and Telegraph company.

1883   James Ritty and John Birch patent an advanced model of "the incorruptible cashier," the first practical cash register. In the following year the National Cash Register Company was purchased by John Henry Patterson, whose vigor and genius for salesmanship made the struggling enterprise an international success. Patterson added a small bell to the device's operation, giving rise to the expression "ring up a sale."

1942   The power to set prices is given to the federal government for the first time. The Emergency Price Control Act was passed by Congress, giving teeth to the Office of Price Administration, which had been established the previous year by an executive order of Franklin Roosevelt.

1981   "That explanation reminds me of the man on trial for murdering his parents who asked for mercy on the grounds that he was an orphan," writes economist Milton Friedman in the *Wall Street Journal*. He was talking about Federal Reserve Chairman Paul Volcker's explanation for large swings in the prime interest rate (regularly over 20 percent) and monetary supply.

2000   Warner EMI Music, the $20 billion joint venture between Time Warner and EMI, is announced. It was the world's largest record company and boasted a stable of stars that included Madonna, Quincy Jones, Garth Brooks, and the Rolling Stones.

JANUARY 31

1795   The resignation of Alexander Hamilton as America's first secretary of the treasury becomes effective. A fiscal and administrative genius who set the foundation of the U.S. economy, Hamilton's politics and personality frequently angered colleagues. America's second, third, fourth, and fifth presidents were among his enemies.

1890   American Tobacco Company is founded by James Buchanan "Buck" Duke, who creates a colossal trust by merging the nation's five largest cigarette companies. This action ended a celebrated "tobacco war" in which price-cutting and advertising concessions had ruined profits. Capitalized at $25 million, American Tobacco aggressively started to absorb corporations dealing in other forms of tobacco products. The trust was broken up by the Supreme Court in 1911.

1893   The Coca-Cola trademark for "nutrient or tonic beverages" is registered. The now-famous flowing script of the trademark was that of Frank Robinson, the accountant for John Styth Pemberton who first blended the elixir in 1886 in a three-legged iron pot in his backyard. Robinson also thought up the name.

1973   Corecipient of the first Nobel Prize in Economics, Ragnar Frisch, dies at 77 in Oslo. It was Frisch who coined the term *econometrics* for the application of mathematical, statistical, and computer-based methods to problems in economics, an approach that he pioneered. He founded the Econometric Society in 1931 and edited its journal. Specific areas he attacked with his numbers-based tools were trade cycles, macroeconomic stability, and the testing of hypotheses.

1990   Giants grow. During one of its great waves of expansion, Wal-Mart opens 36 new stores on this day, from Arizona to Florida. McDonald's opens its first outlet in the Soviet Union in Moscow's Pushkin Square. Hundreds stood in line in frigid temperatures to spend several days' wages on a single meal. Even now, this store remains one of McDonald's busiest.

FEBRUARY

FEBRUARY 1

1633   The tobacco laws for the English colony in Virginia are codified, limiting tobacco production in order to reduce dependence on a single-crop economy.

1828   Meyer Guggenheim is born the son of a tailor in Langnau, Switzerland. At 19 he immigrated to America where he and his father became peddlers of virtually anything—shoestrings, lace, ribbons, and spices. One of their items was stove polish, for which they profited 2¢ a can; Meyer was soon producing his own and making a profit of 8¢. He went into coffee production, then speculated successfully in clothing and foodstuffs during the Civil War. He then went into lye production and sold his company for $150,000, which he put into railroad stocks, which he sold to Jay Gould for $300,000 more than he'd paid. He then went into the importing of European laces and embroideries and began bringing his seven sons into his business. This was all before the Guggenheims went into the industry that made them famous, very rich, and world dominant: mining.

1898   History's first automobile insurance policy is issued by the Travelers Insurance Company of Hartford, Connecticut, to Dr. Truman J. Martin of Buffalo, New York. The premium was $11.25, covering a liability up to $10,000, to protect Dr. Martin from possible lawsuits brought by owners of horses frightened by the sight and noise of his car.

1960   Twenty-nine U.S. oil companies go on trial in a federal district court in Tulsa, Oklahoma, charged with conspiring to raise and fix the prices of crude oil and gasoline. All were acquitted several weeks later, with Judge Royce H. Savage finding, "The evidence does not rise above the level of suspicion."

1963   "There is one difference between a tax collector and a taxidermist—the taxidermist leaves the hide." —Mortimer Caplan, director, Internal Revenue Service, in *Time*

FEBRUARY 2

1865   John D. Rockefeller buys out his partner in his first oil business. Rockefeller, 25, paid $72,500 to the fractious Maurice Clark and handed over his half of their commodities business in return for full ownership of their Cleveland oil refinery. Rockefeller later said, "I had worn out the knees of my pants" begging bankers for the loan of the cash.

1870   Three news agencies—Reuters of England, Havas of France, and Wolff of Germany—sign the first in a series of press treaties whereby they divide up the world among themselves and establish a monopoly on world press services for many years.

1942   Barry Diller is born in San Francisco. Blessed with a rare combination of both creative and managerial talent, Diller rose rapidly to leadership of ABC, then Paramount, then Twentieth Century Fox, which he built with Rupert Murdoch into a successful fourth television network. To the shock of many, he abruptly quit Fox in 1992 ("It's not mine" was his simple explanation) to pursue domination of Internet commerce. "Everyone thinks 'Hollywood vs. this?'" said Diller. "Hollywood is mostly a pain in the ass."

1981   A remarkable streak ends. Every year since 1921—through various wars, the Great Depression, and constant technological and competitive challenges—General Motors had reported an annual profit. That streak ended today, with the announcement of a loss of $763 million ($2.65 per share) for 1980. When the streak began in 1921 (at the start of GM's rise to become the world's largest corporation), the company was just one of 86 automakers; it comprised a collection of scattered, sometimes feuding and badly coordinated companies, and it was just emerging from insolvency under the leadership of William Crapo Durant, who had been forced out of his own company for the second time in 1920.

FEBRUARY 3

1637   Holland's tulip market suddenly begins to crash. After years of "tulipmania" speculation that had driven prices to inexplicable heights, prices fell to near-nothing in a matter of days. Just weeks before, one collector had paid 1,000 pounds of cheese, 4 oxen, 8 pigs, 12 sheep, a bed, and a suit of clothes for a single bulb of the Viceroy tulip.

1690   The British colony of Massachusetts establishes a provincial bank, which soon prints the first paper money in the New World. Issued in denominations of 2 shillings to £5, the notes' purpose was to quell the dissatisfaction of unpaid soldiers who had unsuccessfully attacked Quebec expecting that they would be paid in plunder from that city. Other colonies saw how easy it was to print money and followed suit. But the system was abused, and by 1780 for every £1 of silver there were £40 of notes in circulation. A pair of shoes in Virginia cost about $5,000.

1815   The first commercial cheese factory is established in Switzerland.

1826   "No real Englishman in his secret soul was ever sorry for the death of a political economist" was one of the observations of Walter Bagehot, the political economist born on this day in Langport, England. Renowned as the editor of the *Economist* (from 1860 until his death on March 24, 1877) who made it the world's leading business journal for a century, Bagehot made original contributions in various social sciences; his own political aspirations were ruined by his lack of ability as a public speaker. "Had I command of the culture of men," wrote President Woodrow Wilson, "I should wish to raise up for the instruction and stimulation of my nation more than one sane, sagacious, critic of men and affairs like Walter Bagehot."

1975   The president of United Brands (aka United Fruit Company), ex-rabbinical student Eli M. Black, smashes the window of his office on the 44th floor of New York's Pan Am Building and throws his briefcase and then himself through it. His conglomerate was in financial trouble, his executives were plotting a coup, and his role in illegal bribes to foreign governments would soon come to light.

1995   IBM drops its ironclad dress code in favor of casual wear. Word spread through watercooler chat at the Armonk, New York, headquarters that the standard starched white shirt, dark suit, and tie would no longer be required, culminating a trend begun in 1993 when Louis V. Gerstner, Jr., took over as chairman and began wearing blue shirts. Retired executive Francis Rodgers said in his memoirs that the old code, though unwritten, was "as effective as if it were engraved in steel—or if it had a loaded gun behind it."

FEBRUARY 4

211   "Make your soldiers rich and do not bother with anything else" was the advice of Emperor Septimus Severus to his sons, Geta and Caracalla. Septimus died on this day at 65 in York, England, the last Roman emperor for 80 years to die in his bed. Caracalla soon established the tenor of his tenure by having his brother murdered in his mother's arms. Besides treachery, cruelty, and mass killing (some 20,000 of Geta's supporters), Caracalla is famous for the huge Baths of Caracalla and for his tax policies. He was very generous to his soldiers: in the wake of Geta's assassination, he gave the military a sum equal to everything Septimus had gathered in all the treasuries. Anxious to raise more revenue, he doubled the inheritance tax to 10 percent. Noting that the tax applied only to citizens of Rome, Caracalla extended the franchise of citizenship to all free male adults in the empire in an edict of 212, thereby immediately expanding his tax base.

1848   Advertising pioneer Francis Wayland Ayer is born in Lee, Massachusetts. Ayer developed advertising practices we now take for granted: the advertising agency that works for a client advertiser rather than a newspaper or other ad medium; a catalog of newspapers, their circulation, and their ad rates (his *The American Newspaper Annual* was begun in 1880); and a national ad campaign to establish brand identity, involving coordinated packaging, name, and trademark (for Uneeda Biscuits in 1899).

1941   "The slipperiest substance of earth," Teflon, is patented by Dr. Roy Plunkett, the DuPont chemist who accidentally discovered it (see April 6).

1971   Rolls-Royce, Ltd. declares bankruptcy, having lost huge sums developing a jet engine for the first Lockheed Tri-Star Airbus. The collapse threatens jobs and whole companies in the defense, automotive, and aerospace industries, and eventually both the British and American governments provide loan assistance.

1985   Dennis B. Levine begins work as an investment banker at the New York offices of Drexel Burnham Lambert Inc. He was immediately assigned to Drexel's first foray into the world of junk bond–backed hostile takeovers, a plan by Coastal Corporation to acquire American Natural Resources Co. (ANR). Ten days later he committed his first insider-trading fraud, ordering $7 million worth of ANR stock through a third party in Switzerland. Levine was the first in the "greed is good" gang of Michael Milken and Ivan Boesky to be investigated and arrested in May 1986.

FEBRUARY 5

1750   "Dispatch is the soul of business, and nothing contributes more to Dispatch than Method." —Lord Chesterfield, English statesman and diplomat, in a letter to his illegitimate son, Philip Stanhope

1850   The first adding machine to employ depressible keys is patented (U.S. Patent 7,074), by Du Bois D. Parmelee of New Paltz, New York. The device was a failure, being neither practical nor widely used, but the name Parmelee coined for it has become generic and immortal: the calculator.

1878   Andre-Gustave Citroën, the engineer and industrialist who introduced Henry Ford's methods to the European automobile industry, is born in Paris. Citroën made his first splash in the early 1900s when his management helped the Mors firm increase its production from 125 to 1,200 cars per year. At the outbreak of World War I, he convinced the French army to mass-produce munitions; the factory he designed became his auto plant after the war. He lost control of his company during the Great Depression, but his name lives on in automobiles all over Europe. He died July 3, 1935.

1991   Publishing magnate James L. Knight dies at 82 in Santa Monica, California. In 1931 Knight quit college to begin working under the business manager of the *Akron Beacon Journal* in Ohio; the experience proved invaluable when he and younger brother John inherited the debt-ridden newspaper two years later. Knight's financial acumen produced a series of successful media acquisitions, culminating in the 1974 merger with Ridder Publications to form Knight-Ridder Inc.

1996   "Don't study the idea to death with experts and committees. Get on with it and see if it works." —Kenneth Iverson, U.S. industrialist/chairman and CEO of Nucor Corporation

1999   At a joint news conference in Washington, Commerce Secretary William Daley and chairman of the Federal Trade Commission Robert Pitofsky announce that the federal government will begin tracking sales on the Internet, calling it "a major indicator of the nation's economic health."

FEBRUARY 6

1659   The earliest known check is written, on a British bank. It would be another 60 years before printed checks as they're known today would be issued. Around 1722 a private London firm, Mssrs. Child & Co., gave customers printed forms to use.

1807   Hiram Sibley is born in North Adams, Massachusetts. Educated in a village school, his first employment was as a shoemaker's apprentice. By his mid-30s he had made a small fortune by starting and selling off several businesses when he met Samuel F. B. Morse in Washington and helped get congressional backing for the construction of the first telegraph line in 1844. In 1851 he organized the New York and Mississippi Valley Printing Telegraph Company, which bought 11 small lines north of the Ohio River. In 1856 the company was renamed the Western Union Telegraph Company, with Sibley as its first president. Under his leadership the first transcontinental telegraph line was built in 1861. By 1865 he was on his way to ringing the globe in telegraph wire when his health forced him into semiretirement, after which he pursued interests in the seed and nursery business and in railroad stocks. He died, the largest single owner of improved land in the United States, on July 12, 1888.

1882   Western Electric wins the contract to produce telephones for the Bell Company, which later acquires the firm, forming the colossus AT&T.

1911   Luxury automaker Rolls-Royce, Ltd. adopts the "Spirit of Ecstasy" mascot, the silver-winged hood ornament that became the company's symbol (some called it a "symbol of excess").

1934   Paris erupts in rioting over the "Stavisky affair." The violence continued until February 9 and was followed by a general strike. Russian-born promoter Serge Stavisky committed suicide in January amid allegations that for years he had been issuing fraudulent bonds under the protection of corrupt ministers and deputies. This and other schemes cost French citizens $40 million and the collapse of the government of Premier Camille Chautemps.

1997   A marriage shocks Wall Street and shatters the universe of investment banking. In a crowded New York auditorium three grinning executives (Richard Fisher and John Mack of Morgan Stanley and Philip Purcell of Dean Witter Discover) hold up their brand-new Discover credit cards, announcing their secret $21 billion merger. It was the first time that an investment-banking powerhouse (Morgan Stanley) had meshed with retail financial services (commercial banking, insurance, credit cards, small stock and bond accounts, and so on). "Class Meets Mass" was the *BusinessWeek* summary of the deal, which Wall Street loved; within weeks the market price of both stocks increased 25 percent.

FEBRUARY 7

1771   "The greater the power, the more dangerous the abuse." —Edmund Burke, British statesman, in a speech to the House of Commons

1804   John Deere is born in Rutland, Vermont. A wandering black-smith until he reached Grand Detour, Illinois, at age 33, Deere discovered that plows brought from the East worked poorly, often clogging up in Midwestern soil. From his invention of the self-cleaning steel plow, to a series of improvements and ever-increasing plow sales, to the establishment of a first-class, ever-developing organization in Moline, Illinois (where John moved in 1847 after selling out to his partner), Deere and Company has become America's, if not the world's, largest manufacturer of farm equipment. Its reputation as a great company was secured during the Great Depression, when it continued to advance credit to its customers on its most expensive equipment, even though it often took years to collect on debts that were written off in the mid-1930s. This kindness wrought repeat business from successive generations.

1935   The classic game of greed and real estate, Monopoly, is mass marketed for the first time by the Massachusetts firm Parker Brothers. They had rejected the game the year before, but successful sales in Wanamaker's department store in Philadelphia convinced them to pick it up.

2002   This day in the history of scandalized businessmen: CEO Bernard Ebbers of soon-to-be-bankrupt WorldCom tells analysts, "To question WorldCom's viability is utter nonsense. I highly recommend everyone step back and focus on reality rather than the fear factor." Elsewhere today in sworn testimony to a House subcommittee, Enron mastermind Jeffrey K. Skilling confides, "On the day I left, I absolutely and unequivocally thought the company was in good shape."

FEBRUARY 8

1835   Cyrus Hall McCormick's closest business associate, his wife, Nettie Fowler McCormick, is born in Brownsville, New York, to a dry goods merchant. She met McCormick in a Chicago church at 22 (he was 49), and they married the next year. Blessed with a sharp business sense and firm grasp of the endless details of manufacturing, she was his private secretary, helped formulate company policies, suggested economies that were introduced to the harvester plant, helped expand the business in Europe, and had seven children. When the Chicago fire of 1871 destroyed Cyrus's factory and he wanted to give up the business, it was Nettie who convinced him to rebuild. Upon his death in 1884 she became the effective leader of the company, overhauling corporate structure and pressing for industry consolidation that eventually produced the behemoth International Harvester Company in 1902. She died July 5, 1923.

1883   "It was not enough to produce satisfactory soap, it was also necessary to induce people to wash," wrote banker/lawyer/government minister/sociologist/economist Joseph Schumpeter (born this day in Triesch, Czechoslovakia) in 1939 about what makes businesses successful. He was known for his theories and writings on capitalist history, business cycles, and the role of entrepreneurs (coining the term *creative destruction*). Schumpeter once said that he had three goals in life: to become the world's greatest lover, the world's greatest horseman, and the world's greatest economist. He noted wryly that he had achieved only two out of the three.

1906   Inventor of the Xerox machine, Chester F. Carlson, is born in Seattle. While employed in the patent department of an electronics firm, Carlson was plagued by difficulties in getting copies of drawings and specifications, so he investigated methods to make quick copies of what he needed. Certain that large companies were already working on photographic and chemical means, Carlson hit on the idea of using electrostatics. Four years later, in 1938, he created the first dry-copy image (the name he chose for the process comes from the Greek *xeros*, "dry"). More than 20 companies turned him down for funding over the next six years. A nonprofit research organization, Battelle Memorial Institute, gave him several thousand dollars in 1944, but that was soon gone. Finally, the Haloid Company (later called Xerox) of Rochester, New York, raised the necessary funds (another $3.5 million) in return for the commercial rights, and 11 years later Xerox introduced its first office copier. Carlson died September 19, 1968.

1908   After years of frustrating negotiations, Wilbur and Orville Wright finally sign their first contract to produce an airplane for the

U.S. government. The plane was delivered on time ("within 200 days") to Fort Myers, Maryland, but it crashed during a September test flight, injuring Orville and killing his passenger, Lieutenant T. E. Selfridge.

1924   John Joseph Carty (vice president and chief of research for Bell Telephone) delivers the first coast-to-coast radio broadcast, a speech at the Bond Men's Club at the Congress Hotel in Chicago, which is heard by an estimated 50 million people. Exactly four years later, in **1928**, the first continent-to-continent television image was received in Hartsdale, New York, by Robert M. Hart; it was a picture of Mia Howe sent across the ocean by short wave from Purley, England, by John Logie Baird, who ran the Baird Television Development Company in London.

2001   Financial advice firm Motley Fool Inc. announces that its business performance is so bad that it has been forced to lay off a third of its workforce.

FEBRUARY 9

1819   Perhaps the best known American woman of the 19th century, Lydia Estes Pinkham is born into a family of reform-minded Quakers in Lynn, Massachusetts. Her husband's real estate speculations drove the family into poverty during the panic of 1873, and it was then that she took the advice of one of her sons to market her home-brewed herbal remedy. Bottled with about 18 percent alcohol as "solvent and preservative," Lydia E. Pinkham's Vegetable Compound went on sale in 1875 and eventually proved a nationwide success—partly through the marketing zeal of her sons; partly through the appealing, homey style of the ad copy she wrote herself; partly through her popular campaign of personally answering every customer's letter (her "Department of Advice" later extended to successful books on sex and reproduction); and partly because there were few products and little sympathy in the medical community for "women's weakness." She died May 17, 1883.

1824   Two days after his 12th birthday Charles Dickens begins work in a squalid, rat-infested London factory, Warren's Blacking, to support his family because his father had been cast into debtor's prison. For 12 hours a day, under a hateful boss (and for 6 shillings a week), Dickens wrapped pots of blacking in oil paper, then in blue paper, and then tied and labeled each pot. The experience deeply affected his psyche and his writing, which in turn caused many to rethink the glories of the Industrial Revolution. He wept when visiting his father, overcome with "depression of spirit and sinking of heart" as he mingled with the imprisoned men who had "lost friends, fortunes, home and happiness."

1955 "As quickly as you start spending federal money in large amounts, it looks like free money." —President Dwight D. Eisenhower

1955 Twenty years of civil war ends in Miami Beach, as executives from the American Federation of Labor and the Congress of Industrial Organizations reach agreement on merger terms, creating a joint membership of 12 million. The AFL-CIO merger is made official on December 5. CIO chief Walter P. Reuther announces that he will cede leadership to "the Honest Plumber," George Meany, who holds the presidency for more than 23 years.

1993 NBC News announces that it has settled a defamation lawsuit brought by General Motors over the network's November feature on *Dateline* called "Waiting to Explode?" which showed GM trucks bursting into flame upon rear impact. It turned out the crash tests were rigged by NBC to create a spectacular show. Though not directly involved, Michael Gartner, president of NBC News, resigned the next month.

FEBRUARY 10

1824 Samuel Plimsoll is born on this day in Bristol, England, and would become a politician/reformer whose name was attached to two commercial entities. His campaign against "coffin ships" (unseaworthy, heavily loaded, heavily insured merchant vessels that put profit over lives) produced the Merchant Shipping Act (1876) and the "Plimsoll line" (marks on ships' hulls, showing the safe limit to which the ship could be loaded; now an international standard). The *plimsoll* is the generic British term for rubber-soled canvas shoes.

1872   John Augustine Hartford (the marketing mastermind behind A&P's rise to become the world's largest food retailer and America's largest food processor) is born in Orange, New Jersey, the youngest son of A&P's founder, George Huntington Hartford. As a young executive, John literally saved the company in the panic of 1907; during a run on the banks he bought a man's place in line for $450 and was able to recover the company's deposits. In 1912 he cemented his reputation with a field test. Firmly convinced that the enterprise had unwisely drifted from its core strategy of low prices and limited services, he argued mightily with his father and brother (who called his idea "crack brained") and was allowed to put up a "cash and carry" of his own design in Jersey City, right around the corner from the company's most profitable store. Within six months, John's "economy store" had driven its rival out of business, and his model became the company standard in the greatest retail expansion the world had ever seen. Each outlet was exactly the same; it was said that John could walk blindfolded into any of the thousands of stores and find the beans. Hartford died September 20, 1951.

1897   The famous slogan "All The News That's Fit To Print" first appears on the *New York Times*.

1942   A standard in retail sales is introduced as the first "gold record" is presented to Glenn Miller, whose 1941 hit "Chattanooga Choo Choo" has been sprayed with gold by RCA-Victor, in recognition of being history's first recording to sell one million copies.

1969   "In solving our problems, we should beware of creating worse ones." —Indira Gandhi, later assassinated after attempting various reforms, which included nationalization of India's banks

1998   After 30 years and $500 million in development, Procter & Gamble's olestra makes its national debut in several snack foods, including WOW! potato chips from Frito-Lay. P&G even funded a study published in the *Journal of the American Medical Association* claiming that the fat substitute (which purportedly tastes and feels like real fat but is not absorbed into the bloodstream) does not cause more intestinal distress than foods with conventional fats. The product immediately caused a stir, becoming synonymous with various intestinal problems and the brunt of jokes on late-night television. It is still on the market but remains controversial and the subject of various websites, both pro and con.

FEBRUARY 11

1875 Founder of the Triangle Publications media group, Moses (Louis) Annenberg is born in Kalwischen, East Prussia. His family moved to Chicago in 1885; Moses joined his father's junk business and also worked as a bartender and a messenger before being hired by publisher William Randolph Hearst. He rose to the position of circulation manager of the new morning paper the *Examiner*. Its introduction sparked virtual gang warfare for street position; Annenberg was successful, but his methods tarnished his reputation forever. He branched out on his own into a variety of companies, the most successful being a wire service that connected racetracks with bookies across the country; at one point he was AT&T's fifth-largest customer. He died July 24, 1942. Triangle Publications was sold by his son Walter Annenberg to Rupert Murdoch in 1988 for $3 billion.

1937 The first major labor dispute in the U.S. auto industry ends at noon. Representatives of General Motors and the United Auto Workers union signed an agreement in a Detroit courtroom that ended a 44-day sit-down strike that crippled car production. GM president Alfred P. Sloan announced a $25 million wage increase to workers and recognition of the union. It was the first major victory in the unionization of America's basic industries by the Congress for Industrial Organization. Workers evacuating the three plants in Flint, Michigan, hugged each other with joy. "Let us have peace and make automobiles," said GM vice president William S. Knudsen.

1974 Eighty-one-year-old J. Paul Getty, oil executive, financier, and one of the wealthiest people in history, said in a newspaper interview, "I've always had a place for every dollar that came in. I've never seen the day where I could say that I felt rich. Generally you have to worry about paying the bills."

FEBRUARY 12

1294   Kublai Khan dies at about 80 in Ta-tu ("the Great Capital," now Beijing), hub of the Yuan empire that he established. Kublai's economics were partly traditional (entrenched in forced labor and continual conquest) and partly progressive (including enormous tax breaks for merchants and entrepreneurs, a flourishing and far-flung trade network on land and sea, roads, a census and postal system, a cabinet of foreign advisers, and paper money). "One may well say that the great Khan is a perfect alchemist," exclaimed admiring Marco Polo about Kublai's administration of paper currency. Alas, paper money contributed to the Yuan demise; its unregulated production brought on inflation, which led to a flow of specie abroad and distress at home. The dynasty ended in 1368.

1970   Joseph Louis Searles III becomes the first black member of the New York Stock Exchange, now about 200 years old. He was a partner in the brokerage firm of Newburger, Loeb and Company.

1989   "Doing business with Alan Bond is like wrestling with a pig. You both get sprayed with mud and the pig loves it." —Anonymous Texas banker on Bond's famously aggressive business tactics, in the *Sunday Times*

2004   Erbitux—the cancer drug that got Martha Stewart into so much trouble for insider trading in 2001—is approved by the Food & Drug Administration. It went on sale later in the month at a cost of $2,500 per dose. Its stock price had been rising for months. Sam Waksal, who founded the company ImClone, still had six years left on his prison sentence.

FEBRUARY 13

1800   The Banque de France is founded at the instigation of Napoleon "to counteract . . . [impairing] influences arising from the

French Revolution and expensive wars." His country was in the midst of an inflation-driven slide toward bankruptcy. In the same year he raised 5 million francs from French and Italian bankers and 9 million from a national lottery, reformed tax collection, and cut the budgets of all ministries. Confidence returned among the bourgeoisie, and bond prices climbed steadily.

1959   The Barbie doll is introduced by the Mattel toy company at the American Toy Fair in New York City. It is an immediate hit and has tremendous fiscal legs (by century's end, the doll, accessories, and spin-off friends had become a $1.9 billion industry). Every second, three Barbies are sold somewhere in 150 different countries. Speaking about those legs, if translated from doll size into reality, Barbie would be seven feet tall, possess a 40-22-36 figure, and have five-foot-long legs. The doll was designed by the cofounder of Mattel, Ruth Handler, who observed that her daughter Barbara preferred playing with the more shapely paper dolls in her collection.

1990   Drexel Burnham Lambert Inc. declares bankruptcy. Tracing its origins back 153 years to 1837, the firm was brought down by junk bond tycoon Michael Milken, whose dirty dealings and super-risky investments collided with sharp investigators and a dull economy. The activities of Milken's ring saddled Drexel with fines of $650 million and a debt burden that could not be met.

1997   The Dow Jones Industrial Average closes above 7,000 for the first time, just four months since it topped 6,000, and six months since topping 8,000. The tech/Internet bubble was at full-speed inflation.

FEBRUARY 14

1876   The application for history's "most valuable patent"—the telephone—is filed by Alexander Graham Bell in the patent office in New York City. His machine still did not work. Two hours later Elisha Gray filed papers for the same device in the same office, beginning a famous legal battle, the first of hundreds that Bell fought over his invention.

1924   Thomas Watson, Sr., changes the name of his Computing-Tabulating-Recording Company to IBM after purchasing a small Canadian firm with that name. Forward-thinking Watson liked the name and decided to keep it, though his company at this time was neither international nor a specialist in office equipment.

1958   "In some advertising, the selling message ends with a period. In other advertising, the selling message ends with a sale. In either event, it costs the advertiser just as much to run a poor ad as it does to run a good one." —Young & Rubicam Inc., in *Advertising Agency Magazine*

1968   The Penn Central Railroad is created by a merger of the Pennsylvania and New York Central lines. Both were in trouble, battered by competition from cars and trucks (which used publicly funded roadways) and airlines (which used publicly funded airports). The new $5 billion corporation was scandal-ridden and bankrupt within two years.

1968   Labor leader Cesar Estrada Chavez announces a hunger strike in Delano, California, to dramatize the plight of exploited farm workers, who have been on strike against grape growers for three years. "I will eat nothing. I will pray for forgiveness for the violence of some of our members. I will pray that there will be no more violence," he said. Senator Robert Kennedy and 8,000 laborers broke bread with Chavez when he ended his fast 25 days later in Delano Memorial Park. Chavez had lost 35 pounds. At Mass, Kennedy praised Chavez as "one of the greatest living Americans." The strike ended in grand victory for the laborers after five years because of Chavez's unfailing leadership, his expansion of the action into a national boycott of grapes, and his ability to enlist the support of housewives and large labor unions. In 1975 California passed the Agricultural Labor Relations Act, still the nation's only law that protects the rights of farm workers to unionize.

FEBRUARY 15

1845   Robert Wood Johnson is born in Carbondale, Pennsylvania. After serving an apprenticeship in pharmacy, he took a job in drug retailing, then became a drug broker in New York City, by which time he had conceived improvements in wound dressings. The firm of Seabury & Johnson was established in 1874 to manufacture plasters with an India rubber base. A critical turning point was a lecture given by Sir Joseph Lister in 1876 that Johnson attended; Lister's theories and methods to combat airborne germs were resisted by the medical establishment, but Johnson jumped on them. In 1885 he formed a partnership with brothers James Wood Johnson and Edward Mead Johnson. In a former wallpaper factory in New Brunswick, New Jersey, they began making antiseptic, individually wrapped surgical dressings. It was the birth of the great Johnson & Johnson health care corporation.

1954   "You have to do a little bragging on yourself even to your relatives—man doesn't get anywhere without advertising." —John ("Cactus Jack") Nance Garner, Franklin Roosevelt's conservative vice president during the progressive New Deal

1971   Britain adopts metric currency, ending the existence of the fabled shilling.

1995   "Paradigm Shift: a euphemism companies use when they realize the rest of their industry has expanded into Guangdong while they were investing in Orange County." —Anonymous, in *Fortune*

FEBRUARY 16

1843   Henry Martyn Leland, the engineer/executive whose innovations and rigorous standards helped launch the auto industry, is born in Danville, Vermont. He created the Cadillac, the Lincoln, the V-8 engine, and the electrical self-starter. His relatively weak financial ability brought his career to a rather sad end (he sold the bankrupt Lincoln Motor Company to Henry Ford in 1922 on his 79th birthday), but his engineering prowess was legend (see February 29).

1852   Pennsylvania-born wagon maker Clement Studebaker and older brother Henry form H&C Studebaker, a blacksmith and vehicle-making enterprise in South Bend, Indiana. Brother John M. was making wheelbarrows for gold miners in Placerville, California, but joined the firm in

1853 with his savings of $8,000. Brothers Peter I. and Jacob joined thereafter, establishing the Studebaker Brothers Manufacturing Company, which prospered during the Civil War on its way to becoming the world's largest maker of horse-drawn carriages. It enjoyed some, but less, success when it switched to horseless carriages and was absorbed by the Packard Corporation in 1954.

1901   John Rex Whinfield, the inventor of polyester, is born in Dorking, England.

1957   "The reader deserves an honest opinion. If he doesn't deserve it, give it to him anyhow." —John Ciardi, in the *Saturday Review*

1960   Eighteen executives from five major electrical companies (General Electric, Westinghouse, Allis-Chalmers, I-T-E Circuit Breaker, and Federal Pacific Electrical) are indicted on charges of rigged and collusive bidding in sales to government and private industry. All 18 defendants pleaded guilty or no contest. They had met dozens of times in cities all around the country and decided among themselves which company would get what percentage of government contracts and which company would submit the "low" (but still artificially high) bid in each sealed bidding event. In sales to private utilities and manufacturers, they devised a formula (which they called "phase of the moon") under which they took turns in submitting the "low" bid. As economist Adam Smith wrote in 1776, "People of the same trade seldom meet together, even for merriment and diversion, but the conversation ends in a conspiracy against the public, or in some contrivance to raise prices."

FEBRUARY 17

1844   Aaron Montgomery Ward, the merchant who created the mail-order method of selling and established the great retail house that bore his name, is born in Chatham, New Jersey. After a series of menial jobs he found his niche in the retail trade, first in a general store in St. Joseph, Michigan, for $6 per week plus board. He was the manager after three years. He worked at Marshall Field's in Chicago for two years, then for a dry goods house; when that failed he became a traveling salesman in rural areas, which led to his breakthrough. He soon became aware of the hard-pressed farmers' resentment of the middlemen's profits, having to sell their produce at wholesale prices but buy goods at retail prices. He shattered the system with a single insight: he bought wholesale for cash and sold via mail for a small markup, easily beating the prices of country stores. In August 1872 (capitalized with $1,600 of his own and $800 from his brother-in-law and operating out of a loft in a livery stable) he issued his first catalog, a single sheet listing about 150 items. The next year he got a tremendous break, becoming the official supply house of the National Grange, which had been searching for a way to "cut out the middleman." By 1893 his catalog was called *The Great Wish Book*, weighed two pounds, and contained 544 pages. Ward died December 7, 1913.

1913   Oregon passes legislation that produces the nation's first commission to establish a minimum wage. Massachusetts had passed a similar law the previous year, but it did not take effect until after the Oregon commission was established and wrangling with the issue. The body had three members, one to represent the employer, one the employee, and one the public.

1958   "The presence of humans, in a system containing high-speed electronic computers and high-speed, accurate communications, is quite inhibiting. Every means possible should be employed to eliminate humans in the data-processing chain." —Stuart L. Seaton, engineering consultant, addressing the American Institute of Electrical Engineers, in *Time*

1966   The great designer and implementer of the modern corporate structure, Alfred P. Sloan, Jr., dies in New York City at age 90 (see May 23). "The only report we ask from all of our units is one page a month," he wrote while he was president of General Motors and making it the world's largest corporation.

1972   The 15,007,034th Volkswagen Beetle rolls off the assembly line in Wolfsburg, Germany, overtaking the Ford Model T as the most-produced car in history.

1997   ABC News reports this evening that Incubus, the name currently in use by Reebok International Ltd. for a woman's running shoe, is that of a mythical demon that savaged women in their sleep. "I'm horrified and the company is horrified," said Reebok spokesperson Kate Burnham the next day. "How the name got on the shoe and went forward I do not know."

FEBRUARY 18

1879   Frederic-Auguste Bartholdi receives a design patent for the Statue of Liberty.

1905   The first investment banker to form an underwriting syndicate in the United States, Jay Cooke, dies at 83 in Ogontz, Pennsylvania. Born August 10, 1821, the son of a lawyer/politician, Cooke joined the Philadelphia banking house of E. W. Clark & Co. at 18 and three years later was made a partner. In 1861 he formed his own Philadelphia bank. Through his brother, Cooke met Salmon P. Chase, who was then governor of Ohio and later secretary of the treasury during the Civil War. Chase enlisted Cooke to float several war bond offerings, and Cooke became famous for his success and for the creative ways he achieved it (see April 8). The underwriting syndicate was formed to finance construction of the Pennsylvania Railroad; eight firms agreed to take a block of bonds and sell them independently; the syndicate handled all distribution and advertising costs. In 1870 Cooke undertook the financing of the Northern Pacific Railroad construction, but during the project his firm failed as the panic of 1873 erased the value of securities nationwide. He recovered and was wealthy again by 1880.

1963   "I do everything for a reason. . . . Most of the time the reason is money." —Suzy Parker, actress and model, in *Newsweek*

2003   A spokesperson for the credit card industry in New York announces that a hacker recently gained access to 5.6 million MasterCard and Visa card numbers. The felon apparently broke through the security of a company that processed transactions for merchants. Visa

USA said there had been no reports of frauds, card-issuing institutions had been notified, and Visa was monitoring the situation.

FEBRUARY 19

1785 "The wisest prophets make sure of the event first." —Horace Walpole, in a letter to Thomas Walpole

1878 Thomas Edison patents the phonograph. "Mary Had a Little Lamb" was the first recording.

1906 Battle Creek Toasted Corn Flake Company is incorporated by Will Keith Kellogg and St. Louis insurance executive Charles D. Brolin, who invested $35,000 to market the cereal products developed by Will and his older brother, Dr. John Harvey Kellogg. W.K. was business-minded, had pushed for the venture for years, ran the business, and had his initials on every box of cornflakes. John, who was superintendent of the Battle Creek Sanitarium where the products were developed, had a different view: "It is exceedingly distasteful to me to have my name associated with the food business or with anything commercial—but we sometimes have to swallow bitter pills, much against our will." The brothers had been creating popular foods for years, but John's aversion to capitalism led others to exploit his products; on the day Kellogg's began, there were 42 other cereal companies in Battle Creek alone.

1954 Young engineer Kazuo Iwama mails the second of the famous *Iwama Reports* from Allentown, Pennsylvania, to eager colleagues Masaru Ibuka and Akio Morita at their Totsuko company in Tokyo. The firm would later revolutionize the global consumer electronics industry as the Sony Corporation, but for now they knew very little about transistors. Iwama spent three months studying the new transistor industry at the Bell, Western Electric, and Westinghouse labs, observing and grilling personnel during the day and typing up notes in motels at night. His seven reports, still preserved at Sony headquarters in Tokyo, taught the Japanese how to make transistors. By 1955 Iwama was making advances in the Sony labs beyond what the Americans had been able to do; he rose to become the second president in the firm's history.

1988   "If we are to be more prosperous we need more millionaires and more bankrupts." —Keith Joseph, on taking business risks, in his maiden speech to the House of Lords

FEBRUARY 20

1852   The first through train from the East reaches Chicago by way of the Michigan Southern Railway. The event sparked an explosion in the growth and economic importance of the city. It soon became the nation's chief rail center; came to dominate industries such as meat, lumber, and grain; and saw the Chicago Board of Trade become the nerve center of the commodities market.

1893   Railroads, as do other forms of transportation, often drive economic events. The Philadelphia and Reading Railroad goes into receivership with $125 million in debts; transportation of coal is crippled. Several other major railroads soon shut down; stock prices fell sharply in May; the market collapsed in June; and by year's end 600 banks, 15,000 businesses, and 74 railroads had closed their doors. The panic of 1893 began a four-year depression.

1921   "Love your neighbour is not merely sound Christianity; it is good business." —David Lloyd George, British prime minister, in the *Observer*

1933   Adolf Hitler first meets Gustav Krupp. Five years earlier Hitler had gone to the Krupp works in Essen as a tourist and had been turned away at the gates. But now things were different; Hitler had just been appointed chancellor of Germany and was only a month away from the government act that would give him dictatorial powers. Still, he needed heavy industry for his wider aims. Tonight's gathering in Berlin, at the house of the president of the Reichstag (Hermann Göring), was attended by the 25 richest industrialists in Germany and marked the marriage of big business to the Nazis. Gustav Krupp, head of the world's largest munitions company and chairman of the Federation of German Industries, became a huge contributor, cheerleader, and henchman overnight. In the words of fellow industrialist Fritz Thyssen, "after Hitler was appointed chancellor, Herr von Krupp became a super-Nazi."

1958   ". . . there is something radically wrong with so-called 'free enterprise.'" —Garfield Bromley Oxnam

1968   Southwest Airlines receives approval from the Texas Air Commission to begin service. The very next day three big airlines (Braniff, Texas International, and Continental) filed legal papers to stop Southwest, which has continually prospered and grown over the past 30 years while its bigger competitors have been continually diseased and dying.

FEBRUARY 21

1825   "Never buy what you do not want, because it is cheap; it will be dear to you." —Thomas Jefferson, in *A Decalogue of Canons for Observation in Practical Life*

1931   Alka-Seltzer is introduced by the Dr. Miles Laboratories of Elkhart, Indiana. It was developed and sold well as a treatment for colds and headaches, but sales skyrocketed when the rumor spread that it relieved hangovers—just as Prohibition ended in 1933. Until this time Miles had been "a small, rather static company"; the great success of Alka-Seltzer ended that meager status. The product was discovered by chance by Miles president Hub Beardsley when he happened to go into a local newspaper (the *Truth*) during the flu epidemic of 1928; none of the staff were sick. The paper's editor explained that he dosed employees with a combination of aspirin and baking soda at the first sign of disease. Beardsley took the formula to his chief chemist, Maurice Treneer, who developed the tablet that has the distinct "plop, plop, fizz, fizz" sound, a gimmick that established brand identity and boosted sales.

1988   "Arguably the only goods people need these days are food and nappies." —Terence Conran, British business executive/retailer/founder of Habitat, in the *Observer*

FEBRUARY 22

1863   On this day in New York City a well-attended autopsy is performed on Joice Heth, reputed to be the 161-year-old nurse of George Washington and star of P. T. Barnum's show (see June 2). The procedure showed her to be about 80. The deception made national headlines; Barnum did not deny the facts but claimed that he was as much a victim as anyone.

1879   Frank Winfield Woolworth, 26, opens "the Great Five Cent Store" in Utica, New York. It was the forerunner of Woolworth's hugely successful five-and-dime chain that eventually dotted the globe. The Utica store, his first, closed after a few weeks of daily receipts as low as $2.50.

1954   "I have a hankering to go back to the Orient and discard my necktie. Neckties strangle clear thinking." —Lin Yutang, Chinese-American philosopher

1999   The First Internet Bank of Indiana, the first full-service bank available only on the Internet, opens for business.

2001   Wal-Mart Stores Inc.—the successor to Woolworth's concept of low-price, high-volume general merchandise—announces its first-ever quarter with profits that exceed $2 billion. The earnings were $2.004 billion (45¢ per share) on sales of $56.56 billion. Executives attributed the increased profit to price reductions and expanding food offerings.

FEBRUARY 23

1744   The most famous of all European banking dynasties begins in a Jewish ghetto in Frankfurt with the birth of Mayer Amschel Rothschild. The family name came from the red (*rot*) shield on the ghetto house his ancestors once inhabited. Mayer studied originally for the rabbinate, but his parents' early deaths drove him to an apprenticeship in a bank. He and his sons rose from traders to financiers of governments, wars, and large-scale industries. Each of his five sons headed operations in a different European center: Frankfurt, London, Paris, Vienna, and Naples. In 1815 their well-coordinated communication network produced one of the greatest coups in investment history: in London, son Nathan secretly received word by carrier pigeon of Napoleon's defeat at Waterloo; he feigned gloom publicly, drove down the prices of securities by selling short, had his agents buy securities at distressed prices, and reaped an enormous fortune when prices skyrocketed with news of Britain's victory.

1954 "It's a terribly hard job to spend a billion dollars and get your money's worth." —George Humphrey, secretary of the treasury, in *Look*

1958 Eric Johnston, four-time president of the U.S. Chamber of Commerce, warns against the trend toward enormity in business: "The dinosaur's eloquent lesson is that if some bigness is good, an overabundance of bigness is not necessarily better."

1995 Barings Brothers, the world's oldest merchant bank, is dead in the water after 232 years, insolvent and just days from declaring bankruptcy and being purchased for £1. Only one man had an inkling of the trouble. Nick Leeson, a 28-year-old derivatives trader, spent this hectic day at work in the Barings Singapore office (buying heavily in a falling market, chalking up millions in losses), drank with colleagues at lunch at a bar called Escape, avoided supervisors who had questions about irregularities in his paperwork, and then disappeared. Over the past 30 months Leeson had accumulated and hidden more than $1 billion in losses in unauthorized futures trading on the Asian markets. Executives had largely turned a blind eye to his activities because they thought he was making huge profits for the firm, as much as $10 million a week (see March 2).

2004 You *can* do well by doing good. Researchers at Georgia State University and Institutional Shareholder Services report that corporations with the best governance (that is, with a board of directors that is conscientious, independent, knowledgeable, ethical, and genuinely concerned about its company) score best on various measures of financial performance (including price-earnings ratios and return on equity). The best-governed firms have five-year average annual returns nearly 8 percent above industry averages, while firms with inferior or rubber-stamp boards of directors return 4 percent less than industry averages (presented in today's *BusinessWeek*).

FEBRUARY 24

1552   England abolishes the trading privileges of the Hanseatic League. Once a major political and commercial force in medieval Europe, the league was now in slow decline. England, on the other hand, was in rapid ascent, bent on making itself into a great sea trader and warrior. The league was begun in the 1200s by merchants banding together to protect themselves against pirates and to build bargaining power in foreign lands. At its height it claimed some 160 member cities throughout Northern Europe (mostly on seacoasts or on rivers connected to the sea). Gradually it dissolved through internal tensions and self-development of the areas it had dominated.

1911   Upton Sinclair weighs in on the controversy over the latest rage in industrial relations. Scientific management's founder, Frederick Winslow Taylor, had just published the first in a series of articles in *American Magazine*. Sinclair rebutted, "I shall not forget the picture which he gave us . . . of the poor old laborer who was trying to build his pitiful little home after hours, and who was induced to give 362 per cent more service for 61 per cent more pay."

1955   The driving business force behind Apple Computers, NeXT Software, and Pixar Animation Studios, Steven Paul Jobs is born and is soon adopted by the Jobs family of Mountain View, California. The family later moved to Los Altos because of Steve's troubles at school; there his classroom attendance remained spotty, but he found something that grabbed him deeply—the Hewlett-Packard electronics company in nearby Palo Alto.

1958   "I believe that the able industrial leader who creates wealth and employment is more worthy of historical notice than politicians or soldiers." —J. Paul Getty, in *Time*

FEBRUARY 25

1819   The first savings bank in America to actually receive money on deposit—the Philadelphia Saving Fund Society, on Seventh and Walnut streets, Philadelphia—is chartered. The bank employed 12 managers and had been taking money since 1816. Its secretary-treasurer, George Billington, was paid $250 per year.

1820   A famous expression in all areas of human endeavor—*bunk,* to indicate "nonsense" or "hot air"—is born. Felix Walker, a congressman from North Carolina, delivered a long-winded speech against the Missouri Bill, making frequent references to his beloved Buncombe County. This and several similar speeches by Walker made Buncombe County well known and synonymous with blowhard rhetoric.

1848   Stock speculator and railroad magnate ("the last of the robber barons") Edward Henry Harriman is born the son of a poor clergyman in Hempstead, New York. He dropped out of school at 14 to clerk for a Wall Street broker and made his first investment killing at age 20 in the Black Friday panic of 1869. Harriman caused the panic of 1907 in a wild bidding fest against J. P. Morgan for control of the Northern Pacific Railroad; stock prices went from near $100 to $1,000 in a day, spelling doom for banks, brokerages, and thousands of investors who had financed speculations on a falling price. "Giants of Wall Street, in Fierce Battle for Mastery, Precipitate Crash that Brings Ruin to Horde of Pygmies," read one banner headline at the time.

1901   The first corporation to be initially capitalized in excess of $1 billion—U.S. Steel—incorporates. Begun with stock valued at $1.4 billion, the company joined seven ex-competitors and controlled 65 percent of the American market. The first president was Charles M. Schwab, who forged the merger. Other big winners were Andrew Carnegie, who became "the richest man in the world" for selling his steel interests for $250 million, and J. P. Morgan, who controlled two of the seven merged companies and received massive fees for underwriting the deal.

1957   "A decision is the action an executive must take when he has information so incomplete that the answer does not suggest itself." —Admiral Arthur W. Radford, chairman, U.S. Joint Chiefs of Staff, in *Time*

FEBRUARY 26

1829   Levi Strauss, creator of blue jeans and the company that bears his name, is born in Bavaria. He immigrated to New York, where he learned the craft of sailmaking, then moved on to San Francisco at the age of 20 during the Gold Rush with a large supply of sailcloth, thinking he would service the growing West Coast ports. He soon discovered a much bigger market for his canvas: making durable trousers for the miners, and an apparel revolution was born. "Levis" is just one nickname for the garments he created, which are now ubiquitous throughout the world and across the fashion spectrum. The famous rivets in the pants were designed and patented by Jacob Davis, a tailor and Russian-Jewish immigrant to Nevada, as a way to repair torn pockets. Davis wrote in 1872 to the "Gents" of the Strauss company, offering a half-share in his discovery if the company would pay the $68 cost of the patent application. "The secratt of them Pents," he wrote, "is the Rivits that I put in those Pockets."

1852   John Harvey Kellogg—physician and health food pioneer, whose chance discovery of cornflakes was largely responsible for the birth of the flaked-cereal industry—is born in Tyrone, Michigan.

1960   "I hate this 'crime doesn't pay' stuff. Crime in the U.S. is perhaps one of the biggest businesses in the world today." —Dr. Paul Kirk, professor of criminalistics, University of California, in the *Wall Street Journal*

1965   Hobie surfboards trademark is registered.

1995   Eddie George, governor of the Bank of England, shocks the financial world by announcing that Barings PLC, the world's oldest merchant bank, is suddenly bankrupt (see February 23).

FEBRUARY 27

1831   A steam-powered coach carries paying passengers over a regularly scheduled route for the first time. Using a locomotive built by Goldsworthy Gurney, the nine-mile route from Gloucester to Cheltenham, England, was covered round-trip four times each day until June, when the noise, smoke, and destruction of roadways led to public outrage and cancellation of the service.

1867   An economist who actually made money, Irving Fisher, is born in Saugerties, New York. In 1910 he invented the popular Rolodex index card system, and he helped establish the Remington Rand company; both activities made him a millionaire. He went broke in the stock market crash of 1929 and never really recovered. He died February 27, 1947, at New Haven, Connecticut. Author of more than 30 widely translated books, Fisher created the "quantity theory of money" to explain and predict price levels. All of his brilliance was discolored by just one statement: "Stock prices have reached what looks like a permanently high plateau"; this was just nine days before the market imploded in 1929.

1891   David Sarnoff is born in the village of Uzlian, Russia. As a rising executive in the Marconi Wireless Telegraph Company in 1915, he proposed production of a "radio music box," a commercially marketed radio receiver. Although the idea was slow to get executive support, it eventually gave rise to the radio industry and the Radio Corporation of America (RCA). In 1926 Sarnoff directed the launch of the National Broadcasting Company (NBC), initially as a tactic to sell more radios.

1998   "One thing is certain: if a CEO is enthused about a particularly foolish acquisition, both his internal staff and his outside advisors will come up with whatever projections are needed to justify his stance. Only in fairy tales are emperors told that they are naked." —Warren Buffett, chairman, Berkshire Hathaway, in a letter to stockholders

FEBRUARY 28

1827   The first railroad for commercial transportation of passengers and freight in the United States, the Baltimore and Ohio Railroad Company (the B&O), incorporates. It took its first paying passenger in January 1830 between two stations in Baltimore, but by 1851 it had reached the Ohio River in the American wilderness.

1913   A sensational report published today by the House Committee on Banking and Currency describes the "money trust" that controls the country's financial power. A tiny band of Wall Street tycoons sat on the boards of multiple companies ("interlocking directorates") and doled out credit at their discretion and profit. Chief among them was J. P. Morgan. In addition to large positions in major banks other than his own, Morgan and his dozen partners held more than 72 directorships in 47 major corporations of different types.

1967   Henry Robinson Luce, cofounder of the Time-Life publishing empire, dies at 68 in Phoenix, Arizona. "No other American without a political office—with the possible exception of Henry Ford—has had a greater influence on American society," said the German weekly *Der Spiegel* (see April 3).

1997   "If you aren't willing to own a stock for ten years, don't even think about owning it for ten minutes." —Warren Buffett, chairman, Berkshire Hathaway, in a letter to shareholders

2003   Coca-Cola sells 49 percent of Hindustan Coca-Cola Beverages, its bottler in India, to Indian investors and employees. The move was the latest in a series of smart steps to improve relations with the Indian government and customers. Coke's market share among colas was small (16.5 percent, compared to 23.5 percent for archrival Pepsi) but growing, thanks to Sanjeev Gupta. His first move after promotion to operations manager in 2000 was to revitalize Thums Up (whose market share among carbonated beverages had fallen from 60 percent to 15 percent under Coke ownership). He then attacked costs, container size, pricing, and advertising, adapting all of them to local tastes and conditions. "Coke had to break a lot of rules for India," observed one beverage executive, admiring a one-year, 24 percent leap in overall company sales.

FEBRUARY 29

1908   Three Cadillacs are disassembled, the parts scrambled, the cars reassembled with random assignment of parts, and then the three remade cars are given a 500-mile road test. They perform flawlessly, winning their creator Henry Leland the Dewar Trophy.

1920   John Maynard Keynes is savaged personally and professionally in a *New York Times* review of his newly published *The Economic Consequences of the Peace*. Columbia history professor Charles Downer Hazen challenged Keynes's thinking ability, critical standards, emotional balance, and patriotism, calling the Versailles Treaty "a great document in the history of human freedom." Of course, Keynes got it right, predicting that the Versailles reparations would cause wild inflation and chaos in Germany and threaten stability everywhere—the effects that produced Hitler and World War II. Keynes's book was a bestseller and established him as the premier economist of the century.

1988   "I'm no managerial genius. But I keep my eye on the bottom line and my people know it. As for management style, I go in with no nonsense. . . . Most CEOs got their jobs because their predecessors and the directors liked them. They slapped the right backs and laughed at the right jokes. It's reverse Darwinism." —Carl C. Icahn, corporate raider icon, in *Fortune*

MARCH

MARCH 1

1382   Shortly after new war-driven sales taxes on wine, salt, and other merchandise are announced, the tax revolt of the *Maillotins* begins in Paris. A woman street merchant beat off one of the king's tax collectors who was trying to seize her goods. "Down with taxes!" she screamed. A crowd fell on the official and murdered him. A police armory of 3,000 long-handled leaden mallets (called *maillets*, hence naming the uprising) was seized from the Hotel de Ville. The *Maillotins* closed the gates of the city and hunted down notaries, jurists, and anyone connected with taxes; the Jewish quarter was also looted. The *Maillotins* were crushed in January.

1933   Andre Citroën hires Andre Lefebvre. Within a year the young engineer had designed, perfected, and built the first car with front-wheel drive, the control system that now dominates the automobile industry. The system was on the market almost a year to the day after Lefebvre was hired.

1947   The International Monetary Fund begins operation.

1960   The first Xerox 914s are shipped. The $200 million copier market is already crowded with 30 companies, including 3M and Eastman Kodak, but the 914 is simpler and faster, makes copies on plain paper, and does not require a master—the original is simply placed facedown on a glass plate.

1976   Tracing its roots back to the City Bank of New York (formed two days before the War of 1812 broke out), the First National City Bank of New York changes its name to Citibank, and its holding company is named Citicorp.

1987   "Being good in business is the most fascinating kind of art."
—Andy Warhol, in the *Observer*

MARCH 2

1904   One of the pioneers who made industrial design a distinct profession, Henry Dreyfuss is born in New York City. At 17 he was designing sets for Broadway productions when a store commissioned him to study its merchandise from an aesthetic viewpoint; he opened his own product design office in 1929. Among his notable designs were airplane and ocean liner interiors, as well as a series of telephones for the Bell company, including the "Trimline," which incorporated all functions in the handset (a now-standard design). "When the point of contact between the product and people becomes a point of friction, then the industrial designer has failed," he wrote in one of his several books.

1973   MCI chairman Bill McGowan arrives at the New York offices of AT&T chairman John deButts to discuss MCI's legal access to AT&T telephone lines (a threat that AT&T is fighting with all of its resources, including its 900 lawyers). McGowan was made to wait three hours, and when he was shown in, deButts was on the telephone with his back turned for another 15 minutes. "You know, we eat guys like you every day of the week" was deButts's greeting. "You're not going to swallow this guy," warned McGowan. "We're going to fight [you] at the FCC, and we have better relations with the FCC than you do. We also have a number of friends in Congress. I have plenty of money. I can spend it on litigation, or I can spend it on construction." The meeting was short and ugly; McGowan was frustrated, but deButts was shaken. "Nothing about MCI can be treated as business as usual," he later confided.

1995   Just as Dutch financial giant ING is negotiating to buy Barings PLC merchant bank, the man who brought Barings from health to bankruptcy, trader Nick Leeson, is arrested with his wife in Frankfurt, having been on the run for a week from Singapore. Under his arm is the Tom Clancy thriller, *Without Remorse* (see February 23).

2004   Bernard Ebbers, who "reshaped the competitive landscape" of the telecommunications industry in the 1990s, is indicted on federal fraud and conspiracy charges in New York. His former second-in-command at WorldCom, Scott Sullivan, pleaded guilty to the same charges and agreed to testify against Ebbers.

MARCH 3

1826 Founder of the first business school in America at the University of Pennsylvania, Joseph Wharton is born in Philadelphia. His granduncle was Samuel Wharton, the great colonial merchant and land speculator, and Joseph had an excellent education, including chemistry and foreign languages; both would aid his success as an international metals manufacturer. He was doing well in zinc and iron when, in 1862, he got a tip from a friend at the U.S. mint in Philadelphia that the government might use nickel in making coins. Wharton refurbished an idle nickel mine he already owned and went into partnership with one of Europe's leading nickel refiners; within a few years he had developed a virtual monopoly on the U.S. nickel industry. Prussia became a major customer when it began nickel coinage in 1874. Wharton was also a founder of the Bethlehem Steel Company (for many years he and Andrew Carnegie were the country's only suppliers of nickel steel for heavy castings), and in 1898 he hired Frederick W. Taylor, who was still developing his principles of scientific management; it was at Bethlehem Steel that Taylor's revolutionary ideas first came to public attention. Wharton died January 11, 1909.

1841 "All good things are cheap; all bad are very dear." —Henry David Thoreau

1923 *Time* magazine is first published by partners Henry R. Luce, 24, and Briton Hadden, 25.

1961 "One of the greatest pieces of economic wisdom is to know what you do not know." —John Kenneth Galbraith, economist and adviser to President John Kennedy, in *Time*

1998 William H. Gates, chairman of the Microsoft Corporation, testifies before Congress for the first time amid ongoing accusations by government and industry that Microsoft is using its dominant position in operating system software (where it controlled 85 percent of the market) to gain an unfair upper hand in new markets. "Will the United States continue its breathtaking technological advances?" Gates aggressively asked members of the Senate Judiciary Committee. "I believe the answer is yes—if innovation is not restricted by government."

MARCH 4

1858   "Cotton is king!" proclaims James Henry Hammond, senator from South Carolina, taunting congressional critics of the South (the phrase was the title of a book published three years previously by David Christy). "You dare not make war upon cotton! No power on earth dares make war upon it. Cotton is king."

1887   Henry Sturgis Dennison is born into his Boston family's box and paper company. The Dennison Manufacturing Company was begun in 1843 by Aaron Lufkin Dennison, "the father of American watchmaking," when he could not find a supplier of boxes for his watches. Henry was president of the company from 1912 until his death in 1952. He increased sales tenfold—during the Great Depression—but beyond that he pioneered programs in employee benefits, worker welfare, and cooperative management. In 1916 the Dennison Company established the first employer-initiated unemployment insurance system in American history.

1990   "I need problems. A good problem makes me come alive." —Tiny Rowland, British entrepreneur, in the *Sunday Times*

2000   Sony PlayStation2 (PS2) goes on sale, and 980,000 units are bought in the first 48 hours, making it the fastest-selling game console in history. Of these, 380,000 were sold over the Internet, which was also a record. The toy is powered by a 128-bit RISC chip known as the "Emotion Engine"; it could generate 66 million polygons per second.

MARCH 5

1817   The New York Stock Exchange adopts a constitution, assumes the name New York Stock and Exchange Board (in 1863 it became known simply as the New York Stock Exchange), and soon rents space at 40 Wall Street. Its first president was Nathan Prime. The new organization quickly established minimum commissions that members charged each other for trades; nonmembers could also trade with members, but at higher commission rates. Although the prices at which deals were struck were recorded daily, this information was not regularly made public for years.

1836　The great cattleman-trailblazer Charles Goodnight is born in Macoupin County, Illinois. His family moved to Texas while Charles was still a child. After establishing several local cattle ranches, Goodnight entered his first venture of national significance in 1868 with partner Oliver Loving, driving a large herd of cattle from Texas to Wyoming (where the animals could be transported to many states by established rail lines) along a route they forged themselves, the Goodnight-Loving Trail. In 1877 Goodnight and John George Adair began the JA Ranch, which rapidly grew to a million acres with one of the world's largest and finest herds of beef cattle. Goodnight also founded the first cattleman's association in the Texas Panhandle, developed new equipment for cattle drives, and developed a new subspecies of cattle—the "cattalo"—through breeding experiments. For these experiments he was nicknamed "the Burbank of the Range." When his wife of 55 years, Mary, died, Goodnight remarried at age 91 (to a woman named Goodnight) and fathered a child the following year.

1954　It has taken a quarter century, but for the first time since October 26, 1929 (when the stock market was in free fall and the world's economy headed toward the Great Depression), the Dow Jones Industrial Average hits 300 again.

MARCH 6

1819　The Supreme Court rules against states' power in *McCulloch v. Maryland*, deciding that states cannot tax any "instrumentality" of the federal government. In this precedent-setting case, Maryland was not allowed to tax the Baltimore branch of the Bank of the United States.

"The power to tax is the power to destroy," declared Chief Justice John Marshall.

1899   Aspirin is patented by Felix Hoffman, a young chemist with the Bayer company in Dusseldorf; he originally prepared it in 1893, in hopes of relieving his father's arthritis. The very first acetylsalicylic acid was created and abandoned in 1853 by Alsatian chemist Charles Frederick von Gerhardt. The *a* in the name is from *acetyl*, the *spir* is from *Spiraea* (a plant used in the compound), and the *in* is a common suffix for medications. The world's most prescribed drug, aspirin was declared a generic name in 1921 by Judge Learned Hand; Aspirin with a capital *A* became plain aspirin.

1930   Birds Eye Frosted Foods go on sale for the first time, in Springfield, Massachusetts. General Foods (formed the previous year through a merger of the Postum Company and the underfinanced fish-freezing business of Clarence Birdseye) introduced frozen peas, spinach, raspberries, cherries, loganberries, fish, and various meats. Although the products were a novelty and relatively expensive, and although frozen food cabinets (other than for ice cream) did not yet exist, the products succeeded, going national the following year.

1937   Ivan "Greed Is Good" Boesky is born in Detroit, the son of a Russian immigrant milkman-turned-pub owner. An uninspired student and an uninspired securities analyst, Boesky found his niche in merger arbitrage (buying the stock of takeover "target" companies and selling it for huge profits if the takeover happened). At his peak, Boesky controlled $3 billion worth of stock purchasing power and was named to *Forbes*'s list of America's 400 wealthiest individuals in 1985, the year before he told a commencement audience at the University of California, Berkeley, "Greed is all right. . . . Greed is healthy. You can be greedy and still feel good about yourself." Three months later he was giving quite a different speech to government investigators, agreeing to become an undercover agent against his fellow conspirators.

1989   "If the automobile had followed the same development as the computer, a Rolls-Royce would cost $100, get a million miles per gallon, and explode once a year, killing everyone inside." —Robert X. Cringley, in *Infoworld*

1990 In a 350–3 vote, the Soviet parliament approves a property law giving private citizens the right to own the means of production—to hire people, own small factories, and operate other business enterprises—for the first time since the early 1920s.

MARCH 7

1893 Print Patent 1 is issued to the H.J. Heinz Company of Pittsburgh, Pennsylvania, for "Heinz's Preserves, Celery Sauce, Ketchup." It showed a pickle with three circular designs. (A patented print could be used as an advertisement but not as a trademark).

1897 Cornflakes are first served at the Battle Creek Sanitarium in Michigan; they are loved immediately. The basic process for producing them was discovered there accidentally by Dr. John Harvey Kellogg and W. K. Kellogg. Experimenting with ways to make vegetarian foods more palatable, the brothers had placed some boiled wheat on a baking tin when Dr. Kellogg was called away for an emergency operation. When they returned the next day, they ran the wheat through a roller, expecting it to come out as a single sheet. What emerged were individual flakes, the forerunner of all ready-to-eat cereals.

1930 The Great Depression has hardly begun, but President Herbert Hoover is optimistic. "All the evidence indicates that the worst effects of the Crash upon unemployment will have passed during the next sixty days." Two years later the stock market was still falling.

1949 The first homes at Levittown, the Long Island housing development, go on sale. Built by Levitt and Sons, Inc., the community was an early example of a completely preplanned and mass-produced housing complex. Situated just outside Manhattan, its name became a national symbol for suburbia. The company's first experiment at such a project—1,600 homes near Norfolk, Virginia—was a failure but convinced William J. Levitt that the right market, right customers, and right economic conditions could produce a success.

1995   "The true investor welcomes volatility . . . a wildly fluctuating market means that irrationally low prices will periodically be attached to solid businesses." —Warren Buffett, chairman, Berkshire Hathaway, in a letter to shareholders

MARCH 8

1776   Four months before America's Declaration of Independence, there is an economic declaration of independence: in Birmingham, England, James Watt first demonstrates his steam engine. In the words of Howard Means, "No longer would factories be held ransom to the vagaries of drought or freeze. No longer, for that matter, would industries have to locate themselves on the banks of rivers or streams. Power would come to them. . . . And what muscle this new power had: Even the relatively primitive steam pump being put through its paces that day could do the work of a hundred men . . . The right man and the right idea had just intersected with exactly the right moment in history, in just the right place, to give birth to the Industrial Revolution."

1938   The Richard Whitney scandal becomes public. Five minutes after trading began on the New York Stock Exchange, at 10:05 A.M., a gong announcing a halt was sounded, and a somber statement was read that the investment firm of Richard Whitney & Co. was insolvent and had been suspended from the NYSE. Whitney was the president of the NYSE from 1930 to 1935, a rigid disciplinarian who often made speeches on the need for personal and professional honesty among brokers. But for an entire decade he had been a crook, stealing from his clients and looting an Exchange fund to aid the widows and orphans of members. Saddled with extreme intelligence and arrogance, Whitney led the obstruction to government oversight, calling the NYSE a "perfect institution" at the Pecora hearings of 1933. But his downfall was the last straw, and within months the Securities and Exchange Commission was able to impose stiff new rules on the NYSE, the first major reform in its history.

2001   An elderly ex-smoker becomes the first person to actually collect court damages from the tobacco industry over a smoking-related illness. Lawyers in Jacksonville, Florida, acting for Grady Carter, 70, received a wire transfer of $1.8 million (damages plus interest) from the Brown & Williamson Tobacco Corporation of Louisville, Kentucky. "Brown & Williamson paid $750,000, but I paid with a lung," said Carter, whose cancer was in remission and who now played golf three times a week. The judgment was just the second time in 40 years of antismoking litigation that a cigarette maker was ordered to pay damages to a smoker; in the first case, the family of Rose Cipollone of New Jersey won $400,000 at trial, but the verdict was overturned on appeal.

2004   *BusinessWeek* reports a nine-month, worldwide survey by Strativity Group Inc., which reveals that 45 percent of executives do not believe their corporation deserves the loyalty of its customers.

MARCH 9

1776   London printers William Strahan and Thomas Cadell release a 1,000-page, two-volume masterpiece: *An Inquiry into the Nature and Causes of the Wealth of Nations* by Adam Smith. It sold out within months but was not reprinted until 1778. The *Wealth of Nations* revolutionized world economics by laying out the rationale for laissez-faire, market-based economics. The book sold originally for 36 shillings (about $5); in 1989 a collector paid $450,000 for an original copy. Smith himself was a modest man. "I am a beau in nothing but my books," he wrote. This opinion was shared by others. "He speaks harshly, with big teeth, and he's ugly as the devil," wrote Madame Riccoboni, the French novelist. "He's a most absent-minded creature . . . but one of the most lovable."

1793   Imprisonment for debt is abolished in France about a month after Louis XVI is guillotined.

1959   Barbie is introduced to her new home: store shelves.

MARCH 10

1746   "Whatever is worth doing at all is worth doing well." —Earl of Chesterfield, statesman/diplomat

1815   A complete list of the securities traded on the New York Stock Exchange is published for the first time, in the *New York Commercial Advertiser*. There were 24 offerings. Most were government bonds and bank stocks; there were no railroads and just one manufacturer.

1911   Kansas (not usually known as a bastion of progressivism) passes America's first "blue-sky" law "for the regulation and supervision of investment companies and providing penalties for the violation thereof." Soon passed by every state in the union except Nevada, blue-sky laws were designed to protect investors in dealing with companies that sold stocks and bonds, generally requiring that both the dealers and the securities they sold be registered. The nickname was adopted quickly, but its origin is cloudy: some say it was because unscrupulous promoters would sell stock in the "blue sky"; others say they will sell stocks that were backed by "nothing but the clear blue sky."

1996   "Talent is cheaper than table salt. What separates the talented individual from the successful one is a lot of hard work." —Stephen King, supersuccessful author, in the *Independent on Sunday*

2000   The NASDAQ (the stock market specializing in tech stocks and dot.com start-ups) hits its all-time peak, closing at 5,132. It had just completed a year of 84 percent growth and was headed into a year of 70 percent loss.

MARCH 11

105   Ts'ai Lun, a eunuch in the court of Han emperor Hedi, creates the first process for making paper that is suitable for writing. Vegetable materials in the sheets of paper included the bark of mulberry trees, hemp, linen, and scraps of fishing net.

1744   Sotheby's auction house has its beginnings when London bookseller Samuel Baker auctions a private book collection. Future auctions would be done in partnership with nephew John Sotheby, and the growing operation would be taken over by John's nephew Samuel Sotheby. Samuel's son Samuel Leigh Sotheby then headed the firm until his death in 1861, and the house expanded to have auction rooms worldwide.

1909   The term *star* (to connote a person who excels) is coined today in the *New York Times*, in a letter from Brooklyn titled "Moving Picture 'Stars.'"

1931   Media baron Rupert Murdoch is born on Cruden Farm, about 30 miles south of Melbourne, Australia. His father, Sir Keith Murdoch, an influential World War I correspondent, acquired substantial positions in various newspapers, radio stations, cable services, and the newsprint industry during peacetime. According to the *Australian Dictionary of National Biography*, "[Keith] Murdoch had forged the first national media chain." It was the model his son followed, only on a global scale that involved billions of dollars instead of thousands.

1991   "Nothing focuses the mind better than the constant sight of a competitor who wants to wipe you off the map." —Wayne Calloway, CEO of Pepsico, in *Fortune*

MARCH 12

1832   Charles Cunningham Boycott is born in Burgh St. Peter, England. In 1880 he was involved in a disagreement with renters in Ireland that forever lent his name to the "collective and organized refusal to buy goods or services" (see September 23).

1877   John Wanamaker opens "a new kind of store" in a converted railroad depot in Philadelphia. It was one of the world's first department stores and soon became one of its largest. Among the many firsts introduced by Wanamaker was the full-page newspaper advertisement on a regular basis. "I know half the money I spend on advertising is wasted, but I can never find out which half," he quipped.

1958   "I can't help from making money, that is all." —Helena Rubenstein, on the cosmetic business that made her worth more than $100 million, in the *New York Journal American*

1973   Federal Express—creator of the next-day delivery industry— has its first day in business, with planes flying into its hub in Memphis from all over the country . . . with a total of *six* packages. Its next day of deliveries in April was not much better, and by the end of its first fiscal year in business it showed an accumulated loss of $4.4 million.

MARCH 13

1770   Formed by 20 merchants in Fraunces Tavern in New York City two years before, the first state chamber of commerce in America is incorporated under a royal charter from King George III. Its motto was *Non Nobis Nate Solum* ("Not born for ourselves alone").

1907   The "great panic of 1907" has its introduction with a sudden plunge in stock market prices. Industrials fell 12 percent in two days; railroads dropped more than 11 percent. Widespread margin calls sank a number of brokerage houses, but by summer a lot of the ground was recovered. The press was full of stories about bankers in the "Money Trust" purposely driving down prices, but the fact was that the market was already at bubble conditions, and the money supply sorely lagged behind demand. "There isn't money enough in the world today to do the world's work," wrote Frank Munsey. The system came unglued in the autumn (see October 23).

1950   "What the French criticize [in Coca-Cola] is less the drink itself than the civilization, the style of life of which it is a sign . . . a symbol . . . red delivery trucks and walls covered with signs, placards and advertisements . . . it is a question of the whole panorama and morale of French civilization." So ran an editorial in *Le Monde*, on a bill pending in the National Assembly to ban the sale of the American soft drink, a reaction to what had come to be called "the Coca-Colonization" of France.

1986   Microsoft goes public; shares start at $21 and reach $28 by day's end. By 2000, one of those shares was worth $10,000.

MARCH 14

1794   Eli Whitney patents the cotton gin, which would revolutionize the cotton and textile industries. His model had already been stolen, and illegal copies of his device were already being made.

1874 Dutch industrialist Anton Frederick Philips is born in Zaltbommel, The Netherlands. After working as a stockbroker, Anton joined his father's small manufacturing firm of incandescent lamps in 1895 as a salesman, climbing to partnership in 1899. Lightbulb sales flourished throughout Europe, and in 1914 the firm began the Philips Laboratories to perform original research and development. Anton took sole control of the firm when brother Gerard retired in 1922, turning it into a multinational company involved in all aspects of electronics.

1932 Seventy-seven-year-old George Eastman, creator of the large-scale amateur photography industry, dies at his home in Rochester, New York. Crippled with a disease of the spine, he wrote a short note, put the cap back on the pen, smoked a cigarette, carefully stubbed it out, and shot himself through the heart. "To my friends, My work is done— Why wait?" read the note left beside a sewing basket that had belonged to his beloved mother (see July 12).

1957 "This is nice and I appreciate it very much. But who ever heard of Paul Revere's horse?" —Charles Lawrence, at a dinner honoring him for developing the engine used in Charles Lindbergh's plane during his nonstop flight to Paris, in the *New York Journal-American*

2002 The once-illustrious accounting firm Arthur Andersen LLP is indicted by the U.S. Justice Department for obstructing justice by shredding documents and deleting e-mails and computer files relating to its ex-client Enron. The *Chicago Sun-Times* headlined its story: "Feds to Andersen: Shred This!" This was the first indictment of any person or company associated with the famous collapse of Enron. Apparently dozens of large trunks were used to haul documents from Enron's offices to Andersen's Houston offices when it became clear that Enron was going to be investigated; Andersen offices in Oregon, Chicago, and London were also involved in document destruction. The case was the last in a string of high-profile, crooked accounting jobs by Andersen in the 1990s. By year's end the firm, begun in 1913 with the maxim "Think straight. Talk straight," had put itself out of business.

MARCH 15

1884   The first accident insurance bill is presented to the Reichstag by Chancellor Otto von Bismarck. His comprehensive system of state insurance for workers (providing accident, sickness, and old-age benefits) was only one of his socioeconomic accomplishments. Canals, railroad nationalization, assistance to agriculture and industry, universal suffrage, a uniform code of civil laws, a uniform currency, and creation of a central bank were others.

1909   The first large department store in Britain, Selfridge's, opens on London's Oxford Street, with the slogan "Anything from a pin to an elephant." Harry Gordon Selfridge had acquired the skills and finances to create the 42,000-square-foot facility from 25 years' experience at Marshall Field's in Chicago. "The Great Principles on which we will build this Business are as everlasting as the Pyramids," he said in a preliminary announcement of the opening.

1975   The swashbuckling shipping magnate and pioneer of supertanker construction, Aristotle Socrates Onassis, dies at 69, or maybe 75, in a hospital in Neuilly-sur-Seine, France. Various organs were either missing or malfunctioning. His wife, Jacqueline, was 3,000 miles away in New York City, and his last remaining child, daughter Christina, left the hospital with a slit wrist. "In business we cut each other's throats," he said in 1969, "but now and then we sit around the same table and behave—for the sake of the ladies."

2002   One day after being indicted on a single count of obstruction of justice for its part in the Enron scandal (see March 14), accounting giant Arthur Andersen LLP begins receiving punishment: the government bans the firm from future federal contracts (Andersen currently holds $60 million to $90 million in government business), and four Fortune 500 companies (Sara Lee, Abbott Laboratories, Northeast Utilities, and Brunswick Corp.) sever decades-long relationships with the firm. Andersen had denied the charge but was already in talks with other Big Five accounting firms to sell off its assets.

2003   Many members of India's lower parliament, opposed to the finance minister's proposal to raise the price of fertilizer, perform a version of the filibuster by screaming raucously for more than four straight hours until the minister withdrew his measure.

MARCH 16

1662   History's first public transport system begins operation. Designed by mathematician/philosopher/scientist Blaise Pascal in 1661 and financed under royal supervision that January, the system began with four coaches that traveled between Porte Sainte-Martin and Porte du Luxembourg in Paris every eight minutes. The line generated much interest but too little revenue and eventually went bankrupt; the medieval streets were too crowded, too narrow, and too bumpy to allow smooth, fast transport.

1798   The entrepreneur who established the first steamship line between Europe and South America, William Wheelwright, is born in Newburyport, Massachusetts. His big break came in 1823 when he was shipwrecked off Buenos Aires. He spent some time on the South American continent exploring its coasts and soon envisioned business potential. Between 1835 and 1840 he raised the necessary capital in England to form a steamship line that linked Chile with Panama and Panama with England. In 1851 he built Chile's first railroad line to connect the mining region of Copiapo to the port of Caldera, and he subsequently introduced the electric telegraph, gas lighting, and water sanitation systems to several cities in Chile and Peru. He also planned the famous trans-Andean railroad between Argentina and Chile. Wheelwright died September 26, 1873.

1830   The dullest day in Wall Street history: just 31 shares are traded on the New York Stock Exchange; only two issues, a total of $3,470, change hands. The market was in an extended depression that had started in 1824, when the year's volume was 400,000 shares.

1958   "The First Duty of a newspaper is to be Accurate. If it is Accurate, it follows that it is Fair." —Herbert Bayard Swope, legendary editor/gatherer of great writers and critics/creator of the op-ed page, in a letter to the *New York Herald Tribune*

1958   The Ford Motor Company produces its 50 millionth car, a Thunderbird (thus averaging nearly a million produced per year since the company's inception). On this day in **1966** an Oldsmobile Toronado rolled off the assembly line as the 100 millionth car that General Motors had built.

1999   At 10 seconds before 8:51 A.M. the Dow Jones Industrial Average surpasses 10,000 for the first time, rising to 10,001.78 for about a minute, before retreating back to four-digit territory. Traders on the floor of the New York Stock Exchange looked up, waved their hands in the air, whooped, hollered, threw some confetti, and got back to work after about 30 seconds.

MARCH 17

1814   "Merchants have no country. The mere spot they stand on does not constitute so strong an attachment as that from which they draw their gains." —Thomas Jefferson, in a letter to Horatio G. Spafford

1845   The rubber band is patented by Stephen Perry of London.

1883   Inventor of the word *capitalism* and arguably the world's most influential economist, Karl Marx, is buried in London's Highgate Cemetery. The grave was virtually unmarked (a monument stands there now), and fewer than 20 people attended.

1906   The term for investigative journalism, *muckraking*, is coined today by President Theodore Roosevelt in a speech to the Gridiron Club in Washington. The origin was ironic. Speaking against sensationalist "yellow journalism," Roosevelt borrowed the term from John Bunyan's *Pilgrim's Progress* ("the Man with the Muckrake . . . who could look no way but downward"). However, "muckraker" soon became the nickname of great journalists who exposed miserable abuses—forced child labor, predatory finance, marketing of unsafe food and drugs—in causes that Roosevelt strongly supported. (Roosevelt famously repeated the phrase about a month later in a speech before the U.S. House of Representatives.)

1919   "Labor can do nothing without capital, capital nothing without labor, and neither labor or capital can do anything without the guiding genius of management; and management, however wise its genius may be, can do nothing without the privileges which the community affords." —W. L. Mackenzie King, three-time prime minister of Canada, in a speech to the Canadian Club, Montreal

1987   Brought to the brink of annihilation in the 1960s and 1970s by fierce Japanese competition, a recession, and its own mismanagement and poor workmanship, America's last motorcycle maker, Harley-Davidson, turned itself around in the 1980s, helped in part by a whopping 1983 tariff on Japanese imports. On this day, the company was in robust health and officially asked the government to remove the tariff, a year before it was due to expire. The *New York Times* celebrated the move as "a masterful stroke of public relations."

MARCH 18

1747   Notorious as America's first inside trader, William Duer is born in Devonshire, England, to a wealthy Caribbean plantation family. In the 1770s he established himself in New York, where he led a kind of double life: esteemed public servant (delegate to the Continental Congress, New York judge, signer of the Articles of Confederation) and wildcat investor (speculating in land, banks, and commodities). Sometimes he mixed the two roles, enriching himself by supplying the army during the American Revolution. When the Department of the Treasury was formed in 1789, Duer was appointed by friend Alexander Hamilton to be its first assistant secretary. Duer immediately began to gather precise information about the government's financial position and to speculate in government securities based on that knowledge. He was charged with malfeasance and resigned after six months. He died in prison on May 7, 1799.

1954   RKO Pictures Corporation stockholders approve the sale of their company to Howard Hughes. His check for $23,489,478 made him the first individual ever to be the sole owner of a major motion picture company.

1961   The Pillsbury Dough Boy is introduced as a marketing and brand symbol.

1984   "The Treasury could not, with any marked success, run a fish and chip shop." —Harold Wilson, British prime minister, in the *Observer*

1996   "There is no human feeling to the U.S. securities markets and sometimes no discernible evidence of human intelligence either. But they work." —Robert J. Eaton, U.S. automobile industry executive and engineer

MARCH 19

1831   On this Saturday an American bank is robbed for the first time, when two doors of the City Bank, Wall Street, New York City, are opened with duplicate keys. The amount of $245,000 was removed by Englishman Edward Smith (alias Jones, alias James Smith, alias James Honeyman), who was later caught and sentenced to five years of hard labor at Sing Sing.

1834   Six members of the Friendly Society of Agricultural Laborers in Tolpuddle, England, are sentenced to seven years in an Australian penal colony for organizing trade union activities. Such activity had been legal since 1824, but shaken by the French Revolution and alarmed at the dimensions of working class discontent, the Whig government was determined to suppress unionism. In this case the men were arrested on trumped-up charges ("administering false oaths"), and the jury was rigged and headed by the home secretary's brother-in-law. After two years of nationwide protests, the "Tolpuddle martyrs" were pardoned, but it was not until 1871 that legislation was passed that exempted unions from prosecution because of "restraint of trade."

1948 The Taft-Hartley Law is invoked for the first time. Workers in the Atomic Trades and Labor Council could not walk off their jobs at the Oak Ridge National Laboratory until a "cooling off" period of 80 days had passed (allowing for investigation of a settlement). The action came just seven hours before the strike by these workers, deemed necessary for national security, was set to begin. The law had originally been vetoed by President Harry Truman, who used it today.

MARCH 20

1856 Frederick Winslow Taylor, the father of scientific management, is born the son of a lawyer in Philadelphia. Taylor intended to follow in his father's footsteps, but abandoned the plan when excessive night studying at Harvard temporarily ruined his eyesight. He then signed on as a laborer in Philadelphia's Midvale Steel Company, where he rose rapidly to chief engineer. In 1881 he introduced scientific time study (now known as time-and-motion study) at Midvale. His idea was that factory efficiency could be improved by carefully observing workers and eliminating wasted time and actions. His methods were successful, made him famous and hated, and revolutionized factory work.

1963 "Advertising is what you do when you can't go see somebody. That's all it is." —Fairfax Cone, advertising agency partner, quoted in the *Christian Science Monitor*

1964 "I don't think anybody yet has invented a pastime that's as much fun, or keeps you as young, as a good job." —Frederick Hudson Ecker, insurance executive and chairman of Metropolitan Life, quoted in his *New York Times* obituary

1995 "Wiper inventor wins millions; still broke" reads the headline announcing today's Supreme Court victory for Robert W. Kearns in his suit against Chrysler for stealing his patented invention of the intermittent windshield wiper, now on virtually every car made. Kearns collected $21 million from Chrysler, but he had already spent $11 million on legal and other fees since inventing the device in 1963, and he expected the court to award another $11 million to his attorneys in the

Chrysler case, even though he had fired them some time ago. His wife was gone, and he was once committed to a psychiatric hospital during the ordeal. "I don't really want to live this way," said Kearns, "but you don't understand what it's like to be in litigation." Kearns slept on an air mattress surrounded by stacks of loose papers and the boxes that held his clothes.

2000   Jean-Francois Theodore, head of the Paris exchange, announces that the stock exchanges of France, Belgium, and Holland will soon merge to form Euronext, the largest single exchange on the Continent. "It is not a link. It is not an alliance. It's a merger, a full merger," said Theodore. Market capitalization of all the listed companies would equal $2.3 trillion.

MARCH 21

1667   "It is pretty to see what money will do." —Samuel Pepys

1924   America's first mutual fund, Massachusetts Investors Trust, is established in Boston.

1966   The *New York Herald-Tribune*, *Journal-American*, and *World-Telegram & Sun* announce a three-way merger after two months of fighting a Newspaper Guild charge of unfair labor practices by all three. The *Herald-Tribune* would now publish in the mornings, the *World-Journal* in the afternoons, and the *World-Journal & Tribune* on Sundays. The guild struck in April, and all three papers stopped publication. The *World-Journal & Tribune* restarted publication in September but closed for good the following May after 18 work stoppages in eight months. At a distance, it certainly looked like the three newspapers were being squeezed by competition, which made them squeeze their workforce; even after the three papers went out of business, New York City still had three daily newspapers.

1983   The cover of today's issue of *Time* magazine features automobile executive Lee Iacocca as "Detroit's Comeback Kid." Part of the cover had a blurb on Henry Kissinger's "New Plan for Arms Control." Unfortunately, the first 200,000 copies read, "Contol," without an *r*, leaving

Time executives with a big decision. They made it quickly. The presses were stopped, the misspelling corrected, and the faulty covers destroyed. The action cost $100,000 and delays of a full day for 40 percent of newsstand copies. In its 60 years this was the first such foul-up for *Time*.

1986   The smoking gun: an invoice from Drexel Burnham Lambert for $5.3 million to Ivan Boesky is created and dated at the Drexel offices in Beverly Hills, California. Michael Milken at Drexel was demanding immediate payment of his share of illegal insider trading profits he had made with Boesky, and there wasn't enough time to hide the payment within legitimate securities trades as they'd done in the past. Milken later claimed the invoice was for research work done for Boesky, but Boesky's revelation of the truth convinced authorities, which convinced Milken to confess (see February 13).

1989   "The very best takeovers are thoroughly hostile. I've never seen a really good company taken over. I've only seen bad ones." —James Goldsmith, British entrepreneur/financier/corporate raider/politician, in the *Financial Times*

MARCH 22

1642   The French monarchy liberalizes its policy on interest rates. An edict today from the court of Louis XIII restored to moneylenders in the conquered region of Savoy the right to "stipulate the interest which can be charged" on bonds and other forms of loan. The area had evolved its own traditions relating to government bonds, usury, and interest, generally setting rates in line with those of neighboring provinces. But in 1601 Henry IV seized the region and dictated his own policy, including an immediate lowering of rates. When recalcitrant lenders were arrested, tried, and sentenced, the market dried up; in the words of a contemporary chronicler, "The search spread panic, and no one dared sign any interest agreements." Europe was just awakening to the benefits of sensible credit.

1919   International airline service debuts, on a weekly basis between Paris and Brussels.

1931   Secretary of Commerce Robert P. Lamont judges that America's economy has turned around and declares "there undoubtedly will be appreciable decrease in the number of unemployed by mid-summer." Lamont soon announced job cuts in his own department, and he urged division heads to do the same.

1954   "All progress has resulted from people who took unpopular positions." —Adlai Stevenson

2000   History's largest sex-discrimination lawsuit ends after 23 years, when the U.S. government agrees to pay $508 million to settle the suit brought by 1,100 women against the now-defunct U.S. Information Agency and its broadcast branch, the Voice of America. In addition to the $508 million—approximately $450,000 before taxes to each plaintiff—the federal government also had to give the women nearly $23 million in back pay and interest, and pay the fees of their attorneys, who intended to bill the government for 90,000 hours over the 23 years.

MARCH 23

1680   The wealthiest man in 17th-century France, Nicolas Fouquet, dies at 65 in prison, on the eve of a pardon. Through inheritance and marriage he amassed considerable wealth, which he then ballooned by serving as the king's financier and banker. His ostentatious residences and lifestyle stirred jealousy (in the king, among others), and when he became finance minister to Louis XIV, he became the object of active plotters. He was convicted of embezzlement under prosecution by Jean-Baptiste Colbert, who wanted his job and suppressed records that would have partially cleared him. His possessions, wealth, and the artisans who beautified his homes ended up in the king's palace at Versailles.

1815   Parliament passes the most famous of the Corn Laws ("corn" meaning grains, especially wheat). The laws were generally intended to keep the price of wheat and bread artificially high, in favor of landowners at the expense of the poor, by placing tariffs on imported wheat. The law passed today contained a mechanism to stabilize prices: wheat could be imported duty-free if the domestic price rose above 80 shillings per bushel. Corn laws were finally repealed in 1845 in the wake of the Irish potato famine, during which the Irish could not afford bread, so they became dependent on potatoes. One million Irish died of starvation after several years of failed potato harvests in the early 1840s.

1839   Imperial envoy Lin Tse-hsu cordons off the factory district of Canton, China. Sent by the emperor to end the opium trade, Lin summoned the opium merchants and threatened to strangle them if they did not end their activities. Lin further demanded surrender of the 20,000 chests of opium sitting in some 20 ships in the harbor. When only 1,000 chests were offered in compromise, the opium was forcibly removed from all foreign vessels. In London Lord Palmerston declared that the opium trade, which accounted for half of the British exports to India, was essential for the nation's balance of payments. China was condemned for her "provocations" and "arrogance," and the Opium War was declared.

1880   The flour rolling mill is patented (U.S. Patent 225,770) by John Stevens of Neenah, Wisconsin. Termed a "grain crushing mill" in the patent, Stevens's device not only increased production by 70 percent, it produced superior flour that sold for $2 more a barrel.

1932   The Norris-LaGuardia Act is passed by Congress. Named for Republicans George William Norris and Fiorello Henry La Guardia, the act prohibited the use of injunctions in labor disputes (except in defined conditions) and outlawed "yellow dog contracts" that made workers promise not to join a union. It helped establish the right to picket, boycott, and strike.

1999   After public outcry, the "Know Your Customer" regulations are abandoned—for the time being. Proposed by the Federal Deposit Insurance Corp., the comptroller of the currency, and two other federal banking agencies to fight money laundering, the regulations specified strict monitoring of all transactions for all bank customers—verifying customer identities, determining where their money came from, and tracking each transaction.

MARCH 24

1855   Andrew William Mellon is born in Pittsburgh. Andrew dropped out of college to found a lumber business with his 14-year-old brother, Richard. They remained lifelong partners, although their first venture was sunk by the depression of 1873. Mellon then joined his father's bank, also in trouble, and was running it by age 27. Mellon was good with figures, but the key to his coming fantastic successes in business (most notably in aluminum, oil, steel, and finance) lay in his talents to foresee the ability of small firms to grow into large ones and assess the qualities of would-be borrowers/collaborators. He won acclaim as secretary of the treasury also (reducing the national debt, reforming the tax code with the Mellon Plan, and overseeing the prosperity of the Roaring Twenties, but his later years were clouded by scandal, the advent of the Great Depression, his favoritism to the rich and to large corporations, and his infamous recommendation of "Liquidate labor, liquidate stocks, liquidate farmers" to President Herbert Hoover as the economy slid into a depression. He died August 26, 1937.

1903   A new type of financial institution, Bankers Trust Company, incorporates. Conceived by Henry P. Davison and organized with Thomas Lamont (both men were to become partners in J. P. Morgan & Co.). Bankers Trust arose out of the panic of 1901, when numerous banks were crushed by the weight of bad loans during a sudden collapse in the stock market. There was no national bank or central organization to help buoy them in the crisis, so a group of banks and insurance companies pooled funds for future emergencies. Bankers Trust was also set up to handle trust banking of private citizens (handling estates, wills, family trusts, and so on), which commercial banks were barred from doing; it was called a "captive" relationship because a bank in Bankers Trust could refer customers with trust business to one of its own extensions.

1990   "I've spent 30 years going round factories. When you know something's wrong, nine times out of ten it's the management . . . people aren't being led right. And bad leaders invariably blame the people." —John Harvey Jones, British management adviser/author/former chairman of ICI, in the *Daily Telegraph*

2004   Microsoft is dealt two blows. First, it received a $613 million fine from the European Union, the largest penalty in EU history. "Microsoft has abused its virtual monopoly power over the PC desktop in Europe," said EU antitrust chief Mario Monti in Brussels. "The illegal behavior is ongoing." Second, Hewlett-Packard announced at the "BrainShare" conference in Salt Lake City that it would equip computers it sold to businesses with Linux software, a competitor. The fine would be of little consequence to the behemoth Microsoft (it had taken in $32 billion income the previous year, and its lawyers could block the fine payment indefinitely), but the rise of tiny Linux could hurt. Just a spot in Microsoft's rearview mirror at the time, Linux was not only much cheaper (it could be downloaded free off the Internet), but it was also open source, which means that its users continually improve it, and it had a populist aura, as opposed to the imperialist aura of Microsoft. The stock price for both Hewlett-Packard and Red Hat (makers of Linux) rose at the announcement.

MARCH 25

1584   Queen Elizabeth I signs a patent to Walter "Ralegh" to explore and colonize America. The patent was for six years and reserved for the queen "the fift part of all the oare and silver" that might be found.

1872   The short, dramatic life of the South Improvement Company comes to an end. Later branded by investigating congressmen as the "most gigantic and daring conspiracy" in business history, the SIC was a double collusion: America's major railroads setting prices secretly among themselves while in cahoots with a cabal of oil refiners. Refiners in the SIC received excellent shipping rates through rebates and "drawbacks"; nonmembers were ruined. John D. Rockefeller didn't design the SIC (Pennsylvania Railroad's Tom Scott had that distinction), but Rockefeller became its greatest organizer and potential benefactor. On this night, however, Rockefeller knocked at the door but was denied entry to the meeting between New York refiners (heretofore excluded from the SIC) and railroad executives in the Grand Opera House in New York City. Rather than seeking entry to the SIC, the New Yorkers had banded with also-excluded Pennsylvania refiners and convinced the railroad men to abrogate the SIC contracts and institute standard rates for all. As a result of the incident, Rockefeller's name appeared for the first time in the *New York Times*; it was misspelled as "Rockefellow."

1893   Premium coupons appear in an American newspaper for the first time. The New York City *Recorder* began a series of offerings in which 20 coupons could be exchanged for a 17- × 25-inch color reproduction of a celebrated painting; ten different works of art could be had.

MARCH 26

1937   Frederick Lewis Maytag, founder of the company that still bears his name, dies at 79. Beyond the technical superiority of his machines, Maytag's success stemmed from his salesmanship and his spotless dealings with investors, suppliers, and customers.

1980   Through the 1970s the prices of precious metals rose constantly, and Texas oil brothers Nelson Bunker Hunt and W. Herbert Hunt bet heavily (largely with borrowed money) that the trend would continue, amassing more than 120 million ounces in silver bullion and futures contracts by the time the price hit $52.50 per ounce in January. They were in sight of cornering the market when two unforeseen events occurred: new supplies flowed into the market (attracted by the increased price), and the governing body—the Commodity Exchange of New York—changed its rules to discourage speculators from hoarding. Prices dropped and the Hunts could not meet margin calls from their creditors. On this day Bunker announced that they were selling silver-backed bonds, a sure sign they were in trouble and needed cash. The market collapsed, with silver dropping to $10.80 the following day.

1987   "You don't go broke making a profit." —Nicholas Shehadie, Australian sportsman and business executive, in the *Sydney Morning Herald*

MARCH 27

1775   "There are few ways in which a man can be more innocently employed than in getting money." —Samuel Johnson, in Boswell's *Life of Samuel Johnson*

1840   Financier and bank executive George Fisher Baker is born in Troy, New York, son of George Ellis Baker, a shoe merchant, state legislator, and private secretary to statesman William H. Seward (see May 2).

1860   The corkscrew wine and champagne opener is patented (U.S. Patent 27,615, to M. L. Byrn of New York City), and 138 years later (**1998**) Viagra is approved by the Food and Drug Administration.

1980   "Silver Thursday": as panic follows the sudden collapse of the attempt of the Hunt brothers (Herbert and Bunker) to corner the silver market, the price of silver plummets to $10.80 per ounce, half its value the previous day and down from over $50 in January (see March 26). Neither the Hunts, their main brokerage (Bache Halsey Stuart Shields), nor the price of silver ever fully recovered from the episode.

1995   Founder of the modern Gucci fashion empire, Maurizio Gucci, is shot to death in the foyer of his Milan office by a henchman of his ex-wife, Patrizia Reggiani. "Quality is remembered long after the price is forgotten" is the Gucci business slogan.

2000   The price for one share of Yahoo! Japan closes at $1.12 million. By the end of trading the following day the price settled to $518,200. The drop of $610,100 set a record as the biggest change in share price in a single day.

MARCH 28

845   Earning income the old-fashioned way—by pillage, terror, and ransom—Vikings traveling up the Seine River, probably under Ragnar Lodbrok, invade Paris for the first time. The city itself was spared after a tribute of 7,000 pounds of silver was paid. The raid came at the beginning of a century of rough tourism of France by the Norse. Bordeaux repulsed them in 847, but the following year the city was captured, pillaged, and burned to the ground, with the population slaughtered. Paris was sacked in 856, again in 861, and burned in 865.

1836   Beer Baron's Day: Frederick Pabst is born on this day. August Anheuser Busch, Jr., was born on the same day in **1899**.

1865   Andrew Carnegie, 29, quits work at the Pennsylvania Railroad, never to have another boss.

1980   A shocking "black day" for the American semiconductor industry comes when Richard W. Anderson of Hewlett-Packard reveals the results of performance tests on 300,000 memory chips, half from HP's three Japanese suppliers and half from American suppliers. All the Japanese firms outperformed the very best American firms. The report, now known as "The Anderson Bombshell," caused a number of American firms to abandon memory chip construction; among them was Intel, which had based a huge part of its success and growth on such chips.

1992   "Our managers are all white, middle-aged men, and they promote in their own image." —Anonymous woman in the financial services industry, reported in the *Economist*

MARCH 29

1848   John Jacob Astor dies in New York City at 84. His estate of $20 million made him America's richest man. When he arrived in America at age 20 in the spring of 1784, he possessed little more than $25 and seven flutes. How did he turn that into an immense fortune? It began on the voyage from Europe; on board he met a fellow German who traded furs with Indians, and Astor chose that as his future occupation. In New York City he established a shop that dealt both furs and musical instruments, and he began making fur-buying trips to the frontier. The Jay Treaty of 1794 was another boost, opening up Canadian sources. Astor was a shrewd bargainer with suppliers and also served as a financier to many of them; when they fell into debt, he demanded they deal only with his company. By 1800 Astor was rich, was the dominant figure in the fur trade, and had begun to purchase New York real estate. In 1808 he and some partners formed the American Fur Company, the nation's first monopoly.

1859   Oscar Ferdinand Mayer is born the son of a professional forester in Germany. At 14, Oscar immigrated to America with relatives;

by 1883 he had spent several years working for the Armour meat company in Chicago, when he branched out on his own and bought a small sausage shop. His brothers were a great help: Max kept the books, and Gottfried had already served as an apprentice to master *wurstmachers* in Nuremberg. Their Bavarian-style sausages were immediately successful, and five years later they bought land for a new, two-story facility. The current Oscar Mayer plant sits on that property.

1886   John S. Pemberton begins advertising his "esteemed Brain Tonic and Intellectual Beverage": Coca-Cola. He concocted it as a headache and hangover remedy. In May he persuaded fountain man Willis E. Venable at Jacob's Pharmacy in Atlanta to sell the beverage on a trial basis; Venable added carbonated water to the syrup, and by year's end Pemberton had sold 25 gallons at $1 per gallon. Advertising costs of $73.96 were triple receipts, however, and Pemberton sold two-thirds of his rights to Coca-Cola for $1,200 the following year.

1918   Samuel Moore Walton, founder of Wal-Mart, is born in a farmhouse near Kingfisher, Oklahoma.

1999   The Dow Jones Industrial Average closes above 10,000 for the first time, at 10,006.78. It had taken 99 years to reach its first 5,000 and just 4 years to reach its second.

MARCH 30

1858   The pencil with the attached eraser was patented on this day by Hyman L. Lipman of Philadelphia (U.S. Patent 19,783).

1887   The nation's first mutual liability insurance company, American Mutual Liability Insurance Company, incorporates in Boston. In October it opened for business, writing 22 policies covering the liability of employers to injured workers. The rate was 30¢ per $100 of payroll.

1947   Independent automobile entrepreneur/inventor Preston Tucker announces plans for his first car, the Tucker. Nicknamed "Tin Goose" and the "Tucker Torpedo," the machine was full of performance and safety innovations (including the padded dashboard, rear-mounted engine, and independent suspension), and the market was right (a postwar economic boom was under way, and no new model car had been introduced since 1942). Money was Tucker's problem. To help raise it he sold franchises to prospective dealers, who put up $50 for every car they anticipated selling. The SEC took him to court on the grounds that he was selling unauthorized securities; by the time he won his case, 51 Tuckers had been built, but Preston was financially ruined.

1951   The first commercial computer, UNIVAC, is given a rigorous 17-hour acceptance test by the Electronic Control Corporation. The machine was marketed by Remington Rand (now Sperry Rand), which bought the rights to and redeveloped ENIAC, the first electronic computer. The UNIVAC was accepted by the U.S. Census Department, and the government ordered five more the following year.

1980   "Hiccups in the international business scene are not new to us. Wedgwood china has survived upheavals before—the Napoleonic Wars, the Franco-Prussian War, the world wars. We do have a sense of continuity." —Arthur Bryan, chairman of Josiah Wedgwood & Sons Ltd., in the *New York Times*

MARCH 31

1913   The greatest financier since Nebuchadnezzar, John Pierpont Morgan dies in Rome's Grand Hotel. Within hours, the pope and 3,697 others have telegraphed condolences to his family.

1921   British miners launch the "Great Coal Strike."

1928   "Now is the time to get out of debt. Sell enough securities to lighten your obligations or pay them off entirely. . . . We do not urge that you sell securities indiscriminately, but we do advise in no uncertain terms that you take advantage of present high prices and put your own financial house in order," reads today's letter to clients from the great Charles E. Merrill, cofounder of Merrill Lynch. The letter was remarkable for its prescience of the coming stock market crash and for its altruism; while many brokers were pumping up client greed in the Roaring Twenties in order to line their own pockets, Merrill was urging restraint and health.

1958 "I've never been poor, only broke. Being poor is a frame of mind. Being broke is only a temporary situation." —Mike Todd, movie producer and theatrical entrepreneur, in *Newsweek*

APRIL

APRIL 1

1778 The dollar sign ($) is created by Oliver Pollock, a New Orleans businessman.

1940 The revolutionary stock brokerage firm of Merrill Lynch, E.A. Pierce & Cassatt opens for business. It was largely designed by Charles E. Merrill, who was thoroughly honest, sincerely interested in his clients' welfare, and highly experienced in retail mass marketing. Among his innovations in the securities industry were branches in small cities, advertising, free seminars, salaried salespeople, and catering to small accounts. "We must bring Wall Street to Main Street," he said, "and we must use the efficient, mass merchandising methods of the chain store to do it."

1948 The firm of Skadden, Arps, Slate, Meagher & Flom—the world's foremost specialists in mergers and acquisitions—is founded by Marshall Skadden, Leslie Arps, and John Slate. Each had been passed over for partnership at an old-line Wall Street law firm. By 1960 they employed 10 lawyers; by 1996 they employed more than 1,000.

1963 New York City newspapers resume publication after a strike of nearly four months. A ranking official of the Publishers' Association of New York was quoted in the *New York Times*, "Our professionals miscalculated on every major point. . . . Always their approach was 'Give 'em nothing—and do it retroactively.'"

1965 The great cosmetics manufacturer, Helena Rubinstein dies at 94 in New York City (see December 25). "I believe in hard work. It keeps the wrinkles out of the mind and spirit," she once said.

1981   Jack Welch, 45, begins work as the eighth chairman in the 89-year history of General Electric. "I was like the dog who caught the bus," he said of the awesome responsibility.

APRIL 2

1799   The legislature of New York State grants a charter to the president and directors of the Manhattan Company to provide water to New York City. A clause in the charter allowed the company to invest excess funds in banking. It was Aaron Burr, one of the company's founders, who insisted on the clause, purely as a scheme to break the monopoly of Alexander Hamilton on New York City's banking. When the company (later to become the Bank of Manhattan and still later to merge with Chase National Bank) bought a house at 40 Wall Street for $30,000 in September, Burr's Republican Party had their bank, Hamilton's Federalist monopoly ended, and the ugly conflict between the two men deepened.

1853   The first significant merger in the first "big business," railroads, is authorized by the New York State legislature. The New York Central was created by consolidation of ten short-line railroads between Buffalo and Albany, with an aggregate capitalization of $23,085,000.

1866   "Work is the grand cure of all the maladies and miseries that ever beset mankind." —Thomas Carlyle, British historian and philosopher

1993   The famous "Marlboro Friday" price slice occurs when tobacco giant Philip Morris announces a sudden, dramatic 25 percent slashing of the prices of all its brand-name cigarettes. Why? To regain market share that generics had been steadily stealing for years. It was a tremendous gamble by (nonsmoking) CEO Michael Miles: the move was unorthodox, profits were immediately jeopardized, and the brand image of superiority was completely undercut. No longer could branded cigarettes demand twice the price of generics, and no longer could the prices be raised annually to fatten profits. PM's share price plunged 23 percent in the first day after Marlboro Friday but then gradually recovered. Market share, profits, and sales all climbed.

APRIL 3

1860   The first Pony Express riders leave St. Joseph, Missouri, and deliver mail to Sacramento, California, just 10 days later. A financial disaster from the start (perhaps it is telling that the route went through the Donner Pass), the Pony Express was organized for the firm of Russell, Majors and Waddell by William Hepburn Russell, who seemed to specialize in incredibly expensive, doomed ventures in the desert. The service covered 1,800 miles, involved 157 manned stations, and kept 80 riders in the saddle day and night. Russell, Majors and Waddell was driven to bankruptcy by the Pony Express, which became obsolete after 18 months with the completion of transcontinental telegraph service. As well as being a classic example of how technology drives business change, the Express remains a symbol of the romantic Old West. The ominous phrase "orphans preferred" on help-wanted ads for riders seems to have been a fiction.

1872   "Increased means and increased leisure are the two civilizers of man." —Benjamin Disraeli, British prime minister, in a speech to the Conservatives of Manchester

1898   Publisher Henry Robinson Luce is born in Tengchow, China, to missionary parents. The family barely escaped death during the Boxer Rebellion of 1900 but stayed on for years. Luce was educated in China until age 14, when he entered the Hotchkiss School in Connecticut on a scholarship. There he met Briton Hadden; they were rival editors on different school publications, and a similar competition persisted at Yale. In 1922 Luce and Hadden became partners to publish the weekly newsmagazine *Time* with $86,000 raised from 72 shareholders. The magazine was successful, influential, and spawned the Time-Life publishing empire. Luce was a missionary himself for the American way of life and thinking; his various magazines were accused of being "masterpieces of bias." His response? "I am a Protestant, a Republican and a free enterpriser, which means I am biased in favor of God, Eisenhower and the stockholders of Time Inc.—and if anybody who objects doesn't know this by now, why the hell are they still spending 35 cents for the magazine?"

1968   At a rally for striking sanitation workers in Memphis, Tennessee, Martin Luther King, Jr., delivers his famous "mountaintop" speech. He is murdered within 24 hours.

1986   IBM unveils the PC Convertible, the first laptop computer.

1997   By a vote of 4–0, the Federal Communications Commission (FCC) approves a plan to make digital television the national standard.

APRIL 4

1800   The nation's first bankruptcy act is passed "to establish a uniform system of bankruptcy in the United States." The law, repealed in December 1803, contained 64 sections, applied only to merchants, and did not permit voluntary bankruptcy.

1878   The Atchison, Topeka and Santa Fe Railroad cuts engineers' pay 10 percent. Most engineers and firemen went on strike, the railroad was closed for five days, and troops were called in at Emporia, Kansas. One of the militia killed an innocent bystander, which led to the arrest of strike leaders.

1958   "I hitched my wagon to an electron rather than the proverbial star." —David Sarnoff, chairman, RCA, on receiving an honorary high school diploma from the New York high school he quit in 1906, in the *New York Times*

2000   Underwriters set the value of 202 million shares of the MetLife insurance company at $14.25 apiece, thus readying them for sale on the New York Stock Exchange. MetLife was the latest insurance provider to convert from mutual ownership by policyholders to public ownership. When the second part of the conversion was completed, with shares being issued to some 9 million policyholders, MetLife became the nation's, if not the world's, most widely held stock, easily surpassing Lucent Technologies' roster of about 4.7 million shareholders.

APRIL 5

1858   The first to make a success of the mail-order seed business, Washington Atlee Burpee is born in Sheffield, Canada. The keys to his success seem to have been his skill as a nurseryman, extensive sources in Europe, and absolute truth in advertising. He employed progressive business methods and conducted field trials for his crops; this ensured quality and often improved yield and taste. By the time he passed the company on to his son (see below), it employed 300 people and handled 3,000 orders daily.

1887   "Power tends to corrupt and absolute power corrupts absolutely. Great men are almost always bad men. There is no worse heresy than that the office sanctifies the holder of it." —Lord Acton, in a letter to Bishop Mandell Creighton of Cambridge University

1893   David Burpee is born in Philadelphia. David became head of his father's firm in 1915, when sales were about $900,000; by the 1950s sales had risen to $6 million, making it the world's largest mail-order seed company. David continued his father's tradition of sound business and product innovation. Twenty thousand orders per day were handled during peak season, and David oversaw the introduction of more than 50 new flowers and vegetables. During World War I, when food shortages and rising prices threatened cities across the country, Burpee established demonstration war gardens that taught citizens how to grow their own food—a good gesture that increased seed orders significantly.

2002   The world's largest bank, Mizuho Financial Holdings of Tokyo, completes its first week in existence on a distinctive note: around 30,000 customers discover that they have been billed twice for the same credit card purchases, and about 100 more complain that they have been debited for withdrawals they never made. The bank's opening day, April Fool's Day, saw its computers crash during opening ceremonies, leaving customers without access to cash. A later glitch blocked millions of money transfers nationwide, preventing account holders from paying their bills. "We take the problems seriously," said chief information officer Fumito Ishizaka. "I think they have substantially damaged our reputation."

APRIL 6

1777   "Sir, I have just been honoured with a Letter from you, dated 26th past, in which you express your self as astonished, and appear to be angry that you have no Answer to a Letter you wrote me of the 11th of December, which you are sure was delivered to me. . . . Whoever writes to a Stranger should observe 3 Points; 1. That what he proposes be practicable. 2. His Propositions should be made in explicit Terms so as to be easily understood. 3. What he desires should be in itself reasonable. Hereby he will give a favourable Impression of his Understanding, and create a Desire of further Acquaintence. . . . Now it happen'd that you were negligent in *all* these Points." —Benjamin Franklin, in a tutorial on business letters from France to a stranger who identified himself only as "Lith"

1808   The American Fur Company is incorporated in New York State by John Jacob Astor. Headquartered in St. Louis, the enterprise dominated the fur trade in the central and western United States for decades, using its size, influence, and sharp business practices to either absorb or crush rivals. It has been called America's first monopoly. Pelt animals were hunted to complete or near extinction in favorite territories: around the Great Lakes, the Rocky Mountains, the Missouri River valley, and Oregon. Trapper and trader activity did much to prepare these regions for white settlement. Astor sold his interests in the company in 1834 after realizing that many source areas were then barren. By that time it was America's largest commercial organization, and Astor would die America's richest man (see March 29).

1930   Hostess Twinkies ("the original junk food") are invented by James Dewar.

1938   Dr. Roy Plunkett, a DuPont chemist, accidentally discovers Teflon while working on coolant gases for use in refrigerators. On this morning he examined a container that should have held a very cold gas but instead found that the chemical had congealed on the sides of the container. He was amazed at how slippery it was and how impervious it was to all sorts of corrosive chemicals he applied to it. The name he gave it was short for its chemical name: tetrafluoroethylene. The substance is now found on space ships, microchips, heart valves, and cookware throughout the world.

1998   The Dow Jones Industrial Average closes above 9,000 for the first time.

1998   "In Largest Deal Ever, Citicorp Plans Merger with Travelers Group." Thus blared the *New York Times* headline announcing today's megamerger that created a $70 billion company between two financial goliaths. The biggest merger in history—creating Citigroup, Inc.—showed just how far Depression-era finance regulations had been eroded. Citigroup would operate in every major financial service, from insurance to banking to stock underwriting. Fearful that such collaboration could lead to abuse of customers and create a national crisis if trouble in one segment cascaded into the others, Congress had passed the Glass-Steagall Act in 1933 specifically to separate these functions. But by 1998 regulators had carved loophole after loophole in that law, culminating in today's marriage, which virtually shattered Glass-Steagall.

APRIL 7

1720   Parliament passes the South Sea Bill, granting the South Sea Company the ability to issue stock in payment of the national debt. The stock price rose, then crashed dramatically (see January 21), creating the phenomenon forever known as the South Sea Bubble.

1902   To exploit the great oil strike at Spindletop, Texas (see January 10), oilman Joseph Cullinan, investment banker Arnold Schlaet, and financier John "Bet-A-Million" Gates form the Texas Company—now called Texaco—in Beaumont. Wherever they drilled around Spindletop, oil spouted . . . until the area suddenly failed. By that time Texaco had fields elsewhere and had established processing and marketing facilities.

1922   The "Teapot Dome Scandal" is brewing. Secretary of the Interior Albert B. Fall secretly promises Harry F. Sinclair of Mammoth Oil Company exclusive rights to develop the Teapot Dome naval oil reserves in Wyoming. In return for this and for the legitimate contract that specified that Mammoth would keep all profits other than a minority royalty that went to the government, Fall secretly received $233,000 in bonds, $85,000 in cash, and some livestock for his New Mexico ranch. Fall made a similar deal with Edward L. Doheny of the Pan American Petroleum Company for leases of the Elks Hills and Buena Vista Hills reserves in California. Fall was briefly imprisoned; Sinclair and Doheny were acquitted.

1947   "It will take a hundred years to tell whether he helped us or hurt us, but he certainly didn't leave us where he found us," remarked Will Rogers about Henry Ford, who dies on this day at age 83 in his bedroom in Dearborn, Michigan. The room was lit with candles and warmed by a log fire, as in the farmhouse of his birth. In Ford's pockets on the day of his death were just a comb, a mouth harp, and a pocketknife.

1958   "The reason the Yankees never lay an egg is because they don't operate on chicken feed." —Columnist Dan Parker, on the most successful team in baseball history, in *Sports Illustrated*

1964   The first mainframe computer, the IBM System/360, is introduced at the company's lab in Poughkeepsie, New York. In addition to greater speed and power, the machine (nicknamed "big iron") allowed unheard-of flexibility: users could upgrade an existing system rather than replace it, the same machine could be used in a variety of applications, and software programs could be swapped between mainframes.

APRIL 8

1863   "[Jay Cooke] has succeeded in popularizing the great five-twenty loan, and now finds the people so anxious to convert their currency into bonds that it is only with difficulty he can meet the sudden and increasing demand," trumpets today's *Philadelphia Press* about the unprecedented success that investment banker Cooke had in selling bonds that were callable in five years and matured in twenty to finance the Civil War. The bonds had sat idle and unwanted for months when Secretary of the Treasury Salmon Chase tried to sell them to usual investors, such as merchants, banks, and foreign buyers. Desperately needing a new approach, Chase turned to Cooke, whose innovations were several: (a) forget the large sellers, and enlist many small agents in small towns, such as local bankers, insurance salesmen, and realtors; (b) coordinate sales via the newly developed telegraph (this effort made Jay Cooke & Co. the first "wire house"); (c) advertise extensively and aim at the common man. Cooke's success not only helped win the war, but also changed the marketing of securities.

1997　"The growing technical prowess of nations such as India unnerves some people . . . who fear a loss of jobs and opportunities. I think these fears are misplaced. Economics is not a zero-sum game." —Bill Gates, chairman and founder, Microsoft, in the *New York Times*

1997　An 1804 silver dollar, only one of 15 in existence, becomes history's most valuable coin by fetching $1,815,000 at auction in New York City. The coin came from the collection of banker Louis Eliasberg of Baltimore, the only person to own a complete set of U.S. coins.

APRIL 9

1492　The last patriarch of the de Medici banking empire, Lorenzo "the Magnificent," dies at 43 in Florence (see January 1).

1893　"America's Sweetheart," Mary Pickford, is born in Toronto. She was four when her father died, and her mother's alcoholism left her feeling responsible for the family as a child. She negotiated her first acting job at age five, approaching the manager of a Toronto theater company by herself and telling him she could play the part that she'd heard was open in "Bootle's Baby." The incident set the tenor of her career—very talented actress (she was one of the first and richest movie idols) but also a shrewd, gutsy, well-prepared negotiator. She understood contracts like a lawyer and understood business like the moguls she bargained with. "True, there are occasional accidents of career, but the greatest successes are not accidental; they are designed," she said. In 1919 she took the big plunge and designed her own studio, forming the very successful United Artists Corp. with luminaries D. W. Griffith, Charlie Chaplin, and Douglas Fairbanks, Sr. That company and her investment portfolio, which was full of California real estate, made her worth an estimated $50 million at her death.

1919   Founding father of the computer age, John Presper Eckert, Jr., is born in Philadelphia. In 1946 Eckert and John W. Mauchly unveiled ENIAC, the first general-purpose electronic digital computer. It weighed 30 tons; filled an entire room; and used some 18,000 vacuum tubes, 70,000 resistors, and 10,000 capacitors. They began the work in 1943 at the University of Pennsylvania for the U.S. government, and by December 1945 the machine solved its first problem—calculations for the hydrogen bomb. The Eckert-Mauchly Computer Corp. was acquired in 1950 by Remington Rand, which merged in 1955 to form Sperry Rand, and later merged again to form Unisys, from which Eckert retired in 1989 with 87 patents.

1969   "Business is like sex. When it's good, it's very, very good; when it's not so good, it's still good." —George Katona, academic and business analyst, in the *Wall Street Journal*

1990   "We feel the spear of the marketplace in our back." —Tony O'Reilly, executive chairman of Independent News & Media/former CEO of Heinz Corporation/former Irish rugby star, in *Fortune*

APRIL 10

1709   England's Copyright Act of 1709—the first of its kind in any country—takes effect. It is "An Act for the encouragement of Learning, by vesting of the copies of printed books in the authors or purchasers of such copies during the times therein mentioned." Authors and/or printers were given exclusive rights to their printed materials for 14 years "and no longer"; though this time limit was criticized and changed, the act was a revolutionary attempt to balance the good of society with that of authors to limit both privacy and piracy.

1790 America's first patent law is passed, an "act to promote the progress of useful arts." The first members of the patent board (placed originally in the Department of State) were Secretary of State Thomas Jefferson, Attorney General Edmund Randolph, and Secretary of War Henry Knox.

1934 Six weeks before being gunned down with partner Bonnie Parker, bank robber Clyde Barrow sends this glowing testimonial to Henry Ford: "Dear Sir: While I still have got breath in my lungs I will tell you what a dandy car you make. I have drove Fords exclusively when I could get away with one. For sustained speed and freedom from trouble the Ford has got ever[y] other car skinned, and even if my business hasn't been strictly legal it don't hurt anything to tell you what a fine car you got in the V8. Yours truly, Clyde Champion Barrow."

1988 "If you do anything just for the money you don't succeed." —Barry Hearn, British sports promoter, in the *Sunday Telegraph*

APRIL 11

1586 "The Genoese merchants that were wont to furnish [Philip II of Spain] with money in time of necessity . . . begin to draw back," notes Queen Elizabeth's principle secretary, Sir Francis Walsingham, about the toll that Francis Drake and other privateers are having on Spain. For years, without any declaration of war or official standing, these freebooters had been attacking Spanish ports and ships, seriously hurting the flow of gold and other supplies to Spain. Now Walsingham noted that money markets were beginning to dry up. Philip's credit rating had been downgraded. By 1588 Philip could stand no more, and he launched the Spanish Armada.

1846 Thomas Adams, Jr., the founder of America's chewing gum industry, is born in Brooklyn, New York. In 1866 he journeyed to Mexico, where he was introduced to chicle, a gum substance from the sapodilla tree. Unable to make commercial rubber out of it, Adams decided to turn it into a food item (following observations of that use in local Indians). He established a small factory in New Jersey but was unable to attract much interest, even when giving his product away as a premium with candy purchases. The addition of flavorings and sugar did the trick.

1932   The famous Pecora Hearings begin in the U.S. Senate in Washington, although it wouldn't be until the following January that Judge Ferdinand Pecora actually joined them. His sharp, dogged questioning of major investment bankers—Aldrich, Dillon, Forrestal, Otto Kahn, J. P. Morgan, Wiggin—exposed the corruption behind the crash of 1929. The term *bankster* became popular. The testimonies had great influence on the Truth in Securities Act and the Glass-Steagall Bank Act, both in 1933.

1938   On this day Richard Whitney, president of the New York Stock Exchange and brother of George Whitney at Morgan, is sentenced to a prison term of five to ten years by Judge Owen W. Bohan in New York City. The first witness at the Pecora Hearings (see above), Whitney spent the night in the Tombs prison and the following day was shipped to Sing Sing in the company of two extortionists who used to be lawyers, a gunman, and a man convicted of rape (see March 8).

1962   ". . . The American people will find it hard, as I do, to accept a situation in which a tiny handful of steel executives whose pursuit of private power and profit exceeds their sense of public responsibility, can show such utter contempt for the interest of 185 million Americans." —President John Kennedy, reacting in controlled anger to the announcement of U.S. Steel that steel prices were being raised just days after Kennedy had leaned heavily on the United Steelworkers union to accept a wage increase far below what they had wanted

APRIL 12

1770   The British parliament repeals most of the Townsend Revenue Act of 1767, removing duties directly payable at American ports by the colonists on lead, glass, paper, and paint. The duty on tea remained. With blood on the streets already, the action came too late. The Revenue Act was one of four Townsend Acts of 1767 whose main purpose seems to have been to control more than revenue; Chancellor of the Exchequer Charles Townsend himself estimated the taxes would bring in only £40,000. Shrewd observers predicted that the colonies would be lost for the sake of this paltry sum.

1857 Founder of the Underwood Typewriter Manufacturing Company, John Thomas Underwood, is born in London, the son of John Underwood, a chemist who had invented copiable writing and printing inks and special papers. The elder Underwood moved to the United States in 1872 and began manufacturing paper and ink in a barn in New Durham, New Jersey. His sons followed in 1873, the first year that the typewriter was being manufactured on a commercial scale by E. Remington & Sons. The Underwoods became pioneer manufacturers of typewriter supplies, making carbon paper, ribbons, and related items. In 1895 John Thomas purchased the rights to Franz X. Wagner's "frontstroke" typewriter, the first to allow the typist to see the letters as they were being typed. In 1897 Underwood began selling the machines, and by 1915 he had created the largest and most complete typewriter factory in the world, producing 500 machines a day and employing 7,500 people.

1888 Ludwig Nobel dies of heart trouble in Cannes, France, but a newspaper mistakenly runs an obituary of his brother, famous explosives inventor Alfred Nobel. The obituary called Alfred a "merchant of death," which hurt him deeply. This chance event spurred him to change the public's image of him and was key to his decision to establish the Nobel Prizes. His most lucrative invention, dynamite, also occurred by chance. In 1866, Nobel discovered that a cask of nitroglycerin had leaked into its packing material—diatomaceous earth. This unplanned combination of substances gave nitroglycerin just the stability it had previously lacked; it was finally commercially viable.

1989 "I always say to executives that they should go and see *King Lear*, because they'll be out there one day, wandering on the heath without a company car." —Charles Handy, British business executive and management theorist, in the *London Times*

APRIL 13

1813   Founder of the Morgan dynasty of financiers, Junius Spencer Morgan is born in West Springfield, Massachusetts, son of wealthy businessman Joseph Morgan. Junius began in dry goods, then worked in several brokerage houses, finally becoming a partner in the powerful London international banking firm of George Peabody & Co. in 1854. The firm changed its name to J.S. Morgan & Co. upon Peabody's retirement 10 years later. It became the most prominent issuing house in London in 1870 when it raised a $50 million loan for the French government to fight the Franco-Prussian War. Morgan died in a coma in Monte Carlo on April 8, 1890, five days after being thrown against a stone wall when a train startled the horses pulling his carriage.

1852   Retail giant Frank Winfield Woolworth is born near Rodman, New York. To escape the family farm he took salesclerk jobs in surrounding towns but surprisingly showed little aptitude for the work—making incorrect change, filling out sales tickets incorrectly, and having little rapport with customers. But he did have a knack for display. His employer decided to try a "five-cent counter"; he purchased $100 worth of cheap miscellaneous items (safety pins, collar buttons, baby bibs, thimbles, soap, crocheting needles, buttonhooks, and harmonicas) and had Woolworth array them on a long table surmounted by a placard advertising the price. They sold out in a day. Woolworth ran with the idea, borrowing $315 in merchandise from his boss and opening The Great Five Cent Store in Utica, New York, in 1879. He had seven stores in 1886, 28 stores by 1895, and 59 by 1900. By the time of his death on August 8, 1919, his empire consisted of more than 1,000 Woolworth stores in the United States, others overseas, the "Cathedral of Commerce" (the Woolworth Building in New York City, then the world's tallest building, opened by President Woodrow Wilson in 1913), and a fortune of $27 million.

1860   The Pony Express completes its first successful delivery of mail to Sacramento from St. Joseph, Missouri. Hundreds cheer as Tom Hamilton gallops up to the post office and hands over the mail satchel containing 49 letters and three newspapers (see April 3).

1968   "It takes less time to put up a factory than to train men of competence to run it." —Indira Gandhi, Indian prime minister

APRIL 14

1720   The South Sea Company offers shares for sale to the public for the first time; £2 million of stock is put up for sale at £300 per share, three times its nominal value. There was no way of knowing the stock's actual value, because hype from the government, from the company, and within the public had already blurred reality and common sense. The issue sold out in an hour (see January 21).

1778   "The insolence of wealth will creep out." —Samuel Johnson, in Boswell's *Life of Samuel Johnson*

1902   James Cash Penney opens his first store, The Golden Rule, in the frontier town of Kemmerer, Wyoming, with his wife. It was the beginning of the J. C. Penney chain. The first day's receipts were $466.59 after the store stayed open from dawn to midnight. The first year's receipts were $29,000.

1986   "If my boss calls, be sure to get his name." —Anonymous ABC executive, quoted by William S. Rukeyser in a television report on the swift shifts of personnel in television management

1994   The top executives of the seven largest American tobacco companies raise their right hands and pledge to tell the truth before today's congressional hearing on smoking, and then each makes exactly the same claim in rapid-fire succession: "I believe that nicotine is not addictive." The front page of the following day's *New York Times* carried a famous photograph of the seven being sworn in; from left to right they were Donald S. Johnston (president, American Tobacco Co.); Thomas Sandelur, Jr. (chairman, Brown & Williamson Tobacco Corp.); Edward A. Horrigan (chairman, Liggett Group Inc.); Andrew H. Tisch (chief executive, Lorillard Tobacco Co.); Joseph Taddeo (president, United States Tobacco Co.); James W. Johnston (chief executive, R.J. Reynolds); and William I. Campbell (chief executive, Philip Morris).

2000   The tech-heavy NASDAQ composite index posts its biggest drop ever, 355.49 points, nearly 10 percent of its aggregate value; the Dow Jones Industrial Average drops 617 points, also a record loss. The dot.com bubble of the 1990s had burst.

APRIL 15

1892   General Electric incorporates in New York State. The company was another industry-dominating merger engineered by J. P. Morgan between Henry Villard's Edison General Electric Company and Charles A. Coffin's Thomson-Houston Electric Company, creating a combined capitalization of $25,400,000.

1955   Ray Kroc opens the fourth McDonald's restaurant, in Des Plaines, Illinois. It is the first one, however, under his control, since he cut a deal with Maurice and Richard McDonald for the rights to franchise the name and the model operation they had created. The deal was that Kroc would sell franchises for $950 and would take just 1.4 percent of sales; the McDonalds would get 0.5 percent of sales. The deal was not very favorable to Kroc because marketing and overhead costs would come out of his percentage; however, Kroc was desperate at the time because of events in his business. The day's receipts in Des Plaines were a respectable $366.12, and the restaurant was soon profitable.

1965   With 710 outlets spread across 44 states, $171 million in annual sales, and a healthy balance sheet, McDonald's goes public. Ray Kroc immediately earned $3 million; share price leaped from $22.50 to $30 by day's end and soon hit $49.

1989   "The idea is to grind the opposition into the ground. That's on and off the table." —Barry Hearn, British sports promoter, on his work as a snooker impresario, in the *Independent*

APRIL 16

1813   Craftsman and arms manufacturer Simeon North wins a government contract to produce 20,000 pistols at $7 each, to be delivered within five years. It was the nation's first contract to specify interchangeable parts (other than Eli Whitney, there seem to have been few, if any, engineers working on interchangeability at the time). The contract stipulated that "component parts of the pistols are to correspond so exactly that any limb or part of one pistol may be fitted to any other pistol of the 20,000." The work of North's factory outside Middletown, Connecticut, was obviously good; several years later he got another contract for 6,000 rifles.

1851   The telegraph line between Brussels and Aachen, Germany, is completed, ending a brilliant little communications monopoly that Julius Reuter had been running. Every day pigeons would be taken by train from Germany to Brussels; at dawn the next morning a written report of stock market activity would be attached under the wings of three birds, which would then be released to fly back to the loft of their German owner. He would then pass the reports to Reuter, who would sell the information to news-hungry investors. Reuter learned how profitable information could be and how powerful the telegraph could be. In 1851 he moved to London and set up a telegraph office near the stock exchange. He later expanded to news of all types, founding the first news agency, which still bears his name.

1924   The Metro-Goldwyn-Mayer film corporation is formed in Hollywood by merger.

1982   The United Auto Workers union signs a 30-month contract with General Motors that freezes wages and reduces the number of days off. This was a bitter pill for the UAW, especially after recent firings by GM chairman Roger Smith in which one in six GM workers lost his job. On the same day the General Motors annual proxy statement was made public, revealing a new plan by Smith that made it easier for 6,000 executives to get bonuses. The juxtaposition of events caused a furor. The *Detroit Free Press* nominated Smith's bonus plan as the auto industry's "Dumbest Move of the Year." "Has GM, under chairman Roger Smith, lost its management touch?" asked *Newsweek*. The influential *Automotive News* said it showed that Smith and other executives lived and worked "far, far away from the real world." Smith was unrepentant: "If you say I'm tough, I'd say, yeah. And I'll tell you, *times* are tough."

APRIL 17

1492   The contract between the Spanish government and Christopher Columbus for his search for a new route to Asia is signed by King Ferdinand. To finance the voyage, royal minister of finance Luis de Santander borrowed 1,400,000 *maravedis* from a fraternity of which he was treasurer, he added 350,000 from his own pocket, and Columbus raised 250,000 from various sources. Then or later Ferdinand gave Columbus a letter to the Khan of Cathay; it was China, not India, that Columbus hoped to reach, and until the end of his life he thought he had found it.

1709   The nation's first successful newspaper debuts. The Boston *News-Letter* was edited by a postmaster, John Campbell, and printed in small pica type on 7½- × 12½-inch sheets by Bartholomew Green in a back room of his home. The paper was without competition for 15 years and reached a circulation of 300.

1837   John Pierpont Morgan is born in Hartford, Connecticut.

1844   The cylinder and flatbed combination printing press is patented (U.S. Patent 3,551) by Robert Hoe of New York City, who also created the first practicable cylinder printing press in 1831. It was originally operated by hand, and then by steam, and used to print the monthly *Temperance Recorder*.

1944   An acute labor shortage prompts this advertisement from a Seattle restaurant owner: "Woman wanted to wash dishes. Will marry if necessary."

1958   "Federal Reserve policy alone is not adequate to curb the excesses of boom periods or to turn recession into recovery. Neither monetary policy nor fiscal policy can maintain economic stability if psychology runs rampant," said Federal Reserve Vice Chairman C. Canby Balderston. And 1958 turned out to be a boom year for Wall Street (the seventh highest percent return in the century) despite a sharp decline in the autumn of 1957.

1991   The Dow Jones Industrial Average closes above 3,000 for the first time.

APRIL 18

1864   The early 1860s witnessed a proliferation of mining companies in the United States, which spawned stock swindles and a gold bubble. There was a pattern to how mining companies were formed and financed, often including agents, called "bubble-blowers," whose job was to lure large investors. On this day one of the largest and most flamboyant of the mining brokers, "the lightning calculator" Anthony Morse, saw his brokerage fail, which caused a panic. Mining stocks fell by an average of more than 90 percent. Mark Twain, himself a lifelong victim of mining securities and other bad investments, quipped, "A mine is a hole in the ground with a liar standing next to it."

1920   On this Sunday morning anarchist and escaped mental patient Thomas Simpkin enters Saint George's Church in Stuyvesant Square, New York City, because he knows it is the Morgan family church. He had come to America from England to murder J. P. Morgan, only to discover that the great financier was already deceased. In the church he shot the family doctor, James Markoe, in the forehead from close range, mistaking him for Morgan's son Jack.

1985   Ted Turner and Bob Wussler of Turner Broadcasting announce a hostile offer to buy CBS for $5.4 billion in stock and junk bonds. Wussler had been fired by CBS after 21 years' service. CBS countered by filing an ugly report on Turner with the FCC and looking for a "white knight" investor who would maintain the company's structure and management. Laurence Tisch of the Loews Corporation conglomerate agreed to play the role, but once inside the company he stripped its assets, fired massively, pumped up the stock price, and got out—typical raider behavior.

1991   "It is beginning to dawn on people that the influence of a nation is not measured by the size of its military budget, but by its industrial strength." —Tony Benn, member of British parliament

1995   Struggling to shed its image as a symbol of workplace violence, the U.S. Postal System holds a forum of postal managers in Washington, unveiling a program to identify problem workers and head off troubles. The term *going postal* has since been established to describe a berserk employee, though postal workers are actually less prone to violence than workers in other industries.

APRIL 19

1772   Credited with systematizing and giving classical form to the rising science of economics, David Ricardo is born in London, the third child in a family of at least 17 and maybe as many as 23. His father, Abraham Israel Ricardo, was a broker in the London Stock Exchange, where David began work at 14. At 21 he married a Quaker and was immediately disinherited and thrown out of his parents' house. "Ricardo's mind was the greatest that ever addressed itself to economics," said John Maynard Keynes. Ricardo's first major work, *The High Price of Bullion, a Proof of the Depreciation of Bank Notes* (1810) demonstrated a close connection between prices and the volume of bank notes. Because he was so successful as a stock trader and government loan contractor, Ricardo was able to retire at age 42 and devote the remainder of his life to theoretical works on economics. Mark Skousen rated him "the richest economist in history." Ricardo died September 11, 1823.

1909   The Glasgow branch of the Bank of Scotland begins selling shares in the Anglo-Persian Oil Company, founded on the strike in Iran at Masjid-i-Suleiman ("Mosque of Solomon"). It was the first oil found in the Middle East and the world's largest reserve at the time. The bank witnessed an unprecedented mob scene, with the public standing ten deep at the counter clutching application forms. Entry to the building was impossible for much of the day. The scene in Persia had its own chaos, created by the clash in cultures. Arnold Wilson, acting consul in the region and de facto adviser to the company, observed, "I have spent a fortnight upon Oil Company business, mediating between Englishmen who cannot always say what they mean and Persians who do not always mean what they say. The English idea of an agreement is a document in English which will stand attack by lawyers in a Court of Justice: the Persian idea is a declaration of general intentions on both sides, with a substantial sum in cash, annually or in a lump sum."

1955   "Adam and Eve ate the first vitamins, including the package."
—E.R. Squibb advertisement advocating a balanced diet rather than
reliance on vitamins, first-place winner in the sixth annual advertising
awards of the *Saturday Review*

1996   "Failing is good as long as it doesn't become a habit." —Michael
Eisner, chairman and CEO, Disney Corporation

APRIL 20

1841   Founder of the Diamond Match Company, Ohio Columbus
Barber is born in Middlebury (later Akron), Ohio, son of a cooper who
started to produce matches commercially several years later. Barber
began in the company as a salesman at 16 and was a natural at it. He
took over the entire company in 1862 and made it prosper to the point
where it was one of several competing for national domination. Barber
instituted several methods that would come to characterize industrial-
ization: (a) monopolistic consolidation—Barber combined with his three
largest rivals in the late 1870s to carve up the country among themselves, controlling about 85 percent of the market; (b) automated production—the partners pooled the best of their independently developed
machines to come up with the first modern, continuous automatic match
machine; and (c) vertically integrated manufacturing and sales organization—the city of Barberton was formed around the company, which
had its own raw materials, produced its own packaging, and had its own
sales and distribution network. In the 1890s the company built the
world's largest match factory in Liverpool, England, and spread into
Peru, Switzerland, Chile, and Germany. Barber died February 4, 1920.

1909   Mary Pickford, 16, begins her motion picture career with Biograph Pictures for less than $200 per week. By 1916 she had begun
asserting herself as an executive and earning $10,000 per week plus 50
percent of the profits from her films (see April 9).

1914   Armed company militia enter an encampment of striking miners near Trinidad, Colorado, rake the tents with gunfire for hours, soak
them with kerosene, and torch them. Dubbed the Ludlow Massacre,

the event saw 100 wounded and 21 killed, including 2 women and 11 children who were caught in the fire.

APRIL 21

1720   The directors of the South Sea Company institute a tactic that virtually ensures the price of their stock will climb quickly and to bubble proportions: easy credit is made available for stock purchase. The company stated that a £5,000 limit would be placed on each stockholder's borrowings, but that limit was ignored (see January 21).

1917   The first national advertising for Del Monte foods appears in the *Saturday Evening Post*. The campaign was created by the McCann-Erickson agency and established Del Monte as one of the best-known brand names in America. The name "Del Monte" was first used on food in 1891; executives of the Oakland Preserving Company were inspired by Charles Crocker's Del Monte Hotel in Monterey.

1946   John Maynard Keynes dies at 62 of a heart attack, in Firle, England.

1986   "Capitalism without bankruptcy is like Christianity without hell." —Frank Borman, astronaut and business executive

APRIL 22

1720   Some are becoming suspicious of the stock of the South Sea Company, though the South Sea Bubble is far from fully inflated (see January 21). The famous printer/investor Thomas Guy begins selling his shares, and at about this time the great physicist Isaac Newton, now master of the mint, decided to unload his £7,000 of South Sea, remarking, "I can calculate the motions of the heavenly bodies, but not the madness of the people."

1778   A founder of the Industrial Revolution through his invention of the "spinning jenny," James Hargreaves, dies in Nottinghamshire, England. His birth date is unknown.

1779   The phrase "not worth a Continental" stems from rampant inflation and uncontrolled money printing during the American Revolution. On this day Benjamin Franklin, 73, writes sarcastically to Samuel Cooper, "This Currency, as we manage it, is a wonderful machine. It performs its Office when we issue it; it pays and clothes Troops, and provides Victuals and Ammunition; and when we are obliged to issue a Quantity excessive, it pays itself off by Depreciation."

1922   Architect Edward Buehler Delk completes the blueprints for the first shopping center catering to automobile-driving customers. Begun in November, the Country Club Plaza outside Kansas City, Missouri, had its first tenant in March 1923. The center occupied 40 acres and had 150 stores, a 2,000-seat auditorium, and parking for 5,500 cars.

1985   "To All Pepsi Bottlers and Pepsi-Cola Company Personnel: It gives me great pleasure to offer each of you my heartiest congratulations. After 87 years of going at it eyeball to eyeball, the other guy just blinked. Coca-Cola is withdrawing their product from the marketplace, and is reformulating brand Coke to be 'more like Pepsi.' . . . There is no question the long-term market success of Pepsi has forced this move. . . . Best regards, Roger Enrico, President, Chief Executive Officer, Pepsi-Cola USA." Enrico sent this memo to celebrate the arrival of New Coke, which had not even been announced yet (see April 23), but which archrival Pepsi-Cola already saw as their biggest victory yet in the "cola wars."

APRIL 23

1959   "Love the soil. The work is hard and sometimes the return is little. . . . But you will find in the good earth and fields a sure refuge from dangerous materialism." —Pope John XXIII, himself a tenant farmer's son, to an audience of 35,000 farmers

1969   Britain issues its first 5- and 10-pence coins, moving its currency completely to the decimal system.

1983   On this Saturday night in New York, Rupert Murdoch is informed that the eminent historian Lord Dacre now thinks the *Hitler Diaries* are forgeries. Not only had Murdoch paid handsomely for the publication rights, but the following day's *Sunday Times* trumpeting their authenticity and serialization had already been printed. *Times* editors in London wanted to know what to do about the embarrassment. "Fuck Dacre. Publish" were the boss's instructions. It turned out to be a coup; Murdoch was refunded the entire rights fee, and circulation of the *Times* rose by 60,000 while the controversy raged in the press; 20,000 of those readers stayed with the *Times* after the controversy died. "After all," Murdoch said, "we are in the entertainment business."

1985   After four years in development, New Coke is announced to replace the 99-year-old formula of Coca-Cola, perhaps the world's most favorite beverage since the invention of water. The flood of harsh customer comments (over 40,000 letters and 6,000 phone calls per day) brought original Coke back before the summer ended. "Sewer water," "furniture polish," and "two-day-old Pepsi" were some of the comparisons drawn with New Coke.

APRIL 24

1620   Founder of the science of demographics and one of history's first formal statisticians, John Graunt, is born in London, whose populace was the first he studied. In 1662, more or less by accident (though he quickly saw that it could be a tool in a primitive form of market research for his own dry goods business), he found himself reading death records of London parishes and began to detect patterns (such as urban death rates exceeding rural rates, and male birth rates exceeded female rates but survivability showing the opposite trend). Graunt looked for a relationship between occupation and mortality, and he constructed the first age-class mortality statistics, now a fundamental tool of insurance. In his own words, he found "some Truths, and not commonly believed Opinions, to arise from my Meditations upon these neglected Papers, I proceeded further, to consider what benefit the knowledge of the same would bring to the world." He died April 18, 1674.

1788   Karl Mayer Rothschild is born in Frankfurt, the fourth of the five famous banking brothers.

1856   Isaac Gimbel, retail magnate, is born in Vincennes, Indiana.

1913 History's first building over 750 feet, the Woolworth Building (the "Cathedral of Commerce") is opened in New York City when President Woodrow Wilson presses a telegraph key in Washington that rings a bell in the engine room and dining hall and causes 80,000 bulbs on all 55 floors to illuminate. Designed by Cass Gilbert and standing 792 feet, it was taller than any man-made structure in the world except the Eiffel Tower.

2002 AOL Time Warner Inc. posts a first-quarter loss of $54.2 billion, the largest quarterly loss in U.S. corporate history. Its stock closes the day at $19.30, a fraction of the $72+ share price when AOL and Time Warner merged in January 2000 to form "the world's first fully integrated media and communications company for the Internet Century."

2004 Cosmetics queen Estée Lauder dies of cardiopulmonary arrest at age 97 in her Manhattan home. "I have never worked a day in my life without selling. If I believe in something, I sell it, and I sell it hard." From a start of blending face creams in her kitchen, she built a Fortune 500 empire with revenues of $4.7 billion in 1998, when Lauder was the only woman on *Time* magazine's list of the 20 most influential business geniuses. She learned marketing skills as a child in her father's New York City hardware store. Her training as a chemist also began in childhood when her uncle, a European skin specialist, came to stay with the family at the outbreak of World War I; she became his apprentice, learned his trade secrets, and participated in the creation of new formulas from natural ingredients.

APRIL 25

1627 The Company of the Hundred Associates, founded by Cardinal Richelieu, is given control of New France, entailing land grants and a monopoly on the fur trade from Florida to the Arctic Circle.

1903 Nipper the dog, the white terrier with black ears listening quizzically to the speaker horn of a Victrola, makes his American debut as a center-spread advertisement for the Victor Talking Machine Company in the *Saturday Evening Post*. One of the great trademarks of all time, Nipper was based on a real obese fox terrier. His original owner died in the 1890s; the owner's brother, a London artist named Francis Barraud, took Nipper in. One day he saw the dog peering with cockheaded curiosity into the speaker horn of an early Victrola; the artist immediately envisioned a sentimental painting. Barraud borrowed a shiny new brass horn from London's Gramophone Company and painted the scene of the curious dog and machine with the deceased master in a casket behind. The Gramophone Company loved the final painting, entitled "His Master's Voice," and persuaded Barraud to sell the rights (for £100) but paint out the mortuary details in the background. Nipper was sitting *on* the coffin in the original painting. The managing director of the Gramophone Company gave strict orders to company firemen that the first thing they were to do in case of fire was carry out the original painting from its place of honor on the wall of the director's boardroom. Victor acquired the U.S. rights to Nipper in 1901, and these were taken over by RCA in 1929 when they purchased Victor.

1935   Walter Sherman Gifford, president of the American Telephone and Telegraph Company, picks up the receiver and places a call to Thomas G. Miller. The call went from New York to San Francisco to Java to Amsterdam to London and finally to Miller's office in New York, about 50 feet away from Gifford's. Having traveled over 23,000 miles of telephone wire and radio, it was the first round-the-world telephone conversation.

1961   Robert Noyce patents the semiconductor device-and-lead structure called the integrated circuit, or "chip," which becomes the key to the computer revolution. Noyce was a vice president and general manager with Fairchild Semiconductor but was not particularly fond of either upper management or the company. In 1968 he formed Intel with Gordon Moore.

1990   "The more opinions you have, the less you see." —Wim Wenders, filmmaker, in the *Evening Standard*

APRIL 26

1478 The Pazzi family of bankers attacks their rivals the Medici in Florence's cathedral during High Mass on Easter Sunday (the priest's raising of the Host was apparently the signal to commence the assault). Francesco de Pazzi and a confederate killed Giuliano de Medici, stabbing him 19 times. Lorenzo de Medici was set upon by two others, one of whom was a priest. Lorenzo defended himself and received only minor wounds as a protective crowd gathered around him. During these events Iacopo de Pazzi (head of the Pazzi), Archbiship Salviati, and others attempted to incite a mob against the Medici in the Palazzo Vecchio, but the Medici were popular and powerful civic leaders and the mob turned against the Pazzi. Iacopo de Pazzi was struck down, carried naked through the streets, and dumped in the Arno. Francesco de Pazzi and the archbishop were hanged next to each other. Some 70 other suspected conspirators were murdered.

1812 Alfred Krupp is born in Essen, Germany, the year after his father, Friedrich, founded the family's cast-steel factory. Alfred perfected the technique of casting steel while manufacturing rails and railroad wheels, and began the manufacture of weapons. The "Cannon King" became the world's largest manufacturer of munitions.

2000 AT&T launches the largest initial public offering of stock in U.S. history. The company offered 360 million shares (valued initially at $10.62 billion) in the AT&T Wireless Group, the corporation's mobile telephone operations, for sale. At the time of the offering, AT&T Wireless had 18,700 employees and over 12 million subscribers, making it the second largest U.S. mobile phone operation behind Verizon.

2002 Robert Lavagna, a trade specialist, former commerce minister, and Argentina's ambassador to the European Union, is named as Argentina's new economy minister. He had a tough job; since the one-to-one pegging of the peso to the dollar was abandoned in January, inflation had run wild and the peso had lost 70 percent of its value. Lavagna was the sixth person in a year to serve as economy minister.

APRIL 27

1898   ". . . in freeing peoples, perishing and oppressed, our country's blessing will also come; for profit follows righteousness," said Albert J. Beveridge ("Beveridge the Brilliant"), a retired statesman, in a speech at the Middlesex Club in Boston. He urged war in Asia, war in Cuba, and neocolonialism for the betterment of the American economy around the world.

1959   "One man's brain plus one other will produce about one half as many ideas as one man would have produced alone. These two plus two more will produce half again as many ideas. These four plus four more begin to represent a creative meeting, and the ratio changes to one quarter as many . . . —Anthony Chevins, vice president, Cunningham & Walsh ad agency, in *Advertising Age*

1970   The first ATM opens in Los Angeles, at the Surety National Bank's Civic Center branch. The automated "tellerless" bank contained six stations equipped with closed-circuit cameras monitored by a human teller. Checks were validated instantly by code rather than by signature, and a money machine dispensed cash in envelopes.

1981   Xerox introduces the first computer with a mouse and point-and-click convenience; it costs $16,500.

2002   Barbie's mother passes away. Ruth (née Mosko) Handler, who not only created the wildly successful Barbie doll but also cofounded the Mattel toy company, died at 85 in Century City Hospital, Los Angeles, of complications from colon surgery. Although feminists have seen Barbie as an icon of female subjugation, Handler saw her as just the opposite. "My whole philosophy of Barbie was that through the doll, the little girl could be anything she wanted to be. Barbie always represented the fact that a woman has choices." Handler saw her great career at Mattel come to an end in 1978 with her indictment and sentencing for mail fraud and securities fraud. She then established a second successful career around the Nearly Me breast prosthesis.

APRIL 28

1884   The term *white elephant* is illustrated. For several years P. T. Barnum had been looking for an animal to match the box office success he had achieved with Jumbo the Elephant and had been intrigued by the legendary sacred white elephants of the Far East. He purchased one, and on this day the beast, named Toung Taloung, arrived from Burma on a steamer in New York City Harbor. Rather than the pure milk-white color that Barnum had advertised, the animal was a dirty gray except for a few light pink spots and pink eyes. The animal was a commercial flop; Barnum was roasted in the press; and his leading circus rival, Adam Forepaugh, soon began drawing large crowds with his own elephant, which was pure white. An investigative reporter, Alexander Kenealy, snuck into the animal's enclosure and washed paint off its body with a wet sponge. Rather than publishing, Kenealy sold the information to Barnum, who then blasted the news across the country.

1914   Printer and organizer in a union of typesetters A. J. Portenar writes a seven-page handwritten letter to Frederick Winslow Taylor, thoughtfully expressing one of the key problems with Taylor's system of scientific management in which human output was analyzed as if it was coming from a machine: "I have tried to read and think about it without prejudice. I have tried to be impersonal. . . . But sitting at my machine, and noting the variations in my own hourly output, I have felt that it would be terrible to know that I am in the grip of a remorseless, unfeeling, unknowing system, that has set me a task that taxes my powers *at their best*, while I realize that I am *not always able to do my best*. There are days when I can with ease do much more than on other days I can do with effort. But nervous energy is sure to be burned more rapidly than it can be replaced under the artificial stimulus of your task and bonus."

1967   The McDonnell-Douglas Corporation is created when Douglas Aircraft is absorbed by the McDonnell Aircraft Corporation, a 39-year-old maker of military equipment. The action came after a year in which Douglas lost $27.6 million on sales of over $1 billion; Douglas's working capital had shrunk to $38 million, down from $187 million in 1958 when rival Boeing introduced the 707.

APRIL 29

1863   William Randolph Hearst is born a twin, on Nob Hill, San Francisco, son of George Hearst, a mining entrepreneur and politician who bought several newspapers to further his political career. After expulsion from Harvard young Hearst showed an interest in newspaper work and served an apprenticeship on Joseph Pulitzer's New York *World* until 1887, when he assumed editorship of his father's struggling San Francisco *Examiner*. In two years he made it profitable, using lessons and methods learned from Pulitzer. In 1895 Hearst purchased the New York *Journal* and began a circulation war against Pulitzer. Hearst cut his price to 1¢ (causing large deficits), stole some of the *World*'s best talent, used many illustrations and a lot of color, and sacrificed accuracy for sensationalism. The battle between these titans created "yellow journalism," and by 1900 Pulitzer abandoned the field to Hearst. Hearst died August 14, 1951.

1956   *Mas Tiempo para el Amor* ("More Time for Love") is an advertising slogan credited with swift sales of washing machines in Spain.

1971   "Take my advice: get people alongside you who make up for your weaknesses. If you are strong in production and weak in strategy, have a strategist as your right arm. . . ."—The great advertising executive David Ogilvy, to the "syndicate heads" of his firm, Ogilvy & Mather

1993   Lloyd's of London announces it is forced to abandon 300 years of tradition and will begin accepting limited liability investments, replacing its only previous policy in which wealthy investors put their entire fortunes on the line in exchange for a share of any profits. Some of its more spectacular insured properties included the *Titanic*, Betty Grable's legs, and a grain of rice with the portraits of Queen Elizabeth II and her husband on it. Today's announcement was forced by enormous recent payouts involving asbestos, the *Exxon Valdez*, and several hurricanes.

APRIL 30

1879   Stanley Burnet Resor, one of the great advertising executives, is born in Cincinnati. Mentored by J. Walter Thompson, "the father of modern advertising," Resor bought him out in 1916 for $500,000. Resor turned JWT into the largest single integrated advertising agency in the world. One of his first moves was canceling 200 of its 300 accounts, focusing on large customers only. He gathered a great staff, and he invested heavily in research. John B. Watson, originator of the school of psychology called behaviorism, was one of his hires. In summing up his career, *Advertising Age* said Resor's greatest contribution came as a "predictor of human behavior."

1952   Mr. Potato Head becomes the first toy advertised on television.

1981   Shortly after 7 A.M. the first People Express airplane with paying customers takes off from the Newark airport. "Please, let it make it back," murmured the airline's founder, Don Burr. When the plane returned from Norfolk, Virginia, dozens of reporters and officials were on hand to celebrate. By midsummer the airline was making the magic 60 percent load target that Burr estimated to be the break-even point with his absurdly low fare of $23 ($35 during peak hours) compared to the $82 charged by major airlines.

1999   The Tokyo trading floor closes after 120 years. From now on all stock trading in Japan would be done through computer, as is the method in all the major exchanges except for New York and Frankfurt. Hand signals and face-to-face trading were conducted for the last time by the dozen or so veterans still using the floor; only 0.2 percent of Tokyo volume was still being conducted this way. There was a small celebration with confetti and noisemakers at the close of trading.

2002   The man and woman who rob the Starbucks coffeehouse this morning in Monroe, Washington, are not satisfied with what they find in the safe, so they work the drive-through window for about a half hour and pocket the cash. About 25 cars were served before the pair escaped. Customers did not think anything was amiss, but "we heard that he makes a crummy cup of coffee," police said.

MAY

MAY 1

1774   One of its earliest known uses of the term *speculation*, which acquired an economic meaning only in the late 18th century, occurs today in a letter written by Horace Walpole. He describes Sir George Colebrooke, the MP and banker, as a "martyr to what is called speculation" after Colebrooke was bankrupted in a failed attempt to corner the market on alum, a substance used in textile dying.

1794   America's first two labor unions were both of shoemakers in Philadelphia. The first was formed in 1792 but existed for such a short time that its name has apparently been lost. The second, the Federal Society of Journeymen Cordwainers, was organized today. They obtained the nation's first union contract in 1799 after a strike of ten weeks but were disbanded in 1806 during a trial for conspiracy.

1880   Advertising genius Albert Davis Lasker is born in Freiberg, Germany, the son of a self-made businessman and banker. Lasker discovered how to make radio pay big profits as an advertising medium by instituting hard-sell messages that provided reasons to buy, which replaced the industry standard of merely telling the listener that the product was available. He coincidentally is credited with starting more people on the habit of smoking than anyone else due to his teaming with George Washington Hill of the American Tobacco Company. Lasker produced a handful of innovations to society as well as advertising but paid an emotional price. After three marriages and three nervous breakdowns, he underwent psychotherapy, relaxed, dissolved his ad agency (which was reborn in 1942 as Foote Cone and Belding), and turned his efforts to civic betterment. He died May 30, 1952.

1941   Cheerios is introduced by General Mills and will quickly become the company's largest selling ready-to-eat cereal. Sales were undoubtedly boosted by the 2–3 percent sugar content.

1975   Wall Street's fixed commission rate ends by order of the Securities and Exchange Commission. Institutional investors (such as bank trust departments, insurance companies, and pension programs) immediately started negotiating lower rates, and reductions in fees as large as 90 percent were realized. Some brokers and dealers are forced out of business; others were forced to merge. More money was freed up for investment, mutual funds became more popular, and brokers reduced services to compensate for lowered revenue.

MAY 2

1670   The Hudson Bay Company (officially The Governor and Company of Adventurers of England Trading Into Hudson's Bay) is chartered by King Charles II.

1931   Financier, bank president, and philanthropist (he endowed the Harvard Business School) George Fisher Baker dies at 91 in New York City. When the national banking system was created in 1863, Baker joined with John Thompson and sons to help establish the First National Bank of New York City. Beginning as a teller and small stockholder, he rose to cashier, then manager, then president of the bank. By 1909 when he became chairman of the board and director of many companies, Baker ranked with J. P. Morgan and James Stillman as a major force in U.S. finance.

1985   In Scranton, Pennsylvania, lawyers for the brokerage house E. F. Hutton plead guilty to charges that it engineered a massive check-writing swindle, in which $4 billion in checks had been written on client bank accounts from 1980 to 1982 without a single penny of interest being paid. The firm consented to pay $10 million in fines and restitution, but U.S. Attorney General Edwin Meese III ordered that none of the 24 executives involved be prosecuted on the grounds that they had not "personally benefited" from their "corporate scheme."

2001 Former Sotheby's chairman A. Alfred Taubman is indicted on price-fixing charges by a federal grand jury in Manhattan. Also indicted was Taubman's counterpart at Christie's, Sir Anthony Tennant. The pair allegedly conspired to fix auction commission rates charged to sellers from 1993 to 1999, for a total of $400 million in commissions charged to more than 130,000 customers. "These guys were incredibly arrogant. . . . They worked in a rarefied insular world and felt that the rules of law don't apply to them," remarked art appraiser Andrew Decker.

MAY 3

1469 Management guru Machiavelli is born in Florence to a once prominent family. His father was a lawyer who had been disbarred from public office as an insolvent debtor and who eked out a living from his meager property and from small, clandestine legal assignments. Machiavelli later wrote that he "learnt to do without before he learnt to enjoy."

1768 America's first arbitration tribunal is established by the chamber of commerce in New York City and consists of seven members to adjust "any differences between parties agreeing to leave such disputes to this Chamber." A different group of seven was appointed for each meeting.

1886 At the McCormick Harvester plant in Chicago, locked-out strikers attack strikebreakers outside the plant. Police intervened, killing several strikers. August Spies, a member of the anarchist International Working People's Association, witnessed the mayhem and prepared a circular calling for revenge. The stage was set for the Haymarket bomb (see May 4).

1941 By a 5–2 vote, the Federal Communications Commission (FCC) orders NBC to sell one of its two radio networks, either the Red or the Blue. There is only one other major broadcast company in the nation, CBS. A third, much weaker company, the Mutual Broadcast System, felt endangered by the two giants and had sought government action to restrain their power. The ruling was appealed by NBC to the Supreme Court, where it was upheld. NBC sold off the Blue network, which became ABC.

1963   "There is a danger when the better mousetrap is better at catching people than at catching mice." —Charles Eames, industrial designer, in *Time*

2003   Warren Buffet had not had a pay raise since 1980, receiving the same $100,000 salary as chairman and chief executive of Berkshire Hathaway Inc. for more than 20 years. His company stock, however, had appreciated nicely. The proxy statement and company report distributed for today's annual shareholders meeting at the Omaha Civic Auditorium, Nebraska, revealed that his 476,198 A shares and 60 B shares were now worth about $32.8 billion. At the start of March they were worth about $29.4 billion. Buffett made some $3.5 billion in two months, no doubt sleeping soundly for much of the time that his money was working.

MAY 4

1886   Haymarket Square in Chicago is the scene for a torchlight meeting to protest the previous night's killing of workers on strike at the McCormick Harvester plant (see May 3). The crowd seemed to be dispersing when a bomb exploded, setting off panic and police gunfire. Seven police were mortally wounded by the bomb, and some sixty others were injured by the bomb and police gunfire. The perpetrator was never found or identified, but a wave of hysteria swept from Chicago throughout the country. Eight anarchists were arrested. Though none were directly connected to the bomb, one was sentenced to 15 years imprisonment, and the rest were sentenced to death; of these, one committed suicide, four were hanged, and the sentences of the other two were commuted. The country's main labor union, the wholly innocent Knights of Labor, also suffered from the Haymarket Square bomb; its membership dropped sharply (from 730,000 to 260,000 members in two years), and it was soon supplanted by the American Federation of Labor.

1975   "It might be said that it is the ideal of the employer to have production without employees and the ideal of the employee is to have income without work." —E. F. Schumacher, British economist and conservationist, in the *Observer*

1984   At the behest of financier Michael Milken, Ivan Boesky begins buying small blocks of stock in Fischbach Corporation, a New York construction company. The action helped one of Milken's clients gain control of the company. By midsummer Boesky had purchased over 10 percent of Fischbach stock, at which point he filed a false 13-D disclosure statement with the SEC, failing to mention Milken's interest in the deal and the fact that Boesky had been guaranteed a no-loss position by Milken. It was the first outright crime the pair committed in the insider trading scandal that destroyed the investment firm of Drexel Burnham Lambert Inc. (see February 13).

1999   "On-line investing requires old-fashioned elbow grease like researching a company or making the time to appreciate the level of risk. I'm often surprised by investors who spend more time deciding what movie they'll rent than on which stock to buy." —Arthur Levitt, Jr., former chairman of the Securities and Exchange Commission, in a speech to the National Press Club

MAY 5

1905   With a card table, a borrowed chair, and 25¢ in capital, Robert S. Abbott, 36, founds the *Chicago Defender*. Four pages long and the size of a handbill at first, the *Defender* became the most spectacular business success during the black migration era in Chicago. In fact, the paper played a large role in encouraging black migration from the South to the North. By 1918 the *Defender* had a circulation of about 125,000 in 71 towns nationwide. The Chicago riots of 1919 caused its white printers to cease production for fear of retaliation by white rioters. Abbott then purchased a press, installed it in a building on Indiana Avenue, and began anew in 1921. With 68 employees and a plant valued at nearly $500,000, the *Defender* was by far the largest black business in Chicago and one of the largest in the nation.

1921   Chanel No. 5 is introduced by couturiere Gabrielle "Coco" Chanel. It was a breakthrough perfume: it was devoid of any feminine floral scent; it came in a revolutionary cube-shaped bottle; and it was the first designer-named fragrance. It soon became the world's largest seller.

1966   Advertising executive Alex F. Osborn, credited with coining the terms *creative thinking* and *brainstorming*, dies at 77 in Buffalo, New York.

1997   A jury in Jacksonville, Florida, finds R.J. Reynolds Tobacco Co. not responsible for the death of lifelong smoker Jean Connor. The six-member jury concluded that RJR cigarettes were not "unreasonably dangerous and defective." On Wall Street the stocks of all major tobacco companies rose in excess of 10 percent, which helped lift the entire market to a record high closing.

1999   An automatic fire alarm brings firefighters to the secluded mansion of money manager Martin Frankel in Greenwich, Connecticut. They found a blazing file cabinet and two fireplaces stuffed with burning documents. Among the papers was an astrological chart intended to answer the questions "Will I go to prison?" and "Should I leave?" There is also a to-do list with "launder money" as task number one (see May 15).

MAY 6

1835   The *New York Herald* begins publication under the direction of cross-eyed Scottish immigrant journalist James Gordon Bennett, who started the four-page penny newspaper with $500, two chairs, and an old dry goods box in a cellar office. His third try at establishing a newspaper, it became a huge success, and Bennett shaped many of the methods of modern journalism.

1870   Founder of the Bank of America (the world's largest bank at the time of his death) Amadeo Peter Giannini is born in San Jose, California, the son of Italian immigrants. Amadeo's working life began as an entry clerk in his stepfather's produce company, but by 19 he was a partner in the firm, showing himself to be a brilliant merchant (see June 3).

1884   The New York investment firm of Grant & Ward declares bankruptcy, leaving former president Ulysses S. Grant almost penniless. His son Ulysses, Jr., was a partner, and Grant had not only put his own capital at the firm's disposal, he had convinced family and friends to do likewise. The firm had been swindled by its other partner Ferdinand Ward.

MAY 7

1847   The American Medical Association is founded in Philadelphia.

1888   George Eastman launches the Kodak camera in New York, using the slogan "You push the button, we do the rest." Eastman's invention revolutionized photography by enabling any amateur to take satisfactory pictures. The small, lightweight $25 camera came loaded with a film roll for 100 shots; the entire camera was sent back to Rochester, New York, for development of the pictures, and a new roll was inserted for $10. Eastman's slogan and product name are considered some of the best in business history; both were created without market research. For the product name, Eastman always liked the letter *K* because it was the first letter of his mother's maiden name, Kilbourn. He created the rest of the name around that: "I knew a trade name must be short, vigorous, incapable of being misspelled to an extent that will destroy its identity, and, in order to satisfy the trademark laws, it must mean nothing."

1946   Totsuko, the forerunner of Sony, incorporates in Tokyo. In the company's founding prospectus, cofounder Masaru Ibuka said, "The first and primary motive for setting up this company was to create a stable work environment where engineers who had a deep and profound appreciation of technology could work to their heart's content."

MAY 8

1532   The first known limited liability partnership contract is signed in Florence. By ensuring that investors could lose no more than the amount they invested, the invention of limited liability was critical to the development of large-scale industry because it encouraged investment and freed up capital.

1884   "It's a recession when your neighbor loses his job; it's a depression when you lose yours."—Harry S. Truman, born on this day in Lamar, Missouri, the son of a mule trader and farmer

1886   Coca-Cola first goes on sale to the public, at Jacob's Pharmacy in Atlanta, Georgia, as a headache and hangover remedy.

1914   W. W. Hodkinson founds Paramount Pictures. Initially a distributor, in 1916 it also became a production company when it was taken over by Adolph Zukor and Jesse L. Lasky, whose pictures it had previously distributed. With Zukor as the chief executive and Lasky as the creative force, Paramount signed such great talents as Mary Pickford, Cecil B. DeMille, and Rudolph Valentino, and emerged as one of Hollywood's most powerful studios. It was purchased by Gulf & Western in 1966 and was absorbed by Viacom in 1994.

1992   "It's just one of those freaky deals that sometimes happens," explains Dale Ihry, head of the North Dakota office of the Agricultural Stabilization and Conservation Service, which had just issued a check for more than $4 million to farmer Harlan Johnson for participating in a crop program. The trouble was that Mr. Johnson was only entitled to a check for $31. Ihry further explained that $4,038,277.04 was a number that occasionally popped up on agency records without warning.

MAY 9

1882   Industrialist Henry J. Kaiser is born in rural Spout Brook, New York, to German immigrants. Henry dropped out of school at 13 to help support the family as a dry goods clerk, then worked as a traveling salesman and junior partner for a photographic supply shop. Within a year he had purchased the firm and set up branches in Miami, Daytona Beach, and Nassau in the Bahamas to cater to the tourist trade. At his death on August 24, 1967, Kaiser controlled more than 80 companies, including Willys Motors, which manufactured jeeps and America's first compact car, and had assets of about $2 billion. "Trouble is only opportunity in work clothes," he said.

1901   "The greatest general panic that Wall Street has ever known" is the way the *New York Times* describes today's events. For weeks, two opposing coalitions (James J. Hill and J. P. Morgan vs. Edward H. Harriman and Kuhn, Loeb & Co.) had been trying to buy up every last share of Northern Pacific Railroad stock in an effort to control western rail traffic and access to Chicago. Neither side was exactly sure who had more shares, so just a few shares could mean control. Share price was beyond actual value, which had attracted a third party of sharks, the short sellers, who sold enormous numbers of shares that they had borrowed on paper (in order to make a killing when the price dropped). In the last 24 hours it had been realized that more shares had been sold than existed, which meant that the short sellers had to pay anything asked for Northern Pacific in order to repay the shares they had borrowed. The market was cornered. Northern had closed on May 8 at about $200; it was at $400 shortly after opening today; by noon it was over $700, and a little after 2:00 shares sold for $1,000. To raise cash to pay these ridiculous prices, brokers were selling other stocks in a frenzy, and those share prices crashed. "All sense of value and sanity was gone," observed Bernard Baruch, who was just beginning his fabled career on Wall Street. By 2:15, the deadline for short sellers to pay back the borrowed shares, the crisis was effectively over because Morgan had forged a truce with Harriman, and lenders announced they would make Northern shares available at $150.

1914   Charles William Post—founder of the Postum Cereal Company, the parent company of General Foods—commits suicide at age 55 (see October 26).

1950   In Bentonville, Arkansas, Sam Walton, 32, takes the keys to the front door of the old country store upon which he will found the Wal-Mart empire. The building had no back door and only 25 feet of road frontage. Walton ascended the rickety stairs to the loft that would become his office and nailed an orange crate to the wall for a bookshelf. He slammed a piece of plywood on two sawhorses to create the desk he would use for the next five or six years. He then covered what he could with oilcloth and plastic because the roof leaked and the worst rain in the history of Bentonville was falling, 12 inches in 24 hours.

1961   A now-famous phrase to describe television—"vast wasteland"—is coined. New chairman of the FCC, 35-year-old Newton Minow throws down the gauntlet at the National Association of Broadcasters convention in Washington, D.C.: "I invite you to sit down in front of your television set when your station goes on the air, and stay there. You will see a vast wasteland—a procession of game shows, violence, audience participation shows, formula comedies about totally unbelievable families . . . blood and thunder . . . mayhem, violence, sadism, murder . . . private eyes, more violence, and cartoons . . . and, endlessly, commercials—many screaming, cajoling, and offending."

1962   The Beatles sign their first recording contract with EMI Parlophone.

1970   Labor leader Walter Reuther is killed with his wife when their chartered plane crashes in rain and fog near Pellston, Michigan (see September 1).

MAY 10

1727   Anne-Robert-Jacques Turgot—the finance minister who was Louis XVI's last good chance to save the French monarchy and his own royal neck—is born in Paris to a family of distinguished public servants. A gifted intellect, Turgot first trained for the church but abandoned that under influence of Enlightenment philosophies. He became a physiocrat (regarded as the first scientific school of economics, it stressed removal of artificial control of markets). As minister of finance his unforgivable mistake was devising sensible and needed reform: abandoning forced labor, reducing taxes on agriculture, freeing the grain market, abolishing the monopolistic/exploitative medieval guilds, and balancing the budget. It was too much. A coalition of financiers, aristocrats, and clergymen isolated Turgot from the young king at court, then had him fired two days after his 49th birthday. After the king's head was removed and the revolution quieted down, most of his reforms were adopted.

1872   Wall Street's first female stockbroker, Victoria Claflin Woodhull, today becomes the nation's first female nominee for president. Woodhull, 33, was chosen as the candidate of the National Woman Suffrage Association at their convention in Apollo Hall, New York City. The abolitionist, orator, and former slave Frederick Douglass was selected as her running mate, but he refused to take part.

1893   The Supreme Court decides what a tomato is. The Tariff Act of 1883 specified that fruits, but not vegetables, could be imported duty-free. When John Nix was charged duty on a cargo of tomatoes he brought from the West Indies to New York in 1886, he protested that it was a fruit—as any botanist would know. In 1893 he took the case to the Supreme Court. Justice Gray announced the decision: "Botanically speaking, tomatoes are the fruit of the vine, just as are cucumbers, squashes, beans, and peas. But in the common language of the people . . . all these vegetables . . . are usually served at dinner . . . and not, like fruits generally, as dessert." The tomato was technically a fruit but legally a vegetable.

2000   In Cairo, Egypt, the Coca-Cola Company is cleared by the mufti Nasr Farid Wasel of charges that it embedded the anti-Islam message "No Mohammed, No Mecca" in the famous script Coca-Cola label, a rumor that has persisted for months in several Mideast countries. With alterations and backward reading that message could be seen, but several panels of Islamic scholars concluded "there was no defamation to the religion of Islam from near or far."

MAY 11

1894   "We struck at Pullman because we were without hope," says one of the participants in the nationwide Pullman Car Strike that begins on this day. George Pullman enacted a fierce, paternalistic control over his workers, demanding exorbitant rent in the company town. In the depression of 1893 wages were cut 25–40 percent, but the rents stayed the same. Earlier this month a group of workers had implored Pullman to redress the situation; he fired three of them. Gatling guns and federal troops crushed the strike in midsummer.

1926   Maxwell House Coffee registers its "Good to the Last Drop" trademark. The product and its name go back to 1886 in the Maxwell House hotel in Nashville, Tennessee. The hotel served its own blend of coffee that was perfected by Joel Cheek; he was persuaded by satisfied guests to market his brew.

1928   General Electric station WGY, Schenectady, New York, begins broadcasting the first regularly scheduled television programs.

1931   With financial panic and economic depression rolling over the entire globe, the Credit Ansalt in Vienna announces bankruptcy. It was not only Austria's largest bank but probably the most important bank in central Europe. A rescue plan announced by the Austrian National Bank and the Rothschilds only served to alert the world to greater trouble and bring on bank runs elsewhere.

1959   "Socks are a universally recognized symbol of the role relationship between a man and his wife. When a woman won't wash or darn her husband's socks, she is seen by both men and women as being lazy, dissatisfied with her husband, and in general a 'no good wife.' Or, if she is a good wife, something must be wrong with him." —Research report of the E.I. du Pont de Nemours company advising that advertising for men's socks should be directed primarily to women, in *Advertising Age*

1998   French foreign minister Dominique Strauss-Kahn hits a start button at the mint in Pessac, and the machine stamps out the first coins for Europe's single currency, the euro. Strauss-Kahn then bit one of the coins "to see if it's real."

MAY 12

1653   Construction begins on the Wall Street wall in New York City.

1898   George Rufus Brown, partner–cum–board chairman of giant international construction company Brown & Root, is born in Belton, Texas. One of the company's more adventurous contracts involved drilling a $42 million hole five miles into the bottom of the Pacific Ocean to the outer edge of the earth's core; this 1962 "Mohole Project" ran into technical difficulties and then a Senate investigation.

1902   Mine work at the turn of the century was dismal: foul and dangerous conditions, paltry pay, company towns that exploited the dependence of the miners. On this day United Mine Workers chief John

Mitchell led 147,000 anthracite coal workers out of the pits to begin a five-month strike that had deep effects throughout the nation. Coal went from $5 to $30 a ton. President Teddy Roosevelt grew impatient and pressured both sides to negotiate. The mine companies, largely in control of imperious railroad barons, rebuffed both the union and Roosevelt, who finally threatened to have the army run the mines. This brought the owners to the bargaining table, and by October the strikers returned to work. A commission of arbitration was formed, and in the spring after an investigation it recommended more pay, fewer hours, and union recognition. One writer called the settlement "the greatest single event affecting the relations of capital and labor in the history of America."

MAY 13

1884 Inventor, industrialist, and founder of the firm that became the International Harvester Company, Cyrus Hall McCormick dies at 75 in Chicago. "By 1880 the sun never set upon McCormick machines," wrote historian William Hutchinson. Late in life McCormick was still making business trips to Europe; on one of those in 1878 the French emperor Napoleon III himself affixed the cross of the Legion of Honour to McCormick's chest, and the French Academy of Sciences honored him as "having done more for the cause of agriculture than any other living man."

1958 The Velcro trademark is registered. The inspiration for this great fastener came to engineer Georges de Mestral during a hike in the Swiss Alps in 1948 while he contemplated the pesky seed burrs that stuck to his clothing. A microscope revealed that the burrs were covered with teensy hooks. It took de Mestral nearly a decade to produce the hook-and-hole design he so easily envisioned. The name comes from the French *velours* (velvet) and *crochet* (hook).

1980 Douglas A. Fraser, president of the United Auto Workers union, is named to the board of directors of the Chrysler Corporation, becoming the first union representative to ever sit on the board of a major U.S. corporation. Born in 1916 in Glasgow, Scotland, to a Socialist father,

Fraser came under the wing of UAW executive Walter Reuther, also an immigrant with a Socialist background. Fraser was no ideologue, however; he believed in reasonable compromise and flexibility (for which he was accused by more hard-line brothers of being a panderer). When Chrysler was facing collapse, Fraser negotiated away millions of dollars already guaranteed to his union in order to save the company. In return, Chrysler traded stock options to the union and rewarded Fraser with today's appointment. "His word is enough for us," explained one executive. "He gets into plant problems like no other union leader I know."

1999   ATM money machines that identify legitimate customers by scanning the irises in their eyes are first used in the United States at branches of Bank United in Fort Worth, Houston, and Dallas, Texas. "It knows you just by looking at you," said Ron Coben, the bank's executive vice president. He cited the system's high-tech cachet as one of its appeals. "It has a very high cool factor. We think of it as James Bond meets stocks and bonds."

1999   Sears, then the nation's largest department store chain, begins selling 2,000 major brands and models of appliances over the Internet, becoming the nation's first old-line, "brick-and-mortar" establishment to sell large-ticket items in cyberspace.

MAY 14

1771   Manufacturer-turned-reformer Robert Owen is born in Newtown, Wales, which he departed at age 10 to become a clothier's apprentice in London. He took full advantage of his employer's good library and by 19 was superintendent of a large cotton mill in Manchester, which he developed into one of the foremost establishments of its kind in Great Britain. In 1797, at 26, he headed a group of investors that purchased a large mill in New Lanark, Scotland, from David Dale (soon to become his father-in-law). The town contained 2,000 inhabitants, 500 of whom were children from the poorhouses and charities of Glasgow and Edinburgh. It was here that Owen began the community and industrial reforms that made him famous. At his firm's expense—and to the frequent frustration of his partners who were considerably more oriented toward short-term profits—sanitation and housing were soon overhauled, and a company store was set up that sold goods at near cost. In 1816 Owen formed the first infant school in Great Britain and thereafter gave it his close personal supervision.

1887   "An act to extend and regulate the liability of employers to make compensation for personal injuries suffered by employees in their service" is passed in Massachusetts, the nation's first legislation requiring industrial and on-the-job accident reports.

1959   "The phenomenon I refer to . . . is the tidal wave of craving for convenience that is sweeping over America. Today convenience is the success factor of just about every type of product and service that is showing steady growth." —Charles Mortimer, president, General Foods Corporation, in an address to the American Marketing Association

MAY 15

1846   "The public mind is polluted with economic fancies: a depraved desire that the rich may become richer without the interference of industry and toil." —Benjamin Disraeli, British prime minister, in a speech to the House of Commons

1911   At 4 P.M. Supreme Court Chief Justice Edward White begins a 49-minute verdict, reading in a low, monotonous voice, "I have also to announce the opinion of the Court in No. 398, the United States against the Standard Oil Company." After 41 years, Standard Oil was ordered to be split up. Five major companies and several smaller concerns were created from the giant. Standard founder John D. Rockefeller, 71, was golfing on his estate at Pocantico, New York, with Father J. P. Lennon when he got the word. "Father Lennon, do you have some money?" he asked. The priest said no and asked why. "Buy Standard Oil," Rockefeller wisely advised.

1923   The Listerine mouthwash trademark is registered. The product was brought into the Warner-Lambert group of companies by Elmer Holmes Bobst as part of a series of acquisitions that turned the firm around from the 1940s onward.

2000   "We live in an economy where knowledge, not buildings and machinery, is the chief resource and where knowledge-workers make up the biggest part of the work force. Until well into the 20th century, most workers were manual workers. Today . . . 40% of our total work force are knowledge-workers." —Peter F. Drucker, management consultant/theorist, in Forbes.com

2002   The weird odyssey of Martin Frankel ends in Connecticut, when his lawyer announces that Frankel will plead guilty to racketeering, conspiracy, securities fraud, and wire fraud. The money manager had vanished two years earlier from a smoldering mansion (see May 5) with as much as $3 billion of other people's money looted from insurance companies in five states, an unlicensed securities company, and the St. Francis of Assisi Foundation that he had established in the Virgin Islands.

MAY 16

1631   *La Gazette*, France's first newspaper, debuts under the editorship of Theophraste Renaudot, a protégé of the powerful Cardinal Armand Richelieu.

1742   "Delay is preferable to error." —Thomas Jefferson, in a letter to George Washington

1832   Philip Danforth Armour, entrepreneur and innovator whose extensive Armour & Co. helped make Chicago the world's meatpacking center, is born in Stockbridge, New York. Armour's first great killing came in the pork futures market at the end of the Civil War, when, anticipating a fall in prices, he and associates contracted to deliver pork to New York at $40 a barrel but were able to buy it at $18 a barrel when the Confederacy and pork prices collapsed. With his share of the $2 million profit, he formed H.O. Armour & Co. with brother Herman. The firm became Armour & Co. in 1870 and moved to Chicago in 1875. It was among the first to bring live hogs to the city and to supervise its own slaughtering. The brothers also pioneered the utilization of former waste products, capitalized quickly on Gustavus Swift's innovation of refrigerated railroad cars, and expanded rapidly—first to eastern cities, then to Europe. "I do not love money," Philip once said. "What I do love is the getting of it. . . . What other interest can you suggest to me? I do not read. I do not take part in politics. What can I do?"

1927   Despite the fact that the manufacture and sale of alcoholic beverages are unlawful, the U.S. Supreme Court rules that bootleggers must file income tax returns.

1956   General Motors dedicates its $125 million GM Technical Center in Warren, Michigan. Overseeing its funding and development was Alfred P. Sloan; overseeing its design was Harley Earl, famous for being the automobile industry's first "stylist." Hired by Sloan in the 1920s and given his own department, Earl made his mark with the 1927 LaSalle, the first of many distinctive projects. It was the first production car with sleek, long, rounded looks, a theme he returned to repeatedly. Earl explained, "My sense of proportion tells me that oblongs are more attractive than squares, just as a ranch house is more attractive than a three-story, flat-roofed house or a greyhound is more graceful than an English bulldog."

2000   People's love-hate relationship with money is revealed in a study released today by AARP of citizens of all ages, races, and income and education levels. Almost three-quarters of those surveyed said they would like to be wealthy, but two-thirds believed that wealth promotes insensitivity to others, and 87 percent expressed fears that wealth would make them greedy.

MAY 17

1792   The Buttonwood Agreement is signed by two dozen stock traders in downtown Manhattan, forming the basis of the future New York Stock Exchange. The name "Buttonwood" came from the fact that the men regularly met and traded stocks under a specific buttonwood (sycamore) tree at 68 Wall Street. The pact really had two causes. The first was that these men wished to set themselves apart from others who dealt stocks, most notably commodity dealers who auctioned stocks in a corrupt fashion. The second was the March collapse of Bank of New

York stock resulting from the scheme of William Duer to manipulate its price through huge purchases and the spreading of rumor. America's first investment panic ensued, causing New York investors and speculators to lose some $5 million, an amount equal to the worth of all the buildings in the city; Boston and Philadelphia sustained losses of $1 million each.

1848   Andrew Carnegie, 11, sails from Scotland for America with his family. His father William, a handloom weaver, had been put out of business by the new technology of steam power.

1886   Pioneer manufacturer of farm implements, John Deere sees his last day above the soil at age 82 in Moline, Illinois (see February 7).

2000   Opened for just six months, Boo.com sells its remaining assets for $2 million and closes its web doors forever; it had burned through $135 million in venture capital seed money on expenses such as $150,000 salaries for founders Ernst Malmsten and Kajsa Leander, $100,000 for their London apartments, and an additional $100,000 for decorating costs. Billed as a "gateway to world cool" by Malmsten, the fashion website spent more than $650,000 on promotional gewgaws, $600,000 for a PR firm, and $42 million on an ad campaign. When reporters suggested that the founders had spent their venture capital too extravagantly, Leander bristled. "I only flew Concorde three times, and they were all special offers."

MAY 18

1912   The first baseball strike takes place at Shibe Park, Philadelphia. Nineteen Detroit Tigers refused to play against the Athletics in sympathy for outfielder Ty Cobb, who had been suspended by league president Byron Johnson for mauling a spectator at a recent Tigers-Yankees game. The strikers were fined $50 a day. Tigers manager Hugh A. Jennings recruited a scrub team (each player was paid $50) and was defeated 24–2 in front of 15,000 fans. It was the first major-league game in which one team scored 24 runs.

1923   Alfred P. Sloan presides over his first meeting of the executive committee since becoming president of General Motors. The roster of attendees read like an all-star list from business history: Pierre du Pont, William S. Knudsen, and Charles F. Kettering were old members, while Charles Stewart Mott and Fred Fisher were attending for the first time. Sloan immediately attacked the problem of the copper-cooled six-cylinder engine, which showed enormous promise and which GM had devoted huge resources and time to developing but which remained on the launch pad. The engine, also known as the "air-cooled" engine, and all its revolutionary promise were soon scrapped.

1943   Henry Ford is told that his son Edsel is dying. Ford refused to believe it, insisting that the doctors at the Henry Ford Hospital could save him. He did not visit his son, instead spending hours tramping through the woods at Fairlane. He commanded Harry Bennett to smash every liquor bottle in Edsel's home. Edsel, 49, died in a coma a week later. Stomach cancer, ulcers, physical and nervous exhaustion related to company work, and a lifetime of psychological abuse from his father were all implicated in his death. The final straw was undulant fever, which Edsel had contracted from unpasteurized milk that Henry insisted would cure his condition.

1986   "Greed is all right. . . . Greed is healthy. You can be greedy and still feel good about yourself." —Ivan Boesky, financier convicted of securities fraud in 1987, in a commencement address to the graduates of the University of California, Berkeley.

MAY 19

1828   President John Quincy Adams signs the Tariff of Abomina-tions into law, raising duties on a variety of raw materials and manufac-tured goods. One of the most extreme protective tariffs in the nation's history, it managed to unite North and South, farmer and manufacturer, in their hate of it and helped to ensure Adams's defeat in the upcoming presidential elections—just the outcome desired by supporters of Andrew Jackson, who devised the tariff. "I fear this tariff thing," warned one of Adams's backers too late, "by some strange mechanism, it will be changed into a machine for manufacturing Presidents, instead of broad-cloths and bed blankets."

1907   Henry Huttleston Rogers, one of John D. Rockefeller's key lieutenants at Standard Oil and a founding director of U.S. Steel, dies at age 67, exhausted from the last two great business ventures of his life: founding the Atlas Tack Company (the largest concern of its kind in the United States) and constructing the $40 million Virginia Railroad, unique in transportation industry history because it was financed by one person (see January 29).

1958   "There is nothing as universal in this world as human thirst . . . Our market is as big as the world and the people in it." —Lee Talley, on being elected president of Coca-Cola, in *Newsweek*

1983   Wesray (an investment partnership owned by former Treasury Secretary William E. Simon and investment manager Ray Chambers) takes Gibson Greeting Card Inc. public, selling about 30 percent of the company for $96 million and giving the whole company a value of $330 million. About a year before, Wesray had purchased Gibson in a famous leveraged buyout for $80 million, of which $79 million was borrowed. The two deals made Simon and Chambers look like geniuses: they had earned a $250 million pretax profit on a $1 million equity investment.

MAY 20

1818   Cofounder of Wells Fargo and American Express, William George Fargo is born, the eldest of twelve children, in Pompey, New York. At age 13 he entered the delivery business, carrying mail twice a week over 30 miles. In 1844 after several ventures, Fargo teamed up with Henry Wells and Daniel Dunning to form Wells & Co., the first express delivery company to operate west of Buffalo. This company merged in 1850 with two others to form American Express. Wells Fargo was formed two years later as a side venture to service the California goldfields when one of the partners balked at going so far west. Europe was soon added to their roster of regions. Fargo died August 3, 1881.

1856   The printing telegraph ticker is patented (U.S. Patent 14,917) by David Edward Hughes of Louisville, Kentucky, who has already sold the rights to it for $100,000 to the Commercial Company. Although the printing telegraph ticker was closely associated with stock trading and market activity, it was not until 1867 that a brokerage first used such a machine; a Daniel Drew company, the Gold and Stock Telegraph Company, began renting them at $6 per week to Wall Street.

1958 "There is no such thing as 'soft sell' and 'hard sell.' There is only 'smart sell' and 'stupid sell.'" —Charles Brower, president, Batten, Barton, Durstine & Osborn advertising agency, in a speech to the National Sales Executives Convention

2003 Richard Grasso, chairman of the New York Stock Exchange, is elected to the board of Home Depot, a company he is supposed to police.

MAY 21

1929 An automatic electronic stock quotation board is first used on Wall Street. Manufactured by the Teleregister Corporation (later Bunker-Ramo Corp.) of Stamford, Connecticut, the device was placed in operation in the brokerage office of Sutro Bros. & Co. It automatically changed figures as activity unfolded and showed the day's open, high, low, and latest price. Just in time for the Great Depression.

1936 E.I. du Pont de Nemours & Co., Wilmington, Delaware, begins commercial production of the ubiquitous plastic Lucite (polymethyl methacrylate). It was crystal clear, low in moisture absorption, and highly nonconducting of electricity, and it had the interesting property of bending light that passed through it.

1942 The huge German firm IG Farben establishes a factory outside Auschwitz, Poland, to exploit the slave labor in the Nazi concentration camp there.

2001 Ford Motor Company announces that it will recall and replace an additional 10 million to 13 million Firestone tires on its vehicles. The announcement follows one earlier in the day by Firestone/Bridgestone that it will no longer sell tires to Ford, ending a 95-year relationship begun in 1906 when Henry Ford was standardizing the Model T and ordered 8,000 tires from his friend Harvey Firestone. Both companies agree that the tires are partly to blame for an extraordinary number of accidents, deaths, and lawsuits in recent years, but they disagree on the culpability of the Ford Explorer, the world's leading SUV. "Business relationships, like personal ones, are built upon trust and mutual respect," Bridgestone/Firestone chief John Lampe wrote to Ford CEO Jacques Nasser. "We have come to the conclusion that we can no longer supply tires to Ford since the basic foundation of our relationship has been seriously eroded."

MAY 22

1755   Tench Coxe, Alexander Hamilton's chief adviser in the Treasury Department, is born the son of a prominent merchant in Philadelphia. He entered his father's counting house after studying at the University of Pennsylvania. In the nation's first Treasury he was appointed assistant secretary (1789) and then commissioner of revenue (1792). Hamilton was the master strategist for designing America's economic development, and Coxe was the chief tactician, playing an especially significant role in Hamilton's famous reports on a national bank and industry. Coxe had been publishing on economics for years before teaming with Hamilton. He was especially optimistic about the future of American industry and convinced Hamilton of this view, but he also pointed out critical problems such as the shortage of labor. He was instrumental to the introduction of cotton farming in the South and to the development of cotton goods manufacturing, and he was among the first to see the promise of Pennsylvania's mineral resources.

1837   Critic and chronicler Philip Hone decries the loss of life connected with American steamboats, especially in Western waters. Such accidents were rare in Europe, even with its denser population, "but we have become the most careless, reckless, headlong people on the face of the earth. 'Go ahead!' is our maxim and password; and we do go ahead with a vengeance, regardless of consequences and indifferent about the value of human life. What are a few hundred persons, more or less?

There are plenty in this country, and more coming every day; and a few years in the life of a man makes very little difference in comparison with the disgrace of a steamboat being beaten in her voyage by a rival craft."

1928   Described as a corporate raider, a greenmailer, a communist, even a piranha, Thomas Boone Pickens is born in Holdenville in the oil patch of the Oklahoma panhandle where his father was an itinerant broker who put together deals between farmers and oil companies. With a degree in geology, Pickens first went to work for Philips Petroleum, a company he would later bring to its knees. Disillusioned with the company's bureaucracy, he quit at 26 and in 1956 with two partners and $2,500 formed Mesa Petroleum. As it grew into the largest independently owned oil and gas company in the United States, Pickens was soon rubbing elbows with elite CEOs whom he saw as only interested in furthering their own personal gains to the detriment of their stockholders and their country. That's when he became a corporate raider.

1997   "When the meek inherit the earth, lawyers will be there to work out the deal." —Sam Ewing, author, in the *Wall Street Journal*

2003   The Cleveland Cavaliers basketball team wins first pick in the NBA draft lottery, ensuring that they will be able to draft local sensation LeBron James. An avalanche of calls for season tickets immediately hit the team offices, which was staffed with 25 sales representatives to handle "LeBron Mania." The Akron high school senior was sure to become a multimillionaire with his team contract, but that is not where the big money lies. Today James, 18, signed a $90 million contract with the Nike shoe company, and contracts with HBO and MTV soon followed. "Put it this way," said Cavaliers spokesman Tad Carper about his team's bonanza, "this is salesman's nirvana."

MAY 23

1712   Con man Richard Town is hanged in London on his birthday for secreting 15 tons of tallow on a ship and attempting to flee with money from defrauded creditors. On the scaffold, displaying the same calm and moxie that had got him there, Town belted out to the open-air crowd, "My friends, this is my birthday. I see you have come to help me honor it." Turning to an attractive lady in the crowd, he continued, "Madame, my compliments, and thank you for coming to my adventure." He then adjusted his cap and signaled for the drop.

1788   Lewis Tappan, father of the credit rating industry, is born in Northampton, Massachusetts (see August 1).

1875   The great manager, creator of "the very idea of the modern American corporation," Alfred P. Sloan, Jr., is born the eldest of five in New Haven, Connecticut. His father was a wholesaler of coffee, tea, and cigars who soon moved the family to upscale Brooklyn, New York. Sloan graduated from MIT in just three years with an engineering degree and went to work for Hyatt Roller Bearing in 1895. At that time its chief product was billiard balls; when it was purchased by General Motors in 1916, Sloan had become its owner and turned it into a leader in the fledgling auto parts industry. Sloan rose to be president and chairman of GM in 1923; in partnership with Pierre S. du Pont, he unified what had been a chaotic agglomeration of many companies. He invented an entirely new form of corporate structure ("federal decentralization" became an international standard) and made GM the largest industrial enterprise the world had yet seen.

1908   "If there is a man on this earth who is entitled to all the comforts and luxuries of this life . . . it is the man whose labor produces them. . . . Does he get them in the present system?" —Eugene V. Debs, politician and labor leader, in a speech at Girard, Kansas

1937   John D. Rockefeller, 97, dies in his sleep at his winter home, The Casements, in Ormond Beach, Florida. The day before, he had paid off the mortgage to the Euclid Avenue Baptist Church in Cleveland; it had been a great source of peace to him in his adolescence.

1950   Having just announced profits for the previous year of nearly $637 million—the highest in corporate history—General Motors today shares the booty with its workers, inking a five-year contract that grants UAW employees pensions and wage boosts.

MAY 24

1626   "The greatest real estate bargain ever" takes place when Peter Minuit, colonial governor of New Amsterdam, buys the entire island of Manhattan for $24 worth of beads, needles, fabric, buttons, and fishhooks, allowing the Dutch to establish a settlement there. Now here's the rest of the story: Minuit was swindled. He'd paid the Canarsee Indians, who didn't even own the place. The rightful owners, the Weckquaesgeeks, were enraged when they found out, warred sporadically with the Dutch for years, and eventually were also paid by the Dutch West India Trading Company. The smooth-talking Canarsees had nothing on the Raritan Indians, however, who sold nearby Staten Island six times.

1763   "Mankind have a great aversion to intellectual labor; even supposing knowledge to be easily attainable, more people would be content to be ignorant than would take even a little trouble to acquire it." —Samuel Johnson, in Boswell's *Life of Samuel Johnson*

1878   The industrial engineer who pioneered time-motion studies, Lillian Moller Gilbreth, is born in Oakland, California. In 1904 she married management consultant Frank Gilbreth, and the two formed a famous team of industrial psychologists who merged the new findings and theory of humanistic psychology with the rigid, mechanistic approach of Frederick Taylor's scientific management. She died January 2, 1972.

1898   Communications magnate Samuel Irving Newhouse is born in Bayonne, New Jersey. Newhouse originally trained as a lawyer and was admitted to the bar, but he lost his first case and never practiced law again. In 1922 he began his media empire by purchasing the *Staten Island Advance* for $98,000; he turned the paper into a financial success and used the profits to buy another newspaper. He seemed to have a collector's fascination for acquiring media companies; among subsequent purchases was Condé Nast Publications and Booth Newspapers Inc. Newhouse never set up a formal office but conducted his business out of a battered briefcase. He died August 29, 1979.

MAY 25

1805   The Cordwainers union of shoemakers, America's first trade union of note, witnesses the first time that management uses the judicial system and armed force to squash a strike. Several Cordwainers, on strike in Philadelphia for better wages, were arrested for criminal conspiracy under a judge's orders. Specifically, they were accused of violating English common law that barred schemes aimed at improving wages. The union disbanded with their trial in 1806.

1916   A famous, and almost always misquoted, saying is minted today by Henry Ford in the *Chicago Tribune*, a newspaper that is bitterly opposed to Ford's antiwar activities. Ford told a *Tribune* reporter that the past meant nothing to him. He continued, "History is more or less bunk. It's tradition. We don't want tradition. We want to live in the present and the only history that is worth a tinker's damn is the history we make today." An editorial appeared separately in today's paper calling Ford an "ignorant idealist" and an "anarchist."

1919   Cosmetics manufacturer and developer, as well as the first black female millionaire, Madame C. J. Walker, dies at her estate, Villa Lewaro, in Irvington, New York (see December 23).

1990   "A specialist is someone who does everything else worse." —Ruggiero Ricci, violinist, in the *Daily Telegraph*

MAY 26

1908   Shortly after 4:30 A.M. the Middle East oil industry is born, in Iraq's Zagros Mountains at a desolate site called Masjid-i-Suleiman ("Mosque of Solomon"). Drillers for the British firm Burmah Oil Company were suddenly drenched with a 50-foot-high gusher; they nearly suffocated in the accompanying gas. It was the world's largest oil reserve. Burmah had been drilling fruitlessly in the region for six years, and a letter was already on its way from London to the field crew to stop exploration because the money had run out, when this morning's gusher erupted.

1934   The Securities and Exchange Commission is created. Senate and House negotiators reached an agreement in Washington on the provisions of the Stock Exchange Regulation Bill. The SEC would consist of five presidential appointees and would administer the Securities Act of 1933. "I think that the stock market bill will purge the securities market of the evil practices shown to have existed in the past," said Ferdinand Pecora, the Senate counselor whose 1933 hearings exposed stock market corruption behind the great crash of 1929. Calling today's bill "a very happy compromise," Pecora saw a bright and clean future for Wall Street. "The bill spells the end of the manipulator, jiggler and pool operator."

1937   The Battle of the Overpass: labor activists Walter Reuther, Richard Frankensteen, and a few others are preparing to distribute leaflets outside the Ford River Rouge plant in accordance with the permit they have obtained from the Dearborn city council, when a pack of goons from the Ford service department challenges them: "This is Ford property, get the hell out of here." The labor leaders started to leave when their path was blocked and they were attacked and beaten. The four bleeding and semiconscious men were dragged to the end of the overpass leading to the plant and thrown over the edge onto concrete steps. There were 39 steps leading to the parking lot; Reuther later recalled, "The end of my spine hit every one."

1938   Hitler lays the cornerstone for the first Volkswagen factory at Wolfsburg on the Mittelland Canal, 40 miles east of Hanover. It would be the world's largest auto assembly plant under one roof. The official Nazi name for the car was the "Strength-Through-Joy Motor Car," or KdF (the German abbreviation of the title). Many aspects of the KdF were borrowed from the Ford business model, from production techniques to marketing; a pricing/savings plan was established to allow every German to own a KdF.

1943   Edsel Ford dies at 49 of "Ford stomach" at his home in Gaukler Point, Michigan (see May 18).

1985   "The trouble with a free market economy is that it requires so many policemen to make it work." —Dean Acheson, statesman, in the *Observer*

2005   Business leaders in Liverpool, England, report that one in every five workers called in sick or otherwise failed to show up at their jobs today, following Liverpool's dramatic come-from-behind defeat of AC Milan in a championship soccer match last night. Hangovers are believed to be the major reason for the whopping absenteeism, but it is also believed that many fans of Everton (cross-town rivals of Liverpool) also failed to show up "to avoid the gloating of their colleagues." The events weren't all bad for business; Sainsbury's supermarket chain estimates that 10,000 bottles of champagne were drunk in the city that night.

MAY 27

1794   The first American to build a megafortune, Cornelius Vanderbilt, is born in a small Staten Island farmhouse, the fourth of nine children. His "plodding and lazy" father kept the family poor, and his shrewd mother once saved the farm from foreclosure by pulling out $3,000 she had squirreled away in the kitchen grandfather clock (see below).

1810   Phebe Vanderbilt goes to the kitchen grandfather clock, pulls out $100, and loans it to 16-year-old son Cornelius, who has just finished ploughing, harrowing, and planting a stumpy, rocky eight-acre tract. The two had struck a deal several weeks before: if he could have the field ready and planted by his birthday, she would lend him the money to buy a boat. Vanderbilt started a ferry service in New York Harbor with his boat, the *Swiftsure*, and soon developed a reputation for hustle and for reliability in fierce weather. The old salts with whom he competed called Vanderbilt "Commodore." By his next birthday he had repaid Phebe and given her an additional $1,000 profit for safekeeping. The next year brought the War of 1812, and it was a bonanza for Vanderbilt when the British blockaded New York City Harbor; he transported men and materials while fortifications were being built, won a contract to carry provisions to six garrisons, and used spare hours to bring food down from the Hudson Valley and sell it from his boat. Profits were used to buy ownership in two more boats. He was just getting started.

1956 "I've run more risk eating my way across the country than in all my driving." —Duncan Hines, on researching his guides to good restaurants

1970 The worst bear market in eight years touched bottom yesterday when the Dow Jones Industrial Average fell to 631. In partial recovery, the Dow today leapt 32.04 points to 663.20, the greatest one-day advance in its history.

1996 "Everything is always impossible before it works. That is what entrepreneurs are all about—doing what people have told them is impossible." —R. Hunt Greene, venture capitalist, in *Fortune*

MAY 28

1796 "An act for the relief of persons imprisoned for debt" is passed today by Congress. It is the nation's first debt law, and it prevents imprisonment of persons for debts of less than $30.

1816 ". . . banking establishments are more dangerous than standing armies . . ." —Thomas Jefferson

1962 An enormous selling wave swamps Wall Street. The Dow Jones Industrial Average fell 34.95 points, the second largest drop in its history (second only to the 38.33 fall in 1929); $20.8 billion of corporate valuation vanished. "In the past this clearly would have been called a panic," explained Charles R. Geisst, "but the very next day, the exact opposite occurred. The market staged one of its sharpest one-day rallies in history, regaining all of the loss and adding a couple of percentage points. After the smoke cleared, it became apparent that a new phenomenon had struck the Street. . . . Stock price fluctuations were possible without the implications of a panic or a crash. The age of volatility had begun."

1990   Engineer and executive Taiichi Ohno dies at 78 in Toyota City, Japan. Ohno revolutionized manufacturing methods with his just-in-time system in which parts are produced only as needed and delivered to the production line just in time for use. With additional methods to pinpoint defective parts, reduce costs, and improve quality, Ohno was key to turning the Toyota Motor Co. from near bankruptcy to a world leader.

1998   "I think large organizations have a real tendency to block bad news from moving around the organization. [H]aving it just be a matter of course that you get the bad news out there, and everybody is . . . talking about it on an open basis, I think is really fundamental." —Bill Gates, cofounder and CEO, Microsoft, in a speech to CEOs in Seattle

MAY 29

1902   The London School of Economics and Political Science opens.

1912   The *New York Sun* reports that the editor of the *Ladies' Home Journal*, Edward Bok, has fired 15 young women from their jobs at the Curtis Publishing Company in Philadelphia after he observed them dancing the turkey trot during their lunch break.

1922   The U.S. Supreme Court unanimously rules that organized baseball is primarily a sport and not a business, and therefore is not subject to antitrust laws and interstate commerce regulations. In the case of the Baltimore Federal League suing Organized Baseball on antitrust violations, Justice Oliver Wendell Holmes explained that the business of giving baseball exhibitions for profit was not "trade or commerce in the commonly-accepted use of those words" because "personal effort, not related to production, is not a subject of commerce"; nor was it interstate, because the movement of ball clubs across state lines was merely "incidental" to the business.

1943   Norman Rockwell's portrait of Rosie the Riveter graces the cover of the *Saturday Evening Post*. An enduring and memorable symbol, Rosie was a recruiting image and a tribute to female workers in defense plants during World War II. "Equal pay for equal work" was proclaimed at the time; a new age had dawned. But in actuality women earned $34.50 weekly at the time, while men earned $57.50. Many unions admitted women during the war, often out of the fear that women would undercut union wage scales if not admitted. The Teamsters admitted women only "for the duration," until men returned from the war to reclaim factory jobs. This has been called "the myth of Rosie the Riveter." (See May 31 for the fate of the real Rosie.)

MAY 30

1846   The man who inlaid the golden eggs—Fabergé eggs—is born in St. Petersburg, Russia. Peter Carl Fabergé inherited his father's jewelry business in St. Petersburg at age 24. He incorporated his sons and the brilliant Swiss designer Francois Berbaum into the business; established workshops in Kiev, Moscow, and London; and made the bold decision to entirely abandon conventional jewelry for objects of fantasy, many inspired by the decorative arts in the court of France's Louis XVI. Fabergé became famous for exquisite and ingenious masterpieces. The first of the famous Fabergé eggs was commissioned in 1884 by Alexander III for his tsarina. Alexander's successor, Nicholas II, continued the tradition until the Russian Revolution, when both Fabergé and Nicholas lost their jobs. Fabergé died in Swiss exile in 1920.

1933   New York's RCA Building opens at 30 Rockefeller Plaza, as Rockefeller Center construction proceeds throughout the Great Depression. The RCA Building was renamed the GE Building in 1990.

1965   "I wouldn't be human if I didn't feel pride and something that transcends pride . . . humility." —J. C. Penney, founder, J. C. Penney stores, at the dedication of his company's Manhattan headquarters

MAY 31

1786   The first union strike benefit in American history is authorized on this day at the Philadelphia home of Henry Myers. Protesting against a recent wage reduction, 26 members of the Typographical Society pledged "that we will support such of our brethren as shall be thrown out of employment on account of their refusing to work for less than $6 per week." They won their demands.

1887   An Atchison, Topeka and Santa Fe Railroad train first reaches Los Angeles, igniting a rate war with Collis P. Huntington's Southern Pacific. The Santa Fe had been able to reach the lucrative market by purchasing the Los Angeles and San Gabriel Valley line. Passenger fares from Kansas dropped to $1, and Los Angeles had a land boom.

1895   The patent for cornflakes (specifically for "flaked cereals and process for preparing same") is filed by one of its two discoverers, John Harvey Kellogg of Battle Creek, Michigan. The patent (No. 558393) was awarded in April 1896.

1921   The Teapot Dome Scandal is set in motion. President Warren G. Harding transferred supervision of naval oil reserves, one of them named Teapot Dome, from the navy to the Department of the Interior. The impetus for this transfer remains uncertain (the most popular theory is that Interior Secretary Albert B. Fall lobbied heavily for control of the reserves), but what is certain is that Fall soon accepted enormous bribes to grant the development rights and majority profits to two businessmen, Harry F. Sinclair and Edward L. Doheny.

1985   Steve Jobs is stripped of power in his own company, Apple Computers.

1997   Rose Will Monroe—Norman Rockwell's model for his 1943 inspirational painting "Rosie the Riveter" (see May 29)—dies at 77 in Clarksville, Indiana, survived by six sisters, several daughters, nine grandchildren, and 13 great-grandchildren. Unlike many women who returned to the kitchen after World War II (whether they wanted to or not), Monroe kept working: she drove a taxi; operated a beauty shop; and started her own Indiana construction company, Rose Builders, which specialized in high-quality custom homes.

JUNE

JUNE 1

1860   "In the last few months I have fortunately struck out what I have no doubt is *the true Theory of Economy*, so thorough-going and consistent, that I cannot now read other books on the subject without indignation." Thus writes the economics prodigy William Stanley Jevons to his brother Herbert about his discovery of the principle of marginal utility, which actually warranted Jevons's immodesty. The principle opened the modern era in economic thought and finally provided a satisfying theoretical resolution to one of the discipline's oldest and most vexing contradictions, the paradox of value: why is an essential substance like water so cheap, while a frivolous commodity like diamonds so expensive?

1863   Hugo Munsterberg is born in Danzig, Prussia. He was frequently regarded as "the founder of applied psychology" for extending the fledgling science into business, management, law, medicine, teaching, and industry.

1892   The General Electric Company (GE) begins operating under its own name following the merger of the Edison and the Thomson-Houston companies. Charles A. Coffin, who had little knowledge of electricity but was blessed with superior organizational skills and the ability to pick good people, was its first president. On its first board of directors were its main financiers, Henry L. Higginson and the ubiquitous J. P. Morgan.

1896   Baron de Zuylen's Peugeot becomes the world's first stolen car.

1958   IBM ends its design of machines containing electronic tubes. "The development people were awfully mad," remembered Thomas J.

Watson, Jr., the chairman and president who mandated the change, "but I kept giving them transistor radios. I ordered 100 of them, and whenever an engineer told me transistors were undependable, I would pull a radio out of my bag and challenge him to wear it out."

1966   This day in oil: Philips Petroleum announces the discovery of an enormous oil field in the North Sea. In 1972 on this day, Baghdad nationalized Iraq Petroleum's Kirkuk oil field; it was the first major seizure by a Persian Gulf nation and produced immediate retaliatory action by Iraq Petroleum. In 1979 on this day, the government-imposed ceiling on oil prices in America was removed to allow U.S. oil companies to compete with OPEC prices; to deal with this and other aspects of the energy crisis, President Carter proposed a windfall profits tax, research into alternative energy sources, fuel assistance to low-income families, and more public transport.

1980   Cable News Network (CNN) goes on the air at 6:00 P.M. when owner Ted Turner flicks a switch and delivers a speech: "We won't sign off until the end of the world—and we'll cover that live."

1999   The chairman of Merrill Lynch, David Komansky, announces that the brokerage firm will soon allow its customers to buy and sell stocks over the Internet: "It appeared foolish to us to ignore that part of the market. So we decided to attack it."

JUNE 2

1835   P. T. Barnum, 24, launches his first traveling show, with the central attraction being Joice Heth, an elderly black woman reputed to be the 161-year-old nurse of George Washington. Later, when interest in her began to falter, Barnum planted an anonymous letter in a leading newspaper that read in part, "The fact is, Joice Heth is not a human being at all. What purports to be a remarkably old woman is simply a curiously constructed automaton, made up of whalebone . . ." (see February 22).

1896   Britain awards Guglielmo Marconi his first patent for a radio telegraphy device.

1952   A 6–3 decision by the U.S. Supreme Court specifies that President Harry Truman usurped Congress's power when he seized steel mills in April and ordered them run by the government. The decision immediately caused the workers to go out on strike and the mill owners to raise prices, the very things Truman tried to avoid through negotiation and then bluster.

1956   "The instability of the economy is equaled only by the instability of the economists." —John H. Williams, professor, Harvard University, in the *New York Times*

1964   Comsat (the Communications Satellite Corp.) has its initial public offering of five million shares at $20 a share. Despite no earnings history or immediate prospects of earnings, the stock was admitted to trading on the New York Stock Exchange and soon tripled in value.

1985   Capitalism creates strange bedfellows: cigarette maker R.J. Reynolds opens merger talks with Nabisco, known for its family- and child-oriented baked goods. Their marriage was actually the latest and largest diversification move by Reynolds into the food industry, a strategy begun in the 1960s. Investors were not inspired, however, and in 1989 stock undervaluation resulted in the famous, record-setting leveraged buyout by Kohlberg Kravis Roberts & Company.

1987   Paul Volcker resigns as chairman of the Federal Reserve Board. President Ronald Reagan announced the nomination of free-market economist and ex-professional clarinetist Alan Greenspan to take his place.

1990   The term *kamikaze capitalism* is coined by Michael Lewis in the *Spectator* to describe the Japanese bubble economy of the 1980s.

2001   On this day CIT Group, the huge commercial-finance corporation, begins operation as Tyco Capital, having recently been purchased by the conglomerate Tyco International Ltd. under the direction of high-living CEO Dennis Kozlowski. "I think CIT will be one of the best deals we've ever done," Kozlowski predicted, despite the risky nature of commercial finance, the exorbitant price paid for CIT, and the fact that Tyco had no experience in the field. CIT showed an enormous and immediate change in fortune, going from a loss of $78.8 million in the two months prior to Tyco ownership to a profit of $71.2 million in the first four months as Tyco Capital. The miraculous turnaround was attributed to tough but effective management; it was a lie. Kozlowski, with a background in auditing, and his lieutenants pulled a number of shady "accounting alchemy" tricks to artificially darken the performance of CIT and brighten the performance of Tyco Capital. On the one-year anniversary of Tyco Capital's birth (**2002**), the board demanded Kozlowski's resignation. Two days later he was on national television in handcuffs.

JUNE 3

1621   The Dutch West India Company is chartered, granting the company a 24-year monopoly in trade and colonization in Africa and America. A further inroad by Holland into Spain's overseas empire, the charter soon led to the European settlement of Manhattan Island, hefty dividends for investors, and a declaration of war by Spain.

1857   Charles Herman Steinway, the man who brought the Steinway & Sons piano corporation into the modern age of marketing, is born in New York City. Grandson of the founder, Charles spent years studying practical piano making but then devoted himself to the commercial side of the business, rising to its presidency in 1896 upon the death of his uncle. Charles introduced modern methods of advertising, and the volume of business increased by 100 percent during his administration.

1864   Ransom Olds, the first man to mass-produce a moderately priced automobile, is born in Geneva, Ohio, the son of a machine-shop owner. The three-horsepower Oldsmobile was the first commercially successful vehicle in America, and it spurred a boom. Between 1904 and 1908, 241 automobile manufacturing companies sprang up in the United States.

1900   The International Ladies' Garment Workers Union is founded by cloakmakers in a small hall on New York's Lower East Side. By 1904 the ILGWU boasted 5,400 members in 66 locals in 27 cities.

1932   "I pledge you, I pledge myself, to a New Deal for the American people." —President Franklin Roosevelt

1946   Hungary issues the one sextillion (10^{21}) pengo note to deal with history's worst case of inflation, estimated at "several million million million" percent in 1945–46. The note was withdrawn July 11.

1949   Amadeo Peter Giannini (founder of Transamerica Corporation and the Bank of America, which by this day is the world's largest bank) dies at 79, leaving nothing to his two remaining children, whom he loved dearly. They expected nothing. According to Giannini, "I believe in using money to help worthy causes while one is still living, and thus get some fun out of it. Of course, it is every man's duty to strive to give his children the best possible equipment for life. But to leave millions to young sons is dangerous. Each of us is better for having to make our own way in the world. God meant us to work." Although he could have been a millionaire many times over, Giannini gave money to charities as much as necessary to keep from reaching that mark every time he neared it (see also May 6).

2002   The world's business community is informed that the office desktop is 400 times dirtier than a toilet seat! The office keyboard was a mere 60 times more bacteria-ridden than the toilet seat. A "bacteria cafeteria on their desks" is the way microbiologist Chuck Gerba described his major finding (reported in today's *BusinessWeek*), explaining that food and beverages are regularly consumed and/or spilled at a desk, which is usually not cleaned properly, while the toilet is disinfected on a regular basis.

JUNE 4

1694   Economist and intellectual leader of the physiocrats (the first systematic school of political economy), Francois Quesnay, is born near Paris. (He was also such a good doctor that he became the personal physician to Madame de Pompadour, mistress of King Louis XV.) Quesnay did not publish his first book on economics until he was 60. Perhaps his greatest role in economic history was as a profound influence on the thinking of Adam Smith, during Smith's visit to the Continent in the 1760s. Smith proclaimed Quesnay a "very ingenious and profound author" and considered dedicating *The Wealth of Nations* to him, but the Frenchman died prior to publication.

1886   A local paper in Mannheim, Germany, announces that history's first successful gas-driven car (the Motorwagon, built by Germany's Karl-Friedrich Benz) has completed its initial test run in Mannheim. The item appeared under the heading "Miscellaneous."

1896   At 2 A.M. Henry Ford, 32, takes an ax and rips out the door frame of the work shed behind his house on Bagley Street, Detroit, so that he can take out the Quadricycle (the first car he built himself, which he has just finished fitting with an engine) on its maiden drive through the city's dark streets (see below).

1917   Guns or margarine: the executive committee of the DuPont company authorizes $105,000 to investigate the production of vegetable oil. This was part of its historic diversification from munitions into other areas, mainly in chemicals, that could exploit its new facilities and management expertise gathered during World War I.

1924   The 10 millionth Model T Ford leaves the company factory at Highland Park, Michigan.

1937   The first supermarket carts are put into service, at the Humpty Dumpty store in Oklahoma City, beginning a revolution in food buying. Storeowner Sylvan N. Goldman created the contraption to allow customers to buy more than could fit in a basket. His prototype involved putting wheels on a folding chair, raising the seat to accommodate an upper and lower basket, and using the chair back as a push handle.

1947   The U.S. House of Representatives overwhelmingly approves the Taft-Hartley Labor Relations Act, intended to limit the power of unions by restricting their weapons. Among the act's provisions were the banning of "closed shops" (in which employees were required to join a union before getting a job) and empowering the president to call an 80-day "cooling off" period (in which striking workers had to resume work if national security was affected by the work stoppage). Unions were outraged, and President Harry Truman vetoed the act, thereby regaining some union support after previous aggressive antiunion actions, but Congress passed the measure over his veto.

1984   Harold Geneen, who turned a faltering ITT into a giant conglomerate, completes and dates the one-page final chapter of his treatise, *Managing*. He noted, "I think it is an immutable law in business that words are words, explanations are explanations, promises are promises—but only performance is reality. . . . That is why my definition of a manager is what it is: one who turns in performance."

JUNE 5

1718   Renowned furniture designer Thomas Chippendale is baptized (his exact date of birth is unknown) in Otley, Yorkshire. His genius was to combine the popular Queen Anne and Georgian styles with Chinese, Gothic, and rococo elements. In effect, he established a solid brand identity. His was the first style of furniture in England to be named after an artist rather than a monarch. Contemporary architect Mies van der Rohe has observed, "A chair is a very difficult object. A skyscraper is almost easier. That is why Chippendale is famous."

1723   Economist and social philosopher Adam Smith is baptized (the exact date of his birth is unknown) in Kirkcaldy, Scotland. Very little is known of his childhood; at age four he was kidnapped by gypsies, who released him when chased by townspeople. Smith's *An Inquiry into the Nature and Causes of the Wealth of Nations* (1776) is acknowledged as the first great work in political economy; it presents the theory of the "invisible hand" of competition as the mechanism that produces order and efficiency in economic systems in which each citizen pursues his own self-interest.

1833   Charles Babbage first meets Ada Lovelace. Babbage's invention, the "difference engine" was the forerunner of modern computers. The lovely teenaged Ada, Lord Byron's only legitimate daughter, was a mathematical prodigy who was fascinated with the machine, befriended Babbage, and published scientific works promoting it. It was in need of promotion; the British government initially sponsored the device, but when support was ultimately withdrawn for good, Prime Minister Robert Peel remarked, "How about setting the machine to calculate the time at which it will be of use?"

1883   Celebrated economist John Maynard Keynes is born in Cambridge, England. Unlike many geniuses, Keynes was popular and well adjusted, and enjoyed many interests, including the stock and commodity markets, in which he made a small fortune. He is famous for making his business decisions in bed. Near death he expressed a single regret in life: that he had not drunk more champagne.

1933   The United States goes off the gold standard, as President Franklin D. Roosevelt signs the congressional resolution that government and private bonds, including paper money, are no longer redeemable in gold. Despite gloomy predictions by scholars and economic advisers (Roosevelt's own budget director announced solemnly that rejecting the gold standard "meant the end of Western civilization"), the economy reacted buoyantly; foreign trade, prices, and stocks all began to rise.

1966   The largest object ever stolen by a single person, the 10,640-ton SS *Orient Trader*, is hijacked on this moonlit night in the St. Lawrence Seaway by N. William Kennedy. He was armed only with an ax, with which he hacked through the mooring lines, allowing the ship to drift out to a black-out tug and from there on to Spain, as part of a violent wildcat waterfront strike.

1977   The first commercially successful personal computer, the Apple II, goes on sale for the first time.

1980   "As scarce as truth is, the supply has always been in excess of the demand." —Henry Wheeler Shaw, in *Rocky Mountain News*

1988   Perhaps in honor of Keynes's birthday (see above), the longest flight of a cork from an unheated, untreated bottle of champagne is recorded today at the Woodbury Vineyards Winery in New York. Professor Emeritus Heinrich Medicus, of RPI, sent the stopper 177 feet 9 inches.

1997   In a "stunning about-face," the New York Stock Exchange votes to scrap its 200-year-old policy of expressing stock prices in fractions; decimals will be used in the future, as soon as computer systems can be reset.

2002   The Houston Astros announce that Enron Field will henceforth be called Minute Maid Park.

JUNE 6

1778   Congress passes a bill abolishing debtors' prisons in the United States.

1854   The charter for the first U.S. clearinghouse (an association of banks, the main function of which is to facilitate the exchange of checks between its member banks) is formally adopted. The New York Clearing House had actually been operating since October 11, 1853. Its first headquarters were at 14 Wall Street; it had 38 member banks; and its first day's clearings were $22,648,109.87.

1863   The board of directors for America's first national bank (the National Bank of Davenport, Iowa) is elected. The bank opened on June 29, and for two days it was the only national bank in operation under the National Bank Act of 1863.

1925   Walter Percy Chrysler founds the Chrysler Corporation.

1932   A federal tax on gasoline is first levied in the United States.

1933   Radio is causing massive unemployment in one particular segment of the world economy—clock setters. According to a report filed today with the *New York Times*, "Before the coming of the radio numbers of clockmakers were employed in paying periodical visits to houses to wind big clocks and keep them in order. People now do the winding themselves. This has thrown a large number of men out of work."

1934   Franklin D. Roosevelt signs the act creating the Securities and Exchange Commission (SEC) to prevent unfair practices in the stock market.

1941   Louis Chevrolet, famous automobile designer, dies at age 62 in Detroit.

1948   Automobile and refrigerator manufacturer and creator of American Motors, Charles Nash, dies at 84.

1976   Jean Paul Getty dies at 83 outside London. During his life his work and investments in oil and 200 other concerns made him the world's richest man; at death his personal fortune was estimated between $2 billion and $4 billion. His will contained 21 codicils, which is the most of any will ever admitted to probate (see December 15).

2000   Unilever agrees to buy Bestfoods for $20.3 billion, creating the world's largest food company.

JUNE 7

1566   Sir Thomas Gresham lays the cornerstone of England's Royal Exchange in London. London was soon the financial center of Europe.

1860   *Malaeska, the Indian Wife of the White Hunter* is published in New York City. Written by Mrs. Ann Stevens and advertised as "a dollar book for only a dime! 128 pages complete, only ten cents!!!," it was history's first "dime novel" (an inexpensive, fast-paced thriller).

1877   George J. Mecherle is born on the family farm outside Merna, Illinois. His desire to create "an honest insurance company" led to his founding the State Farm Insurance group, which was well on its way to becoming one of the world's largest insurance organizations at the time of his death in 1951. Exactly 45 years after his birth (**1922**) the original license for his first company, State Farm Mutual Automobile Insurance, was dated. The following day the first board meeting was held, and the first action by the board was to halve its pay.

1882   The first U.S. tariff commission is authorized.

1899   Carrie Nation conducts her first raid against the liquor industry. "I have come to save you from a drunkard's fate!" she proclaimed, storming into a saloon in Kiowa, Kansas, and proceeding to smash the bar mirror, front windows, and every bottle in the place with the bricks she'd brought.

1921   The executive committee of General Motors agrees to establish a small manufacturing plant to produce air-cooled automobiles. Revolutionary and highly promising (prototypes achieved runs of about 1,000 miles per gallon), the air-cooled engine was heavily supported within the corporation by the administrative brilliance of Pierre S. du Pont and the technical brilliance of Charles F. Kettering, but it was finally scrapped after six years' development because of persistent production flaws and because sales of conventional cars were skyrocketing.

1961   In the first-ever sale of Japanese stock on Wall Street, Sony Corp. offers two million shares at $1.75 each. The entire issue was bought out in two hours, with a closing price of $2.40. Yoshio Terasawa, the New York agent for underwriter Nomura Securities, instructed his secretary to answer the ceaselessly ringing telephones with the greeting "Sony, sold out" and then left for the day.

JUNE 8

1887   The granddaddy of IBM is born. Herman Hollerith, 27, patents his punch-card tabulating machine. A precursor of the electronic computer, the machine won a Census Bureau competition in 1889, proved a great success in America's 11th census in 1890, and led Hollerith to form the Tabulating Machine Company in 1896. In 1911 Charles R. Flint merged this company with two others to form the Computing-Tabulating-Recording Company (C-T-R), which changed its name to International Business Machines Corporation (IBM) in 1924.

1911   The Firestone Tire & Rubber Company begins production at its first custom-built factory, Plant 1 in Akron, Ohio. It already needed expansion. Fabulous growth was the hallmark of Firestone through the early 1900s; constant innovation in product, technology, and production methods fueled the growth. History's first Indianapolis 500 auto race was won with Firestone tires just 10 days before today's factory opening. Harvey Firestone used the race year after year to test and publicize new products.

1912   Universal Pictures is created by Carl Laemmle with the merger of his Independent Moving Picture Co. and several other small film companies. Legend has it that Laemmle chose the name after seeing a Universal Pipe Fittings truck drive by. Small, portly, and eccentric, Laemmle was known affectionately as "Uncle Carl" by his employees, among whom he sought to build a family atmosphere; he had a reputation as being the best natured and least neurotic of studio bosses. He was a major force in the successful battle of independent producers to break the attempted control of American film production/distribution by Edison's Motion Picture Patent Company, and he founded Hollywood's "star system" by giving actress Mary Pickford a huge salary and huge billing. The conventional wisdom of the time was to withhold significant naming and billing of stars because it might lead to huge salaries; Laemmle gave her both.

1994   Buckling under political and corporate pressure that threatens its very existence, the Financial Accounting Standards Board (FASB) announces that it will not require companies to expense stock options. This is the ruling that opened the floodgates to the accounting scandals of the early 2000s.

JUNE 9

1768   Samuel Slater, founder of the U.S. cotton textile industry, is born in Belper, England, into a prosperous farming family that provided him a good education and encouragement to his mathematical ability. He was apprenticed at 14 to the partnership of Jedidiah Strutt and Richard Arkwright, who had built the world's first spinning mill in 1768 and then the world's first water-powered spinning mill in 1771. At age 21, Slater emigrated to New York with a firm memorization of the blueprints of the Arkwright machines. He thus evaded the law against exporting drawings of textile machinery. He also evaded the law against the migration of skilled mechanics by identifying himself as a farm laborer at the point of embarkation. In 1790 Slater and Moses Brown established America's first cotton spinning mill at Pawtucket, Rhode Island.

1931 Dr. Julius Klein, the assistant secretary of commerce, announces in a speech to the Radio Manufacturers Association in Chicago, "The depression has ended. . . . In July, up we go."

1958 "It is, of course, a trite observation to say that we live 'in a period of transition.' Many people have said this at many times. Adam may well have made the remark to Eve on leaving the Garden of Eden." —Harold Macmillan, British prime minister, in the *New York Times*

2003 Art Cooper, the editor who turned *GQ* from an obscure fashion publication into a slick, international men's magazine synonymous with a suave lifestyle, dies of a stroke in New York City at age 65. He had just retired a week previously after 20 years as the magazine's top editor. He expanded its focus from fashion to include general interest and well-written literature, boosting its circulation to 800,000. The term *GQ* (originally short for *Gentlemen's Quarterly*) is now an adjective used to describe high style.

JUNE 10

1943 Hungarian journalist Laszlo Biro (1899–1985) patents the ballpoint pen. The inspiration came one day during a visit to the print shop of the magazine for which he wrote. Noticing how quickly the ink dried, he saw the advantages in a pocket-sized writing implement with that property and set to work on a prototype in 1938. To escape the Nazis, Biro fled to Argentina in 1940 and began selling his pens in Buenos Aires in 1945. His name became a household world; the *biro* is a global synonym for the ballpoint pen.

1947 Saab introduces its first automobile, the Model 92 prototype. Primarily a producer of aircraft, Saab had to shift into another product line with the end of World War II and for a while considered toasters. When automobiles was the final decision, the aircraft engineer Gunnar Ljungstrom was put in charge of the project, which began with his own sketches of an aerodynamic, light, and safe vehicle—sort of an airplane without wings. Noted industrial designer Sixten Sason then prepared production drawings. The name of the car came from a numbering system established for wartime products. The color was Saab's standard "aircraft green." Swedish critics raved at today's unveiling, but the first 92s didn't reach showrooms for another two and a half years.

1978   The Ford Motor Company sends out its first recall notice for the Pinto, a car now remembered for fiery explosions.

1985   Coca-Cola announces that they are reintroducing old Coke under the name Coke Classic. Having taken four years to develop, New Coke didn't survive two months (see April 23).

2001   Almost exactly a year before his life and his company (Tyco International) exploded in scandal, CEO Dennis Kozlowski throws the now infamous 40th birthday party for his new wife, Karen Lee Mayo. The 60 or so guests were all flown to the Mediterranean island of Sardinia and housed at the celebration site, the Hotel Cala di Volpe Resort. Gladiators were posted at every entrance, luxurious foods and beverages were continually served by toga-clad waiters, an enormous cake with exploding breasts was brought in, and a full-sized ice sculpture replica of Michelangelo's *David* dispensed vodka through its penis. Kozlowski decided Tyco should pay about half of the $2,100,000 tab. The event coincided with the announcement of numerous firings at CIT, a company that Tyco had recently purchased.

JUNE 11

1982   Washington announces that heavy tariffs will be imposed on some steel imports in order to help domestic steelmakers whose foreign competition is founded on cheap labor and government subsidy.

1987   Martin Sorrell, chief executive of the WPP Group, shocks the advertising universe of Madison Avenue with a $45 per share hostile tender offer for the JWT Group, the parent of ad agency J. Walter Thompson and the public relations company Hill & Knowlton. When JWT's chairman Don Johnston finally capitulated two weeks later for

$55 per share, the first successful hostile acquisition of an advertising firm was completed, shattering the conventional wisdom that service organizations were immune from hostile takeovers because their main asset, their top people, could simply quit and go elsewhere. But Sorrell made the deal work, managing to hold on to most of the creative people and entrenched clients, and improving financial management so that profit margins rose from a dismal 4 percent to a respectable 10 percent.

2002   The New York Stock Exchange delists Bethlehem Steel after nearly a century. In its last day of trading, the company share price dropped 4¢ to 25¢ per share; it had not been above a dollar for 30 days, triggering its expulsion from the NYSE. Once a symbol of industrial might, even part of the Dow Jones Industrial Average from 1929 to 1997, Bethlehem girders can be found coast to coast, in the Empire State Building and the Golden Gate Bridge. But low-cost foreign steel, combined with high labor and pension costs for its 13,000 active employees and 74,000 pensioners, led to five straight red-ink quarters and a bankruptcy filing in October.

JUNE 12

1792   *New York Morning Post and Daily Advertiser*, the first daily newspaper in New York City, is founded.

1864   Handsome but "congenitally indolent" Moritz Warburg marries the industrious Charlotte Oppenheim in Hamburg, Germany, and the couple soon set up house at 17 Mittelweg. Thus was founded the Mittelweg branch of the Warburg banking dynasty. The children of Moritz and Charlotte included Max M. Warburg (financial adviser to the Kaiser and the German delegation at the Paris peace conference in 1919), Felix Moritz Warburg (a partner in the New York banking firm of Kuhn, Loeb & Co.), and Paul Moritz Warburg (director of Kuhn, Loeb & Co. and founding member and designer of the U.S. Federal Reserve Board; his son James Paul was also a banker and economist of international stature and an original member of Franklin Roosevelt's brain trust).

1931   They finally get Al Capone. "I own the police" was his frequent boast, and up until today it seemed true. The 32-year-old mobster and

68 henchmen were charged with a variety of tax, conspiracy, and prohibition crimes. In October Capone was found guilty of evading $231,000 in income taxes. His career was over. His business card read, "Alphonse Capone, Second Hand Furniture Dealer, 2222 S. Wabash."

1981   "When you're negotiating for a 35 hour week, remember they have only just got 66 hours in Taiwan, and you're competing with Taiwan." —Victor Kiam, CEO, Remington Corporation, in the *Daily Express*

JUNE 13

1835   James Gordon Bennett publishes the first Wall Street financial article to appear in any U.S. newspaper, in the *New York Herald*.

1906   The first federal consumer protection law (34 Stat.L.260) is enacted, "an act forbidding the importation, exportation or carriage in interstate commerce of falsely or spuriously stamped articles of merchandise made of gold or silver or their alloys."

1978   Henry Ford II, chairman of Ford Motor Company, visits the office of company president Lee Iacocca for just the third time in eight years. Ford fired Iacocca weeks later.

2000   Breaking a tradition that is over 200 years old, the Securities and Exchange Commission orders that all stocks traded on U.S. exchanges must be quoted in dollars and cents rather than in fractions. Pilot programs would begin in September, and the plan was to be fully implemented by April. The change was estimated to save ordinary investors $3 million a day in commissions.

JUNE 14

1907   George Baldwin Selden (1846–1922)—the lawyer/inventor who in 1895 was awarded the famous Selden patent that gave him patent rights to any combination of an engine and carriage and thus was the source of royalties for years from every American carmaker except Henry Ford, who refused to pay a penny—today actually produces a machine that runs, on a racetrack near Guttenberg, New Jersey, in front of an audience of lawyers and court officials. Started by an air compressor inside a shed, Selden's machine coughed along for five yards and then stopped dead. The mechanical failure did not stop Judge Charles Merrill Hough from upholding the Selden patent until 1911, when Ford lawyers killed it forever by successfully arguing that its engine was of a fundamentally unique type.

1946   Real estate developer Donald Trump is born the son of a real estate developer in New York City. Trump made his first fortune during a time of financial stress in the 1970s when he was able to purchase prime property cheaply and build with generous city tax concessions; he lost his first fortune during a time of financial stress in the 1990s during a severe recession. According to Trump, "You just have to be the kind of guy to get people to do things."

1951   The first commercial electronic computer, the bungalow-sized UNIVAC I, is demonstrated and dedicated in Philadelphia by staff of the U.S. Census Bureau, which purchased it from the Remington Rand Corporation.

1954   The first proxy battle to capture the attention of mainstream America—the fight for control of the New York Central Railroad—is officially over. Three judges declared at the thrice-recessed stockholders meeting in Albany that railroad executive and financier Robert R. Young had secured a majority of the 5.8 million proxies cast, defeating the incumbent management team headed by William White. Young actually began his campaign for control of the nation's second largest railroad in 1947 with the purchase of large blocks of stock. Repeatedly denied a seat on the Central's board of directors, Young decided to take his fight directly to the shareholders, promising them better management, better profits, better dividends. Today's victory brought neither peace to Young or prosperity to the railroad (see June 15 and January 25).

JUNE 15

1954   Alfred Perlman spends his first full day on the job as president of the New York Central Railroad after being installed by chairman

Robert R. Young, winner yesterday of a historic proxy fight among shareholders (see June 14). Perlman was considered a railroading genius, having turned around several failing lines, and he soon saw a plan for the Central: specialize in freight, abandon its long tradition of excellent passenger service, and cut personnel drastically. Young was crushed by the plan, having taken over the Central with a romantic vision of building a nationwide passenger line, but did not fight it. By 1957 the Central was well on its way to solid profitability when a recession and the increased strength of road and air transport dealt a death blow to Young (see January 25), to dividends, and to the Central itself, which declined throughout the 1960s until it merged with the Pennsylvania to form the Penn Central in 1968, only to collapse in a spectacular bankruptcy in 1970.

1960   "[W]hat is a committee? A group of the unwilling, picked from the unfit, to do the unnecessary." —Richard Harkness, news commentator, in the *New York Herald Tribune*

1961   Sony cofounder Akio Morita is handed a check for $3 million a week after the very successful initial sale of Sony stock on the New York Stock Exchange. According to his wife, Yoshiko, it was the happiest moment in Morita's business career.

1987   "I find it rather easy to portray a businessman. Being bland, rather cruel and incompetent comes naturally to me." —John Cleese, British actor/writer, referring to appearing in industrial training videos, in *Newsweek*

JUNE 16

1812   New York's Citibank—now the financial conglomerate Citigroup—has its origins in the City Bank of New York, which opens today at 52 Wall Street, two days before the War of 1812 begins.

1903   The Ford Motor Company is incorporated with $28,000 raised from 12 shareholders, including the brilliant but fractious Dodge brothers. The papers of incorporation were filed today at the state capitol in Lansing, Michigan. It was Henry Ford's third attempt to form an automobile company, and this one held. He received 225 shares for his design and his 17 patents. Production began in a converted wagon factory on Detroit's Mack Avenue on the $750 Model A, which boasted a two-cylinder, eight-horsepower, chain-driven engine mounted under the seat.

1911   IBM is incorporated in the state of New York as the Computing-Tabulating-Recording Company (C-T-R).

1950   W. Edwards Deming—the quality control theorist whose methods were to revitalize postwar Japanese industry but who was largely ignored in the United States for decades—arrives in Tokyo. It was his second visit there, but his first as a sort of quality control guru by invitation of the Japanese government. "As for remuneration," he had written to host Kenichi Koyanagi of the Union of Japanese Scientists and Engineers, "I shall not desire any. It will be only a great pleasure to assist you."

1958   "I don't meet competition. I crush it." —Charles Revson, founder, Revlon, Inc., in *Time*

1980   The Supreme Court declares that living organisms that are products of human ingenuity are patentable. In the 5–4 ruling in the *Diamond v. Chakrabarty* case, the Court upheld the patent on genetically engineered bacteria capable of breaking down crude oil.

JUNE 17

1952   President Jacobo Arbenz Guzman announces sweeping land reform in Guatemala. Absentee-owned property would be redistributed to his nation's people, with compensation to the previous owners in the form of 20-year bonds and 3 percent interest on declared tax value. Intensively cultivated land would not be touched. The United Fruit Company, which had large plantations in the country, reacted strongly in the form of the U.S. government. Having already stopped selling arms to Guatemala and having seized a Swiss shipment, America pushed through a motion of censure in the Organization of American States and then orchestrated a coup. With American weaponry and six gunships piloted by American volunteers, a rebel army from Honduras and

Nicaragua under the command of Colonel Carlos Costillo Armas (a Guatemalan graduate of the U.S. Command and General Staff College at Fort Leavenworth, Kansas) attacked the country. President Jacobo Arbenz Guzman was deposed with ease.

1985 "The person who knows 'how' will always have a job. The person who knows 'why' will always be his boss." —Diane Ravitch, educator/academic, in *Time*

2004 Results of a 30-state study of credit reports are announced in Washington by the Public Interest Research Group: 79 percent of all credit reports have some sort of error; 54 percent include personal identifying information that is misspelled, outdated, belongs to someone else, or is otherwise wrong; and one in every four has errors serious enough to disqualify a consumer from buying a home, opening a bank account, or getting a job.

JUNE 18

1935 The Rolls-Royce trademark is registered. The logo remains a memorable statement of strength, dignity, and quality. The working partnership of Charles Stewart Rolls (mainly a marketer) and Frederick Henry Royce (mainly a car builder) began in 1904, was incorporated in 1906, and blossomed in 1908 when they moved their factory from Manchester to Derby and focused solely on producing the Silver Ghost, a machine that was driven "14,371 mile nonstop." The Royce-designed Ghost got its name from being nearly silent, and boasted a six-cylinder engine of 40 to 50 horsepower, which proved that a gasoline engine could match the performance of a steam engine.

1941 Harry Bennett shows his boss, Henry Ford, the agreement reached with the United Auto Workers union. Ford was the last automaker to settle with the union, and the company had been especially violent in suppressing union activity (see May 26). Yet the conditions on this agreement were more generous than those given by any other auto company and included back wages for fired union supporters, a closed shop, pay guarantees, and grievance procedures exactly as the UAW wanted. Henry Ford's wife, Clara, was a major cause of the complete change of policy. She was appalled by antiunion violence; she knew son Edsel favored harmony with the union; and perhaps most persuasive, she threatened to leave Henry if there was not an agreement. As Henry later explained, "Don't ever discredit the power of a woman."

1956 "When we know as much about people as hog specialists know about hogs, we'll be better off." —Major General Lewis Hershey, selective service director

1992 Prodigy announces that it will provide subscribers with access to the Internet, thereby becoming the first major online service to let users surf the Web. With the introduction and rapid spread of web browsing programs in 1993, proprietary services like Prodigy began to see memberships drop, which forced it and others to become full-service Internet service providers (ISPs).

JUNE 19

1843 Karl Marx is married in Kreuznach, Prussia, to Jenny von Westphalen, who urges him to stay out of politics. In the words of John Kenneth Galbraith, "For no woman since Mary did marriage portend so much."

1945 Publicity you just can't buy: after a feast in his honor at the Statler Hotel with the nation's press looking on, war hero General Dwight Eisenhower is asked if he wishes anything else. "Could somebody get me a Coke?" he asked. After polishing off the soft drink, he was again asked if he had any requests, to which he replied, "Another Coke."

1956 Founder of IBM, Thomas J. Watson, Sr., dies at 82 in New York City about a month after retiring as CEO. Exactly three years later (**1959**) creator of ITT as an enormous conglomerate, Harold Geneen, 49, took over as president of the then-struggling telephone company. Watson was famous for his slogan "Think," which he plastered in every office and on every desk in the company. Geneen was known for, among other things, his reverence for facts, believing information to be a key to good management. After one 1965 meeting he sent out a memo blasting his executives for playing fast and loose with the term "facts," which he defined as incontrovertible "final and absolute reality." "Apparent facts" or "reported facts" were no facts at all. Once "true facts" were established, management decisions became easy.

1997   One of the longest trials in England's history ends today with a victory (sort of) for McDonald's Corp. Activists Dave Morris and Helen Steel were found guilty of libeling the restaurant chain and fined $98,000. In his 800-page ruling Justice Roger Bell said that McDonald's was "culpably responsible" for animal cruelty, that its advertisements "exploit" impressionable children, and that its food provides "the very real risk of heart disease." McDonald's spent $16 million to win its $98,000 and was left with bad publicity.

JUNE 20

1753   Believing a treasure lies in the British East India Company vaults in Fort William, Calcutta, the chieftain Siraj-ud-Daula captures the fort and forces 146 Britons into a prison cell that measures just 18 feet by 14 feet 10 inches and has two barred windows. It would forever be known as the Black Hole of Calcutta. When the door was unlocked at 5:55 the next morning, only 23 were alive.

1965   Financier, stock speculator, and presidential adviser Bernard Baruch dies in New York City at 94. "When as a young and unknown man I started to be successful I was referred to as a gambler," Baruch wrote of his career, paraphrasing Ernest Cassell. "My operations increased in scope and volume. Then I was known as a speculator. The sphere of my activities continued to expand and presently I was known as a banker. Actually I had been doing the same thing all the time." (See August 19.)

2002   Government auditors in London announce they have discovered that the Ministry of Defense had valued 1,175 brass nuts at $122 million, or $104,000 per nut. The valuation was part of a crash program to economize, in which the ministry claimed to have cut its stock of spares and supplies way beyond target. The auditors recalculated the whole collection of nuts to be worth $1.73.

2002   Levi Strauss & Co. closes its plant in Blue Ridge, Georgia. It was the first of six sewing shops the company would shut by autumn and was part of two trends in modern manufacturing: outsourcing and the conversion of old-line companies from manufacturers to marketers of goods made under contract by others.

JUNE 21

1527   Machiavelli dies at 58 in Florence and is soon buried in the church of Santa Croce, with his tombstone stating, "No eulogy would do justice to so great a name." Just twelve days before, he had been rejected for a position in the new government that had replaced his patrons, the Medici; the rejection had been a blow to him and led to violent abdominal spasms. His great masterpiece on management, *The Prince*, widely printed and quoted in business contexts today, was essentially ignored by the Medici and didn't appear in print until he'd been dead for five years. It has not been out of print since.

1824   British workers gain the right to organize, when Parliament repeals the antiunion Combination Acts at the urging of MP Joseph Hume under guidance of the labor reformer Francis Place. The following year Parliament passed another act, however, which outlawed strikes and provided for summary methods of conviction.

1877   Ten members of the radical labor/terrorist organization the Molly Maguires are hanged for murder in Pottsville, Pennsylvania. Agitating for better working conditions in the coal mines, the Mollies were uninterested in lawful or peaceful means, using violence to intimidate mine bosses, who themselves used illegal methods to control workers and skirt labor laws. The name was taken from an organization of Irish anti-landlord agitators led by a widow, Molly Maguire. Court convictions, adverse publicity, and better economic times brought an end to the Mollies in America.

1879   Frank Winfield Woolworth opens his second five-and-dime store (the first having failed in three months) in Lancaster, Pennsylvania. This one was successful and began his empire in low-cost, open-shelf, self-service retailing.

1963   "Work is much more fun than fun." —Noel Coward, dramatist/composer/producer, in the *Observer*

1970   The nation's largest rail line, Penn Central (formed in 1968), declares the nation's largest bankruptcy. Incompatible management teams, excess debt, an absence of postmerger planning, unrelenting growth of competitors, and ill-advised diversification (mainly in real estate) were blamed. Perhaps the greatest problem lay close to the top: "the fucking railroad" was one way CEO Stuart Saunders referred to the company of 92,000 employees.

2003   The fastest selling book in history, *Harry Potter and the Order of the Phoenix*, by J. K. Rowling, goes on sale at midnight in Britain, America, Australia, Canada, and many other countries. Five million copies were sold on the first day. It was the fifth in Rowling's series about young wizard Harry Potter.

JUNE 22

1792   "Never fear the want of business. A man who qualifies himself well for his calling, never fails of employment." —Thomas Jefferson, in a letter to his nephew Peter Carr

1934   Ferdinand Porsche signs the contracts to produce three Volkswagen prototypes for the RDA (the Automobile Manufacturers Association of Germany). He had 10 months to produce them.

1941   This day in executive stress relief: inventor of Valium, Leo Sternbach, flees with his landlady's daughter and his new bride, Herta, from Switzerland to the United States in fear of a Nazi invasion. "We came with only our clothes," Herta recalled. Rolaids, the medication for upset and stressed-out stomachs, was trademarked on this day in 1954.

1993   Lloyd's of London announces its losses for 1990 are £1,910,000,000, the worst in the firm's 300-year history. Lloyd's had lost nearly £5.5 billion in the previous three years, far more than it had earned in the last 40, and many of its Names (that is, investors) had been forced into bankruptcy.

JUNE 23

1400   Johannes Gensfleisch is born the son of a prosperous patrician in Mainz, Germany. Because *gensfleisch* means "goose flesh" or "goose meat," he used his mother's maiden name—Gutenberg.

1810   John Jacob Astor founds the Pacific Fur Company to complement his American Fur Company, which already dominates the trade in the Missouri River valley, the Rocky Mountains, and the Great Lakes. Astor designed Pacific Fur to monopolize fur trade in the American Northwest and the nation's fur trade with China. In 1811 he established the town of Astoria as his headquarters.

1885   "I can give you the secret. It lies mainly in this. Instead of the question, 'What must I do for my employer?' substitute 'What can I do?' . . . The rising man must do something exceptional, and beyond the range of his special department. *He must attract attention.*" —Andrew Carnegie, in a speech at Curry Commercial College, Pittsburgh

1906   Laws regulating the purity of foods extend back to the Greeks and Romans, who both had regulations against the adulteration of wines. In the United States between 1880 and 1906, 103 bills were introduced in Congress to regulate food and drug commerce, but all failed until today, when the House passed the Pure Food and Drug Act. Opposition was not only historic, but heated. "Is there anything in the existing condition that makes it the duty of Congress to put the liberty of the United States in jeopardy?" asked Republican Nelson W. Aldrich. "Are we going to take up the question as to what a man shall eat and what a man shall drink, and put him under severe penalties if he is eating or drinking something different from what the chemists of the Agricultural Department think desirable?" Two events were critical in the passage of today's bill: publication of *The Jungle* by Upton Sinclair, which exposed the filthy conditions of slaughterhouses; and blackmail by President Theodore Roosevelt, who read *The Jungle*, sent two officials to investigate, and threatened to release their report (which would "be well-nigh ruinous to our export trade in meat") unless Congress acted.

1911   Advertising executive David Ogilvy is born in Scotland. He wrote, "When I was six, [my father] required that I should drink a glass of raw blood every day. To strengthen my mental faculties, he ordained that I should eat calves' brains three times a week, washed down with a bottle of beer. Blood, brains and beer; a noble experiment." *Blood, Brains and Beer* is the title of his autobiography.

JUNE 24

1839   A pioneer in various aspects of the meatpacking industry and in industrial practices in general, Gustavus Franklin Swift is born on a farm in Sandwich, Massachusetts. At 14 he went to work for his brother, the local butcher, and at 16 he conducted his first independent venture: buying a heifer, slaughtering it, and selling the meat door-to-door. By 20 he was making regular trips to the mainland to buy a steer and then selling the slaughtered meat the next day on Cape Cod. He then opened several meat markets, established a distribution territory, and became a shrewd cattle buyer. In 1872 he formed a partnership with James Hathaway and moved headquarters to Chicago, then the center of the beef universe. Hathaway quit the partnership when Swift began experiments in shipping dressed beef to the East; Hathaway thought the concept foolish. The experiments led to the groundbreaking refrigerated railroad car and an enormous fortune.

1872   "The secret of success is constancy to purpose." —Benjamin Disraeli, prime minister, in a speech to the House of Commons

1990   "I suffer no slings and arrows. I just sail on. That's the secret of success in life." —Robert Maxwell, British publisher/business executive/politician, in the *Observer*

JUNE 25

1868   The first federal law relating to an eight-hour workday is enacted by Congress and will be signed by President Andrew Johnson. It provided that "eight hours shall constitute a day's work for all laborers, workmen, and mechanics who may be employed by or on behalf of the Government of the United States."

1930   The *Rochester Democrat and Chronicle* publishes a glowing advertisement for a medicinal cure-all called Sargon: "Labor Official Praises Sargon for New Health . . . Regained 18 Lbs. Of Lost Weight and Troubles Disappeared, Says Kimber." This was a pretty good testimonial from a man who had been dead for six days and whose obituary had just appeared in the same newspaper.

1985   In one of the most extraordinary memos in the history of personal computers, Bill Gates and Jeff Raikes of Microsoft write to executives John Sculley and Jean Louis Gassee of rival Apple Computers, urging them to license the technology of Apple's new Macintosh computers. Gates and Raikes presented a complete game plan to their adversaries, providing a detailed statement of the advantages of licensing, a business plan of how to structure the licensing agreements, and a list of companies and individuals to contact for the most advantageous deals. "Apple must make Macintosh a standard. But no personal computer company, not even IBM, can create a standard without independent support. Microsoft is very willing to help Apple implement this strategy. . . . " The memo and a follow-up letter a month later were ignored. Apple's tight-fisted refusal to license any of its revolutionary technology has always been seen as a mistake, one that held Apple down—close to failure at times—and allowed Microsoft to achieve near-total domination of the market with its liberal licensing policy. "I just did not see how it would make sense," Gassee said years later. "But my approach was stupid. We were just fat cats living off a business that had no competition."

1994   "If you have bright plumage, people will take pot shots at you." —Alan Clark, British politician and diarist, in the *Independent*

1998   The Rose Bowl, the granddaddy of all football bowl games, finally succumbs to commercial sponsorship, announcing today that it will now be called "The Rose Bowl Presented by AT&T." Why the change after resisting the trend for so long? "It's the money," admitted chairman Harriman Cronk.

2002   What a day for spectacular scandals: WorldCom announces it has lied about $3.9 billion in expenses and fake profits, Adelphia files for bankruptcy, and Martha Stewart makes her famous clenched-face appearance on the cooking segment of CBS's *The Early Morning Show*. She grimly chopped cabbage with an enormous knife while host Jane Clayson ambushed and angered her with questions about her alleged insider trading of ImClone stock. "I think this will all be resolved in the very near future and I will be exonerated of any ridiculousness. I want to focus on my salad, because that's why we're here," said Stewart.

JUNE 26

1894   His offer to mediate between management and labor having been rejected by George Pullman, Eugene Debs orders his American Railway Union (ARU) to stop handling Pullman equipment. Two dozen railroads serving Chicago then refused to operate without Pullman cars, and the Pullman strike became a nationwide affair.

1974   At 8:01 in the morning, a bar code reader is used for the first time at a supermarket checkout, when a pack of Wrigley's gum is passed through a scanning machine in Marsh Supermarket in Troy, Ohio.

1998   Hormel Foods Corporation announces that Spam is now on display in the Smithsonian Museum. Two cans—one from 1937 when the luncheon meat was introduced and the newest can unveiled in November 1997—were added to the permanent collection of significant cultural artifacts in the National Museum of American History. "Without Spam," wrote Khrushchev in his memoirs, "we shouldn't have been able to feed our army."

2000   "Natural resources are morally neutral. As such they can be a source of great good . . . or dreadful ill. The key element is not the resource itself, but how it is exploited." —Nicky Oppenheimer, South African chairman of De Beers, in a speech to the Southern Africa Business Association

2000   In a White House ceremony, leaders of competing public and private teams announce that the human genome has been mapped. "Today . . . marks an historic point in the 100,000-year record of humanity," said J. Craig Venter, chief scientist of Celera Genomics, a

Rockville, Maryland, company that completed the genome in just nine months using one of the most powerful assemblages of computers in the world. "We have caught a glimpse of an instruction book previously known only to God," added Dr. Francis Collins, leader of the international (six countries) publicly financed ($300 million over five years) Human Genome Project. For some time it looked like rivalry and hostility would prevent a joint announcement, until President Clinton got involved, instructing his scientific advisers to get Collins and Venter together. Shares of Celera reached as high as $135 today, but then finished at $112 after profit taking, off $13.25.

JUNE 27

1857   *Scientific American* warns of a coming economic crunch: "The whale oils which hitherto have been much relied on in this country to furnish light and yearly become more scarce, may in time almost entirely fail." Prices for whale oil were on a sharp rise, from 43¢ per gallon to $2.25 (1823 to 1866). This supply shortage came just as demand for artificial lighting was increasing, with the rise in the nation's literacy and cottage industries. Kerosene replaced sperm whale oils as the next big thing in energy.

1878   Japan adopts a new currency system based on the yen. In August the feudal system was abolished, and in October equitable taxation laws were instituted.

1882   The Bank of Japan is established.

1905   "Bread or Revolution" was one of the threatening slogans of the Industrial Workers of the World (the Wobblies), founded on this day in Chicago by "Big Bill" Haywood (president of the violent Western Federation of Miners), Daniel De Leon (leader of the Socialist Labor Party), and Eugene V. Debs (leader of the Socialist Party). The IWW— "one big union for all the workers"—was formed mainly of unskilled and casual laborers in response to the American Federation of Labor's opposition to unionism for the unskilled, its opposition to revolution, and its fundamental acceptance of capitalism. Revolution was in the air.

In this same year, Moscow saw its Bloody Sunday massacre, the *Potemkin* mutiny, and Lenin's return from exile.

JUNE 28

1794   A cornerstone in America's "military-industrial complex" is laid. Joshua Humphreys (1751–1838) was appointed as America's first warship builder by Secretary of War Henry Knox, at a salary of $2,000 per year. Humphreys designed and supervised construction of the nation's first fleet, including the *Constitution* ("Old Ironsides"), *Constellation*, the *Chesapeake*, and the *President*.

1892   General Electric is traded on the New York Stock Exchange for the first time—about two months after the Edison-Houston merger that created it. Miffed that his name did not adorn the new company, Thomas Edison attended his first, last, and only board meeting in August 1892. "I will not go on the board of a company that I don't control," he growled before selling all his GE shares. His electricity patents stayed with GE.

1939   Twenty-two men and women file casually aboard Pan American Airways' *Dixie Clipper* at Port Washington, Long Island, and settle back in their seats for a 22-hour flight to Europe. It was history's first commercial transatlantic flight. The plane will proceed to the Azores, then Lisbon, then Marseilles. For safety reasons, the flight was in a pontoon plane that could land in the ocean; the *Dixie Clipper* was docked on water and the passengers entered it over a pontoon bridge.

2000   For the first time in public, Lorillard Tobacco Co. CEO Martin Orlowsky admits believing that smoking causes lung cancer and other diseases and is addictive. He was testifying in a Miami courtroom against paying punitive damages to sick Florida smokers.

JUNE 29

1620   King James I bans tobacco growing in England. The action comes out of health concerns . . . for his treasury. He granted the monopoly to the Virginia Company in America in return for a tax of one shilling per pound.

1855 *The Daily Telegraph* begins publication in London following repeal of the Stamp Act by Parliament. Other papers went from weeklies to dailies, but the *Daily Telegraph* doubled the circulation of the *Times* within five years, and by 1870 it was the largest selling newspaper in the world, with a circulation of over 270,000.

1916 A Boeing aircraft flies for the first time. It was a "stick-and-wire" seaplane that William E. Boeing built with Conrad Westervelt in six months in a boathouse on the shores of Lake Union near downtown Seattle. Boeing built the seaplane because he liked to fish; he had purchased the second pontoon plane that Glenn L. Martin ever built, but when Boeing became impatient with how long it took to get spare parts, he decided to build his own plane.

1999 "I have come to view strong corporate governance as indispensable to resilient and vibrant capital markets. It is the blood that fills the veins of transparent corporate disclosure . . . the muscle that moves a viable and accessible financial reporting structure. And without financial reporting premised on sound, honest numbers, capital markets will collapse upon themselves, suffocate and die." —Arthur Levitt, Jr., former chairman, SEC, in a speech to the Audit Committee Symposium, New York City

JUNE 30

1683 Curiously, pirate ships in the 17th century offered employment terms that were highly progressive. Captains were elected by the crews, the workers were paid on a commission basis and acted as free agents, the right to strike was taken for granted, and there was established health insurance. Management was very much a democratic, "bottom-up" affair. In the following contract dated today, for example, the workers decided what the boss would be paid, rather than vice versa. Notice also the dedication of the workers to each other. "Articles of Agreement between us aboard the *Camelion*, Nic Clough commander, that we are to dispose of all the goods that are aboard amongst us, every man to have his full share, only the Commander is to have two shares and a half for the ship, and whom the Captain pleases to take for the Master under him is to have a share and a half . . . as for the Doctor, a share and a half . . . As you are all here present, you have taken your corporal oath upon the holy Evangelists to stand by the other as long as life shall last." A signature or mark for each of the twenty crewmen followed. The vessel was captured three months later; eight of the crew were sentenced in New York to twenty lashes and a year's imprisonment.

1934   The first five members of the SEC are appointed by President Franklin Roosevelt. The first meeting convened two days later. The five were James McCauley Landis (a protégé of Louis Brandeis, a harsh critic of Wall Street, and the body's second chairman), Ferdinand Pecora (of the Pecora Hearings that exposed Wall Street wrongdoing), George Matthews and Robert Healy of the Federal Trade Commission, and Joseph P. Kennedy as the first chairman. Kennedy's presence, let alone chairmanship, caused an outrage because of his shady reputation— including that of a speculator and stock price manipulator—but Kennedy was a strong ally of Roosevelt's, he was an astute businessman, and he would help make the SEC palatable to Wall Street. For a start, he was the only member of the original SEC with any experience in securities markets. He might have been the fox guarding the henhouse, but he knew where the holes in the fence were. It turned out to be a shrewd and successful choice by Roosevelt.

1948   The transistor is unveiled at the Bell Telephone Labs in Murray Hill, New Jersey. The age of the vacuum tube (also developed at the Bell Labs) was over; the age of computers had begun.

1999   Procter & Gamble announces in Cincinnati that it will immediately stop using animals to test many of its household products. Exempted from the ban were current food and pharmaceutical products and cases in which animal testing was required by law.

JULY

JULY 1

1813   The British East India Company loses its monopoly on trade in India but will continue its monopoly on the trade with China until 1833.

1827   The first Spanish newspaper to be published in the United States, *El Redactor*, makes its debut in New York City. Juan Jose de Lerena was its first editor. Other newspapers started this year were London's *Evening Standard* and the *Freeman's Journal*, the first black newspaper in the United States, which also began in New York City.

1899   Fabrica Italiana Automobili Torino (Fiat) is founded in Turin by cavalry lieutenant Giovanni Agnelli (1866–1945) and eight partners, with an initial capitalization of $152,000. By November the company had built 10 three-horsepower cars. Fiat became Europe's largest automaker and Italy's largest industrial firm. To meet the need for parts, Agnelli founded the ball- and roller-bearing industry in Italy.

1908   Cosmetics queen Estée Lauder is born in New York City as Josephine Esty Mentzer. "If you can't smell it, you can't sell it," she said in 1976 (see April 24).

1941   For-profit commercial television is first broadcast legally in the United States, as the licenses issued by the Federal Communications Commission become effective. Ten stations had received licenses on May 2. License number one was issued to W2XBS, NBC, which telecast from the Empire State Building over Channel 1. Today's first legally sanctioned commercial (for Bulova Watch Company) cost $9 for 20 seconds.

JULY 2

1890   The Sherman Anti-Trust Act is passed by Congress. "Every contract, combination in the form of trust or otherwise, or conspiracy in restraint of trade or commerce among the several States, or with foreign nations, is hereby declared to be illegal." The bill took its name from sponsor Senator John Sherman, brother of William Tecumseh Sherman. For years the law was ineffective, known in business circles as the Swiss Cheese Act, until Supreme Court judgments in the 1900s gave the law its intended teeth.

1900   Ferdinand Zeppelin sees the airship that bears his name make its first flight at Lake Constance, Germany (see July 8).

1921   A big day for broadcasting: a heavyweight boxing championship is carried live on the radio for the first time. It was possibly the most-listened-to event so far in radio's history. An estimated 400,000 people heard the broadcast, set up by David Sarnoff, mainly on homemade radios and those in public arenas. It was a great boost to the interest in radio on the part of executives, entrepreneurs, and citizens. In "the battle of the century," Jack Dempsey knocked out handsome French challenger Georges Carpentier in round four at Boyle's Thirty Acres in Jersey City. Approximately 75,000 fans paid $1,626,580 to see the fight, making it the first prizefight to gross $1 million.

1962   Sam Walton opens the first Wal-Mart in Rogers, Arkansas.

1997   The government of Thailand devalues the baht, starting a domino effect of falling economies. The overheated growth in Asia in the 1980s and 1990s produced speculation and overvaluation of local currencies. Banks had overextended themselves to feed the growth. Speculators began buying dollars as a hedge, which spiraled into panic. Similar events followed in the Philippines, Malaysia, South Korea, and Indonesia. International Monetary Fund (IMF) loans and interest rate cuts in the European and American central banks prevented the events from creating a worldwide recession.

JULY 3

1819   The first savings bank in America—the Bank for Savings in the City of New York—opens for business. The first day's receipts were $2,807 from 80 depositors. The statement for the first six months showed a loss of $27, suffered as a result of accepting counterfeit money and a short change loss of $23.92.

1916   The "witch of Wall Street," Henrietta Howland Green, dies the richest woman in America with an estate exceeding $100 million at 80 in New York City. Despite her enormous wealth—started with a sizeable inheritance but then expanded greatly through her own shrewd management and investments in stocks, railroads, Chicago real estate, bonds, and mortgages—she lived her last 20 years in a tiny apartment in Hoboken, dressed shabbily, haggled with shopkeepers, and avoided medical treatment other than what she got at charity clinics. Unfortunately, her penury stretched to her children, and the story goes that her son lost a leg because she refused him proper medical treatment until it was too late. Her practice of maintaining a large pool of liquid assets for lending allowed her not only to survive the panic of 1907 but to thrive; when the smoke cleared many other investors found themselves in debt to her.

1944   John Maynard Keynes lays out his plan for the World Bank at the afternoon session of the banking committee of the Bretton Woods conference in New Hampshire. The conference was organized by the United Nations for the purpose of developing world economic policy once World War II was over. Based on the American Reconstruction Finance Corporation, Keynes envisioned the World Bank as a $10 billion loan fund to finance productive projects of its member nations. The fund would be created by member subscriptions, bond flotations, and net earnings from its loans. Keynes's vision was largely accepted by the conference and the World Bank was established, though with smaller capitalization than Keynes sought. The conference also established the IMF and the system by which world currencies would be tied to the U.S. dollar, which in turn would be tied to gold.

1955   "After you've done a thing the same way for two years, look it over carefully. After five years, look at it with suspicion. And after ten years, throw it away and start all over." —Alfred E. Perlman, president, New York Central Railroad, in the *New York Times*

1998   The meek inherit the earth: maker of the humblest of vehicles, Volkswagen, purchases the maker of one of its most luxurious, Rolls-Royce. Volkswagen's bid of £479 million was preferred by shareholders to the £340 million offered by BMW. The purchase did not include the company that made engines for the Rolls nor the use of the Rolls name or trademarks.

JULY 4

1631   The Bureau d'Adresse—history's first employment agency—is established in Paris.

1817   The first spadeful of dirt is turned in the construction of the Erie Canal, which will link the Great Lakes to the Hudson River. The canal made the markets and resources of the Midwest easily accessible to the East Coast, and thus to Europe. When completed in 1825, the canal reduced the travel time between Buffalo and New York City from 20 days to 6; the cost of moving a ton of freight dropped from $100 to $5. In its first year of operation, when it was open for just part of the season, 13,110 boats and rafts passed through it, and a full seventh of its construction cost (the state borrowed $7,411,770 to build it) was recouped in tolls.

1828   Construction begins on the Baltimore & Ohio (B&O) Railroad, the first commercial rail line in the United States for carrying freight and passengers. It was financed in part by America's richest man (and last surviving signer of the Declaration of Independence), 90-year-old Charles Carroll of Carrollton, who laid the cornerstone. On this same day President John Quincy Adams turned the first spade of dirt to start construction of the Chesapeake & Ohio (C&O) Canal, thus beginning a race between the B&O and the C&O across the Allegheny Mountains. The B&O reached Cumberland, Maryland, in 1842. The

C&O, plagued with financial difficulties, got to Cumberland eight years later and was already obsolete when it was completed.

1834   Unskilled workers in New York City demonstrate against abolitionists, fearing that freed slaves will take their jobs. Rioters broke up an antislavery society meeting at the Chatham Street Chapel, threatening the blacks in attendance. Rioting continued for more than a week, and churches and homes were destroyed.

1885   The most powerful motion picture executive in Hollywood for three decades, Louis Burt Mayer, is born the son of a metal salvager in Minsk, Russia (see November 28).

JULY 5

1841   A railroad train pulls out of Leicester station bound for a one-day excursion to Loughboro, England; it is the world's first publicly advertised package tour and is full of 570 teetotalers and organizer Thomas Cook. Normally there would be 50 passengers for the 48-mile trip, but printer/temperance worker Cook had a brainstorm when Midlands County Railway opened an extension between the two towns; he knew there would be high demand because Loughboro was holding a temperance rally. He persuaded rail officials to reduce the fare (Cook charged 14 pence) if he could guarantee 500 passengers. Today's successful trip marked the birth of the travel agency industry.

1923   The 16-mm Kodak Model A camera and projector are introduced. Although home movie equipment had been available in Britain since 1896, the Kodak equipment was cheap and infinitely easier to use, and therefore accessible to a much wider audience.

1970   "Making money ain't nothing exciting to me. You might be able to buy a little better booze than the wino on the corner. But you get sick just like the next cat and when you die you're just as graveyard dead."
—Louis "Satchmo" Armstrong

1991   The Bank of Commerce and Credit International is shut down by regulators in Britain, the Cayman Islands, France, Luxembourg,

Spain, Switzerland, and the United States. Established in 1972, BCCI at one time operated in 73 countries with 1.3 million customers; its assets of $20.6 billion made it the world's seventh largest privately held bank. It was thoroughly corrupt.

JULY 6

1785   The Continental Congress in Philadelphia agrees unanimously "that the money unit of the United States of America be one dollar; that the smallest coin be of copper, of which two hundred shall pass for one dollar; that the several pieces shall increase in a decimal ratio."

1892   In the predawn dark, 300 armed militia from Pinkerton's National Detective Agency approach the Carnegie steel plant in Homestead, Pennsylvania, on river barges, planning a sneak attack on striking workers. (The strike had begun several days before when Carnegie and his chairman, Henry Clay Frick, demanded that the workers' union be dissolved and announced a new policy that lowered the floor on minimum pay; Carnegie workers were paid according to the market price of steel.) Strikers and townspeople knew about the barges since they had passed Pittsburgh in daylight, and the Pinkertons were pinned down at the riverbank. At one point in the daylong fighting the workers loaded the town's courthouse cannon with dynamite, but it blew up. The workers poured oil on the water and set it on fire, but it was blown by winds in the wrong direction. The workers then loaded a flatcar with blazing combustibles and pushed it down the track toward the barges, but it derailed. The battle lasted all day, until a truce was called in the late afternoon. Ten workers and three Pinkertons had been killed. The workers succumbed to Carnegie's demands in November. The strike and a depressed steel market caused Carnegie's personal income for the year to fall $300,000, sinking to $4 million.

1946   A famous aphorism of competition—"Nice guys finish last"— is coined today, and it is probably the last time it is quoted accurately, even by its author. Brooklyn Dodger manager Leo Durocher was watching pregame batting practice at the stadium of the New York Giants, the

Polo Grounds, with reporter Frank Graham of the *Journal-American*. When the Giants entered, Durocher contemplated them individually as they came onto the field: "Take a look at [Mel Ott]. A nicer guy never drew breath than that man there. Walker Cooper, Mize, Marshall, Kerr, Gordon, Thomson. Take a look at them. All nice guys. They'll finish last. Nice guys. Finish last."

1950   In Tokyo, 11 days after the Korean War began, the Nikkei Average bottoms out at 85 yen. It had fallen by half since the Tokyo Stock Exchange was allowed by occupation authorities to open in May the previous year. Today marked the lowest point the postwar Japanese stock market would hit. Within a generation it climbed beyond 30,000.

JULY 7

1752   Joseph-Marie Jacquard—who established firsts in both the Industrial Revolution and the computer revolution—is born in Lyon, France. He conceived the Jacquard loom in 1790, but the French Revolution intervened (he fought for the revolutionaries), and Jacquard finally made a working machine in 1801. The machine was the first to produce all weaving motions and the first to weave figured patterns. It was such a boost to the textile industry that the conventional weavers in his hometown burned the machines and attacked Jacquard. Eventually it was accepted, and by 1812 there were 11,000 in France. The machine was the first to be controlled by punched cards, the very system that Herman Hollerith used in the most primitive IBM computers about a century later. It was also the first to contain other computer-like characteristics: it was programmable, it involved numerical control, it used coded information, and it had a memory. Jacquard died at Oullins, France, on August 7, 1834.

1891   American Express copyrights its Travelers Cheque, which will be a boon to globe-trotting customers as a protection against theft and other loss of cash. The cheque business began quietly; in its first year of sales only 248 cheques (worth $9,120) were sold, but by 1909 annual sales were $23 million.

1927   This day in record records: Christopher Stone, editor of *Gramophone*, presents the first record program on the BBC in London, thus becoming Britain's first *disk jockey*. Stone hated the term. In **1954** a record by Elvis Presley was first played on the radio; station WHBQ in Memphis broadcast his first recording for Sun Records, "That's All Right (Mama)." In **1989** CDs (compact disks) outsold vinyl record albums for the first time.

1928   After three years of development, the Chrysler Corporation introduces the Plymouth automobile, its answer to Ford and GM rivals in the inexpensive-but-reliable class. Thirty thousand witnessed the event in the Chicago Coliseum, and Amelia Earhart was at the wheel. The Plymouth allowed Chrysler to take its place as one of the world's major auto manufacturers. With a delivery price of $670, the Plymouth sold more than 80,000 units in its first year, which enabled a drastic expansion of production facilities. This success convinced Dodge shareholders to merge with Chrysler. Chrysler was the only car company to pay dividends through the Great Depression, and in 1933 Chrysler was the only carmaker to better its sales of the boom year of 1929. By 1935 Chrysler overtook Ford as America's second largest auto firm.

1965   Despite convictions for jury tampering and theft of $250,000, Jimmy Hoffa is reelected to a five-year term as president of the Teamsters union.

1997   "Their problem is that they play a lot of golf, which is right up there with heroin abuse as a killer of our nation's productivity. The only difference is that golf is more expensive." —Dave Barry, humorist, referring to executives, in *Fortune*

JULY 8

1838   Ferdinand Zeppelin is born into nobility in Constance, Germany. In 1863 while serving as a military observer of the Union army, Zeppelin took his first ride in a balloon at St. Paul, Minnesota, and upon retirement from the military in 1891 devoted himself to developing the flying ships that would bear his name. After exhausting his personal wealth, he had to rely on public support and the patronage of Kaiser Wilhelm II to continue his experiments. He conceived of putting a balloon inside a superstructure made of aluminum, and on July 2, 1900, a zeppelin made its first flight at Lake Constance. The machine was equipped with two engines and a functional steering mechanism. Zeppelins were significant weapons during World War I and achieved success as commercial airliners after the war. Zeppelin died March 8, 1917. The first passenger fatalities in the history of commercial air flight were brought about by the spectacular explosion of the zeppelin *Hindenburg* on May 6, 1937, at Lakehurst, New Jersey. Zeppelin's basic design survives to this day, but the machines are mainly used for advertisement.

1839   John D. Rockefeller is born at night in a bare, 8- × 10-foot front bedroom in a snug house built by his father, William, outside Richford, New York. William was essentially a traveling peddler and flimflam man who took to calling himself "Dr. William Rockefeller, celebrated cancer specialist." Shortly before and after Rockefeller's birth William fathered illegitimate daughters in the same house with the live-in "housekeeper"—his girlfriend, Nancy Brown.

1889   The *Wall Street Journal* is first published by Dow Jones & Company, a financial information service established in 1882 by Charles Henry Dow (1851–1902) and Edward D. Jones (1856–1920).

1932   The Dow Jones Industrial Average closes at 41.88; this is the lowest the index sinks during the Great Depression and represents a 90 percent fall from the heights it had reached in 1929. New underwritings had also fallen off 90 percent from 1929, and 2,000 investment houses had gone out of business. Something of a rally began the very next day, and by September the DJIA had doubled. The following year produced the highest total return on stocks (reflecting both dividends and price appreciation) of the entire 20th century.

2003   Microsoft announces that it will no longer compensate employees with stock options but will give them actual shares of stock instead; furthermore, it will expense the cost of the shares on its books, potentially reducing profits by billions of dollars. The new policy was fairer to employees and fairer to investors. "We want to be a magnet for the best people by paying smarter," said CEO Steve Ballmer.

JULY 9

1795   Real estate is taxed directly for the first time as a source of internal revenue for the federal government under ordinance 1 Stat.L.584.

1853   Matthew Perry makes initial diplomatic contact during the expedition that opened Japan to Western trade after two centuries of isolation. Perry anchored his fleet of seven "black ships" off the town of Uraga, 27 miles from Tokyo. Today he was visited by a town leader, who informed Perry that he must conduct negotiations at Nagasaki. Perry refused. "He was told," noted Perry's diary, "that my intentions were perfectly friendly, but I would allow no indignity. Nor would I permit the guard boats which were collecting about the ships to remain where they then were, and if they were not immediately removed I would disperse them by force." The Japanese official ordered the boats away, but a few remained nearby. Perry then sent one of his own boats to motion them away and show their ready weapons at the same time. This "had the desired effect."

1877   The Bell Telephone Association, the first formal Bell company and forerunner of AT&T, is founded in New York City by Gardiner Green Hubbard, a lawyer and public utilities entrepreneur. Hubbard and his son-in-law, Alexander Graham Bell, were each allocated 30 percent interest in the Bell telephone patent; 10 percent was allocated to Bell's assistant, Thomas A. Watson; and the remaining 30 percent went to investor Thomas Sanders, who put up more than $100,000 to finance Bell's experiments. Hubbard directed the early business strategy: he decided to rent, not sell, the early Bell telephones, and instead of licensing manufacturers to produce and sell the machines, a single company (that later became Western Electric) was contracted to produce phones for distribution by the association.

1925   Oonagh Keogh, 22, becomes the first female member of any stock exchange, when she is admitted to the floor of the Dublin Stock Exchange.

1985   "None of us really understands what's going on with all these numbers," David A. Stockman once confessed. Today he announces his resignation as Ronald Reagan's budget director to take a Wall Street job and write his White House memoirs, for which Harper & Row paid him over $2 million.

JULY 10

1790   In Edinburgh, the founder of economics, Adam Smith, sends for his regular dining companions, renowned chemist Joseph Black and renowned geologist James Hutton. Smith was 67 and one week from death. He insisted that Black and Hutton burn all of his manuscripts except for the few that were ready for publication. Reluctantly, they agreed. Sixteen volumes of the genius's work were turned to ash.

1825   Richard King, founder of the King Ranch, is born the son of poor parents in Orange County, New York. Starting as a steamship cabin boy, King amassed his own fleet of 22 boats by the end of the Civil War. In 1853, acting on the advice of his friend Colonel Robert E. Lee, King paid a Spanish family $300 for 15,500 acres (less than 2¢ per acre) along the Rio Grande River in Texas. One reason for the depressed price was that the previous owner had been killed by Indians, as had the owner before him. A drought in the same year further lowered the price of the land, as well as the price of cattle. King bought his original herd of longhorns for $5 a head. By 1925, when his widow died, the King Ranch was about the size of Delaware and thus qualified as the world's largest ranch.

1832   President Andrew Jackson vetoes the renewal of the charter of the Bank of the United States. The closest thing to a national bank at the time, it enjoyed a monopoly on federal government banking but was held in private hands. "It appears that more than a fourth part of the stock is held by foreigners and the residue is held by a few hundred of our own citizens, chiefly of the richest classes. . . . The bounty of our Government is proposed to be again bestowed on the few who have been fortunate enough to secure the stock and at this moment wield the power of the existing institution. I can not perceive the justice or policy of this course," wrote Jackson in his explanatory note to the Senate. Jackson withdrew all federal funds from the institution in 1833, helping to precipitate the panic of 1837 and the subsequent depression.

1958   "We can lick gravity, but sometimes the paperwork is overwhelming." —Wernher Von Braun, rocket scientist, on bureaucratic red tape, in the *Chicago Sun-Times*

JULY 11

1765   "Idleness and pride tax with a heavier hand than kings and parliaments. If we can get rid of the former, we may easily bear the latter." —Benjamin Franklin, in a letter on the Stamp Tax Act

1838   John Wanamaker is born in Philadelphia, where he would launch one of America's first department stores in 1875. Wanamaker established a number of firsts in retailing, including the use of regular full-page advertisements, which he started in 1888.

1864   Both the North and South suffered wartime inflation during the Civil War. In the first quarter of this year, 100 confederate dollars were worth $4.60 in gold, and on this date the gold value of the northern "greenback" dollar fell to 35¢.

1962   Edward Francis Hutton, the founder of the brokerage house that bears his name and the executive who joined some 15 companies to create General Foods Corp. in 1929, dies at 85 in Westbury, Long Island. On this same day Owen Young, international monetary expert, adviser to six presidents, and chairman of General Electric at a critical juncture (1922–36), dies at 87 in St. Augustine, Florida.

1985   Disaster turns to triumph: Coca-Cola chairman Roberto Goizueta and president Donald Keogh humbly announce that the original Coke is being brought back to market after New Coke flopped. "We have hurt you," said Goizueta, "and for that we are sorry." Denying that the whole thing was an artful scam to generate interest in Coke, Keogh said, "We're not that smart and we're not that dumb." He then continued in the light-hearted vein, reading several letters of complaint, including, "Dear Chief Dodo, What ignoramus decided to change the flavor of Coke?" One of the two executives then coined the term *megabrand* to describe just how important Coke is to the world. Coca-Cola stock closed at a 52-week high.

2000 "One less welcome byproduct of rapid economic and technological change . . . is the evident insecurity felt by many workers despite the tightest labor markets in decades. This anxiety stems, I suspect, from a fear of job skill obsolescence, and one very tangible measure of it is the pressure on our education and training systems to prepare and adapt workers to effectively run the new technologies." —Alan Greenspan, economist/chairman of the Federal Reserve Board

JULY 12

1730 Josiah Wedgwood is baptized (his birthdate is unknown) in Burslem, England, into a family of potters. Wedgwood joined the business as a child and quickly displayed exceptional ability at the potter's wheel. At 14 he was stricken with smallpox and eventually had a leg amputated; Wedgwood used the long period of inactivity to read, research, and experiment in pottery. He eventually formed a fruitful partnership with Thomas Whieldon, the foremost potter of his day, during which he mastered all the established methods and began to produce innovations of his own. By the 1760s Wedgwood had established his own firm, secured royal patronage, and enjoyed a worldwide market.

1793 The first telegraphic communication of complex information over a long distance occurs when engineer Claude Chappe and his older brother, Ignace, direct messages over the nine miles between Saint-Martin-du-Tertre and Paris. Chappe's visual system employed elevated stations, telescopes, and semaphores (arm signals that could indicate 49 different letters and symbols). The Chappe system then appeared in Russia, Sweden, Denmark, Prussia, India, and Egypt.

1854 George Eastman, creator of the amateur photography industry, is born on the family farm in Waterville, New York, where his father ran the farm and two commercial schools 120 miles apart. "I never smiled until I was forty," Eastman once wrote. Part of this may have been due to circumstances that arose shortly after his birth. In 1857 a depression hit the country, and his father's health began to slip. By the time Eastman was seven, his father had died and the businesses and the farm had been sold. The family moved to the city of Rochester, where his mother took in boarders. Eastman remained devoted to her throughout her life. At 23 Eastman had established a career as a bank bookkeeper and was planning a vacation to the Caribbean to investigate land investment when an acquaintance suggested that he buy a camera. Eastman canceled the trip, but the journey of his life had begun.

1979   Another sports promotion gone bad: the Chicago White Sox hold a Disco Demolition Night for this evening's scheduled double-header with the Detroit Tigers. Any fan bringing a vinyl disco record would be admitted for just 99¢; the plan was to collect all the disco records in a dumpster and blow them up with dynamite between the two games. But things did not go exactly as showman/owner Bill Veeck planned. While hometown Chicago was being beaten in the first game, records started flying down on the players from the upper decks. When the explosion did occur, the field was covered with chards of vinyl, and thousands of people poured out of the stands, confronting riot police and still flinging records. Umpires called off the second game before it began. On July 13, the Tigers were given the victory.

1986   "The difficulty is that we have an industrial base with so many characteristics of an industrial museum or of an industrial hospital." —Barry Owen Jones, Australian politician, in the *Sydney Morning Herald*

JULY 13

1568   The beer industry owes much to religious people. Medieval monks were responsible for introducing hops into the recipe, and on this day the dean of St. Paul's Cathedral in London, Alexander Nowell (c. 1507–1602) perfects a method for bottling beer. He discovered the idea behind bottle conditioning after accidentally leaving a container of beer at his favorite fishing spot. Besides beer, Nowell is most famous for writing the catechism that is still used by the Church of England.

1865 In an editorial in the New York *Tribune*, Horace Greeley advises young civil servants dissatisfied with their low salaries in Washington, D.C.: "Washington is not a place to live in. The rents are high, the food is bad, the dust is disgusting and the morals are deplorable. Go West, young man, go West and grow up with the country."

1978 After years of growing antagonism, Henry Ford II finally fires Lee Iacocca as president of Ford Motor Company. Ford fumbled for a reason, "It's just one of those things." Iacocca fired back, "Your timing stinks. We've just made a billion eight for the second year in a row. That's three and a half billion in the past two years. But mark my words, Henry. You may never see a billion eight again."

1984 "I am the proprietor. I am the boss. . . . There can only be one boss and that is me." —Robert Maxwell, British publisher/business executive, in a speech to labor leaders

2000 "Whatever happens, you get your pet back." —Slogan of a Manhattan firm founded by two brothers, one a vet and the other a taxidermist, in *Architect's Journal*

JULY 14

1857 Appliance manufacturer Frederick Lewis Maytag is born the son of German immigrants in Elgin, Illinois, on the family farm. In 1880 Maytag became a salesman for a farm implement maker and then became part owner and chief executive of the Parsons Band Cutter and Self Feeder Company. In 1907, largely to smooth out the boom and bust cycling of farm equipment sales, the Parsons company introduced the Maytag Pastime clothes washer, consisting of a wooden tub and hand-operated dolly. The promise was so great that in 1909 the Maytag Company was formed, capitalized at $750,000, around an improved model of the Pastime. In 1911 the machine became electrified. In 1922 the Gyrofoam was introduced; developed by Howard Snyder, the machine washed clothes through violent water currents rather than rubbing. Despite its relatively small size, the Gyrofoam outperformed and outsold all of its competitors.

1964   From a second-hand printing press in Canberra, Rupert Murdoch watches the first edition of a newspaper he created roll off the presses. The paper was the *Australian*, with a declared purpose "to report the nation to Canberra and Canberra to the nation." It was not only Murdoch's first paper, it was the nation's first national daily. It lost money for years.

1965   "There was a time when a fool and his money were soon parted, but now it happens to everybody." —Adlai Stevenson, who died today in London

2000   Coca-Cola announces that it will begin expensing stock options on its books. The action came after lobbying by one of its largest shareholders, Warren Buffett, and was quickly followed by the same announcement at Bank One and The Washington Post Co.; Ford, H.J. Heinz, and Gillette announced they were considering the same policy.

JULY 15

1867   Maggie Lena Walker is born the daughter of a cook and former slave in Richmond, Virginia. While still in her teens, Walker became a teacher, took business classes, and worked as an insurance agent. She also reconnected with the Grand Order of St. Luke, an African American fraternal and cooperative insurance society, which she had joined as a young girl. Under Walker's leadership the organization went, in 25 years, from a membership of 3,400 to more than 50,000, and from debt of $400 to assets of $400,000. The staff went from a single clerk in antiquated surroundings to 50 people occupying a modern four-story office building in Richmond. In 1903 Walker opened the St. Luke Penny Savings Bank, and during the chaos of 1929 and 1930 the bank absorbed all other black-owned banks in Richmond to become the Consolidated Bank and Trust Company. Walker remained its chairman until she died on December 15, 1934.

1903   The first sale in the history of the Ford Motor Company occurs. The first entry in the company's credit column recorded the following: "(Chicago Ill Trust & Sav)/Dr. E. Phenning/$850.00." The customer's name was misspelled. He was E. Pfennig, a dentist from Chicago, who had paid in full for a Model A.

1916 William Boeing founds the Pacific Aero Products Company. Based on a floating hangar/workshop on Lake Union in Seattle, Washington, the company was the forerunner of the giant aircraft manufacturer, the Boeing Company. Boeing began making planes because he liked to fish in remote places. On this date in **1954** the first jet airliner, the Boeing 707, was given its initial testing.

1933 "Words ought to be a little wild for they are the assault of thoughts on the unthinking." —John Maynard Keynes, in the *New Statesman*

1965 Congress passes an act requiring all cigarette packages to carry a health warning.

1985 The original desktop publishing program, PageMaker, is first shipped for sale to customers by the Aldus company. Designed by Paul Brainard for use in Macintosh computers, it was the first software to enable a single individual to write, lay out, paginate, and print a newspaper or book, including illustrations, using only a microcomputer and laser printer.

JULY 16

1877 "The father of public relations," Ivy Ledbetter Lee, is born in Cedartown, Georgia, the son of a prominent Methodist minister in Atlanta.

1984 " 'You're fired!' No other words can so easily and succinctly reduce a confident, self-assured executive to an insecure, groveling shred of his former self. . . . Handled creatively, getting fired allows an executive . . . to actually experience a sense of relief that he never wanted the job he has lost." —Frank P. Louchheim, business executive, in the *Wall Street Journal*

1995 Amazon.com opens for business. There was no advertising, no press, no hoopla. Founder Jeff Bezos simply told all 300 beta testers to spread the word. During the first month the company sold books in all 50 states and 45 other countries. "Within the first few days I knew this was going to be huge," recalled Bezos.

1997   The Dow Jones Industrial Average closes above 8,000 for the first time, and closes above 11,000 for the first time on this date in **1999**.

JULY 17

1763   The future fur and real estate tycoon John Jacob Astor is born into near-poverty in Waldorf, Germany, the son of an indolent butcher (see March 29).

1787   Friedrich Krupp—the industrialist who started his family's rise to international significance by founding the dynasty's cast-steel factory in 1811—is born in Essen, Germany (see October 8).

1790   The founder and genius of economics Adam Smith dies on this Saturday in Edinburgh at age 67. "I love your company, gentlemen, but I believe I must leave you to go to another world," said Smith a few days before, in refusing the last dinner invitation of famous companions Joseph Black and James Hutton.

1902   "The rights and interest of the laboring man will be protected and cared for—not by the labor agitators, but by the Christian gentlemen to whom God has given control of the property rights of the country and upon the successful management of which so much depends." Now regarded as one of the most hubristic of all business quotes, these words appear today in a letter from Reading Railroad president George F. Baer to photographer William F. Clark. Facing a strike by the United Mine Workers, Baer refused to talk with the miners and refused arbitration or mediation from any outside body, including President Teddy Roosevelt. It finally took intercession by J. P. Morgan to make Baer agree to federal arbitration.

1902   A building is *air-conditioned* for the first time. The term would not be coined for another 40 years, but on this date the air in the Sackett-Wilhelms Lithographic and Publishing Company in Brooklyn, New York, was both cooled and dried by blowing it past coils of cool water. The system was created by young engineer Willis Haviland Carrier for paper, not people. Sackett-Wilhelms found their printing paper was expanding and contracting in the heat and humidity, and was unable to take ink; it was for this problem that Carrier invented air-conditioning.

2001   Publisher and chairman of the *Washington Post*, Katharine Meyer Graham dies in Boise, Idaho, at age 84, following a sidewalk fall several days before at the Sun Valley ski resort from which she had never regained consciousness. On this date in **1959** her father—the eminent financier, banker, and public official Eugene Meyer, Jr.—passed away at age 83. Meyer acquired great wealth in pre-Depression investments, mainly in minerals and in Allied Chemical Corporation. He lost a lot of this in his purchase and unsuccessful management of the *Washington Post*. His daughter made the paper a journalistic and financial success largely by hiring the right people and then treating them well. Meyer also had a checkered record as governor of the Federal Reserve Board and as the first chairman of the Reconstruction Finance Corporation. He was a major force in the creation of the RFC in 1932 but lent its money to large banks, railroads, and insurance companies, and ignored farmers and small businessmen.

JULY 18

1858   Founder of the Avon cosmetics company, David Hall McConnell is born in Oswego, New York. McConnell entered business life in 1879 as a book salesman. As a district manager in Atlanta in 1886 he had a life-altering inspiration: if books could be sold door-to-door, so could perfume. His first venture was the California Perfume Company, in which he produced perfumes in his home and sold them along with the books. But the cosmetics proved so successful that he abandoned the books and established a perfume factory in Suffern, New York. He chose Avon as a business name because of the similarity in landscape between Suffern and Avon, England.

2001   AOL Time Warner Inc., citing an advertising slowdown, reports a net loss of $734 million for the second quarter. Stock price sinks several dollars to $46.10, down from $73.75 which AOL was selling for the day before the two media giants (AOL and Time Warner) merged in January 2000.

2002   AOL Time Warner Inc. announces a management shake-up. Unable to create "synergies" or central control over the sprawling media empire, Robert Pittman left his posts on the board of directors and as the company's chief operating officer. He was replaced by two veteran media executives from the Time Warner side of the organization. Also today, the *Washington Post* published an article detailing "unconventional" deals and bookkeeping to boost on-paper revenues before and after the merger between AOL and Time Warner. The company denied wrongdoing, but stock price fell 5 percent to $12.45.

JULY 19

1788   Prices on the Paris stock exchange collapse; the monarchy is doomed. Unemployment and bread prices were already disastrously high, readying the population for revolt. Bread alone required 60 percent of an average wage. In August, having failed to convince financiers to prop up the government, Lomenie de Brienne declared France bankrupt. Louis XVI fired him as finance minister and restored Jacques Necker, the Swiss banker who had resigned in disgrace in 1783 after lying about state finances. In January Necker imported thousands of tons of grain and flour to avert famine, but in April there was a major riot, which began at the Reveillon wallpaper factory when a pay cut was proposed. Three hundred Parisians were killed by government troops.

1802   French immigrant E. I. du Pont arrives with his wife, children, and dogs at the farm he has purchased on Brandywine Creek near Wilmington, Delaware, to establish his gunpowder factory. Du Pont chose the site for the availability of two kinds of power—water and human labor. Wilmington had a colony of Frenchmen who would work for less than Americans. Du Pont had already had unpleasant dealings with Americans. He was charged more than the going local price for the land (du Pont bought 95 acres for $6,740), and after it was learned he was going to erect a waterwheel and factory, a dam appeared upstream. It threatened his whole operation. Du Pont acquired the water rights on the bank opposite that owned by the dam builder and thus obtained legal right to destroy half of the dam and set the Brandywine flowing strongly again.

1814   Industrialist and inventor Samuel Colt is born in Hartford, Connecticut. In 1833 Colt established a factory to manufacture firearms. He received one of America's first patents, No. 138, and he also created a battery-operated naval mine that was history's first device using a remote-controlled explosive. The business failed in 1842, and Colt lost the rights to all his patents, but the Mexican War brought his first federal contracts and success again. Colt was a progressive factory owner, with both the machines and the people who operated them. He made unprecedented developments in the manufacture of interchangeable parts and the production line, to which he applied advanced ideas concerning working conditions and employee welfare. He died January 19, 1862.

1945   "A professional is a man who can do his job when he doesn't feel like it. An amateur is a man who can't do his work when he does feel like it." —James Agate, British critic and essayist, in his diary

JULY 20

1850   Richard Joshua Reynolds, founder of the tobacco empire that bears his name, is born in Patrick County, Virginia, where his father was one of the largest planters and slaveholders in the state. Reynolds's childhood was spent around tobacco farming, and as a youth he was a traveling salesman for his father's produce business. After a business school education, Reynolds took over as production manager and immediately began to improve the plantation's methods. In 1875, capitalized with $5,000, he established a processing plant in Winston, North Carolina, to take advantage of distribution and labor advantages there. By 1887 he was marketing 86 brands of chewing tobacco. In 1913 his brother and partner William persuaded him to go into the cigarette business; their Camel brand, introduced that year, was the first mass-marketed cigarette. R. J. Reynolds died July 29, 1918.

1858   Fans pay an admission charge for the first time to see a baseball game. In Long Island, the New York Fashion Race Course charged 50¢ each to 1,500 people to watch the New Yorker All Stars defeat the Brooklyn Atlantics 22–18. The money was used to cover the rental of the park and other expenses; it was not until 1863 that players were paid a percentage of gate receipts.

1996   "In the Middle Ages, the rich tried to buy immortality by building cathedrals. These days they set up business schools instead." —Anonymous, in the *Economist*

2004   Software giant Microsoft announces that it will give most of its cash hoard of $75 billion directly to shareholders through a combination of dividends and stock buybacks over the next four years. The dividend payment to chairman Bill Gates was about $3 billion, which alone dwarfed the news-making $1.9 billion dividends paid out recently by MGM. Gates planned to donate the money to charity.

JULY 21

1619   America's first strike ends more than a year before the Pilgrims arrived. In 1608 the British-owned London Company established a glassworks in the Jamestown colony, and its first staff consisted of eight Polish artisans. Their success inspired the hiring of other Poles in the colony. All went well until 1619 when the House of Burgesses decided that they, and anyone else not of "English stock," could not vote. The Poles walked off their jobs, hobbling the economy. On this day their demands of suffrage were met.

1748   "Remember that Time is Money. . . . Waste neither Time nor Money, but make the best Use of Both." —Benjamin Franklin

1816   Paul Julius Reuter, founder of the first news agency, which still bears his name, is born in Kassel, Germany, with the given name of Israel Beer Josaphat. He changed names when he converted to Christianity in 1844, about the same time that he changed careers, from banking to publishing. His political pamphlets earned the hostility of the authorities, and in the great year of European revolution, 1848, he fled to Paris. As a young banker in Gottingen, Reuter had made the acquaintance of Carl Friedrich Gauss, the eminent scientist who was then experimenting with electrical telegraphy. When his nickel-and-dime business of translating articles and financial bulletins went broke in Paris, Reuter went into telegraphy, acquiring operating rights at the new German terminus in Aachen, from which he became a conduit for financial news between various European capitals. It was at this time that he established his ingenious carrier pigeon news service (see April 16). Reuter "followed the cable" to Britain, opening a small office near the London stock exchange and securing a lucrative commission to send commercial news between the London and Paris bourses. He branched into general news, secured contracts with newspapers, and expanded to other continents when undersea cables were laid.

1836   The first Canadian railway opens, linking Laprairie on the St. Lawrence River to St. Johns on the Richelieu.

1904   The Trans-Siberian railway is finally completed. It took 13 years to lay the 4,607 miles of track, with winter work proceeding through snowstorms and temperatures reaching $-85°F$. The chief function was to bring tea, silk, and cotton from China, and grain and cattle from Siberia.

1973   "Sweat is the cologne of accomplishment." —Heywood Hale Broun, broadcast journalist, in a television interview

1977   The *Wall Street Journal* reports that Kellogg Co. has recently reduced the percentage of ground particles of iron in Frosted Rice cereal from 25 percent of the government's "recommended daily allowance" to 10 percent, after consumers discovered they could move the flakes of the cereal with magnets. "We had problems evenly distributing the product's sugar coating," explained a company spokesman.

JULY 22

1913   Charles (Bates) "Tex" Thornton—the visionary who built Litton Industries into one of the first megaconglomerates, and the leader of the "Whiz Kids," the team of army colleagues who turned Ford Motor

Company around in the late 1940s—is born in Haskell, Texas. His father abandoned the family shortly after Thornton's birth. He was reared by his mother, who suggested that he begin buying land at age 12 with money earned at odd jobs. At 14 Thornton owned 40 acres, and at 19 he and a friend opened a gas station and car dealership. He became a clerk in the Department of the Interior and at night completed courses for a college degree. The door to the upper echelons of military intelligence was opened by his report on the financing of low-cost housing, which caught the attention of the assistant secretary of war for the air forces, Robert Lovett, who was looking for someone to help him apply modern management and statistical techniques to planning in the army air force.

1923   In 1921 during a brief period of stability, the German mark was trading at around 81 marks to the dollar. A year later it was 670, and by the spring of 1923 it had fallen to 30,000. On this day the Berlin correspondent of the *London Daily Mail* dispatched, "I was amazed when I found today that one had to pay 24,000 marks for a ham sandwich whereas yesterday in the same café a ham sandwich cost only 14,000 marks. . . . The salary of a Cabinet Minister has been raised from 23,000,000 ten days ago to 32,000,000 marks."

1986   "People assume you slept your way to the top. Frankly, I couldn't sleep my way to the middle." —Joni Evans, publishing executive, referring to her start in publishing as a manuscript reader, in a speech to a conference of female executives

JULY 23

1875   Isaac Merrit Singer dies at 63 in Torquay, England, made wealthy through his talent as a mechanical inventor (his improvements brought the sewing machine into general, domestic use, giving it the ability to make continuous and curved stitching) and his talent as a marketer. Singer had a background in acting and theater management, was a skillful organizer and superb advertiser, and was an innovator in installment credit plans; he created the $5 down, $5 per month purchase plan for his machines.

1888   Scottish veterinary surgeon John Boyd Dunlop files a patent application for the pneumatic tire. The now-universal fixture was created the previous year in his Belfast home when Dunlop fitted his son's tricycle with tires made of garden hose filled with water. The family doctor suggested air instead of water. Dunlop was awarded his patent and went into production in 1890, only to discover that the idea had been patented in 1845. By that time, however, the Dunlop Company held enough accessory patents to secure its viability. The air-filled tire came along just as the automobile was being developed and contributed to the success of motorized vehicles.

1892   Twenty-one-year-old anarchist Alexander Berkman, posing as an agent for a New York employment firm, enters the Pittsburgh office of Carnegie chairman Henry Clay Frick, pulls a gun, and shoots Frick twice in the neck, tearing off part of his left ear. Frick and his assistant, John Leishman, leapt on Berkman, and a third shot went into the ceiling. Berkman freed himself enough to pull a dagger and plunged it into Frick seven times. A crowd gathered in the street, staring dumbstruck as the three men struggled in the window. The police arrived after several minutes. It is said that Frick stayed in his office until the day's work was done, that he refused anesthetic when doctors worked on his wounds ("I can help you probe better without it"), and that he was back at work full-time in a week. Berkman was imprisoned for 14 years. After being pardoned and released in 1906, he and lover Emma Goldman emerged as the top spokespeople of American anarchism. They were both deported in 1919 to his native Russia, where they became disenchanted and outspoken against Communism and had to flee that country. Berkman took his own life in 1936.

1969   Investment banker Sidney James Weinberg, "Mr. Wall Street," dies at 77 in New York City. "Money?" he once said. "Keeps coming in all the time, and hardly means anything." (See October 12.)

JULY 24

1824   The result of the world's first public opinion poll, on voter preference in the 1824 presidential race, is published in the *Harrisburg Pennsylvanian*.

1851   On a farm field outside London, Cyrus Hall McCormick attends the first head-to-head test of his reaper against two other brands, one of which is a highly touted machine from chief rival Obed Hussey. Though he'd sold 3,000 reapers in America, McCormick had yet to break into foreign markets, and he'd figured that the London Exposition of 1851 was the perfect opportunity. His machine was the ugly duckling of the show, "a cross between an Astley chariot, a wheelbarrow, and a flying machine," according to a leading British newspaper. Seventy seconds after today's field test began, the McCormick machine had cut 74 yards of grain, while the two competing machines had broken down. McCormick received several awards, and the European market was his.

1952   Lilli, a risqué adult cartoon character, makes her debut in the German magazine *Bild Zeitung*. Drawn by cartoonist Reinhard Beuthien, the slender, blonde Lilli is shown in her first of many appearances begging a fortune-teller, "Can't you give me the name and address of this tall, handsome, rich man?" Lilli was turned into a three-dimensional doll in August 1955, and Ruth Handler bought three dolls during a vacation in Europe. Handler saw in Lilli a version of the doll she wanted to create—Barbie.

2000   The rates for cable television service have shot up 45 percent since 1996 when the Telecommunications Act was passed and the cable industry was deregulated. This is the finding of a study circulated today by Consumers Union, publishers of *Consumer Reports* magazine. The act was supposed to increase competition and thus bring down consumer costs, but today's figure for rate increase far outstripped the rate of inflation over the same period. Cable industry officials disputed the validity of the report because actual deregulation did not begin until 1999. Even using industry figures, however, cable rates since 1999 had grown at a pace about double that of inflation.

JULY 25

1848   Energy entrepreneur Joseph Newton Pew is born on the family farm in Mercer County, Pennsylvania. Pew taught school for several years, then entered the business world as a real estate broker, which took him to Titusville, site of America's first oil field. He began investing in oil lands and quickly realized the potential of natural gas for heating and illumination. In association with others, Pew brought piped gas to a number of cities, including Pittsburgh; he also invented apparatus for pumping gas. Among the companies he formed was the Sun Oil Company (1880), which became Sunoco. The Pew Memorial Trust extends from the dynasty he began. Pew died October 10, 1912.

1904   Some 25,000 textile workers form a picket line in Fall River, Massachusetts, to protest the deplorable conditions in the mills. The strike lasted for most of the summer and helped focus national attention on the workers' plight. The National Child Labor Committee was formed later in the year.

1955   "After the first million, it doesn't matter. You can only eat three meals a day—I tried eating four and I got sick. You can't sleep in more than one bed a night. Maybe I have twenty suits, but I can only wear one at a time, and I can't use more than two shirts a day." —Jeremy Hirshhorn, multimillionaire, in *Time*

JULY 26

1714   "The patient, like a drowning man, catches at every twig and hopes for relief from the most ignorant when the most able physicians give him none." —Anonymous, on human susceptibility to medical quackery, in the London *Spectator*

1803   Public freight-carrying railroad service commences. Incorporated in 1801, history's first commercial freight line, the Surrey Iron Railway, opened its line from Wandsworth to Croydon, England.

1842   Founder of the neoclassical school of economics, the first authority to popularize supply-and-demand curves, Alfred Marshall is born the son of a tyrannical bank cashier in the slum of Bermondsey ("reeking of evil smells") outside London. Marshall was ashamed of his background, disguising his place of birth and ignoring his parents in autobiographical writings. However, he never lost his concern for social welfare. He defined economics as "a study of mankind in the ordinary business of life," emphasizing "the material requisites of wellbeing" in his breakthrough 1890 text *Principles of Economics*. He died on July 13, 1924, at Cambridge, England.

1877   "The Boy Plunger of Wall Street," Jesse Lauriston Livermore, is born on a Shrewsbury, Massachusetts, farm. At 16, Livermore went to Boston where he got a job with Paine, Webber & Co. writing stock quotations on a display board. Scraping together $10 of his own savings and borrowing the rest from the broker, Livermore's first speculation was on Chicago, Burlington, and Quincy Railroad stock; when he reached a 30 percent profit, he sold. After several similar deals and warnings from his employers that he should stop, Livermore quit and carried on operations in the "bucket shops" of Boston, Chicago, and Denver. By 1906 he was in New York City with a $2,500 stake. In that same year he made $250,000 short-selling Union Pacific, and he began a series of deals with Anaconda Copper that made him a millionaire three times over by the age of 30. In 1908 he attempted to corner the cotton market and lost $900,000. He made it back on Wall Street in several days. Perhaps his biggest deal came in 1925, when he short-sold 50 million bushels of wheat in the Chicago grain market; he timed the market perfectly, obtaining the wheat in a rising market and selling it at peak. His estimated profit was $100 million. He went bankrupt four times and was able to fully repay his creditors all but one of those times. He died November 28, 1940.

1956   Egyptian president Gamal Abdel Nasser seizes control of the Suez Canal. It was the first time an Arab state claimed ownership of its own natural resources in defiance of Western commercial interests. French, British, and Israeli troops moved against Nasser but on the verge of victory called off their invasion under pressure from the Americans who, as historian David Halberstam put it, "were nervous about what seemed to them virtually a restoration of colonial power in that region."

JULY 27

1694   The Bank of England, the first modern central bank, is chartered. A group of merchants headed by Scotsman William Paterson had created a pool of £1.2 million to lend to the king. In return, the subscribers received 8 percent interest on their contributions; had the right to collect consumption taxes on beer, vinegar, and ale; and could loan money to others in the form of printed notes backed by the king's promise to pay. The notes could be used to pay taxes. Headquartered first in London's Threadneedle Street, the bank soon came to control the country's money supply by setting the rate at which money was loaned to commercial banks.

1900 The H.J. Heinz Co. is incorporated. It was the third food-processing/marketing firm that Henry John Heinz had organized; the first went bankrupt, and the second (organized with brother John and cousin Frederick) established national and international prominence. In this same year, the company erected the first large electrical sign in New York City's history, at Fifth Avenue and 23rd Street; six stories high and using 1,200 bulbs, the sign contained a 40-foot pickle.

1971 The first stock brokerage to trade shares in itself on a major exchange was Merrill, Lynch, Pierce, Fenner and Smith Inc. The stock debuts on this day on the New York Stock Exchange, opening at 38¼ and closing at 37, with a total volume of 47,500 shares traded.

1989 Workers at the Japanese-owned Nissan assembly plant in Smyrna, Tennessee, vote not to be represented by the United Auto Workers union. Despite a long and costly campaign, the UAW failed to win approval in any of the Japanese car companies based in the United States.

JULY 28

1851 Samuel Sachs is born in Baltimore, where his German immigrant father ran a private school. In 1882 he became a partner to his father-in-law, Marcus Goldman, who had established a banking business in New York. When other partners were added in 1885, the firm became Goldman, Sachs and Company. It initially dealt solely with short-term financing for firms and corporations through the medium of commercial paper, but when Goldman died in 1904 and Sachs took the helm, he turned the firm into a major underwriter of publicly offered securities. And he did it by exploiting a previously ignored niche: retailers, light industry, and other small entities that were not being serviced by the major bankers. The turning point was in 1906 when the United Cigar Manufacturers and Sears, Roebuck and Company needed substantial funding. Sachs and partner Henry Goldman realized they did not have, nor could they borrow, sufficient monies, so they partnered with Lehman Brothers to successfully underwrite both offerings. Between 1906 and 1924, the two firms managed 114 negotiated offerings for 56 issuers. Together, their prestige and contacts became solid on both sides of the Atlantic.

1907   Earl S. Tupper is born in Berlin, New Hampshire. As a DuPont chemist, Tupper was quick to see the potential of the newly developed plastic polyethylene in home products. He began producing his own line of cups and bowls called Tupperware, in 1942 in a small Massachusetts factory. Two developments, one technical and the other in marketing, made Tupperware a household word. The first was his invention of a snug-fitting lid that expelled air from a bowl when flexed. The second was the development of in-home sales parties, brought to fruition under the management of Brownie Wise, a poor Detroit single mother who began selling Tupperware door-to-door, but then found parties more effective. "A Tupperware party is held every two seconds around the world," said a company executive in 2003.

1959   "Less is more." —Mies Van Der Rohe, architect, on restraint in design, in the *New York Herald Tribune*

1988   "My views about economics are very simple. I think we know very little. We know some things, but our knowledge is limited. . . . It is very important having humility in managing economics." —Alan Walters, British economist and government adviser, in the *Daily Mail*

1997   Its economy in tatters after two decades of uncontrolled growth that had hyperinflated the value of its currency and imperiled its banks (see July 2), Thailand requests a special line of credit from the International Monetary Fund to prevent total collapse.

2003   Two of the world's largest banks, J. P. Morgan Chase and Citigroup, agree to pay fines of about $300 million to settle charges that they knowingly helped the disgraced and defunct Enron hide debt, inflate profits, and defraud investors. Under the settlement, the banks neither admitted nor denied the charges from the Securities and Exchange Commission and the office of Manhattan district attorney Eliot Spitzer. The action followed a similar agreement with Merrill Lynch & Co. by four months.

JULY 29

1908   The first price regulation on a national or state level since colonial times goes into effect today in Louisiana. The state's Act No. 128 "to prohibit unfair commercial discrimination between different sections, communities, cities, or localities in the State of Louisiana or unfair competition therein and providing penalties therefore" was approved on July 2 by Governor Jared Young Sanders.

1955   The Reynolds name is synonymous with two industries: tobacco and metals. Richard Samuel Reynolds, who dies at 73 on this day, was the founder of the Reynolds Metal Company. In his uncle R.J.'s tobacco company in 1902, he distinguished himself as an advertiser and by developing a moisture-saving tin container for the newly introduced Prince Albert Tobacco. Richard left tobacco to start his own soap powder factory, which first burned down and then was declared nonessential during World War I. Richard saved himself from bankruptcy by developing a waterproof ammunition container, which brought government contracts and focused his life's work on metal products. He formed the Reynolds Metal Company in 1928, which came to specialize in aluminum products, the most famous of which is Reynolds Wrap. Reynolds became convinced of aluminum's future during a 1937 trip to Europe in search of new sources of raw materials; he discovered the aluminum capacity of Germany to be 800 million pounds—more than double the combined capacity of England, France, and the United States. He correctly guessed that light metals were crucial to Hitler's industrial plans and immediately sought expansion of his own and his country's capacity.

2002   The market capitalization of Internet software maker Broad-Vision Inc. reaches $98 million. Just two years before, the company had been worth $23 billion, more valuable than Sears Roebuck & Co. and a host of other corporate giants. That meant that today the company was worth less than half of 1 percent of its former value. It got worse. Broad-Vision had $111 million in cash in bank accounts. Investors thought the whole company was worth less than the cash it held (a phenomenon called "trading below cash"). The assets, potential, management, and goodwill of the company added up to a negative. The company was worth more dead than alive.

JULY 30

1774   America's first business publication was the *South-Carolina Price-Current*, a one-sheet broadside, two columns, 6 × 12 inches, published by Crouch & Gray, commission merchants in "Charles-Town," South Carolina. The first known copy was issued today and listed 168 commodities and their prices.

1863   Henry Ford is born on a farm at Dearborn, Michigan. He remembered later, "There is a legend that my parents were very poor and that the early days were hard ones. Certainly they were not rich, but neither were they poor. As Michigan farmers went, we were prosperous. The house in which I was born is still standing."

1909   Famous for Parkinson's law (work expands so as to fill the time available for its completion) and various ancillary laws, including "expenditure rises to meet income," Cyril Northcote Parkinson is born at Barnard Castle, Durham, England. A writer and history teacher for most of his life, Parkinson first became enchanted with the paradoxes and downright follies in organizational life while serving as an army staff officer in World War II, where he observed bureaucrats making work for each other and expanding their staffs in order to enhance their own power and prestige.

1960   "Britain Friday withdrew the farthing from circulation as a coin of the realm because after 800 years it isn't worth a farthing anymore." —UPI dispatch

1975   Tough labor leader Jimmy Hoffa leaves his summer home at Big Square Lake outside Detroit at about 1:15 P.M., telling his wife, Josephine, that he has a meeting with a Detroit mobster, "Tony Jack" Giacalone, and a New Jersey Teamster official, Anthony Provenzano. Hoffa drove to the Machus Red Fox restaurant in Bloomfield Township and waited in the parking lot. At 2:30 he called Josephine—asking whether Giacalone had called to say he would be late. He apparently chatted with a real estate salesman at about the same time in the parking lot. And then Jimmy Hoffa disappeared. "Maybe he took a little trip," theorized Giacalone.

2003   The last Volkswagen Beetle rolls off an assembly line at the VW plant in Puebla, Mexico, 65 miles southwest of Mexico City. It was sent to a museum in Wolfsburg, Germany, where the first was produced in 1938. It was unit number 21,529,464, light blue, covered in flowers. The king of all cars (in terms of longevity of production, number produced, and countries inhabited) is known by some pretty humble nicknames around the world: *Cucaracha* (cockroach) in Nicaragua, *Huevito* (little egg) in Cuba, *Maggiolino* (beetle) in Italy, *Coccinelle* (ladybird) in France, *Bubbla* (bubble) in Sweden, *Tosbaga* (turtle) in Turkey, and in Detroit Henry Ford II called it "little shit box."

JULY 31

1914   Stock exchanges in London and New York close, as do exchanges in a dozen other American cities and the cotton and coffee exchanges in New York. Security markets in Madrid, Montreal, Toronto, and a host of other world capitals had closed in the previous two days. The specter of World War I brought deep fears that there would be massive selling of securities, which could collapse prices and drain the nation's gold reserve. By November the markets had started to reopen, and it became clear that the war was going to be good for many companies and their stock prices. Today is the third time the New York Stock Exchange had closed; it did not open until December 12, a record duration of staying shut.

1928   The MGM roaring lion logo is seen for the first time, introducing W. S. Van Dyke's *White Shadows in the South Seas* with Raquel Torres and Monte Blue. It was the studio's first talking picture.

1948   In Nuremberg, Alfried Krupp is found guilty of charges of wartime plunder and slavery. He was sentenced to 12 years' imprisonment and forfeiture of his property.

1957   "Find out where you can render a service, and then render it. The rest is up to the Lord." —Sebastian Spring Kresge, chain store tycoon, on his 90th birthday

AUGUST

AUGUST 1

1464   The greatest of the Medici bankers, Cosimo "the Elder," dies at 75 in his villa at Careggi, Italy, while listening to one of Plato's *Dialogues*. Cosimo took the successful bank established in Florence by his father, Giovanni di Bicci, and grew it into an empire, with nine major branches throughout Europe, ventures in insurance, money markets, speculation, farming, manufacturing, international trade, and control of state taxation. Cosimo came to manage papal finances, and in 1462 Pius II granted him the Tolfa alum mines monopoly; as alum was indispensable to Florence's famed textile industry, this license alone would have made him rich.

1464   Cosimo de Medici is succeeded by his son Piero "the Gouty," who soon makes the horrible decision to call in Cosimo's loans to influential citizens. It created a panic and a mutiny, which temporarily drove the Medici from power.

1841   The nation's first credit rating agency, Mercantile Service, is founded in New York City by Lewis Tappan, who reasoned in the aftermath of the panic of 1837 that wholesalers would pay good money for reliable credit information on the country storekeepers who wanted to buy their goods. By the autumn he had 133 subscribers. A branch opened in Boston in 1843. By 1848 the firm had hundreds of correspondents and had spawned a number of imitators and competitors; Tappan was earning enough ($15,000 per year) so that he could retire and devote himself to the antislavery and reform issues that were uppermost in his heart. In 1859 the firm was purchased by one of its executives, Graham Dun, who went on to establish the present-day credit assessment firm of Dun & Bradstreet in 1933.

1952   The first Holiday Inn is opened in Memphis, Tennessee, by Kemmons Wilson.

1988   "Administrators are cheap and easy to find and cheap to keep. Leaders—risk takers: they are in very short supply. And ones with vision are pure gold." —Raymond W. Smith, chairman of Rothschild Inc. and former chairman of Bell Atlantic Corporation

AUGUST 2

1824   Ground is broken for Fifth Avenue in New York City, destined to become a world-famous showplace of fashion and fine stores.

1881   The Federation of Organized Trades and Labor Unions is organized. It was renamed as the American Federation of Labor (AFL) at a convention in Columbus, Ohio, in December 1886, when it absorbed a number of trade and labor organizations, including the faded Knights of Labor.

1930   Wonder Bread is introduced by the Continental Baking Company. The world's first sliced bread, Wonder became its largest selling brand.

1937   The new regulatory body, the Securities and Exchange Commission shows its teeth for the first time, expelling the flamboyant trader Michael Meehan from several exchanges for manipulating the price of Bellanca Aircraft Corporation stock. It was a significant public relations triumph for the SEC, which had decided against the lesser punishment of one year's suspension for Meehan.

1985   Montgomery Ward announces the end of its mail-order business. The Ward's catalog—older than Sears's—was discontinued after 113 years in print.

AUGUST 3

1900   Firestone Tire & Rubber is founded in Akron, Ohio, by Harvey Samuel Firestone, who invests $10,000 of his own money to exploit his patent for a method of attaching tires to rims. The event coincided with the **1888** death of rubber manufacturer Benjamin Franklin Goodrich at age 46, who established Akron as the center of the rubber industry in the United States when he moved his operation there in 1870 after seeing an advertisement by the city's board of trade soliciting new industries (see November 4).

1907   In Chicago federal judge Kenesaw Mountain Landis finds Standard Oil of Indiana guilty on 1,462 counts of receiving secret rebates on shipments of crude oil over the Chicago and Alton Railroad. The fine was $29,240,000, the maximum penalty. John D. Rockefeller was in the middle of a golf foursome in Cleveland when a messenger delivered the verdict. Rockefeller played superbly, though seething with anger. During the outing he coolly and accurately predicted, "Judge Landis will be dead a long time before this fine is paid." The verdict was overturned on appeal, which made President Teddy Roosevelt seethe with anger.

1933   The Mickey Mouse watch first goes on sale, for $2.75. The watch was one of the earliest pieces of merchandise tied to a movie and is arguably the best known.

1977   Regarded as the first completely assembled, ready-to-use home computer, the TRS-80 is introduced by Radio Shack at the Warwick Hotel in New York City. *T* stands for Tandy (the parent company), *R* for Radio, *S* for Shack, and the 80 was the product number of the microprocessor provided by the Zilog company of California. The $599.95 system came with a 12-inch black-and-white monitor, cassette tape storage, four kilobytes of RAM, and a 1.77-mHz processor. It was a great success, although the factory could produce only one computer a day until late September.

AUGUST 4

1790   Considered in modern times as one of the safest investments available anywhere, U.S. government bonds are authorized for the first time by congressional act on this day, mainly to pay off the federal debt from the Revolutionary War (including states' debts that were assumed by the federal government). The total issue amounted to $64,456,963.90. Practically the entire issue was retired by 1836.

1816   Financier and railroad speculator Russell Sage is born in a covered wagon in Oneida County, New York, while his parents are en route from Connecticut to Michigan. Sage served two terms in Congress, leaving in 1857 with a determination to make a fortune through his insider political connections and experience. He teamed up with the infamous Jay Gould to conduct deceitful—but very profitable—raids on a handful of properties, including the Chicago & Milwaukee Railroad, the Pacific Mail Steamship Company, the Union Pacific Railroad, the Manhattan Elevated Railroad Company, and Western Union. Like Gould and Jim Fisk, Sage was the target of physical assault, surviving a bomb attack in 1891 that destroyed his office and his assistant. A testimony to Sage's acumen is the market in puts and calls stock options, which he organized in 1872 and which thrives on Wall Street to this day. He died July 22, 1906.

1917   It is a rare occurrence when the New York Stock Exchange closes on a day that trading is scheduled. In its 200-year history it has closed just three times for financial reasons, but it has been closed twice on August 4 for other reasons. Today it closed due to the summer heat, and on the same day in **1933** it closed again—this time at 12:30 in the afternoon for safety reasons after gas bombs exploded nearby.

1988   A key player in the postwar revitalization of Japanese industry, Doko Toshio, dies at 92 in Tokyo. After college Doko went to work as a turbine designer for the Ishikawajima Shipyard, eventually becoming the parent firm's president from 1950 to 1960, during which time he revamped its organization in order to benefit from heavy U.S. procurement during the Korean War. He oversaw the construction of the *Idemitsu maru*, the world's largest tanker. Doko then took the helm of a struggling Toshiba Corp., revitalizing worker and management morale and bringing the firm to prosperity. From 1974 to 1980 he was the chairman of one of Japan's four main business organizations, the powerful Keidanren, comprising about 110 groups from 800 corporations.

1991   "Our belief is that Microsoft has peaked. They have enough hubris now to believe they don't need IBM, that they don't need anybody. I think Microsoft will be a big, struggling company in two years." —George Colony, president, Forrister Research (a Massachusetts market research firm), in the *New York Times*

AUGUST 5

1886   Advertising executive Bruce Barton is born the son of a Congregational minister in Robbins, Tennessee. "In good times, people want to advertise; in bad times, they have to" was one of Barton's quips. In addition to cofounding Batten, Barton, Durstine & Osborn—the world's fourth largest advertising agency at the time of his death on July 5, 1967—Barton was a congressman who bitterly opposed the New Deal and an author whose controversial 1925 bestseller *The Man Nobody Knows* was one of the earliest business books to interpret a historic figure as if he were a business executive. This book portrays Christ as the world's greatest salesman, a top-notch manager who "picked up twelve men from the bottom ranks of business and forged them into an organization that conquered the world." Jesus's parables were "the most powerful advertisements of all time," and the "principles of modern salesmanship on which businessmen so pride themselves, are brilliantly exemplified in Jesus' talk and work."

1891   An American Express Travelers Cheque is countersigned and cashed for the first time.

1899   The Detroit Automobile Company, the first carmaker in the city's history, is incorporated. Detroit was destined to become synonymous with automobile manufacturing, but its first company was destined for failure. More than a dozen investors, including the city's mayor, William Maybury, lost about $90,000 when the company dissolved in just over a year. Twelve vehicles were produced, but serious conflict arose between the backers and the mechanical force behind the company, Henry Ford.

1955   The 1 millionth Volkswagen Beetle rolls off the production line at Wolfsburg, West Germany. At the time, Volkswagen accounted for about half of the country's auto production. A reporter in *Popular Mechanics* tried to explain its success: "The Volkswagen sells because it is, more than anything else, an honest car. It doesn't pretend to be anything it is not."

1984   "The shock of unemployment becomes a pathology in its own right." —Robert Farrar Capon, theologian and writer, in the *New York Times*

AUGUST 6

1859   The first known advertising slogan—"Worth a guinea in a box"—makes its debut on this day in the British newspaper *St. Helen's Intelligencer* in an advertisement for Beecham's Pills.

1890   In the late 1800s the "battle of the currents" raged between General Electric and Westinghouse over which would provide the nation's electrical power. But it was not just a struggle between two different providers; it was between two different types of electricity. Westinghouse had developed alternating current (AC), and General Electrical—a Thomas Edison company—had developed direct current (DC). Edison waged an ugly campaign in the press and in the laboratory to prove that AC was more dangerous. He sponsored experiments in which hundreds of animals were put to death. Edison further urged the New York legislature to adopt Westinghouse-powered electric chairs for executions. On this day, without Westinghouse's knowledge or consent, Westinghouse apparatus was used in the first electrocution of a human being (murderer William Kemmler, in Auburn, New York). Whatever advantage Edison's system might have gained through the demonstration was short-lived, however, as AC proved to be much more efficient and safe enough and was eventually adopted as the international standard. The knockout punch came in 1893 when Westinghouse secured the contract to provide the lighting system for the Columbia Exposition.

1926   A motion picture with sound is first shown to the public by Warner Brothers at a packed Manhattan Opera House. There was a series of short clips prepared by Sam Warner, followed by the full-length *Don Juan*, starring John Barrymore. The sound process, called Vitaphone, was developed by Bell/Western Electric engineers and leased to the Warners. Although it could not carry dialogue and was too expensive to be practical on a wide-scale basis, Vitaphone signaled a revolution in entertainment. Warner Brothers stock shot up from $8 to $65, and the brothers became rich overnight.

1980   Cuban refugee chemist Roberto C. Goizueta, 49, is elected CEO and chairman of the board of Coca-Cola. He was the 11th chief executive in the company's 94 years, and one of its best. He immediately gave Sergio Zyman, a Jewish Mexican marketing specialist, the go-ahead to bring Diet Coke to market. The product revitalized the sales, brand image, and morale of Coca-Cola.

AUGUST 7

1749   "Few people do business well who do nothing else." —Lord Chesterfield, statesman and orator

1783   Pioneering inventor of lace-making machinery (which made him a target of the Luddites) John Heathcoat is born in Duffield, England (see January 18).

1826   Robert Graham Dun—the "Dun" in the Dun & Bradstreet credit rating service—is born in Chillicothe, Ohio, to Scottish immigrant parents. In 1850 he joined The Mercantile Agency, the nation's first credit rating company. Dun became a partner and then the sole owner in 1859. He brought huge growth after the Civil War, keeping pace with the explosion in American commerce and the introduction of new business methods and tools. The first weekly issue of *Dun's Review* of business conditions appeared in 1893, and publication soon spread to Paris,

Germany, Australia, and South Africa. By the time Dun retired, there were 140 offices worldwide, with 10,000 reporters/investigators getting daily reports from 5,000 companies.

1944   The world's first program-controlled calculator is dedicated at Harvard University in Boston. The device was the Harvard Mark I and could perform an astounding three additions or subtractions per second. It could also perform trigonometry and logarithms. Not exactly pocket-sized, it weighed five tons and contained 500 miles of wire. The research was a collaboration of Harvard, the navy, and IBM. Thomas J. Watson, Sr., founder of IBM, regarded the device as interesting but impractical and unprofitable; his son, Thomas J. Watson, Jr., grew an empire from it.

AUGUST 8

1857   The California gold rush led to an overpopulation of small chartered banks that printed up an excess of their own notes. Prosperity begat inflation, which begat the illusion of even more prosperity. There was a boom in western land prices and imported goods, construction blossomed everywhere, and stocks (especially those of railroads and shipping companies) leapt in price. The purchase of all the goodies was largely done with borrowed money. On this day the inevitable correction/bust began, with a sudden fall in stock prices as banks began calling in loans. The panic of 1857—called the Western Blizzard because of its western origins—had begun. The bottom fell out later in the month (see August 24).

1882   Edward John Noble is born in Gouverneur, New York. In 1943 Noble purchased the Blue Network of radio stations from RCA; it was the first sale in media history of a major broadcast network. The following year the name was changed to the American Broadcasting Company (ABC). The deal was financed through earnings from Life Savers candies, a company that Noble had pulled from the jaws of bankruptcy in 1914 when he developed a foil packaging that ended the problem of candies adopting the glue flavor of their previous cardboard tubes. Noble is also credited with inventing the counter display in 1913 as a means to sell more Life Savers; he devised the stand-alone holder to position candies right near the cash register, an early innovation in impulse buying.

1919   Retailer Frank Winfield Woolworth dies at age 67 in Glen Cove, New York. Because he had not completed or signed his will, the document of record was a two-page handwritten will he had dashed off in 1889. It left his entire estate of approximately $67 million (about $1.5 billion in today's currency) to his wife, Jennie, who was mentally infirm and unaware of her surroundings.

1976   "Industrial relations are like sexual relations. It's better between consenting parties." —Vic Feather, British labor leader, in the *Guardian*

1981   The *Wall Street Journal* reports the early retirement of Pan American World Airways' chairman and CEO, General William T. Seawell, who had engineered the previous year's purchase of National Airlines. Once the world's preeminent international airlines, Pan Am was now saddled with enormous debt and virtually drained of cash. It never recovered from "Seawell's folly." Seawell handled one more deal between the National Airlines mistake and his departure, and that was selling off the crown jewel in the Pan American empire, the Pan Am Building in Manhattan. It had been the world's largest commercial office building when completed in 1963; now it was a temporary shield to ward off creditors.

2003   A study is completed by MarketPerform.com, a service that rates the raters and researchers of stocks. The results indicated that investors will do well if they listen to analysts' recommendations—and then do exactly the opposite. The year-long study found that investors who buy stocks with sell recommendations did better than investors who bought the buy stocks. At Morgan Stanley, the buy stocks yielded 13.5 percent gain, but the sell stocks did nearly three times better, with an average gain of 32 percent. Not a single analyst firm did better with its buy picks than its sell picks.

AUGUST 9

1831   The Mohawk and Hudson Railroad begins service when the locomotive *De Witt Clinton* pulls a train of cars between Albany and Schenectady in upstate New York. It was the first link in the line that became the historic New York Central, battleground of business titans in both the 19th and 20th centuries.

1934   Walt Disney, 32, presents his animation team with an outline of the first full-length animated film, *Snow White and the Seven Dwarfs*. Before its debut three and a half years later, the animators had drawn 250,000 separate pictures; the original budget of $250,000 had been busted to over $1 million (largely due to Disney's perfectionism); and the project had acquired the nickname of "Disney's folly." "It was prophesied that nobody would sit through a cartoon an hour and a half long," Disney remembered. Sometimes prophecies don't come true (see December 21).

1960   Standard Oil of New Jersey suddenly announces it is slicing the price of Middle Eastern crude oil by 14¢ a barrel, or about 7 percent. The other refining companies in the West were taken by surprise but also dropped their prices. The oil-producing countries in the Middle East were also taken by surprise and got hopping mad. They would lose significant revenue and had not been consulted on the use of their own resources. Monroe Rathbone, chairman of Standard Oil, dismissing the concerns and growing resentment in the Middle East, said, "Money is heady wine for some of these poor countries and some of these poor people." Within hours of Standard's announcement, Abdullah Tariki in Baghdad telegraphed Juan Pablo Perez Alfonzo in Caracas, and the two would meet in Beirut to plan the meeting that would create OPEC.

1995   Barely a year old and never having shown a profit, software/web browser company Netscape holds its initial public offering (IPO). Five million shares went on sale for $28, double the initial estimate. By the end of the day the stock hit $78 and closed at $58. The company turned its first quarterly profit in the next four months, updated its browser, and announced that 15 million people and more than 70 of the Fortune

100 top companies used its products. Share price reached $170. Market capitalization was now $5 billion, and the company was not yet two years old.

2000 "As entrepreneurs, we have to remember the importance of building bridges . . . to new opportunities. Those links should reach out to all sorts of folks: artists, engineers, teachers, business owners, writers, elders, singles, couples." —Gladys E. Edmunds, travel company entrepreneur, in *USA Today*

AUGUST 10

1821 The first investment banker to form an underwriting syndicate in the United States, Jay Cooke, is born the son of a lawyer/congressman in Sandusky, Ohio (see February 18).

1959 "A new idea is delicate. It can be killed by a sneer or a yawn; it can be stabbed to death by a quip and worried to death by a frown on the right man's brow." —Charles Brower, in a speech to the Association of National Advertisers

1987 The $31 billion merger between Sweden's ASEA and Switzerland's Brown Boveri is announced. The new company, ABB, was the world's largest manufacturer of electrical equipment, created through one of the largest cross-border mergers of the century. The negotiations were done quickly, secretly, and without lawyers; today's announcement was a total surprise to the industry. The merger was widely celebrated for two other qualities: how complementary the two partners were, and the masterful "matrix" organization devised by ASEA's Percy Barnevik to make a single, functional whole out of a group of 1,300 companies employing 210,000 people in 150 countries. The entire organization was run by an executive committee in Zurich, with operations divided by business areas, company and profit centers, and country organizations; "decentralization under central conditions," said chief executive Goran Lindahl.

1998 "Remember when railway companies were the reigning industrial forces? Then, airlines companies came along. . . . How many rail-

way companies became airline companies? None! How many industrial companies will become information companies? Not too many!"
—William Mougayar, consultant and management theorist, in *Emarketer*

AUGUST 11

1919   Andrew Carnegie dies in his sleep in his Berkshire Hills mansion in Lenox, Massachusetts. He was practically broke, having given away almost his entire fortune, $350 million, to charity. His attitude and deeds set the tone for 20th-century philanthropy. "The man who dies rich dies disgraced," he wrote in 1889.

1950   Stephen Wozniak is born in Sunnyvale, California. Twenty-six years later he and Steve Jobs started Apple Computers in Jobs's garage.

1963   "Bigness taxes the ability to manage intelligently. . . . The growth of bigness has resulted in ruthless sacrifices of human values. The disappearance of free enterprise has submerged the individual in the impersonal corporation. When a nation of shopkeepers is transformed into a nation of clerks, enormous spiritual sacrifices are made."
—William O. Douglas, associate justice, the Supreme Court, in a speech to business executives

1968   The Beatles launch their new record company, Apple. Apple Records and Apple Computers (see above) began a legal contest in the 1990s and into the next century over which company owned which rights to the name.

2003   Thailand holds its first-ever auction of lucky license plates. One thousand bidders flocked to the televised event in a five-star Bangkok hotel. The plates cost more than the cars! The highest bid was $95,200 for the number 9999 (the number nine is auspicious to Thais because of its association with King Rama IX); the winning bidder was Communications Minister Suriya Jungrungraungkit, who said he was sure his purchase would be worth it because of the luck it would bring and because he could resell the plate at a profit. "This is better than investing in the stock market," he said.

AUGUST 12

1851   The Singer sewing machine is patented. Isaac M. Singer has gone into partnership with his lawyer, Edward Clark, who defended Singer against patent infringement lawsuits brought by Elias Howe. They lost and were forced to pay royalties to Howe. They were still able to manufacture the machines, however, and they dominated the market worldwide. Singer's marketing talents made himself and rival Howe rich.

1908   "Stronger than a horse and easier to maintain," the Model T Ford is introduced and will soon outsell every other car on the market. It retailed for $850.50, had a wooden body on a steel frame, and only came in black.

1956   "Creation is a drug I can't do without," said Cecil B. De Mille, motion picture director/producer, in the *New York Times*. This was his 75th birthday.

1981   IBM enters the personal computer market with a lavish public introduction of its IBM-PC at the Waldorf-Astoria Hotel in New York City. It was an immediate commercial success, selling 200,000 units in the first year and surpassing Radio Shack's TRS-80 as the industry leader. However, because both its hardware and software were available from outside manufacturers, a group of companies soon began making and marketing IBM clones, essentially the same machine but at a much lower price. The clones hurt IBM tremendously, but they made software company Microsoft rich.

AUGUST 13

1866   The founder of Fiat (Fabbrica Italiana Automobili Torino), Giovanni Agnelli, is born in Villa Perosa, Piedmont, now Italy (see July 1).

1888   Television pioneer John Logie Baird is born in Helensburgh, Scotland. After trying his hand at a variety of business ventures—selling marmalade, French soap, and Australian honey—Baird devoted himself to his dream of creating television. He produced televised objects in outline in 1924, televised the human face the following year, and transmitted images of moving objects in 1926 at the Royal Institution, London. In 1928 he demonstrated color television. When the British Broadcasting Corporation began service in 1936, Baird's system was in competition with one promoted by Marconi Electrical and Musical Instruments; Baird's was essentially a mechanical system, while the Marconi system was electronic and the one selected for further development by the BBC. Baird died June 14, 1946.

1911   "An idea can turn to dust or magic, depending on the talent that rubs against it" was an observation of advertising executive William Bernbach, born on this day in New York City. In 1949 after working in several ad agencies, he joined with Ned Doyle and Maxwell Dane to form the agency of Doyle Dane Bernbach. Starting with just $500,000 in billing, the agency grew to become one of America's largest and most respected agencies. It revolutionized advertising by developing soft-sell policies with believable messages, abandoning hard-sell approaches. Creative meetings had a similar tone; instead of brainstorming with artists and writers, Bernbach preferred quiet roundtable discussions to solicit ideas from his associates. He died October 2, 1982.

1914   The nation's first bus company, Greyhound, has its origins on this day when Swedish-American drill operator Carl Eric Wickman, founds the Mesabi Transportation Company in Hibbing, Minnesota. He used a Hupmobile to transport iron miners on a regular schedule between Hibbing and nearby Alice; he charged 15¢ one-way and 25¢ for a round trip, while local taxis charged $1.50 each way. Wickman soon took a partner, and began creating his own bodies and mounting them on truck chassis. By 1918 he had 18 buses operating in northern Minnesota, with annual earnings of $40,000.

1955   The United Steel Workers union signs a contract with American Can and Continental Can, winning the first 52-week guaranteed annual wage in any major U.S. industry.

1963   "Criticism is never inhibited by ignorance." —Sir Harold Macmillan, British statesman, in the *Wall Street Journal*

AUGUST 14

1834 The infamous system of workhouses is established in Britain with today's passage of the Poor Law Amendment Act. Gone was the centuries-old policy, extending back to Elizabethan times, of the state supplementing especially low wages. The ill and aged still received state aid, but anyone else desiring state help had to live and work in the workhouses, which were designed purposely as "uninviting places of wholesome restraint" where husbands were separated from their wives and children from their parents. Among the tasks that residents were expected to perform were stone crushing and bone grinding.

1834 Called the "Pepys of Wall Street" for his witty diary and published reflections on the financial wranglers who surrounded him, Henry Clews is born the son of a potter in Staffordshire, England. During the Civil War, Clews's brokerage firm became the country's second largest seller of government bonds (second only to Jay Cooke & Company), establishing a reputation for solid performance along limited, conservative lines. Clews witnessed and recorded many of his colleagues being driven crazy by wild speculations and scams at a time when the nation was getting rich and the stock market was a new playground with few rules. He survived the panics and depressions of 1857, 1873, 1893, and 1907, just missing the big one of 1929 by a few years. He died January 31, 1923.

1856 The *Times* of London announces the Bessemer steel-making process to the world. Henry Bessemer had just presented it to a meeting in Cheltenham of the British Association for the Advancement of Science. Steel was now cheap enough to be a practical building and industrial material.

1951 Publisher William Randolph Hearst dies at 88 (see April 29).

1960 "Experience is a hard teacher because she gives the test first, the lesson afterwards." —Vernon Law, professional baseball player, in *This Week*

2001 Jeff Skilling resigns abruptly as Enron's CEO, a post he held for just six months. Enron's stock was worth half of what it was at the start of Skilling's reign. It was about to fall to nothing.

AUGUST 15

1666   "But, Lord, to see what success do, whether with or without reason, and making a man seem wise." —Samuel Pepys

1795   The French franc is created by the revolutionary Convention, the ruling authority in France from the fall of the monarchy, through the "Reign of Terror," to the advent of Napoleon.

1877   Thomas Edison suggests the use of *hello* as the standard telephone greeting, in preference to *ahoy* as suggested by Alexander Graham Bell, the telephone's inventor.

1962   Modern world trade is largely conducted through the use of containerships. America's first containership dock opens for business on this day in Newark Bay, Elizabeth, New Jersey, when Sea-Land Service's S.S. *Elizabethport* docks there in a facility built just south of Port Newark. Employing 730 people and operated by the New York Port Authority, the facility in its first year handled 1,504,021 tons of cargo from 242 vessels, earning a total of $4,015,000.

AUGUST 16

1819   The Peterloo Massacre: a huge crowd has assembled at St. Peter's Field in Manchester, England, to hear activist farmer Henry Hunt deliver a speech on reform of government and repeal of the Corn Laws (tariffs that kept bread prices high to the benefit of large landowners). The assemblage was peaceful, many attending with their families and picnic lunches, but a mounted force of local businessmen in the Manchester Yeomanry assaulted the crowd with sabers. Nine men and two women were killed; 600 were injured. A series of repressive political measures soon passed in Parliament.

1954   Time Inc. begins publication of *Sports Illustrated*, which will lose $26 million before it becomes profitable in 1964.

1976   "Profits are the lifeblood of the economic system, the magic elixir upon which progress and all good things depend ultimately. But one man's lifeblood is another man's cancer." —Paul Samuelson, winner of the 1970 Nobel Prize in Economics, in a speech to the Forum of European and American Economists

1993   AT&T shocks the communications industry by announcing that it will pay $12.6 billion to purchase McCaw Cellular Communications, the nation's largest cell phone network. The move marked AT&T's entry into wireless communication and meant that AT&T would now compete directly for customers with the Baby Bells. It also signaled that the major wave of future telecommunications would be through the air rather than through wires.

2004   Costco Wholesale Corp., known for bulk chicken and selling soda by the case, begins test marketing caskets in two Chicago outlets. Samples were displayed right next to the mattresses. "A casket at Costco, yeah, I think it's pretty bizarre," said a customer, who wondered about buying one from a kiosk with limited samples of fabrics. "When you go casket shopping, you want to see the whole thing." The profit potential was clearly there, especially in light of the funeral industry's reputation for high markup and bundled expenses. "[I]t just needs to be done," said Gina Bianche, a buyer in Costco's corporate office in Issaquah, Washington. An official with the Casket and Funeral Supply Association speculated that overall funeral expenses would have to rise to make up for lost profit if funeral parlors lost market share to outside retailers in casket sales.

AUGUST 17

1809   Industrialist/entrepreneur Matthew Boulton dies at 80 in Birmingham, England, where he had established the Soho Manufactory, one of the largest and most modern production facilities in the world. It specialized in metal objects. Boulton developed the forerunner of modern assembly lines, he offered medical insurance, and he hired artisans as well as the best production people. But his greatest contribution to the Industrial Revolution was his partnership with the inventor James Watt. He financed Watt's work on the steam engine, and he pushed Watt to invent the rotative engine, which could drive other machines.

1851   "All men's employments, all trades and professions, in some of their aspects are attractive." —Henry David Thoreau

1915   Automobiles become even more suitable for the mass market when Charles F. Kettering patents the electric self-starter. Kettering and Edward A. Deeds had formed Delco (Dayton Engineering Laboratories Company) in 1909 as an independent research facility and produced a number of automobile advances. The Cadillac was the first vehicle with an electric starter. Delco was purchased by the United Motors Company in 1916 and was later absorbed by General Motors, whereas the Sloan-Kettering partnership flourished.

1937   Margaret Rudkin approaches a neighborhood grocer near her Connecticut farm—Pepperidge Farm—and asks him if he would care to stock her bread, priced at 25¢ a loaf. Every other bread on the market cost 10¢; the grocer informed her of this and asked her if she was daft. The perspicacious Rudkin buttered some slices and gave them to the grocer and his clerks. "They all reached for more," Rudkin remembered, "and said, 'Well, that's bread!'" By the time she had returned to her farm, the grocer had already telephoned to say that all her loaves had sold out. Rudkin had just launched Pepperidge Farm baked goods. Within a year of baking her first loaf, she had to move the operation off the farm to a bigger facility in town with room for 50 employees. Rudkin pioneered several now-commonplace marketing concepts: the niche for premium products, the demand for all-natural ingredients, and brands perceived as comfort foods.

AUGUST 18

1871   Henry Meiggs receives a contract of £1.6 million to build the first major railroad in Costa Rica. Several days later Meiggs paid £100,000 to Presidente Tomas Guardia. When the political opposition raised a storm, Guardia explained, "The contractor of the railway, Señor Henry Meiggs, without any prior agreement, and purely out of generosity, in accordance with customs in such negotiations, had placed at my disposal . . . the sum of 100,000 pounds. So that I should do with it in the way I thought best." Guardia further stated that he had used all the money in the service of his country. The project thus began as corruption. Fittingly, Meiggs employed his nephew, Minor Cooper Keith, who during the construction began the banana plantings that founded the infamous United Fruit Company.

1896   Having managed the *Chattanooga Times* to prosperity, Adolph S. Ochs acquires control of the *New York Times* for $75,000, most of it borrowed: "It will be my earnest aim that the *New York Times* gives the news, all the news, in concise and attractive form, in language that is permissible in good society, and give it early, if not earlier, than it can be learned through any other medium." Ochs immediately discarded the romantic fiction and the tiny typefaces, beefed up other areas like financial news, started a weekly book review section, and inserted a Sunday magazine.

1937   Toyota Motor Company Ltd. is founded as a division of Toyoda Automatic Loom Works. Sakichi Toyoda received £100,000 from a Lancashire firm in 1929 for the rights to manufacture his advanced loom in England; Toyoda used the money to develop a motorcar prototype and installed his son Kiichiro to run the operation. Kiichiro sent an engineer to the Packard factory in Detroit as a tourist, and he returned with enough information to set up an assembly line.

1947   The Hewlett-Packard electronics company is incorporated.

1956   "Next to the dog, the wastebasket is man's best friend." —San Francisco executive, commenting on the vast amount of reading required of businessmen, in *BusinessWeek*

1982   Once a dominant force in the sale and development of computers, Wang Laboratories files for Chapter 11 bankruptcy, its stock having sunk to 75¢. The company was founded in 1951 by the Chinese-born computer whiz An Wang and grew by the 1970s into a multinational colossus. However, Wang's headstrong tendencies (he was once described as a "humble egomaniac") and the company's failure to keep pace with the growth of personal computers caused its downfall . . . a downfall that was not permanent. In 1993 the company was reborn as Wang Global and once again has achieved success, this time as a systems integrator and information technology provider.

AUGUST 19

1836   "Books have had their day—the theatres have had their day—the temple of religion has had its day."—James Gordon Bennett, publisher, the *New York Herald*

1851   Soft drink entrepreneur Charles Elmer Hires is born on a farm near Roadstover, New Jersey. In 1886 he began selling a ready-to-drink beverage made from 16 different wild roots, herbs, bark, and berries in bottles. Hires selected the name *root beer* when a friend suggested to him that hard-drinking miners would be more attracted to root beer than to herb tea.

1870   Financier, stock speculator, and adviser to presidents during and after the two world wars, Bernard Mannes Baruch is born in Camden, South Carolina, the son of an immigrant doctor. Baruch showed an attraction for gambling as a youth (his father had to drag him from gambling houses on various occasions) and tried to make his first fortune in the Colorado gold mines. Baruch returned to New York and entered the securities trade, being made a partner in the brokerage firm of A.A. Hausman & Co. in 1896. The following year he earned $40,000 on a $200 speculation in the sugar market, and he bought a seat on the New York Stock Exchange with the earnings. He was a millionaire by age 30. "A man can't retire his experience. He must use it. Experience achieves more with less energy and time," he said in 1955 on his 85th birthday.

1883   Gabrielle "Coco" Chanel, the fashion designer/entrepreneur who ruled over Parisian haute couture for six decades, is born near Issoire, France. "Innovation! One cannot be forever innovating. I want to create classics," she once announced. Her legacy to the fashion industry includes the little black dress, men's clothing for women, and the chic of suntans.

1906   Philo Farnsworth, one of the inventors of television, is born.

AUGUST 20

1875 The Prudential Insurance Company of America is first advertised with that famous picture of the Rock of Gibraltar. "The Prudential Has the Strength of Gibraltar" was the slogan; the ad was devised by J. Walter Thompson and appeared in *Leslie's Weekly*. It was the company's debut ad in its first year in business.

1907 One of the great phrases of corporate chastisement, "malefactors of great wealth," is coined in a speech by President Teddy Roosevelt. Just two months later Roosevelt was forced to seek the help of some of those very malefactors he attacked today—J. P. Morgan and a coterie of New York bankers—to deal with the panic of 1907.

1920 Detroit radio station WWJ begins operation. It was the country's first radio station to be owned by a newspaper, the *News*, and thus was the first example of horizontal integration in the media industry.

1972 "To be successful, keep looking tanned, live in an elegant building (even if you're in the cellar), be seen in smart restaurants (even if you nurse one drink) and if you borrow, borrow big." —Aristotle Onassis, shipping magnate

AUGUST 21

1621 Twelve women ("1 Widow and 11 Maides") are sent from London to Virginia to be sold to wife-seeking bachelors for 120 pounds of tobacco each, or approximately one pound of tobacco for one pound of woman.

1914 On this day the Audit Bureau of Circulations is formed in Chicago as a cooperative, nonprofit branch of the Association of American Advertisers. It conducted the first independent audit of newspaper circulations in order to verify circulation figures.

1961 "I suggest the only thing to do is to insist that every cover of *Life* shall say 'important.'" —Henry Luce, publisher and cofounder, Time Inc., in a memo to his staff

1988   Ross Johnson, CEO of RJR Nabisco, throws a gala party at the Castle Pines Golf Club outside Denver to introduce the smokeless cigarette, Premier. Johnson opened packs of Premier after dinner. "Smells like burning lettuce," was one of the earliest comments. Johnson admitted they would take some getting used to, adding, "We're saying in the ads to try them for a week." This brought a tart response from someone else: "I don't know if I could get through a pack." Johnson finally saw that the product was in bigger trouble than he thought but proceeded with the launch a few weeks later. After years of work and a bill of $300 million before a single cigarette was sold, Premier qualified as one of the most expensive consumer product developments in history. Bad tasting, bad smelling (customer reactions to the odor included "like burning tennis sneakers" and "as if you'd just opened a grave on a warm day"), hard to light, hard to draw on, devoid of the sensory satisfactions of conventional cigarettes, Premier was pulled within weeks of its market introduction with the howls of late-night comics still ringing.

AUGUST 22

1450   Johannes Gutenberg, about 50 years of age and needy of cash, enters into a contract with wealthy goldsmith Johann Fust, whereby Gutenberg borrowed 800 guilders (later raised to 1,600 guilders) to further develop his printing press. The press was put up as collateral. Fust pressed for immediate results, for printing jobs to run, for a quick return on his money; Gutenberg resisted and pressed to perfect his machine. A perfectionistic creator clashed with a bottom-line backer. Fust sued for repayment of his money in 1455; when Gutenberg could not pay, Fust took the press. Fust formed a partnership with Peter Schoffer, a former employee of Gutenberg's, and used the press to found history's first commercially successful printing company. Gutenberg borrowed more money in 1456 and began on a new press.

1901   The Cadillac Company is founded in Detroit by Henry Leland, a precision machinist who named his firm after the 18th-century explorer Antoine de la Mothe Cadillac, founder of the city. In 1902 the company got its first salable model when the Henry Ford Company fired

Henry Ford. Leland had been brought into that company as an adviser by its backers; arguments between Leland and Ford led to Ford's dismissal, but the car Ford had designed stayed behind. Its engine was replaced by a one-cylinder engine made by Leland, which was the first Cadillac. The firm was reorganized as the Cadillac Automobile Company in 1902 and immediately began a tradition of production excellence. By 1909 Cadillac was the flagship brand of the fledgling General Motors family.

1997   "Running a company on market research is like driving while looking in the rear view mirror." —Anita Roddick, British entrepreneur/founder of The Body Shop, in the *Independent*

AUGUST 23

1630   The first minimum wage, in fact the first labor law of any kind, in colonial America is passed in the Massachusetts Bay Colony by Governor John Winthrop and his court of assistants who decree that construction workers be paid at the rate of one shilling a day.

1794   "I praise loudly, I blame softly." —Catherine the Great, Russian empress, in a letter

1852   The term *Industrial Revolution* was coined by historian and social reformer Arnold Toynbee, who is born on this day in England.

1853   The first bank clearinghouse in the United States is organized by 16 presidents, 1 vice president, and 21 cashiers representing 38 banks. It was named the New York Clearing House, and today's organizational meeting was held at Merchants Bank in Manhattan. The exchange opened in October at 14 Wall Street; its first day's clearings were $22,648,109.87.

1937   During a trip west to see the woman he loved, David Packard, 25, gets together with close college friend William Redington Hewlett, 24, in Palo Alto, California. It was the first "official" business meeting of what would become the Hewlett-Packard electronics company. The product ideas they discussed were high-frequency receivers and medical equipment, and there was mention that "we should make every attempt to keep up on [the newly announced technology of] television." The proposed name for their company was the Engineering Service Company. In the following autumn the two started working together in a Palo Alto garage. Among their first creations was an audio oscillator that was tried as a muscle stimulator and harmonica tuner, a variable-frequency motor controller for the Lick Observatory on nearby Mount Hamilton, and a signaling device to indicate a foul-line roll for a local bowling alley. The audio oscillator, designed by Bill Hewlett, was their first product.

AUGUST 24

1690   Job Charnock establishes a trading post for the British East India Company on the Hooghly River in West Bengal. Charnock's choice of the site was careful and based on geography (the site was protected on one side by the river and on another by a series of salt lakes) and commerce (it was close to three villages in which Indian merchants were settled). One of these villages was Kalikata, which would be the source of the name of Charnock's trading post—Calcutta. Its advantageous proximity to land, sea, and river helped it grow as a commercial center, and Calcutta became one of the world's largest cities.

1849   Having been expelled from Prussia, Belgium, and most of France, Karl Marx, 31, crosses the Channel to England where he spends the rest of his life.

1857   The Western Blizzard, the panic of 1857, sweeps across the country. Through a process begun, ironically, by the bonanza of the California gold rush (see August 8), the nation's credit system was rotted at its base. On this day the house of cards collapsed; the Ohio Life Insurance and Trust Company in Cincinnati failed, leaving $5 million of liabilities unpaid. Life insurance companies in New York are then forced to make cash demands on their banks, a number of which were forced to suspend specie payments for months. Stocks sold for practically nothing, 20,000 workers in New York City alone lost their jobs, and by autumn 5,000 companies were dead.

1967   The Yippies crash Wall Street: Abbie Hoffman, Jerry Rubin, Stew Albert, and others from the famous protest group show up at the New York Stock Exchange in beards, long hair, and costume. They were blocked from entering the visitors' gallery and told that the balcony was closed for repairs. "Hey, the only reason you won't let us in is because we are Jewish," said Rubin, who was dressed as a cowboy. "Just look at his hair. He's a Nazi for sure." Reporters snapped pictures and took notes as the anti-Semitic accusations continued, and finally the guard stepped aside. Once on the balcony the Yippies started throwing money down on the floor. Trading halted, as the brokers scrambled for the money. When the paper notes ran out, the boys started throwing coins, at which point the brokers started booing. Guards ushered the intruders into the street, where "we burned money, danced, and gave millions of press interviews," according to Albert. A few weeks later the NYSE enclosed the visitors' gallery in bulletproof glass.

1975   Cosmetics king and founder of Revlon, Charles Revson, dies at 68 in New York City (see October 11). "Creative people are like a wet towel. You wring them out and pick up another one," he once said.

1995   Microsoft's Windows 95 goes on sale. It was the most publicized software release in history: 500 reporters attended the official launch at the Microsoft headquarters near Seattle; Jay Leno was the master of ceremonies; the Rolling Stones performed commercials (the group had never allowed itself to do commercials before); and special advertisements ran all over the world. Approximately seven million units were sold within six weeks. For chairman Bill Gates the event was an apotheosis of sorts, firmly establishing his and his company's place on top of the computer revolution. "Gates reminds me of the nineteenth-century industrial barons who by force of will and business genius built monopolies," commented business analyst Stewart Alsop.

AUGUST 25

1819   A founder of the Industrial Revolution, James Watt, dies at 85 in his home at Heathfield, near the manufacturing city of Birmingham, England (see January 19).

1822   Gardiner Green Hubbard is born in Boston, where he became a lawyer and public utilities entrepreneur. One of his daughters, Mabel, was deaf due to scarlet fever, and his activities to improve education for the handicapped brought him in contact with a teacher of the deaf, Alexander Graham Bell. Hubbard became interested in Bell's experiments, which would eventually produce the telephone. In 1875 Hubbard and Thomas Sanders (another wealthy man with a deaf child whom Bell helped) declared a simple oral pact with Bell whereby Hubbard and Sanders would meet half of the costs of developing the phone and all three would share in the profits equally. From then until the telephone was well established commercially, Hubbard was the business manager (see July 9). Bell married Mabel Hubbard in 1877.

1987   The Dow Jones Industrial Average hits a record high of 2,722.42—and then proceeds to make a 1,000-point slide over the next few months, including the worst day in its history (see October 19).

1999   "We're fast approaching the point at which there is really no distinction between the .com companies and traditional businesses. The only distinction will be between the winners and losers, and of course, the pace of change at which companies become winners or losers." —Michael Dell, chairman and CEO, Dell Computer Corporation

2003   Why do businesses fail? *Business Week* today publishes the survey results of 1,900 professionals who help troubled companies. The six main reasons and their relative importance were as follows: too much debt (28 percent); inadequate leadership (17 percent); poor planning (14 percent); failure to change (11 percent); inexperienced management (9 percent); and not enough revenue (8 percent).

AUGUST 26

1801   Robert Morris, 67, is released from debtor's prison. Known as "the financier of the American Revolution" for almost single-handedly managing and raising the funds to keep Washington's troops going for years, Morris spent more than three years behind bars after wild plunges into land speculation with borrowed funds failed to bring the anticipated revenue.

1858   The first news dispatch handled by commercial cable is received from Europe in the offices of the New York *Sun*, which publishes it the following day. It announced the Treaty of Tientsin which ended the Anglo-Chinese War of 1856–58. The transatlantic cable was completed on August 5 and carried communication between government dignitaries on August 16, although today it was used as a tool of commerce.

1919   Coca-Cola's initial public offering of stock is held. Five hundred thousand shares of common, nonvoting stock are offered at $40 per share. By 3:45 P.M. the offering was overscribed by 140,000 shares. By 1991 one share of stock had split into 1,152 shares; if the dividends of that one $40 share were reinvested, it would be worth $2 million.

1993   Home Depot, the nation's largest home-improvement retailer, announces in Atlanta that it will stop selling wood from environmentally endangered areas. The ban included all wood products, from brooms to front doors. "[This] is a great victory for the forests," said a spokesperson from the Rainforest Action Network. Arthur M. Blank, president and CEO of Home Depot, explained, "This is not in response to . . . any extreme group. It's in response to our opportunities, and moreover our responsibilities."

AUGUST 27

1859   "Oh, Townsend, oil coming out of the ground, pumping oil out of the earth as you pump water? Nonsense! You're crazy." So New Haven banker James Townsend was told when he sought investors for an untested method of getting an untested resource out of the ground. Townsend collected very little money for the venture; in fact, he had already sent a "stop work and pack up" letter to his agent in the field, "Colonel" E. L. Drake, when the drill hit oil. It was America's first oil strike. It started quietly. On this Saturday afternoon the drill dropped into a crevice 69 feet below ground and then slid another six inches.

The driller, William Smith, told the crew to knock off for the rest of the weekend, and they did (see August 28).

1877   Charles Stewart Rolls—the business and marketing half of the Rolls-Royce partnership—is born in Monmouth, Wales. In 1902 he formed a company to promote continental cars in Britain before they were popular; this brought him in contact with motor car designer Frederick Henry Royce. Rolls was a lifelong aviation enthusiast; he was the first to fly across the English Channel and back nonstop (June 1910) and was the first British pilot fatality (July 12, 1910).

1882   Samuel Goldfish is born in Warsaw, Poland. Orphaned as a child, he emigrated to London and then to New York, where he began work in a glove factory. By age 18 he was one of the top glove salesmen in the world and a partner in the company. With the name of Samuel Goldwyn, he formed a filmmaking firm with brother-in-law Jesse Lasky, thus beginning his great 30 years as one of Hollywood's most prominent producers; he helped found Metro-Goldwyn-Mayer in 1924. He is also famous for "Goldwynisms" such as "A verbal agreement isn't worth the paper it's printed on."

1923   Several things occur the day after French Premier Raymond Poincare announces that German reparations payments must continue and that the industrial Ruhr region will remain occupied until more payments are made: the value of the Deutsche mark toboggans to an exchange rate of 7 million marks to the dollar; the Reichsbank publishes its most disastrous financial statement ever, with its president, Rudolf Havenstein, saying that wild inflation must continue as there seems no way to check it; and the Bourse (stock market) sees a record-breaking "catastrophe boom," with stocks gaining some 30 million points.

1957   The Ford Motor Company introduces the Edsel to compete with General Motors' Oldsmobile. Despite favorable market research and a low price, the car sold poorly and was pulled from the market after three years. It cost $250 million to develop the Edsel line, and only 110,847 were made. Named for Henry Ford's son, the name is now synonymous with colossal business failure.

1988 "Good economics is good politics." —Paul Keating, former Australian prime minister, in the *Sydney Morning Herald*

AUGUST 28

1859 Having struck a crevice and abandoned work the previous day (see August 27), driller William Smith returns to his experimental oil well in Titusville, Pennsylvania. He peered into the pipe and saw a dark fluid floating on top of water. He drew up a sample with a tin rain spout; it was oil. Drilling for oil was a totally new technique, and Smith was using equipment that was meant for drilling for salt. This was the first oil strike in America's history and immediately set off a mad rush to acquire sites in the area. Oil quickly became plentiful, prices plummeted as supply outstripped demand, and the problem became what to do with the oil. Whiskey barrels were bought out quickly for storage, and the price of barrels became nearly twice that of the oil inside them.

1907 United Parcel Service begins in Seattle, when 19-year-old Jim Casey borrows $100 from friend Claude Ryan and begins a local delivery service called American Messenger Company. He had six messengers, two bicycles, and a telephone. He soon began delivering parcels for merchants in a modified Model T and a year later added seven motorcycles to his fleet. From the start, the delivery people dressed formally, with suits, ties, and caps. By 1918 the company had been renamed Merchants Parcel Company and was handling the deliveries for all of Seattle's major department stores. Today UPS is the world's largest package handler, with nearly two billion deliveries daily in 185 countries and territories.

1922 The first advertisement in broadcast history takes place. The Queensboro Realty Company of Jackson Heights, New York, paid radio station WEAF (later WNBC) $100 for 10 minutes of airtime to publicize a group of apartments called Hawthorne Court.

1937 The Toyota Motor Car Company Ltd. incorporates.

1955 To commemorate the first radio "commercial" (see above), NBC vice president William S. Hedges announces that during the period from 1922 to 1955, sponsors had paid $20 trillion to advertise products over radio and television. "What have you done with my child?" asked one of the inventors of radio technology, Lee De Forest, after the commercial era began. "You have sent him out on the street in rags of ragtime to collect money from all and sundry. You have made of him a laughingstock of intelligence, surely a stench in the nostrils of the gods of the ionosphere."

1962   "The Bell System is like a damn big dragon. You kick it in the tail, and two years later, it feels it in its head." —Frederick Kappel, chairman, AT&T, in *Look*

AUGUST 29

1619   Jean-Baptiste Colbert, the finance minister behind Louis XIV's domination of Europe, is born today into a merchant family in Reims, France. Various administrative posts brought Colbert into contact with the powerful Cardinal Mazarin, who on his deathbed recommended Colbert to Louis XIV. Colbert restructured his nation's economy, starting with the medieval and chaotic tax system, which he simplified and made fairer, thereby opening a new flow of income into royal coffers. He also vastly improved the productive capacity of France (granting privileges to private industries, establishing state manufactories, encouraging immigration of skilled labor, establishing and enforcing product standards), and he built up a merchant fleet to carry the high-quality goods. Colbert once asked a group of businessmen what he could do for them. One of them, Legendre, is supposed to have replied, "*Laissez nous faire*" ("leave us alone"). It is the earliest known reference to laissez-faire as a doctrine in economics in which government stays out of business.

1833   Against the opposition of Tories and many Whigs who subscribe to Adam Smith's laissez-faire principles of 1776, the British Parliament passes a factory act which forbids the employment of children under the age of 9, limits factory work of children aged 9–13 to 48 hours per week and 9 hours per day, specifies 2 hours of schooling per day to children under age 13, and limits working hours of children 13–18 to 69 hours per week and 12 hours per day. The law also established a system of paid inspectors, but it applied only to the textile industry and, abused, soon overcame its safeguards.

1898   The Goodyear Tire and Rubber Company incorporates in Akron, Ohio, based on products made of vulcanized rubber. Founder Frank Augustus Seiberling's drive, business experience, and good fortune of going into the tire business just as automobiles were becoming popular made the company very successful. By 1905 Goodyear was the nation's largest producer of carriage tires, and a decade later it was the world's largest maker of auto tires. A postwar depression swamped the company, and Seiberling was forced out of the firm in a 1920 reorganization.

1956   "The consumer is not a moron. She is your wife." —David Ogilvy, advertising executive, giving advice to advertising copywriters, in the *New York Herald Tribune*

1979   Communications magnate Samuel Irving Newhouse dies at 84 in New York City, having amassed holdings worth hundreds of millions of dollars as the owner of 31 newspapers and five broadcast stations in 22 U.S. cities.

AUGUST 30

1830   The Baltimore & Ohio Railroad, the first railroad in the United States to be chartered as a common carrier of freight and passengers, abandons the horse-powered locomotive for steam power.

1907   John W. Mauchly, cocreator of ENIAC, the first electronic computer, is born.

1930   The "Oracle of Omaha," billionaire investor king Warren Buffett, is born the son of a stockbroker in Omaha, Nebraska, just a few blocks from where he eventually established and managed the investment conglomerate Berkshire Hathaway. From 1965 to 2001 Berkshire's per-share book value grew an average 24 percent annually. It is the most profitable investment vehicle in history.

1933   Air France is founded through the merger of France's Aeropostale and another firm.

1954   Jay Catherwood Hormel dies at age 61, having led the Hormel meatpacking company since assuming its presidency in 1929. Hormel had a variety of accomplishments while an executive at Hormel: creating the first canned ham (1926), initiating the company's executive training program, launching a series of imaginative advertising campaigns to distinguish the Hormel brand, and introducing Spam (1937), which became the world's largest selling brand of canned meat.

1969   BBN, the company selected by the U.S. Defense Department to supply computers for ARPANET, the forerunner of the Internet, ships its first machine to UCLA. Several more machines were shipped during the next few months; they were linked up, and the Internet began.

AUGUST 31

1619   "About the last of August came in a Dutch man of warre that sold us twenty negars." Thus does John Rolfe, founder of commercial tobacco production in Virginia (and husband of Pocahontas), record the first known importation of African slaves into the American colonies.

1837   "I do not see how any man can afford . . . to spare any action in which he can partake. Drudgery, calamity, exasperation, want, are instructors in eloquence and wisdom." —Ralph Waldo Emerson, in a speech to the Phi Beta Kappa Society at Harvard

1995   Just days after the release of Windows 95, Microsoft announces the discovery of a virus that ruins the floppy diskette version of the program.

SEPTEMBER

SEPTEMBER 1

1654 "Necessity hath no law." —Oliver Cromwell, Lord Protector of the Commonwealth of England

1689 Russia imposes a graduated tax on beards.

1795 Publisher James Gordon Bennett is born in Newmill, Scotland, where he trained for the priesthood. After emigrating to North America he worked as a teacher and bookseller before entering newspaper work, first as a writer and then as an owner/publisher. He founded the *New York Herald Tribune* (see May 6). Part salesman, part showman, Bennett considered his function "not to instruct, but to startle."

1862 America's first federal tax on tobacco for internal revenue goes into effect.

1907 Labor leader Walter Reuther is born in Wheeling, West Virginia. His grandfather was a pious man who fled Prussian militarism and oppression. His father, Val, also hated social injustice. Reuther dropped out of high school and went to work for Wheeling Steel as an apprentice tool and dye maker; he was fired from this job for leading a protest movement. In 1927 he went to Detroit, a labor powder keg created by automobile companies and executives growing fat and rich off the labor of underpaid workers in harsh conditions. The town was ripe for a brave, articulate, visionary leader with a passion for organizing and justice.

SEPTEMBER 2

1792 "Boldness, again boldness, and always boldness!" —Georges Jacques Danton, lawyer and leader of the French Revolution, in a speech to the Legislative Committee of General Defense

1936   President and CEO of Intel, Andrew S. Grove, is born as Andras Grof in Budapest, which was brutalized by Nazis and then Communists during his youth. It was Grove's driving managerial style that got Intel to the top of the computer hardware industry; when Grove retired in 1998, Intel chips were in 85 percent of the world's personal computers. He has said, "There are two options: adapt or die."

1991   *BusinessWeek* reports a survey of human resource professionals conducted by a nonprofit organization. Nearly half of these personnel officers thought *a priori* that women had less initiative and took fewer risks than men. And if they did take more initiative and more risk, they risked being rejected for such "nonwomanly" traits.

1998   LTCM—the secretive, multibillion-dollar hedge fund—is in deep trouble, which means that a host of financial institutions around the world are imperiled. John Meriwether contacted all existing investors asking for more money to help weather the storm. Not a single check or pledge was offered. Further, both the Federal Reserve Bank of New York and the fund's clearing broker, Bear Stearns, had begun investigations into the extent of LTCM's heretofore-unreported borrowing (see September 18).

SEPTEMBER 3

1728   The entrepreneur behind James Watt's great steam engine inventions, Matthew Boulton, is born in Birmingham, England (see August 17).

1860   Retail innovator Edward Filene is born in Salem, Massachusetts, to a German immigrant retailer. Filene grew the family store in Boston into the world's largest specialty store. His most famous and successful promotion for customers was the automatic bargain basement, in which prices declined automatically if the merchandise failed to sell within a set period of time. Filene was also a great innovator in the treatment of his employees. He instituted a career advisory board for young personnel; he sought out and trained management talent; he established the nation's first minimum wage for women and girls; and his Employees Credit Union was a prototype for credit unions nationwide. His most controversial plan, implemented in 1911, was to ultimately transfer management of the store to his employees through the Filene Cooperative Management Association, which was organized in 1898. The plan so outraged conservative partners that they sued Filene, ultimately stripping him of power.

1868   The "mother of postscientific management," Mary Parker Follett, is born in Quincy, Massachusetts. Follett was a social activist and community developer, but her most lasting legacy was as a management theorist, pioneering now-common ideas like constructive conflict resolution, participative management, group problem solving, and flatter organizational structures. She developed the argument that authority and leadership are functions of an individual's knowledge, experience, and ability, rather than his rank in the corporate hierarchy. Her democratic urgings greatly influenced a number of progressive executives such as manufacturer Henry Dennison and retailer Edward Filene (see above). Warren Bennis called Follett "a swashbuckling advance scout of management thinking."

1912   The new Filene's with a seven-foot doorman opens in Boston. The building was designed by Daniel Burnham and sat on the corner of Washington and Summer streets.

1929   The Dow Jones Industrial Average closes at 381.17. It was the peak before the crash and the Great Depression. It was decades before 381 was hit again.

1957   "The best investment on earth is *earth*." —Louis Glickman, New York real estate owner, in the *New York Post*

SEPTEMBER 4

1609   Two centers of international commerce, New York and Los Angeles, have beginnings on this day. In **1609**, explorer Henry Hudson, in the employ of the Dutch firm United East India Company, first encounters the wilderness island of Manhattan. In **1781** Spanish settlers found the community that they called "El Pueblo de Nuestra Senora La Reina de Los Angeles de Porcicincula."

1783   The "Ice King," Frederic Tudor, is born in Boston, the son of a prosperous lawyer. Unlike his father and three brothers, Tudor declined to "waste his time" attending Harvard, but he had decided from the age of 13 to be in business. At 21 he and brother William whimsically conceived of exporting the ice around them to the Caribbean; Tudor began a lifelong obsession with the venture once he heard that timbers shipped from New England to the tropics still had ice on the plank-ends after weeks at sea. Dubbed a madman and ridiculed, Tudor invested $10,000 to get 130 tons of ice moved from Massachusetts to Martinique, securing a monopoly on the scheme in Martinique through a well-placed bribe. His first venture lost a net $4,000 when the entire shipment melted after six weeks. Gradually, in between imprisonments for debt, Tudor developed better means of shipping and harvesting, built icehouses in various locations, and established a prosperous business. In 1833 he successfully shipped ice halfway around the world to the British East India Company in Calcutta. In 1856 he shipped 146,000 tons of ice out of Boston in 363 cargoes to 53 different places, including the Philippines, Australia, and China. India had become Tudor's best customer; it was an especially low-cost venture because ships had routinely sailed there with empty cargo holds.

1877   The Quaker Man trademark is registered for Quaker Oats. The original Quaker Man looked like a serious, well-fed colonial lawyer; he was holding a parchment with *Pure* written on it. In 1946 the trademark was changed to just the familiar head and upper body; this is the appearance known to the world today. In 1915 the Religious Society of Friends (the real Quakers) tried to stop the commercialization of their name but failed on the federal level and in all the state courts they tried except Indiana.

1882   The office of J. P. Morgan at 23 Wall Street becomes the first establishment in New York City to have electric lighting, when inventor Thomas Edison throws a switch in the office at 3 P.M., bringing in power from the Edison Illuminating Company station at Pearl Street.

The company soon supplied power throughout Manhattan and became Consolidated Edison Co., the prototype of all U.S. central-station power networks.

1885   The Exchange Buffet opens on this Friday at 7 New Street, across the street from the New York Stock Exchange. It was the world's first self-service restaurant.

2003   In New York, U.S. District Judge Robert Sweet dismisses a class action lawsuit that blamed McDonald's for making people fat. Judge Sweet concluded that McDonald's did not claim its food to be nutritious or part of a healthy diet. Sweet concluded that it was not the role of the courts to protect consumers "from their own excesses."

SEPTEMBER 5

1897   Arthur Charles Nielsen, founder of the radio and television rating service that bears his name, is born in Chicago. Nielsen was a brilliant engineering student. In 1923, borrowing heavily from fraternity brothers, Nielsen began his first product evaluation company, involving industrial equipment. The company was essentially a 10-year failure, but his efforts began to pay off when he hit on a scheme to use drugstores' own records to provide valuable information on buying patterns. His great triumph was adapting the "audimeter" (a device that could detect when and to what frequencies radios were tuned) to the public's use of radios and televisions. It took 17 years and investments of $15 million to bring this service to the break-even point. He died June 1, 1980.

1926   Ford Motor Company plants introduce the eight-hour day, five-day workweek plan.

1929   Roger Babson, an investment guru of the times, delivers a luncheon speech: "I repeat what I said at this time last year and the year before, that sooner or later a crash is coming." At 2:00 that afternoon, just as Babson's words were coming over the Dow Jones news ticker, the stock market went into a nosedive. In the day's last hour of trading 2 million shares changed hands; AT&T went down six points, Westinghouse dropped seven, and U.S. Steel fell nine. It was the first significant set-back in the bull market of the Roaring Twenties, and it was named for Babson (the "Babson Break"), who had been predicting such an event for 18 months. For the first time, a crash seemed a real possibility.

1935   At 4:00 in the afternoon, J. P. Morgan and Company is officially split in two: Morgan Stanley and Company will be an investment bank; J. P. Morgan and Company will carry on the firm's traditional role as a commercial bank. The action came in compliance with the 1933 Glass-Steagall Act.

SEPTEMBER 6

1683   "The art of taxation consists in so plucking the goose as to obtain the largest amount of feathers with the least possible amount of hissing." This insight was attributed to Louis XIV's finance minister, Jean-Baptiste Colbert, who died today in Paris (see August 29).

1873   Founder of both the Hudson Motor Car Company and United Airlines, Howard Earle Coffin is born on a farm near Milton, Ohio. He partnered with Roy D. Chapin to found the successful Hudson company in 1910. During World War I he held several administrative and technical posts, which introduced him to aviation. In 1925 he founded National Air Transport Company, Limited, which later became United when it joined with Boeing Transport in 1930. Coffin died of an accidental gunshot wound November 21, 1937.

1919   The debut strike by actors in the United States ends, following a favorable agreement with Broadway producers. Begun a month earlier, the strike closed 13 New York theaters and had spread to other cities. Affiliated with the American Federation of Labor, the union was the Associated Actors and Artists of America.

1974   The Mattel toy company requests that trading of its stock be suspended on the New York and Pacific stock exchanges, claiming it has discovered enormous misstatements in its financial reports for fiscal 1971 and 1972. The books had been cooked to inflate the stock price. As a result of the scandal, several officers, including the creator of Barbie, Ruth Handler, were dismissed from the company and then indicted. Handler pleaded no contest, and in December 1978 was fined $57,000 and sentenced to 41 years in prison. Both penalties were suspended.

1989   The Banca Nazionale del Lavoro, Italy's leading bank, admits that it has been defrauded of an enormous sum, later estimated to be about $5 billion. It was the biggest bank fraud in history. Its branch in Atlanta had made unauthorized loan commitments to Iraq. The bank's chairman, Nerio Nesi, and its director general, Giacomo Pedde, resigned.

SEPTEMBER 7

1867   Great financiers spawn. J. P. Morgan, Jr., is born today in Irvington, New York. J. Paul Getty, Jr., is born on a freighter bound for Genoa in **1932**.

1914   One of the great mottos about dedication to the job—"Neither snow nor rain nor heat nor gloom of night stays these couriers from the swift completion of their appointed rounds"—is unveiled on this day when the New York Post Office Building is opened in New York City on Eighth Avenue. The inscription was supplied by architect William M. Kendall just for the building façade. It is erroneously believed to be the motto of the entire U.S. Postal Service, but it actually extends back to about 450 B.C. and was written by the historian Herodotus. The U.S. Postal Service has no official motto.

1929   *Business Week* magazine is first published. The stock market crashed 45 days later. Contrary to popular opinion, the opening issue of *Business Week* expressed the view that the economy was not really in great shape. The new McGraw-Hill publication lost $1.5 million by 1936, but then turned a corner and became the leader in business periodicals. It later became the leading magazine of any kind in terms of advertising pages.

1949   George Elton Mayo, made famous by the "Hawthorne experiments," dies at age 68 in Polesden Lacey, England. In 1924 the National

Research Council began a study of the relationships between factory conditions and productivity at the Hawthorne Works of Western Electric Company in Chicago. During the study, MIT engineers were unable to find a significant relationship between good illumination and worker efficiency; the study would have been terminated had it not been for an even more surprising observation—that productivity had increased in both the control group and the experimental group without good illumination. Similar results occurred with other environmental factors: humidity, temperature, lighting, and noise. Mayo was called in at this point to try to explain the paradox. He and coworkers discovered that human interaction and social relationships on the job were more important than environment in determining worker output and motivation. The field of labor relations was changed forever; industrial sociology was born.

1998   Google.com, the Internet search engine that is now a multi-billion-dollar corporation, is launched from a garage in Menlo Park, California.

SEPTEMBER 8

1772   Fur trader Manuel Lisa is born in New Orleans. Around 1790 he moved to St. Louis and became established in the fur trade that was flourishing there. He formed the Missouri Fur Company with several other important traders; William Clark (of Lewis and Clark fame) was their agent in St. Louis. Until his death on August 12, 1820, Lisa made repeated and lengthy journeys throughout the Missouri River valley, covering some 26,000 miles. The trade was profitable, earning up to $35,000 in a season. Lisa's successors, like William H. Ashley, used the trails that Lisa blazed to systematically commercialize the trapping.

1858   Abraham Lincoln, in a speech at Clinton, Illinois, utters a sentence that instantly becomes a maxim in politics, business, and every other realm of activity involving trust: "You can fool all of the people some of the time; some of the people all of the time; but not all of the people all of the time."

1935   Robert Augustus Chesebrough, discoverer of Vaseline and cofounder of Chesebrough-Ponds Inc., dies at age 98. He attributed his longevity to Vaseline; he ate a spoonful of it every day (see January 9).

1974   The Franklin National Bank of New York is declared insolvent, the largest bank failure in U.S. history. Many larger banks received no return or compensation on their loans. Italian financier Michel Sindona, a director in the bank's parent company, was convicted in March 1980 of embezzling $45 million, which catalyzed the collapse.

1992   "With publicity comes humiliation." —Tama Janowitz, author, in the *International Herald Tribune*

SEPTEMBER 9

1890   Harland Sanders is born near Henryville, Indiana, the son of a farmer who died six years later. His mother supported the family by peeling tomatoes during the day and sewing at night, while the children learned to forage for food. This changed when Sanders was 12; his mother's new husband forced the children out of the home. Quitting school in the seventh grade, Sanders began a 25-year odyssey through a variety of jobs, finally opening a gas station in Corbier, Kentucky, in 1929. He began selling meals out of the back of the station, and this proved so popular that he opened Sanders' Cafe. With its offering of family-style dinners and Sanders's original preparation of "finger lickin' good chicken" (he developed a secret blend of 11 spices and used a pressure cooker to seal in flavor and moisture), his restaurant was a great hit, receiving an endorsement in Duncan Hines's *Adventures in Good Eating*. It was at this time that the state of Kentucky awarded him the honorary title of "Colonel." Sanders sold the café and took his magic chicken recipe on the road. By 1964, there were more than 600 Kentucky Fried Chicken franchisees in Canada and the United States. In that year, Sanders sold out most of his interests in the empire to Jack Massey and John Brown; he received $2 million, a lifetime salary of $40,000, and a seat on the board of directors. In 1971 the corporation was purchased by Heublein Corp. and boasted 3,500 franchises in 48 countries and $700 million a year in business.

1924   "Although the geological information we possess at present does not indicate that there is much hope of finding oil in Bahrain or Kuwait, we are, I take it, all agreed that even if the chance be 100 to 1 we should pursue it rather than let others come into the Persian Gulf, and cause difficulties of one kind and another for us." —Sir Charles Greenway, chairman, Eastern and General Syndicate

1926   The National Broadcasting Company (NBC) is created by the Radio Corporation of America (RCA). David Sarnoff's fledgling network soon boasted 31 affiliates and became a leader in television. The growth in radio stations was so rapid that NBC split into two networks, the Red and the Blue, the following year.

1956   "A wide screen just makes a bad film twice as bad." —Samuel Goldwyn, in *Quote*

SEPTEMBER 10

1907   The two-story fashion emporium, Nieman-Marcus, opens in Dallas at the corner of Elm and Murphy Streets. Its first stock sells out in four weeks. Advertising executive A. L. Nieman, his wife Carrie, and his brother-in-law Herbert Marcus started the venture with $30,000; they invested $12,000 in carpeting and fixtures, and leased the premises for $750 per month. Carrie Nieman's original stock was $17,000 worth of furs, coats, dresses, tailored suits, and millinery for the women of Dallas, a town of 86,000 with 222 saloons.

1956   "In the tiny space of twenty years, we have bred a whole generation of working Americans who take it for granted that they will never be out of a job or go a single year without a salary increase." — K. K. DuVall, president, Chicago Merchandise National Bank, in *Time*

1960   Angry representatives from the world's top oil-producing countries meet in Baghdad, Iraq, to discuss options after being told by Western oil companies how much they would be paid for their oil. Perez Alfonso represented Venezuela; Faud Rouhani represented Iran; Sheikh Abdulla Tariki headed the Saudi delegation; Kerim Kassem was the meeting host and chief delegate for Iraq; Kuwait was represented by

Faisal Mezidi. By the time the conference adjourned five days later, the five nations had formed OPEC.

1979   The first Japanese motor vehicle plant in America begins production in Marysville, Ohio. Ten Honda dirt bikes were built today in the 260,000-square-foot plant. The management style was neither American nor Japanese, but a hybrid that began in group discussions (Should there be morning exercises? Should the "associates" wear uniforms? What would management titles be?) after a small nucleus of Americans were hired but before the plant opened. Production was soon increased from 10 units per day to 24,000 per year, other models were added, and the first Honda car plant in the United States began production in 1982.

1998   "Back in 1989 Dell made a massive mistake relating to inventory, and now we're regarded as the best in our industry in inventory. The answer is not having a brilliant conception of all the best ideas before you start a business, but rather learning from your mistakes and not repeating them—and making sure that those lessons are passed along as the organization continues to grow." —Michael Dell, chairman and CEO, Dell Computers, in a speech to the Society of American Business Editors and Writers Technology Conference

SEPTEMBER 11

1785   "Ministers and merchants love nobody." —Thomas Jefferson, in a letter to John Landon

1789   Alexander Hamilton is appointed the first U.S. secretary of the treasury, and Tench Coxe is appointed the first commissioner of (internal) revenue.

1970   The Ford Pinto is introduced. Priced under $2,000, the compact was intended to compete with low-cost, small foreign imports. But the car was rushed to market; among its design flaws was the tragic placement of the gas tank, which made it prone to rupture and explode when the car was involved in rear-end collisions of over 20 mph. It was later discovered that Ford *knew* about this problem *before* the car was released.

The irresponsibility caused an uproar, and in 1978 a California jury awarded a record $128 million to a plaintiff in a Pinto case.

1995   On the 75th anniversary of its Betty Crocker line of products, General Mills announces that it is time for Betty to get a facelift with the help of her customers and computer technology. The plan called for the public to send in their own photos (any race, ages 18 to 118), from which 75 would be selected, and those 75 would be melded digitally into a single, new Betty Crocker. Originally, "Betty Crocker" was the fictitious name that the company used on responses to customer enquiries; she was later portrayed on packages as a matronly, kindly gray-haired woman. Then she became a major brand label.

2001   The two landmark office buildings of New York's World Trade Center are destroyed by airplanes hijacked by Al Qaeda terrorists. Two other planes crash elsewhere—one into the Pentagon and one into a field in Pennsylvania. Nearly 3,000 die. The shock waves throughout the world continue to reverberate.

SEPTEMBER 12

1812   Richard March Hoe, inventor and manufacturer of the first successful rotary printing press, is born in New York City, son of the eminent printing press manufacturer Robert Hoe. Like his father, Richard possessed inventive genius. After entering the family firm, he continued to make improvements on his father's products, with the big breakthrough coming when he abandoned the old flatbed printing surface, for which he substituted a revolving cylinder. This "lightning press," patented in 1847, revolutionized printing, and in a way revolutionized education, commerce, and democracy because of the speed with which it could produce printed sheets. At first it turned out 8,000 sheets per hour, and with further modification it was used with the *New York Tribune* and produced 18,000 sheets an hour. With the Hoe machine, publishers could satisfy the increasing demand for newspapers and other printed materials.

1873   The Remington Company begins manufacturing the first commercially successful typewriter.

1877 The Chase National Bank is chartered under the National Bank Act. Its founder, former schoolteacher John Thompson, named the bank for Salmon P. Chase, who was secretary of the treasury under Abraham Lincoln and who was responsible for the passage of the National Bank Act. After a series of mergers and continued prosperity, the bank acquired the Equitable Trust Company (a Rockefeller holding) in June 1930 and thus became the largest bank in the world. In 1955 a merger with the Bank of Manhattan —cofounded by Aaron Burr in 1799—created the Chase Manhattan Bank.

1958 Jack St. Clair Kilby, a young engineer from the University of Illinois who has recently been hired by Texas Instruments, shows his colleagues a weird construction of two metal plates, wires, components, and what looks like a healthy dose of tar, all on a single surface. It was the world's first integrated circuit, an organization of transistors, resistors, and other components to perform specific functions. Integrated circuits (also called "microchips") are now a major part of every computer, analogous to neurons in the human brain. Six months after Kirby's revelation, Robert Noyce at Fairchild Semiconductor produced a device that had the same function but superior construction. Noyce won the ensuing patent race, but the two friendly rivals considered themselves coinventors.

1995 In a stunning retreat from a disastrous U.S. investment, the Mitsubishi Corporation announces that it is abandoning ownership of Rockefeller Center and is handing the keys back to the mortgage holder. The Art Deco skyscraper complex, a "symbol of American capitalist power and economic might," had been languishing in bankruptcy court for four months because Mitsubishi had been unable to pay the $1.3 billion mortgage. Mitsubishi had lost $100 million a year for the previous six years on the property.

SEPTEMBER 13

1776 "Wonders will never cease." —Sir Henry Bate Dudley, in a letter to David Garrick (an English actor)

1857   Milton Snaveley Hershey is born in his grandfather's farmhouse on the site that is now Hershey, Pennsylvania. His father was an itinerant speculator; Hershey attended seven schools in eight years, never getting beyond the fourth grade. He took his first job at age 14 as a printer's devil in Lancaster, Pennsylvania. He was fired within a year and began work in a nearby confectionary. He completed a four-year apprenticeship and went into business for himself in Philadelphia, making candies at night and selling them during the day. The business failed after several years, and Hershey went to work for a confectioner in Denver, where his father had relocated. The two ran a candy store until the elder Hershey endorsed a friend's bad note. Milton then went to New York and began a candy manufacturing company. When that collapsed in 1886, he returned to the region of his birth and started all over again.

1963   Mary Kay Ash, 45, begins selling her own line of cosmetics, Beauty by Mary Kay, out of a cramped, 500-square-foot storefront in Dallas, Texas. Her husband and business partner, George Hallenbeck, had died a month before, and Mary Kay threw herself into her work: "Richard, Ben, [her sons] and I put in sixteen and eighteen-hour workdays as we struggled to do anything that had to be done." She wrote a five-page consultants' guide (her business model was direct sales, in which "consultants" sold her products through Tupperware-style home parties; the consultants purchased the products from her beforehand, thus minimizing her debt), she produced a newsletter, and she encouraged her sales force vigorously to spread the word about the company. She opened with nine consultants.

1964   Mary Kay Ash throws a party to celebrate her first year in business. Sales totaled $198,000. The firm's 200 employees gathered in a warehouselike new facility at 1220 Majesty Drive in Dallas. Mary Kay prepared chicken and Jell-O salad and awarded the top salespeople with wigs. Mary Kay Cosmetics continued to grow and prosper, reaching annual sales in the next 30 years of $950 million. In 1976 the company became the first with a female chairperson to be listed on the New York Stock Exchange. By then her top salespeople were awarded trademark pink Cadillacs. By the time of her death, on November 22, 2001, Mary Kay was known all over the world.

1989   Britain's biggest-ever, computer-generated bank error gives customers an extra £2 billion in 30 minutes. Reportedly, 99.3 percent of the money was returned.

1999   "International finance is always looking for new opportunities. The challenge for Africa is not just to be attractive to traders and investors, but to offer opportunities which are more attractive than anywhere else in the world." —Peter Hain, British politician, in a speech at the Challenges for Governance in Africa Conference, London

SEPTEMBER 14

1864   The first inexpensive Bessemer steel is commercially produced in America from a two-and-a-half-ton converter at the Kelly Pneumatic Process Company in Wyandotte, Michigan.

1867   Karl Marx publishes *Das Kapital* in Germany. He wrote, "When commercial capital occupies a position of unquestioned ascendancy, it everywhere constitutes a system of plunder."

1901   A steady sell-off hits Wall Street following the announcement of the death of President William McKinley eight days after being wounded by an assassin's bullet. Investors were unsettled because they were losing a business-friendly president and were getting Teddy Roosevelt in his place; Roosevelt was a progressive, activist leader who fought the abuses of big business his whole life. Among his projects to protect the worker and the consumer were the Pure Food and Drug Act, the Hepburn Act, the Elkins Act, a campaign against Standard Oil and other monopolistic trusts, the Anthracite Coal Commission, and the cabinet-level Department of Commerce and Labor.

1990   "There are those who want an economic and monetary union so beautiful, so perfect, that it will never get started, it will never even be born." —Jacques Delors, president, European Commission, in the *Guardian*

SEPTEMBER 15

1830   The principal inventor of the railroad locomotive, George Stephenson, opens the 36-mile Liverpool-Manchester line. It was the first rail line designed to carry primarily passengers (other lines carrying coal had been in operation for years). The event has been called "the birth of the railroad age." The first recorded accident involving a moving railroad locomotive occurred at the opening. Distinguished politician William Huskisson was crossing the tracks after greeting Prime Minister Wellington, when he stumbled and was fatally run over by Stephenson's *Rocket*.

1876   Newspaper chain publisher Frank Ernest Gannett is born the son of a farmer in Bristol, New York. After graduation from Cornell University and several editorial positions, Gannett purchased his first paper, the *Elmira Gazette*, in 1906 and shortly thereafter merged it with three other regional papers in upstate New York to form the Gannett Company. It established a pattern on which an empire was founded: the purchase of daily newspapers in one-newspaper towns and cities. He had hit upon a very profitable formula, because such markets offered great opportunity for lucrative advertising and expandable circulations. Gannett owned more than 30 such periodicals by his death on December 3, 1957, in what has been called a chain of "small monopolies." He took over more newspapers than any other publisher without the help of an inheritance. He personally edited only one of his papers. As a policy he decentralized management, giving the regional editors full control of their own papers. The one thing he insisted on was that intoxicants could not be advertised. The Gannett Company continued to expand into print and broadcast ventures after its founder's death; one of the latest of its papers was *USA Today*, which began publication on this day in **1982**.

1921   The federal government issues its first regular broadcast license to radio station WBZ in Springfield, Massachusetts.

2003   A milestone in the coffee industry and in retailing in general occurs when Procter & Gamble begins selling a line of "fair trade" coffees. The selling of the Mountain Moonlight brand was done directly through mail-order and online. "We brought very serious concerns to P&G, and after considerable dialogue, the company was willing to take action," said Sister Ruth Rosenbaum, director of the Center for Reflection, Education and Action, an activist organization that owns P&G stock and that lobbied at P&G shareholder meetings for several years. The intention of the fair trade movement was to eliminate the middleman, thereby returning more profit to producers. The issue of coffee had recently come to fore because coffee prices had reached their lowest levels in 50 years, hitting the poor growers of Africa, South America, and Central America hard.

SEPTEMBER 16

1893   Alexander Korda is born in Hungary. Korda directed movies in Vienna, Berlin, and Hollywood before moving to England, where he founded London Film Productions and Denham Studios. Among his productions are *The Scarlet Pimpernel, The Third Man, Richard III,* and 1933's *The Private Life of Henry VIII* with Charles Laughton. He was knighted for saving the British film industry and died in 1956.

1906   Douglas McGregor—famous for his "Theory X, Theory Y" analysis of worker motivation—is born in Detroit, Michigan (see October 13).

1908   General Motors Company is incorporated in New Jersey with a token capitalization of $2,000. William Crapo Durant, head of Buick, had intended to form a dominating automobile trust based on the model of U.S. Steel, but both Henry Ford and Ransom Olds wanted $3 million in cash for their companies, so Durant went it alone at first. He soon purchased Oldsmobile, Pontiac, and Cadillac, and then integrated vertically by acquiring a number of the companies that supplied parts. Durant was a better organizer than manager, and despite brisk sales, GM was in financial trouble in two years. Durant was forced out by the banks that bailed out the company, after which he cofounded the Chevrolet Motor Car Company. That venture was very successful, allowing Durant to acquire enough GM stock to oust the bankers and retake the company, adding Chevrolet to its line.

1920   Just before noon on this sunny Thursday, a horse-drawn cart filled with explosives and 500 pounds of iron sash weights stops in front of the J. P. Morgan Bank at the corner of Wall and Broad Streets. The driver disappeared among the passersby, and minutes later the cart exploded. Thirty-eight were killed, 130 were injured; $2 million in property damage resulted. J. P. Morgan's grandson, Junius, received a gash; a young trader named Joseph P. Kennedy, who was walking on the street, was hurled to the ground. The perpetrators were never identified. A row of pockmarks scarred the Tennessee marble on the facade of the Morgan building and can still be seen today.

1960   "Advertising is found in societies which have passed the point of satisfying the basic animal needs." —Marion Harper, Jr., president, McCann-Erickson advertising agency, in the *New York Herald Tribune*

1985   The Department of Commerce announces that the United States is now a debtor nation for the first time since World War I. After years of budget deficits and balance of payment deficits, the nation has come to rely heavily on foreign purchase of Treasury bonds and notes, rather than on domestic taxation.

SEPTEMBER 17

1917   "As in law so in war, the longest purse finally wins." —Mahatma Gandhi, in a lecture to the Bombay Provisional Conference

1928   The first international oil cartel is created in secret on this day in a remote hunting lodge in the Scottish highlands called Achnacarry House. The 17-page document, called the Achnacarry Agreement, was completed after two weeks of talks between the chief executives of the world's three largest oil companies: Walter Teagle of Jersey Standard (American), Sir John Cadman of Anglo-Persian (British), and Henri Deterding of Shell (Dutch). A key provision was the "as is agreement," in which the Big Three agreed to slice up and maintain world markets in proportion to what each controlled in 1928; beyond that, the objectives were to control prices, prevent price wars, and ensure excellent profits. At most, the Big Three held only 45 percent of the world market, and so they were never able to achieve the degree of domination they wanted. After several years the men went their separate ways.

1949   Created by Chuck Jones, the first Roadrunner cartoon is broadcast, introducing the world to Wile E. Coyote (the Roadrunner's hapless pursuer) and to the mail-order company Acme Corp., producer of some of the most worthless and dangerous products ever invented for the screen. Poor Coyote was forever ordering something from Acme, and coming to certain (temporary) death when the product backfired. Among his memorable Acme purchases were Instant Road, Female Roadrunner Costume, and Do-It-Yourself Tornado Kit.

1985   After revolutionizing personal computer technology and its market, then falling out with his own company, Steve Jobs submits his letter of resignation to Apple Computer's vice chairman, A. C. "Mike" Markkula. "The company appears to be adopting a hostile posture toward me. . . . Accordingly, I must insist upon the immediate acceptance of my resignation. I would hope that in any public statement it feels it must issue, the company will make it clear that the decision to resign as Chairman was mine . . . As you know, the company's recent reorganization left me with no work to do and no access even to regular management reports. I am but 30 and want still to contribute and achieve. . . . "

1986   Having been caught in a number of insider trading crimes, Ivan Boesky signs a plea agreement with the Securities and Exchange Commission and immediately becomes an undercover government agent to help snare his former confederates, especially the genius Michael Milken.

SEPTEMBER 18

1837   Charles Lewis Tiffany and partner John B. Young open the Stationery and Fancy Goods Store near city hall in New York City. Twenty-five-year-old Tiffany has borrowed $1,000 from his father in Connecticut to stock the store with pottery, Chinese bric-a-brac, umbrellas, and stationery. Total receipts for the first three days were $4.98; profits for the first week were 33¢. By 1848 the store had moved to 271 Broadway, and Tiffany had started making his own jewelry. A Paris branch was opened in 1850 and a London branch in 1868. The name Tiffany & Co. was adopted in 1853.

1851   The *New York Daily Times* debuts. It was the brainchild of journalist Henry J. Raymond and financiers George Jones and Edward B. Wesley, who declared, "We intend to issue it every morning (Sundays excepted) for an indefinite number of years." The paper was four pages long and sold for 1¢. The change to the current name of the *New York Times* was made in 1857.

1869   Friedrich Engels, 48, retires as a partner in a prosperous textile factory in Manchester, England, and moves to London to plot the overthrow of capitalism with Karl Marx.

1873   Black Thursday: The "Gibraltar of Finance," Jay Cooke & Co., goes belly-up in Philadelphia, closing its doors at quarter past noon. Unable to sell his enormous stock of Northern Pacific Railroad bonds, Cooke had lost the confidence of his creditors and his bank depositors, whose withdrawals helped drain the institution of cash. Paying the Northern Pacific bills was a huge drain. The failure hit the nation as a total shock; the disbelief was such that a paperboy in Pittsburgh was arrested for shouting out the news. The New York Stock Exchange suspended trading, and by the end of the day 37 banks and two brokerage houses in New York had gone under. The event ignited the panic of 1873; when the country and markets had recovered six years later, an estimated 10,000 businesses were gone.

1977   "Never dump a good idea on a conference table. It will belong to the conference." —Jane Trahey, copywriter and author, in the *New York Times*

1998   LTCM is in full-blown crisis. The secretive, multibillion-dollar hedge fund (created by two Nobel laureate economists and a smooth-talking fund-raiser; see October 14) had invested heavily with borrowed money on the merger of two high-tech companies (Tellabs and Ciena). When the merger fell apart the stock of those companies fell deeply, causing brokers to demand collateral from LTCM. Its capital reserves of $3.7 billion in mid-August quickly dropped by two-thirds. Because of LTCM's enormous borrowing and investments, a lot more than just LTCM was now imperiled. Said one Wall Street executive, "And if this firm had to liquidate in distress, the ramifications for the global marketplace would be very negative." When asked how negative, the executive replied, "No one felt they could even quantify it." Once thought too large and in control of too powerful an investment method to fail, LTCM's fate now rested in the hands of others, including angry rivals (see September 23).

SEPTEMBER 19

1812   Mayer Amschel Rothschild, founder of the most famous of all European banking dynasties, dies in Frankfurt at 68 (see February 23).

1926   The Florida real estate boom/bubble of the 1920s ends suddenly when a hurricane destroys the Florida East Coast Railway link to the Florida Keys. Prices had been deflating for about a year (numerous building lots that were purchased unseen turned out to be under water), but this was the last straw. It is said that property owners who had bought land during the boom tried to turn away Red Cross workers after the hurricane because the publicity would damage property values.

1926   "No one . . . has ever lost money by underestimating the intelligence of great masses of the plain people." —H. L. Mencken, in the *Chicago Tribune*

1928   William S. Paley signs an option in Philadelphia to buy 50.3 percent of the stock of the struggling CBS radio network. He immediately hops a train to New York City to make the rounds of advertising agencies with one question: "Is there any future for radio as an advertising medium?" After five days of canvassing, the opinion was unanimous: no. The one exception was the young partnership of John Orr Young and Raymond Rubicam, who had just come to Manhattan to start their own agency; their radio expert, Tony Geohagan, said that it was still early, but he thought radio's future was good. The incident typified Paley's business style: hardworking, cautious, and optimistic. Young & Rubicam turned out to be a hugely successful advertising agency, and CBS turned into a broadcasting empire under Paley's leadership.

1966 "Wall Street indexes predicted nine out of the last five recessions." —Paul Samuelson, Nobel laureate economist, in *Newsweek*

SEPTEMBER 20

1853 Elisha Graves Otis sells his first elevator, which is designed for hauling freight. Orders were slow until the following May when at the Crystal Palace in New York City he demonstrated his safety elevator by having himself hoisted high above the ground and ordering the rope cut.

1873 The New York Stock Exchange closes its doors for the first time due to financial crisis, in the wake of Black Thursday and the failure of Jay Cooke & Co. (see September 18). The NYSE reopened after 10 days.

1926 Charles G. Bludhorn, the "Mad Austrian" who built a car bumper business into one of the world's largest conglomerates (Gulf & Western), is born in Vienna. After immigrating to America, Bludhorn worked for a cotton broker, did a stint in the military, and worked for an importer-exporter before starting his own import-export company specializing in commodities in 1949. Eight years later he began the creation of Gulf & Western by purchasing a controlling interest in the small bumper firm, Michigan Bumper Company; the following year he acquired an auto parts distributing company and merged the two as Gulf & Western, which by 1970 he had built into the nation's 64th largest industrial corporation. At that point he had started to diversify, eventually turning his auto parts business into a conglomerate with interests as varied as racetracks, cigars, panty hose, publishing, mining, and Paramount Pictures. The huge operation came to be known as "Charlie's cats and dogs." Bludhorn died February 19, 1983.

SEPTEMBER 21

1784   The first daily newspaper in the United States, the *Pennsylvania Packet and Daily Advertiser*, appears on the streets for the first time. Selling for 4 pence a copy, the paper was published by David C. Claypoole and John Dunlap in Philadelphia. It was founded in 1771 as a weekly under the title of *Pennsylvania Packet and Weekly Advertiser*.

1893   America's first gasoline-powered car moves for the first time, in Springfield, Massachusetts. It had a one-cylinder engine, an electric ignition, a spray carburetor, and tiller steering. Bicycle-designer Charles Edgar Duryea, 31, got the idea for the contraption when he saw a stationary gasoline engine at the Ohio State Fair in 1886; he conceived of a compact engine fitted to a carriage. His younger brother, J. Frank Duryea, was a toolmaker, and together they built the machine in a rented loft in Springfield. In later years an argument marred the relationship between the brothers; Charles claimed the model was brought to a running condition under his guidance, while Frank claimed he had perfected the engine and transmission while Charles was in Illinois.

1895   America's first automobile company, the Duryea Motor Wagon Company of Springfield, Massachusetts, is incorporated under the laws of Maine. In November, on Thanksgiving Day, the Duryea Brothers won the country's first car race, and the following year the Haynes-Duryea motorcar was the first U.S. automobile to be offered for sale. Total U.S. car production in that first year was 25. The Duryea company produced autos until 1917.

1930   The founder of the Campbell Soup Company, John Thompson Dorrance, dies at 56, leaving the third largest estate recorded up to then: $115 million. A brilliant chemist, Dorrance completed his Ph.D. in chemistry in 1897 at Germany's University of Goettingen, and in that year he went to work for the Joseph Campbell Preserve Company in Philadelphia, where his uncle, Arthur Dorrance, was a partner. He invented condensed soup in 1899. At the time, there were only three soup companies in the country, and all of them shipped in bulky, water-heavy cans, which created problems in distribution, display, and use.

Dorrance's process removed the water from the soup; it immediately solved the problems and was an immediate success. The great product was backed by a great advertising campaign. Campbell's began advertising on New York City streetcars in 1899 and ran its first national ad in *Good Housekeeping* in 1905, by which time sales had already exceeded 16 million cans of soup a year. By 1911 they were selling all the way to California, becoming one of the first companies to achieve nationwide distribution of a brand-name food.

1945   On the first full day of Henry Ford II's term as the new president of Ford Motor Company, someone nearly gets shot. A board meeting was held to record the resignation of company founder Henry Ford, who was so frail that he had to be helped into his seat. Harry Bennett, the company's violent service chief and right-hand man to the elder Ford, snarled, "Congratulations!" at Henry II as he stalked out of the meeting after the resignation letter was read. Bennett had wanted the presidency himself. Later in the day, Henry II sent executive John Bugas to fire Bennett, who had been burning papers all afternoon in his office, and who shouted, "You son of a bitch!" when he saw Bugas. Bennett pulled a .45 automatic out his desk, and ex-FBI chief Bugas pulled a .38 out of his belt. "Don't make the mistake of pulling the trigger, because I'll kill you. I won't miss. I'll put one right through your heart, Harry," he warned.

SEPTEMBER 22

1791   Michael Faraday is born in Newington, England, one of ten children of a poor journeyman blacksmith. Faraday built the first dynamo and the first electric motor, but he had no interest in turning either into a practical tool or a moneymaking venture. His obsession was to discover the relationship between electricity, magnetism, light, and gravity.

1963   "It is a medium of entertainment which permits millions of people to listen to the same joke at the same time, and yet remain lonesome." —T. S. Eliot, poet, on his dislike for television, in the *New York Post*

1980 Procter & Gamble voluntarily withdraws Rely tampons from store shelves. In addition, P&G signed an unprecedented consent agreement with the Food and Drug Administration to run a series of advertisements that discouraged the use of Rely, warned women of a possible link between Rely and toxic shock syndrome (TSS), and informed users how to obtain refunds for purchases of Rely. The move cost P&G an estimated $75 million, or 91¢ a share, but was undertaken when no sign of defect had appeared in Rely and when there was no proven link between TSS and the product. No lawsuits had been filed or scientific evidence presented. So why did P&G take the action? Essentially, to protect the public and to protect its company image. A statistical relationship between TSS and Rely had been reported, and the P&G name was linked with disease in every news story. The company's quick action minimized the number of times that association was repeated, as well as garnering some points for good citizenship. "What we are trying to do is what we think is right," said a P&G spokesperson.

1999 "To be vital, an organization has to repot itself, start again, get new ideas, renew itself. And I . . . should disappear from the company so my successor feels totally free." —Jack Welch, former chairman and CEO, General Electric, in *Fortune*

SEPTEMBER 23

1720 In this month the South Sea Bubble burst, with stock price dropping 75 percent in a matter of weeks. Famous man of letters Alexander Pope writes a letter on this day to Bishop Atterbury, even as his own sizeable investment is vanishing: ". . . Most people thought it [the collapse] wou'd come, but no man perpar'd for it; no man consider'd it would come *like a Thief in the night*, exactly as it happens in the case of death. Methinks God has punish'd the avaritious as he often punishes sinners, in their own way, in the very sin itself: the thirst for gain was their crime, and that thirst continued became their punishment and ruin. . . . *They have dreamed out their dream, and awaking have found nothing in their hands.* Indeed the universal poverty, which is the consequence of universal avarice, and which will fall hardest upon the guiltless and industrious part of mankind, is lamentable. The universal deluge of the S. Sea, contrary to the old deluge, has drowned all except a few *Unrighteous* men. . . . "

1848   Chewing gum is first produced commercially in the United States by John Curtis in his home; he calls it State of Maine Pure Spruce Gum.

1880   Angry tenant farmers in County Mayo, Ireland, go to the home of estate manager Charles Boycott to protest high rents during a deep agricultural depression. The farmers told Boycott's servants to leave, which they did. Suddenly there was no one to tend his house, cook his meals, wash his clothes, or harvest his crops. Shopkeepers were forbidden to deal with him, the local blacksmith agreed not to shoe his horses, and even the local postboy was warned against delivering his mail. "You must show him," said Irish nationalist leader Charles Parnell, who coordinated the action, "by leaving him severely alone." It was history's first boycott. In the end, 50 men were imported from Ulster to harvest the Boycott fields under armed guard by British soldiers. The Boycotts moved into a local barn, but continued community pressure forced them to depart Ireland the following year. In 1881 Parnell's This Land Act was passed, greatly expanding the rights and civil treatment of tenant farmers.

1988   "There's nothing the British like better than a bloke who comes from nowhere, makes it, and then gets clobbered." —Melvyn Bragg, British broadcaster and novelist, in the *Guardian*

1998   The LTCM hedge fund faces bankruptcy, and worldwide markets face disaster (see September 18). On this day sleek black limousines converged on the Federal Reserve Bank of New York, depositing representatives from 16 banks and brokerage firms and various government economists to attempt a salvage operation. At first it was announced that a white knight buyer may have been found: billionaire Warren Buffett. But when the group returned at 1 P.M. from recess, they were told that Buffett had pulled out. Angry arguments and resentful speeches gripped the meeting, but in the end 14 firms committed $100 million to $350 million each to bail out LTCM, thereby preventing a collapse that could have hurt all of them. LTCM had new owners, with its original investors taking big losses.

SEPTEMBER 24

1621   London's first newspaper—*Corante, or newes from Italy, Germany, Hungarie, Spaine, and France*—begins publication.

1869   Wall Street's first Black Friday occurs. Unscrupulous Jay Gould and Jim Fisk had been buying gold heavily, with the aim of driving its price sky-high, then suddenly dumping it for a big killing. A linchpin of the scheme was convincing President Grant not to put treasury gold on the market; Gould had seeded newspapers with articles (written by an "expert" who was secretly paid by Gould) that supported a fairly high gold price, and Gould enlisted Grant's brother-in-law, speculator Abel Corbin, to help convince the president of the policy's wisdom and benefit to America and the Republican Party. As the price of gold steadily rose, so did the grumbling, until finally on this morning Secretary of the Treasury Boutwell was deluged with "tornadoes of telegrams" as gold rose to 162. Grant was playing croquet when Boutwell reached him and convinced him to reverse policy and sell gold immediately. The effect was dramatic; buying bids were replaced by a mad rush to sell. A reporter from the New York *Herald* inside the NYSE happened to hear the bells of Trinity Church on Wall Street strike noon; gold stood at 160 on the NYSE indicator when the bells first chimed, and by the time the bell's last echo had died away gold was at 138. It continued to fall. Hundreds of investment houses and untold number of innocent investors were ruined in the price collapse.

1889   The bane of the late employee, a time clock that records when each worker punches in to work, is patented in the United States by Scotsman Dr. Alexander Dey (U.S. Patent 411,586). Dey's two brothers operated a department store in Syracuse, New York, and together the three formed a company to produce the device. The Dey device printed workers' numbers and clock-in times on a single sheet; it was replaced in general use by the now-common system in which each employee has his own card (see October 30).

1948   The Honda Motor Company is incorporated and will swell to become the world's leading producer of motorcycles and a world leader in car production. The organization was founded by engineer Soichiro Honda as the Honda Technical Research Institute, which focused solely on producing small internal combustion engines. Today's event came on the 40th anniversary (**1908**) of the completion of the first factory-built Ford Model T, for many years the world's largest selling automobile.

1998   The online auction house eBay holds its initial public offering (IPO). The price was $18 per share, but by day's end it had shot up 160 percent to $47. Founder Pierre Omidyar, new CEO Meg Whitman, and other executives were instantly rich. Back at headquarters in San Jose, California, conga lines snaked through the hallways.

SEPTEMBER 25

1725   Designer and builder of the world's first car, Nicolas-Joseph Cugnot, is born in Poid, France. A military engineer, Cugnot returned to Paris after the Seven Years War with a number of inventions in his head that he'd conceived during the campaigning. One of these was a steam-powered tractor, really a tricycle, to haul artillery. He designed and built a two-piston steam boiler (independently of Newcomen and Watt who are famous for their steam engines) and successfully constructed two of his war machines, the first in 1769 and the second in 1770. The second still survives in a Paris museum. It looks like a mechanical beetle with wheels; it has front-wheel drive and ran at 2.25 mph with four passengers. Cugnot died October 2, 1804.

1956   "Farming looks mighty easy when your plow is a pencil, and you're a thousand miles from the corn field." —President Dwight Eisenhower, in a speech in Peoria, Illinois, about "synthetic farmer" experts in Washington

1990   The Soviet Parliament grants President Mikhail Gorbachev free reign to decontrol the Russian economy as he sees fit. Gorbachev moved cautiously, however, as prices and shortages of commodities continued to rise.

1995   The *New York Times* reports that gambling is now the fastest-growing industry in the United States: "A $40 billion business that draws more customers than baseball parks or movie theaters." The article provided the example of Iowa, which did not even have the lottery until 1985, but within a decade had the lottery, ten major casinos, a horse track, a dog track, and 24-hour slot machines. According to the report, 9 out of 10 Iowans said they gambled, with 5.4 percent saying they have a problem, up from 1.7 percent five years earlier. This was in a state where a Catholic priest went to jail for running a bingo game in the 1970s.

1997   The Travelers Group announces its $9 billion acquisition of Salomon Brothers investment firm. For Travelers CEO Sandy Weill it was another risky, high-priced gamble. The new entity immediately became the country's number two underwriter of corporate debt and equities, the fourth most-active merger adviser, and the third largest retail broker. According to one member of the Travelers board, Weill's aim was building "the greatest financial services company in the history of the country and in the history of the world."

SEPTEMBER 26

1855   John D. Rockefeller, 16, takes his first job. It was, perhaps, the best day of his life, and an event he celebrated more heartily than his birthday, each year raising a red flag at his home to commemorate what he called "Job Day." Rockefeller dropped out of high school two months before graduation when his father said he was not going to college; he took a three-month course at a business school and immediately began searching for work. This morning, after six fruitless six-day weeks, he walked into the offices of Hewitt and Tuttle, commission merchants and produce shippers, on Merwin Street. He was interviewed by the junior partner for a bookkeeper's position and told to come back after lunch. In the afternoon he was interviewed by senior partner Isaac L. Hewitt and then heard the magic words, "We'll give you a chance."

1914   Congress establishes the Federal Trade Commission, the main instrument for policing the nation's advertising. It was empowered to regulate "unfair methods of competition" and to stop deceptive advertising in interstate commerce.

1928   William S. Paley, 26, is elected president of the fledgling CBS radio network. By December revenues had tripled.

1969   The *New York Times* reports that the Franklin Simon Company, one of the nation's leading fashion apparel chains, will break ranks with other major department stores and begin accepting bank credit cards.

1979   How can you go wrong minting money? By issuing the Susan B. Anthony dollar. The Treasury Department first issued the quarter-sized dollar in January 1979, predicting that it would save taxpayers $50 million a year in the printing of paper money, which wears out relatively quickly. But it never caught on with the public. The *Washington Post* called it "a federal white elephant," and on this day Jack Anderson in a nationally syndicated column delivered something of a eulogy, calling it "a costly fiasco, rejected by merchants, bankers, and public alike." With 500 million of them still sitting in government storage, production was stopped in March. This famous fiasco joins other currency blunders, like the Eisenhower dollar, the Kennedy half-dollar, and the two-dollar bill. Though it has the same value, all money is not equal.

SEPTEMBER 27

1560   One of the great strokes of Queen Elizabeth I to restore her country's economic prosperity was reminting the nation's debased coinage in order to restore its value. Her father, Henry VIII, had repeatedly diluted the coin with base metals, and with each debasement the credit of English merchants sank. Elizabeth undertook the massive and risk-filled project very early in her reign because of its importance. On this day the proclamation went out for debased coins to be returned to government mints, where they would be replaced by coins of true value. Elizabeth actually pushed the proclamation ahead two days from its original schedule in order to minimize speculative trading, as rumors of the secret program began to filter through the kingdom. The project was a great success and helped establish England as a center of international finance. One 17th-century historian proclaimed that Elizabeth did "achieve to the victory and conquest of this hideous monster of the base moneys," judging it to be her "greater, yea greatest, glory."

1825   The first passenger rail service using a locomotive, the 27-mile Stockton and Darlington Railway, opens. George Stephenson's 15-ton engine *Active* traveled at 10 mph, pulling a tender, six freight cars, the directors' coach, six passenger coaches, and 14 wagons for workmen.

1855   Salt king Joy Morton is born in Detroit, the son of Julius Sterling Morton, Secretary of Agriculture and the founder of Arbor Day. Joy was a bank and railroad executive before joining the salt company of E.I. Wheeler in Chicago, and when Wheeler died in 1885 Morton took control and reorganized it as Joy Morton and Company. He merged with other companies to form the National Salt Company, then the International Salt Company. In 1910 Joy and brother Mark bought out their partners and incorporated as the Morton Salt Company, destined to be the largest and most important firm in the industry.

1938   Queen Elizabeth II launches the Cunard ocean liner named for her at Clydebank Pier in Scotland. It was the world's largest passenger vessel at the time. Twenty-nine years later (**1967**) Cunard's *Queen Mary* completed her last transatlantic voyage, concluding the days of the great ocean liners.

1989   The board of directors of Columbia Pictures approves the sale of the company to the Sony Corporation for $27 per share, or $3.4 billion in cash. It was expensive and Columbia was not doing well, but the merger of Sony's electronics products and Columbia's entertainment programming was seen as a synergistic wave of the future—hardware and content software under one roof. The event marked the peak of Japanese postwar success. Just months later the Japanese stock bubble burst, creating a depression whose effects still linger.

SEPTEMBER 28

1618   The world's first pawnshop opens in Brussels. People in need of cash could borrow money at a low rate of interest if they left a security.

1889   Production genius William Jones is killed when a furnace explodes at the Carnegie steel production complex in Braddock, Pennsylvania. Six others perished instantly in the blast, which was heard 12 miles away in Pittsburgh. A hard driver of men, Jones was brilliant on the production floor, famous for making innovations on the spot. Carnegie replaced Jones with a rising young executive who would one day run the entire Carnegie operation and go on to found the Bethlehem Steel Corporation: Charles M. Schwab.

1901   The Gillette Company (ultimately the Gillette Safety Razor Company) is incorporated. Twenty investors paid $250 each for 500 shares of stock. After a close shave with bankruptcy, taking on additional debt of $12,000, and first-year sales of just 51 razors, the idea of a disposable razor really caught on. By 1904 sales reached 90,844 razors, and company founder King C. Gillette bought out one of the original investors for $62,500—for the stake that had cost just $250 three years before.

1998   "Increasingly, I have become concerned that the motivation to meet Wall Street earnings expectations may be overriding common sense business practices. . . . Managing may be giving way to manipulation. Integrity may be losing out to illusion." —Arthur Levitt, Jr., former chairman, SEC, in a speech to the New York University Center for Law and Business

SEPTEMBER 29

1916   John D. Rockefeller, 77, becomes the world's first billionaire during a stock market boom.

1950   The first telephone answering machine is tested by scientists with the Bell Telephone Company.

1960   "Their dedication is to competitive creativity—a deep desire within the consciousness of each man to create something better today than yesterday's best." —John Orr Young, cofounder of Young & Rubicam, on what makes a great advertising agency, in the *New York Times*

1987   Henry Ford II dies at age 70 of viral pneumonia on the fourth anniversary of his Hall of Fame induction, in a Detroit hospital built by and named for his grandfather. His last rites were delivered by Reverend John Mericantante III, Lee Iacocca's family priest. Ford had fired Iacocca amid great bitterness nine years before. It is unclear how Mericantante got to Ford's bedside, though he had just conducted the marriage ceremony of Iacocca's daughter in Detroit, and he was reportedly driven to the hospital in a Chrysler limousine. Iacocca denied any role in the "grotesque sendoff."

SEPTEMBER 30

1452   The first section of the original Gutenberg Bible, history's first book printed from movable type, is published in Mainz, Germany. Johannes Gutenberg, in his late 50s, completed the Bible in 1456, despite losing a lawsuit in 1455 to his major financial backer, Johann Fust, who sought return of the invested money or control of the printing press.

1861   "Tell 'em quick and tell 'em often" was the promotional dictum of the colorful William Wrigley, Jr., who is born in Philadelphia (see January 26).

1903   Edward H. Harriman becomes a director of the Erie Railroad. A cornerstone of his management style was delegation of authority. During one of the meetings of the executive committee, a manager sought approval of a $10,000 purchase of mules for the company's coal mines. A debate ensued until an exasperated Harriman jumped in: "If the manager in charge cannot be trusted to buy mules without bringing the subject to the Executive Committee, a new manager should be selected. My time is worth about a mule a minute and I can't stay to hear the rest of the discussion. I vote 'Aye' on the requisition."

1908   The Harvard Business School (the Graduate School of Business Administration) opens in Cambridge, Massachusetts, under the direction of Dean Edwin F. Gay. Unlike other professional schools of the time, such as law or medicine, the new school demanded that entrants already have a college degree. According to a statement by Harvard, "The school does not pretend to graduate men who will begin at the top or high up in their several lines of business. It does aim to teach them how to work and how to apply powers of observation, analysis, and invention to practical business problems."

1996   "Downsizing suddenly became news because for the first time, white-collar, college-educated workers were being fired in large numbers, even while skilled machinists and other blue-collar workers were in demand." —Paul R. Krugman, economist, in the *Wall Street Journal*

OCTOBER

OCTOBER 1

1881 Founder of the Boeing Airplane Company, William Edward Boeing, is born in Detroit. Boeing started to make planes in 1916 in a boathouse on the shores of Lake Union near downtown Seattle. In that same year he formed Pacific Aero Products Company. His first commercial aircraft was the B&W two-seat, twin-float seaplane, built in collaboration with Conrad Westervelt. Between World Wars I and II, this model and several others sold well, setting up Boeing's rise to become one of the world's top manufacturers of gigantic seaplanes, bombers, and passenger planes. The Boeing company pioneered the development of jetliners, jumbo jets, and supersonic passenger aircraft.

1945 *Life* magazine publishes an article about the new head of the Ford Motor Company, Henry Ford II, who has just taken over a corporation that is losing $9.5 million a month. The article reached Arjay Miller, one of a partnership of 10 air force officers who had decided to stay together to sell their newly developed expertise in systems analysis to private companies. The group had printed up a brochure and sent it to some businesses but not to Ford. Not until Miller saw the *Life* article. The group, including Robert McNamara and "Tex" Thornton, was soon working for the desperate and inexperienced Henry Ford II and became known as the "Whiz Kids." Their statistical, computer-based analysis of corporate performance and structure not only helped turn Ford around, it changed the face of management.

1958 American Express launches its credit card at a press conference. Although 250,000 people had already requested the cards and 17,500 establishments around the world were lined up to accept them, the company faltered; it entered a field that already had established players, it entered in a very big way, it had purchased the wrong automation equipment, and the effort was poorly managed. The venture lost millions of dollars for four years, until George Waters was put in charge. Among his turnaround tactics were boosting card fees, advertising heavily, cracking down on delinquent accounts, increasing the percentage paid by merchants who honored the cards, using market surveys, changing the color of the card from purple to green, and calling cardholders "members." Waters's assault was essentially on revenues and on brand image.

1984   "I think a lot more decisions are made on serendipity than people think. Things come across their radar screens and they jump at them." —Jay W. Lorsch, sociologist, in the *Wall Street Journal*

OCTOBER 2

1885   Investment banker Harold Stanley—the "Stanley" in Morgan Stanley—is born in Great Barrington, Massachusetts, the son of inventor William Stanley, for whom the General Electric Company's Stanley Works in nearby Pittsfield was named. After Yale and a European tour, Stanley entered investment banking. In 1915 he was hired to head the bond department of Guaranty Trust Company; under his management the department grew so rapidly that a separate company, the Guaranty Company, was formed. As president of Guaranty for 12 years, Stanley had dealings with the House of Morgan; that firm's head, J. P. Morgan, Jr., was so impressed that he stole Stanley to replace a retiring partner. At 42, Stanley was one of the youngest partners in Morgan annals. When the House of Morgan split in two in 1935 (commercial versus investment banking), Stanley was made head of the investment branch.

1975   The once-mighty retail chain, W.T. Grant, files for bankruptcy. The company's origins extended back to 1906, when William Thomas Grant, a buyer for department store bargain counters, noticed that the fastest selling merchandise was priced at 25¢. Hit with an inspiration that would eventually make him a household name, Grant surmised that 25¢ was a "magic price," and he founded his chain on that premise. Sixty years later different management embarked on a huge and doomed program of expansion in two directions: horizontally (erecting 410 supersized Grant outlets all over the map in five years), and vertically (infusing the product lines with higher priced items). Both moves worked against the company, saddling it with over $1 billion in debt and alienating the chain's established customer base. A recession in 1974 sent Grant belly-up. It was the nation's single largest retailing failure.

2002   A clerical error causes the large investment firm Bear Stearns to place orders to sell not the intended $4 million worth of stock, but 1,000 times that amount. Eventually the firm recovered about 85 percent of the missold stock (thereby having sold only 156 times the intended amount) and said that the remaining loss would have no material impact on the company's health. The next day's *Wall Street Journal* reported the accident on the same page as a Bear Stearns advertisement that touted the company's ability to "execute complex transactions flawlessly."

OCTOBER 3

1295   The mercantile interests of England are invited to participate in Parliament for the first time. The Parliament of 1295 became known as the Model Parliament because later gatherings used the same format. King Edward I recognized the advantage of including a wider range of distinguished citizens in government, but there was another reason for including the businessmen of the day in his government: his treasury was virtually bankrupt due to endless warfare with Scotland, France, and Wales.

1776   Two months after becoming a country, the U.S. federal government borrows money for the first time, when Congress approves the borrowing of $5 million at 4 percent interest to halt the rapid depreciation of paper currency, which is being printed to finance the Revolutionary War. Congress further authorized agents in France to borrow an additional £2 million.

1930   At 8:00 at night, in the dark of the Great Depression, Columbus M. Joiner (known as "Dad" for his age of 71 and as "King of the Wildcatters" for his success in finding oil in unlikely places) hits an enormous gusher while drilling on widow Daisy Bradford's farm in Rusk

County, in east Texas. "Put out the fires! Put out your cigarettes! *Quick!*" yelled someone to the oil-soaked crowd of thousands that had gathered over the past few weeks after rumors of an impending strike had spread. Joiner had opened an oil field that was 45 miles long and 5 to 10 miles wide (140,000 acres in all)—by far the greatest oil discovery on the continent at that time. Within days, two effects took over: entrepreneur drillers flooded into east Texas, and oil prices crashed from about $1 per barrel to as low as 2¢ a barrel. Dad Joiner was vulnerable because he had title to just two of 50,000 leased acres, and because he had sold, oversold, and resold more "interests" in his claim than there were interests. He sold one lease 11 separate times (see November 27).

OCTOBER 4

1932   A Chicago grand jury indicts the utilities mogul Samuel Insull and his brother Martin, for embezzlement from several of the Insull companies. It was the first in a series of indictments against Samuel Insull, who had become one of the country's richest men largely through the sale of utility securities during the Roaring Twenties. Stock in Insull Utility Investments, for example, rose from $30 to $147 per share in just eight months in 1929. Following the market crash of that year, Insull borrowed heavily to prop up his companies, but in April 1932 was forced to surrender his stocks, estate, and life insurance to creditors. He and his wife quietly left Quebec for Europe, where they tried to disappear. By September investigators had found a number of irregularities in Insull's records. Amid losses to investors of $700 million in Middle West Securities and $85 million in Corporation Securities, he had shifted collateral between companies, given illegal preferences to favored creditors, transferred assets to pay questionable broker's fees, and spread profits from successful companies as he saw fit to favored associates or to other companies. Insull was found on a Greek tramp steamer bound for Egypt, returned to the United States, tried several times, and never convicted of anything. The saga made world headlines, and Insull was an issue in the 1932 presidential race. The utility holding company, the device he had used so adeptly, was made illegal as a result of the scandal.

1957   Russia's launch of *Sputnik I* on this day produces shock throughout America and Europe, feigned nonchalance by many in the political and military establishment, and a complicated reaction in the business community. By October 21, the Dow Jones Industrial Average had lost 10 percent of its value. Rumors that the Federal Reserve System would loosen credit conditions and then the actual lowering of the discount rate in November helped to spark a market rally that continued through 1958, making that year one of the century's best in total return on stock investment, 43.37 percent.

1957   "The CEO of hip-hop," Russell Simmons, is born into the middle-class neighborhood of Hollis in Queens, New York. As a youth, Simmons was part of the street life, sometimes dealing drugs. He entered college in 1975 but quit just short of graduation in order to concentrate on managing several rap groups, including the groundbreaking Run-DMC (his younger brother, Joey, was "Run"). It was during this period that Simmons founded the Def Jam record label with another promoter, Rick Rubin, an undergraduate at New York University. Ignored for many years, hip-hop was officially recognized by the recording establishment in 1985, when Sony Corp. signed a distribution deal with Def Jam. Simmons sold Def Jam to Universal Music in 1999 for $120 million, though he still remains as its chairman. Simmons now heads the conglomerate Rush Communications, a holding company for ventures in fashion, media, finance, consumer products, and philanthropy.

1958   The British Overseas Airway Corporation (now British Air) inaugurates commercial transatlantic passenger jet service with a flight between New York and London. Pan Am established service the same month, and in just one year airlines were carrying 63 percent of all transatlantic traffic (1.5 million passengers in the air versus 0.9 million in ships). Nevertheless, European companies continued to launch new passenger liners.

1996   History's largest coffee break occurs when 513,659 people drink coffee simultaneously in 14,652 groups throughout the United Kingdom. The event raised $28.46 million for the Macmillan Cancer Relief charity.

2004   Tourist traffic to outer space takes a big step forward when the privately built *SpaceShipOne* soars 62 miles above the earth and safely returns with its pilot, Brian Binnie. The half-hour excursion was the second for the craft in five days; it proved that *SpaceShipOne* could function as a spaceliner and thus won the $10 million "X Prize" that had been offered nearly a decade before to encourage private ventures in space. Patti Grace Smith, associate administrator of the Federal Aviation Authority, reported that excitement around the X Prize had begun to excite the investment community. "I'm starting to get calls from brokers. That's brand new," said Smith.

OCTOBER 5

1888   The earliest "ball pen," with a self-contained ink supply and retractable tip, is patented by Alonzo T. Cross.

1902   McDonald's founder, Raymond Kroc, is born into near-poverty in Chicago. He dropped out of high school the first time to become an ambulance driver in World War I; after the war he dropped out a second time to become a jazz pianist. He took a steady job as a salesman for the Lily-Tulip Cup Company after getting married in 1922, but he soon became musical director for a pioneering Chicago radio station, WGES, where he made his first notable discovery: the comedy team of Amos and Andy. His second notable discovery was restaurant owners Mac and Dick McDonald. He encountered them in 1954 in San Bernardino, California, while selling "multi-mixer" blenders; the McDonalds' small establishment was using more blenders than any of his other clients. He then investigated why. "What do you do when your competitor's drowning?" Kroc once said. "Get a live hose and stick it in his mouth."

1932   The anthem of the Great Depression, "Brother, Can You Spare a Dime?" is performed in public for the first time. The song was written in 1928 by Jay Gorney and E. Y. Harburg.

1981   "Why is it so necessary to sneer at people who are successful?" —Terence Conran, British business executive and retailer, in the *Daily Express*

1982   Johnson & Johnson recalls Tylenol from store shelves after it is discovered that a Chicago assassin has laced the medication with cyanide. Thirty-one million capsules were destroyed. Johnson & Johnson reintroduced Tylenol in triple-sealed safety packages and regained 95 percent of its top market share in three months.

OCTOBER 6

1769   "Let me smile with the wise, and feed with the rich." —Samuel Johnson, in Boswell's *Life of Samuel Johnson*

1908   The Ohio Art Company, makers of the Etch-A-Sketch art toy, is founded by Henry Simon Winzeler.

1927   Al Jolson changes entertainment history with the following words: "Wait a minute! Wait a minute! You ain't heard nothin' yet." They were the first spoken words in *The Jazz Singer*, the first full-length talking film, which opened at the Warner Theater in New York City on this night. It was a smash success, driving Warner Brothers stock from $9 to $132. Sam Warner died of a heart attack 24 hours before the film's triumphant debut. Harry Warner, the business mastermind of the studio, used the film's profits to grow the company, buying radio stations, backing Broadway shows, purchasing record companies, and adding one theater a day to the Warner empire during the height of expansion.

1945   The production of ballpoint pens begins in the United States, 70 per day, under the supervision of Chicago promoter Milton Reynolds. His product originated during a business trip to Buenos Aires, where he saw the pen invented by Ladislao Biro. Upon return to the States, Reynolds modified Biro's design to circumvent existing patents. By the end of the month Reynolds had placed the pens in Gimbel Brothers department store in New York, where they quickly sold out at $12.50 each. Reynolds promised that they could write under water, would not leak at high altitudes, and made it practical to handwrite multiple copies of business and government forms through carbon paper. Initially some banks suggested that ballpoint pen signatures might not be legal.

1956   A beacon of both integrity and business acumen, founder of the Merrill Lynch investment firm, Charles Edward Merrill dies at age 70 (see October 19).

1991   "It's the same each time with progress. First they ignore you, then they say you're mad, then dangerous, then there's a pause and you can't find anyone who disagrees with you." —Tony Benn, British politician, in the *Observer*

OCTOBER 7

1806   Carbon paper—a mainstay of business and legal documentation until the advent of copiers and computers a century and a half later—is patented by R. Wedgwood of Great Britain. His process involved saturating a thin sheet of paper with ink, then drying it between sheets of blotting paper.

1925   Colonial Air Transport, the first private air transport company in the United States, is awarded the first mail-carrying contract from the federal government under the just-passed Airmail Act of 1925. The managing director of Colonial was Juan Trippe, 26, who had founded the airline with chums in the Rockefeller, Whitney, and Vanderbilt families. Trippe, ambitious to carry passengers as well as cargo, soon left Colonial. The next airline he founded was Pan American.

1927   With *The Jazz Singer* having opened the previous evening and already become a phenomenon (see October 6), Adolph Zukor calls 50 Paramount Pictures executives into his suite in New York's Savoy-Plaza Hotel, demanding to know why they had not yet made a talking film. Similar scenes no doubt occurred in other war rooms throughout the movie industry.

1930   "We told you that the time would come when the master would become impersonal, and that powers that have nothing to do with industry would control industry—the powers of gambling with credit." —Ramsey MacDonald, British prime minister, in a speech at Llandudno, Wales

1952 Grandfather to the baby foods industry, Daniel Frank Gerber, Sr., dies at age 79 (see January 12). Creator of the frozen foods industry, Clarence Birdseye, dies at age 69 exactly four years later (**1956**; see December 9).

OCTOBER 8

1826 Friedrich Krupp—the industrialist who started his family's rise to international significance by founding the dynasty's cast-steel factory in 1811—dies in Essen, Germany, of pectoral dropsy at just 39. His health was broken by continual debt, unfulfilled ambition, and business failure. His son Alfred took over his production works and turned it into an empire.

1882 "The public be damned!" William H. Vanderbilt, the first son of Cornelius Vanderbilt, makes this celebrated remark on this day in his private railroad car somewhere between Chicago and Michigan City, Indiana, while reporters are interviewing him about a new rate war between his New York Central line and the Pennsylvania line. Vanderbilt said that the Central could not make a profit on the $15 New York–Chicago fare but was maintaining it to fight the Pennsylvania. "Otherwise, we would abandon it," said Vanderbilt, who adds that the fast *Chicago Limited* extra-fare mail run was being eliminated. "But don't you run the train for the public benefit?" protested freelance writer Clarence Dresser. "The public be damned! I am working for my stockholders. If the public wants the train, why don't they pay for it?" demanded Vanderbilt.

1896 The Dow Jones Industrial Average is first reported.

2003 Stock in Schnitzer Steel closes at $37 per share, marking a one-year increase of 270 percent! And Schnitzer didn't even manufacture steel; it dealt in junk—junk and scrap metals, which it just happened to send to various places, including China. This was the cause for the huge leap in its stock valuation. China was turning scrap into finished steel for building as part of its voracious economic expansion. Another U.S. recycler, Metal Management, was now shipping scrap to China for $188 per ton, twice the price of two years ago.

OCTOBER 9

1746 "Whatever is worth doing at all is worth doing well." —Lord Chesterfield, statesman and orator, in a letter to his son

1779 The first of the Luddite riots begins in Manchester, England. Now synonymous with anyone blindly and vehemently opposing technological change, the Luddites were organized bands of English handicraftsmen who rioted and attacked factories in protest of the modern textile machinery that was displacing them.

1863 Edward William Bok—who in 30 years of innovative editorship of the *Ladies' Home Journal* effected journalistic and social reforms and helped shape contemporary culture—is born in Den Helder, the Netherlands, into a family that will soon be poor immigrants in Brooklyn. Bok began work as an office boy with Western Union while attending night school; entered publishing with *Scribner's Magazine* (where he became its advertising manager at age 24); and finally established the Bok Syndicate Press in 1886, for which he developed the strikingly successful "Bok page," a full page of material devoted solely to material for women. This brought him the editorship of the *Ladies' Home Journal* in Philadelphia, where he became one of the most original, most influential editors in the history of periodical journalism. He devised a group of departments that informed and advised on almost any topic. He broke the media taboo against mentioning venereal disease. Among his other campaigns were women's suffrage, wildlife conservation, power company encroachment on Niagara Falls, and clean towns and cities. In 1892 he announced that his magazine would no longer advertise patent medicines, initiating a movement that won the participation of other editors and culminated in the passage of the Pure Food and Drug Act in 1906. By 1917 readers were sending his office 1 million letters a year asking for public reply. He died January 9, 1930.

1873 The "father of the modern drug store," Charles Rudolph Walgreen, is born on a farm of Swedish immigrant parents near Galesburg, Illinois. In 1909, pharmacist Walgreen formed C.R. Walgreen & Co., which soon blossomed into a nationwide chain of drug stores. Walgreen was a gifted retailer with a scientist's eye for detail. His stores were clean and well lit (atypical for retail stores of the time); he popularized the lunch counter in connection with the soda fountain; he was an early advocate of the open display (the forerunner of self-service); he opened the first "super-drug store" in Tampa, Florida, in 1934; and from early on he manufactured many of the items in his stores. By 1939, when he retired, the company manufactured 25,000 different articles under the company label. "The only really smart thing about me," he often said, "is that I know enough to hire men who are smarter than I am."

OCTOBER 10

1925 Tobacco magnate and founder of the American Tobacco Company, James Buchanan Duke, dies at age 68 in New York City. Just nine days before his death, Duke offered $47 million to Trinity College in Durham, North Carolina, if the school would change its name; today it is called Duke University. Another enormous chunk of his fortune (including $70 million in cash, a slew of town and country mansions, company stock, and a private railroad car called Doris) went to his only child, Doris Duke.

1933 Synthetic detergent for the home is first marketed. It was actually sodium alkyl sulfate made from chlorosulfonic acid and a fatty alcohol, but its creator and marketer, the Procter & Gamble company of Cincinnati, simply called it Dreft.

1951 The transistor is first used in a commercial product. Bell Telephone introduced trunk dialing apparatus and initiated long-distance, direct-dial telephone service.

1993 The Intel Corporation ships the first Pentium processors. With 3.1 million transistors on a single chip, it was the fastest, smallest, most powerful processor on the market—and it had a bug. At first Intel CEO Andy Grove dismissed the flaw as a remote, statistical problem. "If you know where a meteor will land, you can go there and get hit," he said. Eventually, Intel offered to replace the early Pentiums at no charge. The hard-driving Grove later admitted that he had much to learn about dealing with the public.

OCTOBER 11

1844   Processed food manufacturer, Henry John Heinz is born in Pittsburgh, the first of nine children to German immigrants. By age eight he was already selling produce to neighbors out of his family garden.

1906   Cosmetics king and founder of Revlon, Charles Haskell Revson, is born in Boston to Russian Jewish immigrants. He went to work in the garment district of New York City, first as a dress salesman, then as a buyer. He is said to have developed an excellent eye for distinguishing shades of black; years later, in developing shades of lipstick, Revson was credited with being a "color genius." He eventually entered the cosmetics industry, selling nail polish for the Elka Company, whose headquarters were in a small corner of a lamp factory, emblematic of the primitive nature of cosmetics firms. Revson saw an industry he could change. After being refused rights as Elka's national distributor, he founded his own company in 1932 with a revolutionary nail polish. Not only was it opaque, but it also came in a wide variety of shades. Andrew Tobias described Revson's transformation of the entire cosmetics industry: "[He] entered a fledgling, highly unprofessional industry of one-man shows (one-woman shows, really) and, more than anyone else, was responsible for building it into a $5 billion industry [by the mid-1970s]."

1950   CBS is awarded history's first license to broadcast color television. Issued by the Federal Communications Commission, the license was challenged by rival NBC, which claimed that CBS's technology was inadequate. The FCC agreed, issuing a restraining order in November. In June 1951, CBS nevertheless became the first to broadcast a commercial program in color.

2004   When Hurricane Ivan ripped through Florida earlier in the month, among the homes destroyed was that of James Abney of Marianna, Florida. There was one part of the residence left intact: a kitchen faucet, held up by two twisted water lines. Even the kitchen sink was gone. An Associated Press photograph showing the defiant spigot sticking up in the air was published worldwide. Employees of the Delta

Faucet Company recognized the fixture as one of theirs, tracked down the owner, and on this day present Abney with a $10,000 check toward the down payment on a new home.

OCTOBER 12

1789   In the heat of its revolution, France passes its first law allowing interest to be collected on loans. In 1807 the rate of interest was set at 5 percent in civil loans, 6 percent in commercial loans; anything above these limits was declared illegal usury.

1891   Investment banker Sidney James Weinberg is born in Brooklyn. Known as "Mr. Wall Street," he was an adviser to every president from Franklin Roosevelt to Lyndon Johnson and once sat on the boards of 31 blue-chip companies simultaneously. Following a course in penmanship, Weinberg landed his first job on Wall Street at Goldman Sachs . . . as the janitor's assistant. His rise in the firm began by chance when he was ordered to deliver a flagpole to the home of the company's namesake and partner, Paul Sachs. The front door was answered by Sachs himself, who was somewhat charmed by the young hustler and encouraged him to persevere on Wall Street and to attend night school. Following naval duty in World War II, Weinberg returned to Goldman Sachs, where his sociability, analytical skills, and astuteness of pricing recommendations led him to the top. Weinberg was the chief architect/underwriter of two record-setting deals: the 1956 sale of $650 million worth of Ford stock (then the largest corporate financing project in history) and the $350 million sale of Sears Roebuck debentures (then the largest-ever debt offering by a public company). He died July 23, 1969.

1956   ". . . I hate television. I hate it as much as peanuts. But I can't stop eating peanuts."—Orson Welles, motion picture director/actor/producer, in the *New York Herald Tribune*

1993   The 1 millionth Camry rolls off a Toyota assembly line a decade after the model was introduced. By 1997 the Camry was America's bestselling car.

OCTOBER 13

1893   The melody to "Happy Birthday to You"—arguably history's most popular, most sung, most recognized jingle—is copyright registered, by Patty Smith Hill and her sister, Mildred J. Hill, who published it as "Good Morning to All" in their book *Song Stories for the Kindergarten.*

1902   Another J. P. Morgan miracle: the first great labor confrontation of the 20th century effectively ends just before midnight, when Morgan representatives present President Theodore Roosevelt with a statement from mine operators that they will finally agree to accept arbitration to settle the five-month strike by anthracite coal miners. The strike had driven coal prices from $5 to $30 per ton, schools had been shut due to a lack of coal, and a national crisis was envisioned. The mine operators had flatly refused to arbitrate or even to talk with coal miner representatives until Morgan convinced them to cooperate. This was the first U.S. case in which the federal government appeared to be neutral rather than pro-management in a major labor dispute.

1964   Douglas McGregor—famous for his "Theory X, Theory Y" analysis of worker motivation—dies at age 58 in Acton, Massachusetts. Traditional management theory assumed that the average employee disliked work, had little ambition, and shunned responsibility; hence, managers were required to provide direction, motivation, and top-down supervision based on command, coercion, and punishment. McGregor (a long-time teacher of psychology at MIT) called this Theory X, to which he opposed his own Theory Y, which assumed that people would exercise self-direction and self-control if committed to objectives. Furthermore, Theory Y saw self-actualization as a great motivator, and that the average person was not just capable of learning responsibility, he would seek it.

OCTOBER 14

1900   William Edwards Deming—the physicist turned business consultant who changed the face of industrial quality control by infusing it with statistical analysis and by insisting that it be a genuine and high priority of his clients, starting with the worker on the shop floor, as a key element in detecting production errors—is born in Sioux City, Iowa. He established his own consulting firm in 1946 but never achieved notoriety in America until he was invited to Japan, where he became a national hero for his part in the industrial miracle/turnaround of postwar Japan (see June 16). Deming was about 80 when his accomplishments were recognized in his native country. He died on December 20, 1993.

1939   Broadcast Music, Inc. (BMI) is founded by U.S. radio networks to create "an alternate source of music suitable for broadcast" to go into direct competition with the monopoly ASCAP, which had recently boosted license fees.

1943   Life Savers millionaire Edward Noble purchases the Blue Network, one of the two radio networks owned by RCA, for $8 million cash. It was the first sale of a major broadcast network in history. The Federal Communications Commission had recently ordered the divestment by RCA when it ruled that a single company could not have more than one network for fear of monopolistic control. Noble called his new purchase American Broadcasting Systems, changing the name to ABC the following year.

1997   Robert C. Merton and Myron S. Scholes are awarded the Nobel Prize for Economics for devising a mathematical formula that measures the value of a market option (that is, an investment that enables the investor to buy or sell an item in the future at a preset price). Popularly known as the "Black-Scholes model" (named for mathematician Fisher Black who had helped discover it, but who had died by the time the prize was awarded and was thus ineligible to be named as a prize winner), the formula was first published in 1973 when its authors were all under 30 years of age and not one of them an economist. The Black-Scholes model broke open the nascent stock options market and helped spark explosive growth in all the financial markets in the 1970s. "Such rapid and widespread application of a theoretical result was new to economics," wrote the Nobel Prize committee. "Nowadays, thousands of traders and investors use the formula every day." Also unusual in this case was that the Nobel Prize winners formed a commercial enterprise, LTCM, around their discovery and became rich from it. Though fantastic, their wealth was short-lived (see 1998 entry for September 18).

OCTOBER 15

1878   The nation's first electric company—the Edison Electric Light Company of 65 Fifth Avenue in New York City—is incorporated. Overseen by J. P. Morgan, 3,000 shares of stock with a par value of $100 per share were issued for the express purpose of financing Thomas Alva Edison, 31, in his invention of the incandescent lightbulb. Edison received half the stock and produced the bulb the following year.

1914   The Clayton Anti-Trust Act is passed by Congress, toughening the federal government's power against combinations in restraint of trade as outlawed by the Sherman Anti-Trust Act of 1890. Named for Representative Henry De Lamar Clayton of Alabama, the act contained a number of antimonopolistic provisions but specifically exempted labor and the unions from such regulation, declaring "labor is not a commodity." This shut the door on the oldest legal argument that governments and managers had used to squash union activity.

1982   In the rose garden of the White House, President Ronald Reagan, before an assemblage of bankers, politicians, and reporters, signs the Garth–St. Germain Depository Institutions Act of 1982, declaring that it would remove "artificial" regulatory restraints on federally insured savings and loan companies. Reagan called the act "the most important legislation for financial institutions in 50 years," designed to help the S&Ls during a period of rising interest rates. "All in all," the president beamed, "I think we've hit the jackpot." The event began the savings and loan debacle of the 1980s, the biggest financial disaster since the Great Depression. Allowed to promise depositors higher rates of interest, freed to make highly aggressive loans and investments, and essentially unregulated because Reagan budget cuts had gutted the regulatory staffs, many S&L executives leapt into reckless deals. Even without the wild corruption that follows unregulated riches, Garth–St. Germain was a train wreck. In 1988 alone, the S&Ls lost $13.44 billion. In the end, with numerous S&Ls bankrupt and untold numbers of investors in the breach, the bailout cost taxpayers $200 billion immediately and $500 billion in interest by the year 2020.

2002 Sam Waksal, the jet-setting scientist/entrepreneur who founded the biotech firm ImClone Systems, pleads guilty in Manhattan to six counts, including securities fraud, bank fraud, conspiracy to obstruct justice, and perjury. In 2001 Waksal illegally alerted several friends and relatives to an upcoming negative assessment by the Food and Drug Administration (which turned out to be just a temporary setback). The most high-profile of Waksal's confederates was celebrity homemaker Martha Stewart, who on this day exactly two years later (**2004**) posted a message on her website that everything in prison was fine, and "The best news is—everyone is nice."

OCTOBER 16

1861 Officials in San Francisco discover that Henry Meiggs, brother of the city's comptroller, has fled to South America with nearly $400,000 of the city's money. Meiggs had become rich in San Francisco through land speculation and the importation of New York lumber, but a credit crisis in 1854 sent him heavily into debt. Shortly before fleeing, he had obtained a book of city debt notes, presigned by the mayor and the outgoing comptroller, and had received upward of $365,000 for them. Meiggs used part of the money to bribe officials in Chile to win the contract to build the Santiago al Sur Railroad, which he completed in less than two years (succeeding where several other contractors had gone bankrupt) and profited by $1.5 million. He repaid San Francisco.

1868 America's first department store—Zion's Co-Operative Mercantile Institution (ZCMI)—is founded under the direction of Mormon leader Brigham Young in Salt Lake City, Utah, where it still operates today. At first, each department was housed in a separate building; dry goods and carpets in one building, men's clothing in another, groceries in another, and a pharmacy/drugstore in still another. In 1869 all the merchandise was housed under one roof.

1929   Just nine days before the *New York Times* blasts "Worst Stock Crash" across its front page, the eminent economist Irving Fisher proclaims in a speech, "Stock prices have reached what looks like a permanently high plateau. I do not feel that there will soon, if ever, be a fifty or sixty point break below present levels. . . . I expect to see the stock market a good deal higher than it is today within a few months." "Permanently high plateau" is now an immortal phrase, and the statement as a whole is thought by many to be the worst piece of economic analysis in history.

1989   "The last stage of fitting the product to the market is fitting the market to the product." —Clive Jones, in the *Observer*

2001   The investment community is shocked to hear the announcement of Enron CEO Kenneth Lay that the world's largest energy trader will post a $618 million loss for the third quarter. The announcement came out of nowhere and spurred a number of investigations, some by reporters and one by the Securities and Exchange Commission. Soon it came out that a further $1.2 billion had been lost in a labyrinth of partnerships that should have been, but weren't, counted on the company's books. Enron tumbled into history's biggest bankruptcy in December.

OCTOBER 17

1885   Industrial technology on the march: on this day Sir Henry Bessemer patents his blast furnace method for mass-producing the first cheap steel. In **1959** the South African diamond firm De Beers announced it had produced synthetic industrial diamonds. And in **2001**, Lucent Technologies' Bell Labs (the storied research facility that produced the first transistors) announced that it had created nanotransistors made of simple clusters of organic molecules.

1904   Amadeo Peter Giannini tells his young teller, "Vic, you may now open the front door." It was the first day of business for his Bank of Italy in San Francisco. Giannini's lending institution was designed to cater to small businesses and average citizens and to offer a range of banking services. Alone among San Francisco bankers, Giannini encouraged loans as small as $25. He was unorthodox in other ways, such as walking the streets in search of depositors and instituting eye-catching advertisements. Thus was laid the foundation for a financial institution that grew branches first through California, then overseas, finally becoming the world's largest banking corporation, the Bank of America, at the time of his death.

1919 The Radio Corporation of America (RCA) is incorporated. Fearing that important patents in the developing field of radio communications might fall into the hands of foreign governments, Assistant Secretary of the Navy Franklin D. Roosevelt asked General Electric to form a subsidiary (RCA) to take control of the technology. In return for stock, RCA acquired the radio patent rights of a stable of companies (AT&T, Westinghouse, United Fruit, GE, General Motors, and American Marconi) and began making and marketing commercial receivers called "radio music boxes." At the time there were barely 5,000 radios in American homes. Under the leadership of David Sarnoff and with improvements in technology and programming, RCA helped foster a huge demand. By 1924 there were more than 2.5 million radios in use, and RCA made most of them. When Lindbergh made his historic flight in 1927, 6 million sets could tune in to the news.

1967 "The public may be willing to forgive us for mistakes in judgment but it will not forgive us for mistakes in motive." —Robert W. Haack, president, the New York Stock Exchange, in the *Wall Street Journal*

1972 AT&T becomes the first company to have more than 3 million stockholders. Its roster hits 3,001,280 on this day.

OCTOBER 18

1648 The first labor organization in colonial America is authorized when the "shoomakers of Boston" are permitted "to assemble and meete together in Boston, at such time and times as they shall appoynt, who being so assembled, they, or the greatest number of them, shall have powre to chuse a master and two wardens, with fowre or six associates, a clarke, a sealer, a searcher, and a beadle."

1773   "A merchant may, perhaps, be a man of an enlarged mind, but there is nothing in trade connected with an enlarged mind." —Samuel Johnson, in Boswell's *Tour to the Hebrides*

1952   The C.F. Hathaway shirt company correctly anticipates a trend in the shirt industry, publishing in the *New Yorker* on this day the advertisement, "Never wear a white shirt before sundown." At the time, four out of five shirts sold in America were white, but that ratio would swing to just two of five shirts being white over the next 15 years.

2002   The nation's last major shirt factory—C.F. Hathaway in Waterville, Maine—shuts down its sewing machines forever just after noon. Like rivals Arrow and Van Heusen and several major shoe manufacturers in the area, the Hathaway production facilities moved overseas. The brand name lived on, but shirts no longer carried the "Made in the USA" label. Known for its man-with-an-eye-patch logo, Hathaway was founded in 1837 and once manufactured shirts for the Union army during the Civil War. A recent failure to win a key contract making shirts for the air force was the nail in Hathaway's coffin. The nonprofit Made in the USA Foundation was unable to find investors to take over the facility, and Windsong Allegiance Group (which operates Hathaway) could not even give away the factory's equipment to anyone with the finances to keep it going. With the closing, 235 people were put out of work.

OCTOBER 19

1885   A beacon of both integrity and business acumen and the founder of the Merrill Lynch investment firm, Charles Edward Merrill, is born in Green Cove Springs, Florida, where his father was a physician and drugstore proprietor. Merrill worked there and had a paper route as a boy, and after college he played professional baseball and had other short-term jobs until joining the small bond-sales firm of George H. Burr & Co., New York City, in 1911. He excelled as a salesman but found himself pushing the bonds of companies he knew to be teetering on bankruptcy. He loathed the task of informing investors that their money was gone, and Merrill left in disgust, forming his own partnership with Edmund C. Lynch, a former roommate and soda-fountain equipment salesman. They initially specialized in underwriting and selling securities for mass retailers such as the grocer Safeway Inc. and McCrory Stores. "Investigate, then invest" was their motto. Merrill eventually became a director of Safeway, helping it to become the nation's second largest food retailer, while at the same time learning retail techniques that were unknown to the securities industry until Merrill brought them there (see March 31 and April 1).

1904   Frank Bunker Gilbreth, 36, and Lillian Evelyn née Moller, 26, are married, thus forming what is still the most famous husband-and-wife team in the history of business consulting. Frank was a contracting engineer and Lillian a psychologist, so they were able to study the industrial process from both the mechanical and humanistic angles, and they were groundbreakers in applying the findings of social science to industrial management. They pioneered the time and motion study.

1945   The term *human engineering* is coined on this day by labor leader Walter P. Reuther, who declares in a speech to autoworkers, "It is time management realized that human engineering is just as important as mechanical engineering."

1967   "Modern economic thinking . . . is peculiarly unable to consider the long term and to appreciate man's dependence on the natural world."
—E. F. Schumacher, British economist and conservationist, in a speech at Blackpool, England

1985   The first Blockbuster Video store opens in Dallas, Texas.

1987   "By far" the worst day in the history of Wall Street. The Dow Jones Industrial Average loses 508 points, or 22.6 percent of its value. The market had lost 1,000 points since a record high in August, and it was widely believed that a recession is imminent. Again, the experts were wrong, but this time the outcome was positive. In response to today's nightmare, the Federal Reserve quickly lowered interest rates, many companies bought back their own stock, and the market stabilized. Then it recovered. By 1989 all the lost ground was regained. The securities market had come a long way since 1929 when recovery from a really bad patch took 20 years (and a war) instead of 2 years. Investors now see the crash of 1987 as a gigantic buying opportunity, and bad days on Wall Street are widely viewed as opportunities for profit.

OCTOBER 20

1902   The House of Gucci fashion dynasty has its beginnings with the marriage in Florence of Guccio Gucci, 21, and Aida Calvelli, 24, a seamstress and daughter of a tailor. Guccio had escaped his family's failing straw hat business and gone to London, where he found employment in the swank Savoy Hotel. There he fell in love with the guests' jewelry, clothes, and other riches, noticing especially the fine leather luggage. A subsequent job with a touring railroad again impressed him with the trappings of the wealthy travelers. Following his marriage to Aida, Guccio went to work for several leather companies, learning first the technical aspects of leather buying and production, then business management. The couple opened their small Florentine shop, Valigeria Guccio Gucci, on a narrow side street near the river Arno and, more importantly, near the shops that catered to the wealthy clientele that they planned to serve. By the end of the first year they were so successful that 60 craftsmen were employed and the workshop had to be moved to a larger facility.

1918   A cofounder of Litton Industries, the first modern conglomerate, Roy Lawrence Ash is born in Los Angeles, the son of a hay and grain broker. With Tex Thornton, Ash formed the Electro-Dynamics Corporation, which bought Litton Industries, a small producer of microwave tubes. They totally revamped Litton, embarking on a rage of acquisitions in which they astutely swapped shares of stock for ownership in larger companies. These companies had no necessary relationship to each other, which is the essence of a conglomerate. By 1961 they had completed 25 mergers, acquiring some 48 plants in nine countries. Litton sales first hit $1 billion in 1966. Ash was the financial and technical wizard, Thornton the promoter and visionary.

1963   "It takes twenty years to make an overnight success." —Eddie Cantor, actor and comedian, in the *New York Times*

1984   The Chinese government in Beijing announces that it will extend to urban areas the same market- and incentive-based economic reforms that it granted to farmers in 1979: wages and bonuses will be linked to job performance, prices will not be held to "irrational" levels, and each enterprise will be allowed some independence to plan its own production and marketing. The Chinese found that the capitalistic mechanisms it had tried in rural areas boosted both productivity and the standard of living.

OCTOBER 21

1856   Charles Wyman Morse—a bold and talented financier, whose increasingly large swindles culminated in the panic of 1907—is born in Bath, Maine, the son of a successful shipper who handled most of the traffic on the Kennebec River. By 1897 Morse was on Wall Street. There he established through coercion and merger the monopolistic American Ice Company. Capitalized on paper at $60 million, American Ice was one of the earliest and most flagrant examples of overcapitalized promotions in the burgeoning development of corrupt trusts. In 1900 the firm announced that the cost of ice in New York was going from 25¢ to 60¢ per 100 pounds; the public outcry led to newspapers investigating, which revealed that large blocks of American Ice stock were held by Mayor Van Wyck, Boss Crocker, and other Tammany leaders, and the docking commissioner was freezing out other companies with special privileges granted to American Ice. There was a court case and American Ice collapsed, but Morse escaped with $25 million. After similar operations in railroads, shipping, and banking, Morse joined forces with F. Augustus Heinze to take over and manipulate the stock price of the United Copper Company; the price rose from $37 to $60 but then suddenly collapsed (partly due to Morse's secret dumping of the stock). Fear led to a run on banks that Morse and Heinze controlled, which spread to other banks, producing the panic of 1907. After prison, Morse got into shipbuilding and mail fraud, was tried several more times, and ended his days in the guardianship of the probate court when he convinced the court that he was too ill to stand trial again.

1907   Monday: the panic of 1907 nears full stride. Stocks reached their lowest level since 1903 and continued to sink. A run began on one of the nation's largest trust banks, the Knickerbocker Trust Company, with lines of its 18,000 depositors forming outside its headquarters (on the site of the future Empire State Building). The Knickerbocker failed at 12:30 the following day, causing its president, Charles Barney, to shoot himself several weeks later. Major depositors also committed suicide. The 70-year-old white knight who would stop the hemorrhaging and quell the panic, J. P. Morgan, had just returned by train from the Episcopal Convention in Richmond, Virginia, declaring, "They are in trouble in New York. They do not know what to do, and I don't know what to do, but I am going back."

1998   A ban on Internet taxes is signed into U.S. law.

OCTOBER 22

1897   The first used-car dealership opens in London.

1936   History's most successful car, the Volkswagen Beetle, is given its first test-drive.

1938   Chester Carlson produces history's first Xerox copy in a closet at the back of a New York City beauty parlor. The handwritten "10-22-38 Astoria," for the date and section of the city, was the first Xerox image. Carlson's makeshift lab, where he invented the machine, was in an apartment above a bar in the same section of the city. Exactly 10 years later (1948) the first public demonstration of a Xerox machine was made before a conference of the Optical Society of America in Detroit. Joseph C. Wilson, president of the Haloid Company (later called Xerox) presided over the meeting. The machine was a red box that produced a single copy in one minute. Wilson's father, an ex-president of Haloid, predicted, "The first commercial adaptation of xerography, the XeroX Copier Machine, Model A, will be made in 1950." He was ten years too optimistic.

1953   The joys of being Aristotle Onassis: today J. Edgar Hoover informs the New York Bureau of the FBI that warrants have been issued for the arrest of Onassis and two associates, and on this day in 1971 his ex-wife Tina marries his archenemy, Stavros Niarchos.

OCTOBER 23

1823 The Prudent Man Rule is born when, in Boston, one John McLean dies, leaving $50,000 in trust for his wife, who is to live off the "profits and income thereof"; the trustees are to split what remains after her death between Harvard and Massachusetts General Hospital. When widow McLean died in 1828, both institutions sued the trustees for mismanagement because the principle had dwindled to just $29,450. In 1830 Justice Samuel Putnam issued a ruling in favor of the trustees because he felt they had acted "honestly and discreetly and carefully, according to existing circumstances, in discharge of their trusts. . . . Do what you will, the capital is at hazard. . . . All that can be required of a trustee to invest, is, that he shall conduct himself faithfully and exercise a sound discretion. He is to observe how men of prudence, discretion, and intelligence manage their own affairs, not in regard to speculation, but in regard to the permanent disposition of their funds, considering the probable income, as well as the probable safety of the capital to be invested." Putnam's statement became known as the Prudent Man Rule, and it immediately became the legal standard governing the investment and risk-taking conduct of fiduciaries.

1907 Wednesday in the panic of 1907: Morgan stops the bleeding. Stocks continued to fall, the giant Knickerbocker Trust Company had already failed, and by 9 A.M. thousands of depositors were lined up in front of the Trust Company of America. Its president, Oakleigh Thorne, tried to reassure the crowd, but the run began. At noon Thorne made his way through the crowded streets to J. P. Morgan's office and begged for an immediate $2.5 million cash injection. Morgan (whose Wednesday began in darkness with a midnight meeting with Secretary of the Treasury George B. Cortelyou) disliked the instability and reckless greed of the trust companies, but he'd seen years of economic depression wrought by similar panics. After compiling a list of Thorne's collateral and being convinced that his institution was fundamentally sound, Morgan agreed to save him. At 3 P.M. the money was carried out of Morgan's bank in suitcases. Through the day Morgan also organized a group of banks to establish a further $10 million fund to dam up any subsequent bank runs, and he learned that George Cortelyou had placed an additional $25 million at his disposal. Morgan put out the word that if any big speculators did anything to further depress stock prices during the crisis, he would crush them.

1940   The distinguished life of George B. Cortelyou comes to an end at age 78. He was a teacher, principal, and court reporter before entering the White House as the stenographer to President Grover Cleveland. He served as the private secretary of President Teddy Roosevelt, who appointed him as the first head of the new cabinet-level Department of Commerce and Labor. He was later made postmaster general, and in 1907 was appointed secretary of the treasury, where he was central to staunching the Panic of 1907 (see above). He then concentrated on creating a central banking system until 1909, when he entered the private sector as the president of the Consolidated Edison power company.

1960   "The Chinese laundry doesn't have to compete; it's competed against." —C. M. Tan, Chinese Consolidated Benevolent Association, in the *New York Herald Tribune*

OCTOBER 24

1907   Thursday in the panic of 1907: J. P. Morgan keeps the New York Stock Exchange open. Despite the Morgan-engineered infusion of cash, several more banks experienced runs, and trading on the NYSE came to a standstill. Ransom H. Thomas, president of the NYSE, crossed Broad Street to Morgan's office at about noon and told Morgan that unless $25 million was raised immediately, at least 50 brokerage firms were imperiled. Thomas wanted to close the NYSE. Morgan ordered that it close at its normal time, 3:00: "*It must not close one minute before that hour today!*" He knew that an irregular closing would only fuel the panic. At 2:00 Morgan summoned the heads of the city's major banks and warned that unless $25 million were raised in 10 or 12 minutes, dozens of brokerages would fail. By 2:16 the money was pledged.

Morgan then dispatched a team to the NYSE floor, announcing the money was available for just 10 percent interest (earlier in the day, desperate brokers had been willing to borrow at 100 percent interest, but there were no lenders). The floor erupted in joy.

1929   Black Thursday: the *New York World* front-page headline declares "Market in Panic as Stocks Are Dumped in 12,894,600 Share Day; Bankers Halt It." Today began the most devastating of all Wall Street crashes and the Great Depression.

1940   The 40-hour workweek goes into effect under the Fair Labor Standards Act of 1938.

2003   Forbes.com publishes its list of top-earning dead people. Elvis Presley led the group with an annual income of about $40 million. Following the music artist came the cartoonist Charles M. Schulz ($32 million); J. R. R. Tolkien ($22 million); John Lennon ($19 million); George Harrison ($16 million); Dr. Seuss ($16 million); Dale Earnhardt ($15 million); Tupac Shakur ($12 million); and Bob Marley ($9 million). Rounding out the top ten was actress/icon Marilyn Monroe (with a mere $8 million per year).

2003   The age of supersonic passenger travel comes to an end. A triple landing ceremony was held at London's Heathrow airport as the last Concorde, from New York, touched down at 4:05 P.M. "Concorde was born from dreams, built with vision, and operated with pride," said the pilot, Captain Michael Bannister. A technological marvel, Concorde was an expensive commercial flop. It also used enormous amounts of fuel, created wild noise pollution, and emitted unique forms of air pollution. Said a Heathrow-area resident who had no objection to the noise, "It's like wearing stilettos. They hurt your feet, but you know they look a lot sexier than ordinary shoes."

OCTOBER 25

1870   The Averill Chemical Paint Company of New York City registers a "trade-mark for liquid paint." It was the first official trademark in U.S. history and was filed under an act passed earlier in the year, which was eventually declared unconstitutional. The Lanham Act of 1946 established the current system of trademark protection.

1907   Friday in the panic of 1907: J. P. Morgan organizes cash and religious leaders. Eight banks and trust companies had already failed, and the stock exchange remained in peril, as call money available to brokers shot back up to exorbitant rates. Morgan walked to the New York Clearing House (the banker's organization for clearing checks) and convinced its officials to issue scrip as emergency currency to relieve the serious shortage of cash. In the evening he called in religious leaders from different faiths and urged them to preach calm in the weekend's services.

1959   "People don't choose their careers; they are engulfed by them." —John Dos Passos, novelist, in the *New York Times*

1976   "Where would the Rockefellers be today if old John D. had gone on selling short-weight kerosene . . . to widows and orphans instead of wisely deciding to mulct [defraud] the whole country." —S. J. Perelman, humorist and playwright

1997   "A stockbroker is someone who takes all your money and invests it until it's gone." —Woody Allen, filmmaker/humorist, in the *Economist*

OCTOBER 26

1854   Charles William Post—founder of the Postum Cereal Company, the parent company of General Foods—is born the son of a grain and farm equipment dealer in Springfield, Illinois. In 1891, in rapidly failing health, he entered the famous sanitarium in Battle Creek, Michigan, run by the Kellogg brothers. He not only recovered his health, he found his life's calling: the manufacture of healthful foods. He started by founding his own institution in Battle Creek, La Vita Inn, which healed by the practice of mental suggestion. He then began experimenting with a cereal beverage he had been given as a coffee substitute by the Kelloggs. First calling it Monk's Brew, he changed the name to Postum and advertised it heavily as a builder of red blood. That change brought commercial success. In the same year, 1896, he developed Postum cereal, and in the following year he created Grape-Nuts. Among subsequent successes were Post Toasties (like others of his products, this was in direct competition with a product of his saviors, the Kellogg brothers), Post's Bran Flakes, and Post's Chocolate Bar, all of which he advertised heavily. By 1900 Post's factories covered 20 acres in Battle Creek, employed 2,500 people, and formed the largest compound of its kind in the world. By 1914, when he committed suicide at age 59, his fortune was worth $20 million. His daughter, Marjorie Merriweather Post, took over his business and grew it, and it was she who was the principle creator of General Foods in 1929.

1957 "Never invest your money in anything that eats or needs repainting." —Billy Rose, theatrical impresario and composer, in the *New York Post*

1999 Punctuating technology's dominance on Wall Street and Main Street, Intel and Microsoft are to be added to the Dow Jones Industrial Average, announces the *Wall Street Journal*, the creator and custodian of the 30-company index. The two corporations would be the first from the tech-heavy NASDAQ stock market to be listed on the Dow. Indicative of the shift in the entire economy away from "smokestack" enterprises, they replaced the once-great Chevron and Goodyear. It was also announced today that Sears Roebuck and Union Carbide would be replaced on the Dow by Home Depot and the Baby Bell telephone company SBC Communications.

1999 "Whatever you shoot is dead for a while before it starts to stink. The same goes for strategies. How many organizations carry this dead thing around with them, unaware of its irrelevancy until it's too late?" —Gary Hamel, academic/business writer/consultant, in a lecture

OCTOBER 27

1811 Inventor/marketer Isaac Merrit Singer is born in Pittstown, New York (see July 23).

1858 R.H. Macy Company opens as a fancy drygoods store with an 11-foot frontage on Sixth Avenue near 14th Street in Manhattan. Until now Macy (born in 1822) had seemed like an incompetent drifter, shipping out on a whaling ship at age 15, then establishing several failed retail establishments. He enjoyed moderate success in the California gold rush and in small-scale land speculation, and with that money and the advance of some merchandise by jobbers, he was able to stock the two long counters in his store with ribbons, gloves, lace, embroideries, hosiery, and the like. His first day's receipts were $11.06, but gross sales for the following year were $90,000. In the next century Macy's would become the world's largest department store in terms of sales volume. From the outset his policy was buying for cash, selling for cash, setting prices that beat competitors, and using plenty of modern-sounding advertising. Three percent of his sales went to advertising, while his competitors typically spent just 1 percent. Profits were plowed back into the store. The location of the store, at a central crossroads in the city, undoubtedly aided in its great success.

1929   A seminal figure in management history, Peter F. Drucker, 19, publishes his first paper on econometrics in a prestigious European journal. The paper presented a model of the New York Stock Exchange, which proved "with impeccable assumptions that the New York Stock Exchange could only go up." Two days later the stock market crashed. "That's when I stopped—or tried to stop—making predictions," quipped Drucker.

1984   "We are tough and brave in war. We are soft and compromising in business." —Michael Owen Edwardes, British company executive, speaking about British managers

1997   The Wall Street roller coaster hits a milestone. For the first time "circuit-breaker rules" were invoked to halt trading just after 2 P.M. News of a 6 percent drop in the Hong Kong index at the day's start had produced steady sell-off, which picked up intensity and indicated a stampede might be in progress. By 2:00 the Dow had lost a whopping 323.42 points, and it was then that trading was stopped. The circuit-breaker rules were passed in the wake of the 1987 market crash and mandated trading halts, or "cooling off" periods, when extraordinary market drops indicated a disaster might be coming. On the following day, the market rebounded dramatically, with the Dow picking up 337.1 points. It was a record gain.

OCTOBER 28

1847   "The father of modern advertising," James Walter Thompson, is born in Pittsfield, Massachusetts. Thompson got a job in New York City with William J. Carlton, who ran a small advertising agency. Thompson became an advertising solicitor and in 1878 purchased the business and continued it under his own name. He was one of the first to recognize the importance of housewives as buyers and also one of the first to see that magazines were the most effective way to reach housewives. He also realized that there would be great advantage to both the advertiser and the publishers if he could unite a number of different magazines in a widespread campaign. He was the first to mount national ad campaigns—for Mennen Talcum Powder, Eastman Kodak, and the "Rock of Gibralter" campaign for the Prudential Insurance Company. By 1900 JWT had a virtual monopoly on the country's magazine advertising, serving as the advertising representative for more than 100 foreign and domestic magazines. At the same time JWT was gradually changing the role of the ad agency from a seller of space to a representative of the advertisers. Thompson is also given credit for being the first to use the back cover of magazines for ads. He died October 16, 1928.

1907   The second Monday in the panic of 1907: J. P. Morgan saves New York City. At 4:00 in the afternoon Morgan was visited in his library by the mayor of New York, George B. McClellan, and other officials, who said the city would be forced into bankruptcy if $30 million could not be raised immediately to pay on short-term bonds. Knowing that the city's failure could inflame a national financial panic that had flared up repeatedly the previous week, over the next two days Morgan organized a bank syndicate to buy $30 million of the city's 6 percent revenue bonds for cash, with an option to purchase $20 million more.

1929   On this Monday, stocks on Wall Street are slaughtered in all directions, with on-paper losses estimated at $10 billion. The Dow Jones lost 12.82 percent of its value, a record at the time. The following day would be worse.

1955   Cofounder of Microsoft, William Henry Gates III is born the son of a lawyer and a teacher in a socially prominent family in Seattle,

Washington. Intelligent but overactive and prone to trouble in school, Gates was sent to the private Lakeside School at age 11, and it was here that he first became acquainted with computers and Paul Allen, the classmate who would be his partner in starting Microsoft in 1975.

1958   The first woman to serve as a director of a U.S. stock exchange was Mary Gindhart Roebling, of the Trenton Trust Company, New Jersey, who on this day becomes one of the 32 governors of the American Stock Exchange of New York City. She was one of the three public members who were not connected with the Wall Street community.

OCTOBER 29

1896   "Few rich men own their own property. The property owns them." —Robert Green Ingersoll, lawyer and writer, in an address to the McKinley League, New York City

1923   The post–World War I reparations demanded of Germany destroyed its economy. On this day a tourist walks into one of the lesser restaurants in Berlin and instructs the waiter, "Give me all the food an American dollar will buy." The incident was captured by a reporter for the *New York Times*. Soup, several meat dishes, fruit, and coffee were served. The guest was smoking his cigar at the end of the meal when another plate of soup and then another meat dish were brought out. "What does this mean?" asked the astonished diner. The waiter bowed politely and replied, "The dollar has just gone up again."

1929   Four days after President Hoover declared, "The fundamental business of the country . . . is on a sound and prosperous basis," Black Tuesday hits Wall Street. It was a true panic in selling. The Great Depression began from this day when 16,410,030 shares were dumped. Many large blocks of shares were thrown on the market without takers. The Dow Jones Industrial Average lost 11 percent of its value, less than the previous day's loss, but psychologically today's devastation was worse. The bottom had fallen out of the market, and there was apparently nothing holding it up. Bankers' pools, which in the past had stopped all-out selling panics, had proved ineffective days ago. Elliot V. Bell of the *New*

York Times reported, "Groups of men, with here and there a woman, stood about inverted glass bowls all over the city yesterday watching spools of ticker tape unwind and as the tenuous paper with its cryptic numerals grew longer at their feet their fortunes shrunk."

1931   "We are the first nation in the history of the world to go to the poor house in an automobile." —Will Rogers, in a radio broadcast

1982   "If a man goes into business with only the idea of making money, the chances are he won't." This wisdom came from the founder of Hallmark Cards, Joyce Clyde Hall, who dies today at age 90 in Leawood, Kansas (see December 29).

OCTOBER 30

1877   Herbert William Hoover—founder of the Hoover Vacuum Company—is born in New Berlin (now North Canton), Ohio, into a family with a prosperous harness and tannery business. The family shifted with the times and began making parts for automobiles in the early 1900s. Hoover and his two younger brothers entered the family business and became lifelong partners. They remained on the lookout for new products, and the vacuum cleaner was dropped in their lap by James Murray Spangler, an inventor who was down on his luck and working as a janitor. Spangler had developed a chronic cough from theater dust during his cleaning and in 1908 patented his solution to the problem. He demonstrated the machine to his cousin, Hoover's mother. The family took over Spangler's failing business and installed Hoover as the new manager. The marketing was aggressive and wise, employing print ads and door-to-door salesmen. A network of independent dealers not only provided local service and an easy means of demonstration, but also allowed for future growth; 372 machines were sold in 1908, and 3,926 were sold in 1912 (a 10-fold increase in four years).

1894   Daniel M. Cooper of Rochester, New York, patents the familiar—and to some, odious symbol—employee time clock, in which the worker inserts his time card and "punches in." In this original version, the employee pressed a lever to activate the machine after the card was inserted. The recorder, called the Rochester, was manufactured by the Willard and Frick Manufacturing Company.

1956   "Doing business without advertising is like winking at a girl in the dark. You know what you are doing, but nobody else does." —Steuart Henderson Britt, advertising consultant, in the *New York Herald Tribune*

OCTOBER 31

1875   The eminent financier, banker, and public official Eugene Meyer, Jr.—the father of publisher Katharine Graham—is born in Los Angeles, the son of a French immigrant merchant.

1977   *New York* magazine publishes the first review of *Close Encounters of the Third Kind*. Business reporter William Flanagan had snuck into a Dallas theater where the much-anticipated movie was being shown privately, so that he could be the first with a review in print. Titled "An Encounter with 'Close Encounters,'" the review predicted that the film would be a huge commercial failure. "It lacks the dazzle, charm, wit, imagination and broad audience appeal of *Star Wars*, the film Wall Street insists it measure up to," Flanagan wrote. The day the article appeared, the stock of Columbia Pictures, producers of *Close Encounters*, dropped $1.375 a share on a large volume of shares. The following day the influx of sell orders was so great that the New York Stock Exchange refused to permit trading of Columbia shares until noon. The stock promptly dropped another $1.50. Soon *Time* magazine published a rave review by critic Frank Rich, calling it "a dazzling movie [that] reaches the viewer at a far more profound level than *Star Wars*." Eventually the movie and the stock soared, despite the rocky start.

1983   "I doubt if there is any occupation which is more consistently and unfairly demeaned, degraded, denounced, and deplored than banking." —William Proxmire, politician, in *Fortune*

1999   The stock market launch of ENEL, Italy's state-owned electricity producer and marketer, becomes the world's largest-ever initial public offering of stock; $19.26 billion worth of shares are sold.

NOVEMBER

NOVEMBER 1

1798   Irish brewer Sir Benjamin Lee Guinness is born in Dublin where his father runs the Arthur Guinness and Sons domestic brewery. Benjamin assumed control of the company in 1825, destined to make it one of the largest breweries in the world. He developed a large export trade of porter and stout to the United States, England, and Europe, and thus founded his fortune.

1927   The Ford Motor Company begins production of the Model A, its first new model in decades. Though hugely successful, the Model T had outlasted its usefulness and was losing market share rapidly to more powerful, more stylish, more comfortable, and more option-packed cars offered by rival manufacturers. Henry Ford had essentially produced the modern automobile industry but had missed one of its offshoot trends—the desire for continual update, especially updating to more expensive models as one's economic status improved. Ford was not graceful in its changeover from the Model T to the Model A; production lines were shut down abruptly in May and sat idle for half a year while the Model A was developed and the lines retooled. Five million Model As were sold by the time production ended in early 1932. On the day the Model A appeared for sale in December, after a nationwide advertising blitz, 50,000 cash deposits were received in New York alone, and mob scenes at dealerships led to showroom windows being blown out.

1942   "Save your money, young man. Save your energy. Save yourself a lot of disappointment" were the words of discouragement from the great civil rights leader Roy Wilkins to John H. Johnson, who had come to New York to discuss his dream of founding a magazine for black America. When Johnson went for his first loan, the refusal was a harsh

"Boy, we don't make loans to colored people." Johnson, 24, finally found the $500 he needed (from the white-owned Citizens Loan Corporation; Johnson had to put up his mother's furniture as collateral) to mail out 20,000 letters announcing his new *Negro Digest*. The mass mailing elicited 3,000 founding subscribers; the $6,000 they paid in was enough to print the inaugural issue, which hit a few newsstands on this date. Most newsstands would not take it. In the first of many marketing coups in his publishing career, Johnson sent friends to repeatedly ask for *Negro Digest* at the Chicago outlets of the major distributor Joseph Levy. Responding to the grassroots demand, Levy bought out the remaining 2,000 copies of the first issue. Within eight months *Negro Digest* had a national circulation of 50,000. It was the first commercial success for the niche market of black Americans, coming at a time before niche marketing was a concept. Johnson pulled off another coup when he attracted Eleanor Roosevelt to write one of his regular features, "If I Were a Negro" for the October 1943 cover story. "If I were a Negro," began Mrs. Roosevelt, "I would have great bitterness." The article garnered national attention and helped boost circulation to 100,000.

1945   *Negro Digest* publisher John H. Johnson brings the first issue of *Ebony* to the newsstands. Within hours the 25,000-copy press run was sold out, and Johnson ordered another 25,000 printed. Johnson loved putting beautiful black women on *Ebony* covers, and in March 1946 his first four-color cover was graced by Lena Horne. It sold 275,000 copies. The following year *Ebony* became the first black magazine tracked by the Audit Bureau of Circulations, registering a circulation of 309,715.

1951   John H. Johnson brings the first issue of *Jet* magazine to the newsstands, with Edna Robinson (wife of boxer Sugar Ray Robinson) on the cover. Within six months *Jet* had a circulation of 300,000 copies per week.

1988   "I've always realized that if I'm doing well at business I'm cutting some other bastard's throat." —Kerry Packer, Australian entrepreneur, in the *Daily Mail*

NOVEMBER 2

1867 The nation's first fashion weekly magazine, *Harper's Bazaar*, debuts. The "repository of fashion, pleasure and instruction" was 16 pages long, cost 10¢ an issue, and was published by Harper & Bros. in New York City. The first editor was Mary Louise Booth. In May 1901 *Harper's* became a monthly.

1932 William Morris, founder of one of the world's foremost talent agencies, dies at age 59 in New York City. Born in Schwarzenau, Germany, Morris came to New York where he was hired by Klaw and Erlanger to book acts for their chain of vaudeville theaters. When the Keith-Albee United Booking Office, which was seeking to monopolize the industry, bought out Klaw and Erlinger, Morris managed theatrical acts independently, with the popular Harry Lauder as his largest star. When theaters were closed to Lauder, Morris appealed to the "trust buster" President Teddy Roosevelt, who personally backed the opening of the entertainment industry. *Variety* magazine also supported Morris against the monopolies, which helped the William Morris Agency get rooted. Morris's son took over the agency, serving as its president from 1932 to 1950.

1955 Kermit the Frog, the first of Jim Henson's Muppets, is copyright registered.

1983 The Dodge Caravan, the first minivan, rolls off the assembly line at Chrysler's plant in Windsor, Ontario. Called "a breadbox on wheels," the minivan replaced the station wagon as the car of choice to transport families. It was embraced by baby boomers, who made it a fixture in the suburban landscape (the vehicle has largely been pushed aside by Generation X, who have made the SUV the most popular family vehicle). Although all major manufacturers produced minivans of their own, Chrysler always held the lion's share of the market, and by the end of 2003, had produced well over 10 million units.

1986 "Having money is rather like being a blond. It is more fun but not vital." —Mary Quant, British fashion designer, in the *Observer*

NOVEMBER 3

1907   The final Sunday in the panic of 1907: J. P. Morgan brings lasting calm. The crisis had been quiet on Wall Street for several days, but key trust companies and at least one major brokerage were still very shaky; the failure of any of them could reignite the panic. Morgan would cement the calm on Wall Street if the trusts united to create a huge fund to help the shakiest among them. Late on this afternoon 125 financial executives were summoned into the Morgan Library in New York City. In the West Room trust company presidents met with explicit instructions to create a $25 million fund to put the Trust Company of America and Lincoln Trust on firm footing. In the East Room commercial bankers gathered to come up with $25 million more to further support the market and to make solvent the stock brokerage of Moore & Schley. The meetings proceeded all night, with Morgan sitting in a side chamber, alternately cajoling and rumbling at trust executives whom he summoned one at a time. At one point Benjamin Strong of Bankers Trust tried to leave through the main door; it was locked. The key was in Morgan's pocket. At 4:45 in the morning Morgan abruptly entered the West Room to find the trust executives in hopeless indecision. He made the case strongly for a group effort, citing his own efforts and risks to calm the markets. "There's the place, King," he finally said to Edward King, the exhausted leader of the trust presidents, pointing to a signature line on the final agreement, "and here's the pen."

1966   The Fair Packaging and Labeling Act is signed into law by President Lyndon Johnson. Labels now had to provide details of a product's contents and manufacturing, clearly state the net weight of the package, and not use misleading phrases like "jumbo ounces" or fake "cents off" or "economy size" designations. The law stopped short of creating uniform weight standards, asking manufacturers instead to "voluntarily" devise their own standards.

1997   "Oil-price forecasters make sheep seem like independent thinkers. There's no evidence that mineral prices rise over time. Technology always overwhelms depletion." —Michael C. Lynch, Scottish historian, in *BusinessWeek*

1999   Packard Bell, once the largest domestic maker of personal computers in the United States, will cease production by the end of the year, announces Tokyo-based parent company NEC Corp. Packard Bell's decline was rapid, going in just a few years from the number one spot to number six by this summer. Sixteen hundred jobs, including those of 12 of the company's 13 senior executives, were lost.

NOVEMBER 4

1698   With the aim of establishing trade with Africa and the Indies, the first ships of the Company of Scotland reach Darien (the Isthmus of Panama). Among the 1,200 pioneers were William Paterson— founder of the Bank of England—and his wife and child, both of whom would soon perish. They called the country New Caledonia and chose to settle on a well-defended spot with a good harbor midway between two Spanish strongholds. It must have been a sunny day. The venture lasted about a year, ended by disease, lack of provisions, and anarchy. Paterson was carried aboard a homeward-bound ship in June, looking "more like a skeleton than a man."

1841   Rubber manufacturer Benjamin Franklin Goodrich is born in Ripley, New York. With his rubber manufacturing company in Hastings-on-the-Hudson facing stiff competition, Goodrich decided to look for other locales to move to. Goodrich came upon an advertisement from the Board of Trade of Akron, Ohio, trying to lure new industry into the area. Thanks to Goodrich and his eventual success, Akron became the center of the rubber industry in the United States.

1842   "Throw theory into the fire; it only spoils life." —Mikhail A. Bukanin, anarchist whose theoretical differences with Marx split the European revolutionary movement in half, in a letter to his sisters

1907   The last Monday in the panic of 1907: the market recovers and J. P. Morgan gets his payoff. Morgan's plan to permanently calm the panic involved saving the stock brokerage firm of Moore & Schley (see November 3). A major holding of Moore & Schley, the Tennessee Coal and Iron Company, was to be taken over by Morgan's U.S. Steel monopoly. All parties would benefit, but the transaction would be illegal for Morgan under antitrust laws. Only the monopoly-hating President Teddy Roosevelt could let the deal go through. Why should he do it? For a start, Morgan had saved the New York Stock Exchange, had saved the U.S. economy from potentially years of depression, and had saved New York City—all in the last two weeks. Also, if Moore & Schley was still in trouble by the 10:00 opening of the stock markets, all hell could break loose. Early on this day, after a midnight train ride from New York, Morgan lieutenants Henry C. Frick and Elbert Gary reached Washington, and just after 9:00 were in conference with Roosevelt. At 9:50 A.M. Roosevelt made up his mind. His language, normally so emphatic, showed the pressure and conflict he was under: "I do not believe that anyone could justly criticize me for saying that I would not feel like objecting to the purchase under the circumstances." The word spread rapidly over Wall Street. Lines at trust companies dissolved, and on Wednesday (there was no trading on Tuesday due to Election Day), the market showed its first gain in weeks.

NOVEMBER 5

1855   Two of the major checks against abuses by predatory business-men are organized labor and investigative journalists. Two giants in these fields share the same birthday. On this day in Terre Haute, Indiana, the great labor leader Eugene Victor Debs is born; and on this day in 1857, one of the original muckrakers, Ida Minerva Tarbell, was born in Erie County, Pennsylvania, just a few miles from Titusville, where the American oil industry began. Tarbell's career was established by her exposure of corruption and abuses within the oil industry.

1982   In reporting on a study of more than 30,000 business telephone accounts over the past 15 years, syndicated financial columnist Sylvia Porter writes, "Billing mistakes were uncovered in a full 45 percent of them!"

1990   "When nobody wants something, that creates an opportunity." —Carl C. Icahn, financier and corporate raider, referring to buying into Texaco when it was in trouble, in *Fortune*

1991   Czech-born, London-based publishing magnate Robert Maxwell, 68, (née Ludvik Hoch) mysteriously disappears from his luxury yacht off the Canary Islands, and his nude body is later found in the Atlantic Ocean. Maxwell had just bought the strike-bound *New York Daily News* for $40 million in March, and just before his death it was discovered that the proud man had secretly siphoned $1.2 billion from two of his flagship public companies and from employee pension funds in an effort to keep his empire from collapsing. Death by his own hand was thus suspected.

1999   U.S. District Judge Thomas Penfield Jackson declares Microsoft Corporation a monopoly, stating that the software giant's aggressive tactics were "stifling innovation" and hurting customers. "Microsoft has demonstrated that it will use its prodigious market power to harm any firm that insists on pursuing initiatives that could intensify competition," he stated. Billionaire founder of the company Bill Gates had a different, flag-draped opinion: "At the heart of this case is whether a successful American company can continue to improve its products for the benefit of consumers." Wall Street shrugged off the ruling; the Dow Jones Industrial Average, which had included Microsoft for only a week, rose slightly, as did the tech-heavy NASDAQ (reaching a record high for the seventh day in a row). Microsoft lost $1\frac{1}{8}$, down to $89\frac{15}{16}$. The stock of Microsoft's dark horse rival, Red Hat (a leading producer of Linux software), shot up $18\frac{1}{16}$ to 104.

NOVEMBER 6

1851   Charles Henry Dow—the "Dow" in the Dow Jones Industrial Average—is born in Sterling, Connecticut. After several newspaper reporting jobs, Dow arrived in New York City in 1880 as a financial reporter for the Kiernan News Agency. Another employee, Charles Bergstresser, had invented a stylus that could record the news onto 35 sheets or bulletins simultaneously, a technique that quadrupled productivity. In 1882, when Kiernan refused Bergstresser's proposal for equity partnership in return for his time-saving invention, Bergstresser persuaded Dow and another Kiernan reporter, Edward Jones, to form a new company, Dow Jones & Company. Their business was preparing and distributing bulletins (called "flimsies," or "slips") to Wall Street financial houses via messengers. A year later Bergstresser convinced his partners to become the first Wall Street news service to acquire their own printing press, which doubled their productivity. In that same year, they began including a sheet of principle news items with the day's last financial bulletin. Also available separately, that sheet was the forerunner of the *Wall Street Journal* (which was first published under its current name on July 8, 1889). Coincident with the founding of the *Wall Street Journal* was the creation of the Dow Jones Industrial Average, a measurement of how a sampling of key stocks (12 stocks at the beginning) performed on any given day. General Electric is the only company from the original list of 12 that survives on today's list of 30. Dow Jones exploited the telegraph to become the first American financial publisher to cover London and the first in New York to cover Boston (buying bulletins from Clarence Barron for 10¢ a word for their afternoon news sheet). In 1897, again at Bergstresser's urging, Dow Jones installed the first broad-tape ticker on Wall Street; the advance allowed words, not just symbols and numbers, to be printed. Advertising their advanced services with the slogan "News Carried by Electricity, Printed by Electricity," Dow Jones was now a three-product company: ticker, bulletins, and the *Wall Street Journal*.

1893   Edsel Bryant Ford, Henry's only legitimate child and heir, is born in Detroit. His first name came from Edsel Ruddiman, Henry's best boyhood friend.

1923   The best-known and most frequently studied case of hyperinflation was Germany in 1923. On this day the circulation of the Reichsbank mark reached 400,338,325,350,700,000,000. Inflation was 355,700 million times 1913 levels.

1998   "At its most basic level, a market represents an agreement between two people. For that market to sustain long-term health, those two people must honor that agreement. They must trust each other . . . you can have all the technology and global forces you want, but it's useless if basic trust does not exist." —Arthur Levitt, Jr., former chairman, the Securities and Exchange Commission

NOVEMBER 7

1876 America finally gets a good cigarette-making machine when Albert Hook of New York City patents the nation's first cigarette-manufacturing device. It produced a continuous filled tube of indeterminate length, which was then sliced into individual cigarettes. It was invented in 1872 and put into practical commercial use in 1882.

1886 Telephone executive and organization theorist Chester I. Barnard is born in Malden, Massachusetts. *Functions of the Executive* (1938) was his groundbreaking analysis of management. He died June 7, 1961.

1923 "Yet nothing is more apparent than that politically, economically, and philosophically the motive of self-interest not only is, but must be, and ought to be, the mainspring of human conduct. . . . The world continues to offer glittering prizes to those who have stout hearts and sharp swords." —Frederick E. Smith, British politician and former Lord High Chancellor of Great Britain

NOVEMBER 8

1656 The great mathematician and natural scientist Edmond Halley is born in a country home in Haggerston, near London. The intellectual gifts that allowed Halley to calculate and predict the orbit of the comet that bears his name were the same gifts that allowed him to create the first actuarial tables, a cornerstone of the life insurance industry.

1836 Parlor game manufacturer and inventor Milton Bradley is born in Vienna, Maine. He settled in Springfield, where he opened the first lithography business in western Massachusetts. During the Civil War jobs were scarce, so Bradley came up with the idea of printing parlor games. An early creation was The Checkered Game of Life; on the basis of its commercial success (he personally peddled the games throughout New York State), he organized Milton Bradley & Co. with two partners in 1864. The Milton Bradley Company was organized in 1878 when his partners retired. As the company matured, Bradley took a special interest in producing games and printed materials for and about kindergarten-aged children. Bradley was a founder of the American game industry and through that changed the way Americans spent their leisure. His company remains vibrant to this day, though not every product succeeds. "We once had a game called Happiness, which stressed the need to help one another out and was not too competitive," said Dr. Dorothy Worcester, psychologist and vice president of market research, in 1979. "It bombed." Bradley died on May 30, 1911.

1956   Now a synonym for business failure, "Edsel" is chosen as the name for the new Ford automobile. The name was that of Henry Ford's only legitimate child, who served as the Ford president from 1919 until his death in 1943. After 12 months of research and analysis and the amassing of 18,000 possible alternatives by the Ford advertising agency, the choice came down to six final names to be considered on this day by the Ford executive committee. (At the start of the name search, the Pulitzer Prize–winning poet Marianne Moore was asked to contribute ideas. "Utopian Turtletop," "Andante con Motor," and "The Resilient Bullet" were among her offerings.) The committee sat unimpressed through the presentation and discussion of each of the six finalists. Chairing the meeting in place of Henry Ford II was Ernest Breech, who finally said in disgust that he didn't like any of them. "Why don't we just call it Edsel?" he asked.

1964   "Capitalism is using its money; we socialists throw it away." —Fidel Castro, in the *Observer*

2001   *Science* magazine reports an amazing breakthrough in computer technology: transistors made of single molecules. They were so small that 10 million fit on the head of a pin. The invention was the work of Zhenan Bao, Hong Meng, and Hendrik Schon of the Bell Labs, the same organization that invented the first transistors in 1947.

NOVEMBER 9

1801   Food-process inventor and industrialist Gail Borden is born in Norwich, New York, on the family farm. In 1833 Borden was in the developing territory of Texas, where he became familiar with the hardships of pioneer life. One of the most pressing needs was carrying sufficient food on migrations, which sparked the idea of preparing food in concentrated form. Borden was 50 when he conducted his first experiment. He developed a meat biscuit and invested all his money in a manufacturing plant. Though the product had obvious value, Borden was beaten by established army food contractors and lost his entire fortune. While on his way to London in 1851 to receive a medal for the biscuit, he was impressed by the plight of immigrant children who lacked a supply of wholesome milk. It was this that got him working on his first big hit, concentrated milk, the process which he patented in 1856. The Civil War created immediate demand for his products; successful response by the military convinced the general public that his products were wholesome and safe. Borden died January 11, 1874.

1933   Harry Hopkins, the most devoted of Franklin Roosevelt's lieutenants during the Great Depression, pushes through a presidential executive order that establishes the Civil Works Administration. With initial capital of $480 million, the CWA would create immediate jobs for 4 million unemployed people. Hopkins was a strong proponent of getting money directly to the poor. To a congressional appropriations committee member who mentioned the "long-term view," Hopkins shot back, "People don't eat in the long term, Senator. They eat every day."

1961   In Liverpool, England, an unknown record store manager named Brian Epstein enters the Cavern nightclub to hear a little-known local band called The Beatles.

1981   T. Rowe Price astounds Wall Street again. On this day, mortgage money was unavailable and building stocks were pariahs, yet Price recommended 15 of them in *Forbes* magazine. By year's end they had all handily outperformed the averages. Price pioneered growth stock investing in the 1930s but was among the first to recommend cutting back on them in the 1960s when they had become a religion and institutions were buying them eagerly. "I never took a course in economics or investments in school or college," Price said after six decades of successful investing. "I graduated in chemistry. Fortunately, I learned in 1931 that I did not have the ability to guess the ups and downs of the stock market averages or the trends in individual stocks. I learned that most of the big fortunes of the country were made by people retaining ownership of successful business enterprises that continued to grow and prosper over a long period of years. . . . It was obvious that to be a successful investor it was not necessary to know what the stock market was going to do."

NOVEMBER 10

1817   The first monopolistic trust in America is organized on this date by the salt manufacturers of Kanawha, West Virginia. The Kanawha Salt Company was formed for the purpose of controlling the quantity of salt manufactured, the method of manufacture, the packing, the production, and the price. The company disbanded on January 1, 1822.

1918   Sir Pao Yue-kong, one of Asia's richest and most powerful businessmen, with the world's largest independent shipping fleet and a corporate fortune of $4 billion, is born in Ningbo, China. Pao was a Shanghai banker until fleeing from the Communists in 1949 to Hong Kong, where he established an import-export business. In 1955 he bought a second-hand freighter, and by 1980 World-Wide Shipping was a fleet of 200 ships. Pao diversified into finance and valuable Hong Kong real estate when he correctly anticipated a slump in worldwide shipping. He was known for close relations with many world leaders, was knighted in 1978, and unlike many colleagues, maintained good relations with Communist China.

1929   "The stock market is just like a sieve . . . through the holes . . . the little investors go. They pick themselves up, do something to get some money, and then . . . away they go again." —Will Rogers, humorist and social commentator, in the *Tulsa Daily World*

1981   The smash-hit board game Trivial Pursuit is trademark registered.

2004   Another smash-hit quiz product, the television show *Wheel of Fortune*, airs its 4,000th episode from New York's Radio City Music Hall. *Wheel* had been television's most-watched syndicated series since 1984. "With all the technology that's available to us, we stick with this giant carnival wheel that goes clunk, clunk, clunk," said host Pat Sajak. "But people love our clunking."

NOVEMBER 11

1863   Heir to the Armour meatpacking corporation, Jonathan Ogden Armour is born in Milwaukee. In 1901 he took over direction of the firm with the death of his father and its founder Philip D. Armour. Jonathan shared several of his father's business traits: the ability to grow a company (Jonathan brought sales to $200 million in 1900 and to $1 billion in 1920); involvement in the wider business community (both were members of the Chicago Board of Trade and directors of many corporations); and involvement in scandals (Philip was part of the "embalmed beef" scandal of 1898–99, and Jonathan lost financial control of the company in 1923 and faced charges of fraud in 1926). He died August 16, 1927.

1873   The founder of the Campbell Soup company, John Thompson Dorrance, is born in Bristol, Pennsylvania (see September 21).

1901   The Nabisco insignia is trademark registered. The company was born of strife in 1898, when two giant bakery groups, New York Biscuit and American Biscuit, called a truce to eight years of warfare. A number of independent bakers and a third large producer, United States Baking, were brought in at the same time to form the National Biscuit Company. Its first leader was Chicago lawyer Adolphus W. Green, who declared, "We should all fight together, not fight each other." Green successfully united all of the warring parties (melding them into a single network of bakeries nationwide, all producing the same items in the same way) and was instrumental in three other key changes: creating new packaging to keep crackers fresher, establishing a single brand-name cracker across the country (Uneeda was the first baked good to fill this role), and instituting massive advertising at a time when few realized the importance of advertising. As to the familiar Nabisco trademark, consisting of an oval under a double-bar cross, the design is a replica of that used by the Society of Printers in 15th-century Venice; it symbolizes the triumph of the moral and spiritual over evil and the material.

1926   Largely as a way to sell more radios, the National Broadcasting Company (NBC) is launched by David Sarnoff of the Radio Corporation of America (RCA). It was one of the earliest horizontal integrations in the entertainment industry, bringing programming content and customers' listening equipment under one roof. NBC grew so quickly that it soon had two networks, and they dominated the early market so completely that in 1941 the Federal Communications Commission ordered that one of the networks be sold.

NOVEMBER 12

1899   "Drink a *bottle* of Coca-Cola, five cents at all stands, grocers and saloons," reads today's advertisement in the Chattanooga *Times*. It was the first ad run by Benjamin Franklin Thomas and Joseph Brown Whitehead, two lawyers who were able, through guile and downright pestering, to get Coke's Asa Candler to finally agree to have Coke bottled under contract. Thomas was an unusual lawyer; in addition to his practice, he operated a stone quarry, hosiery mill, paving-brick company, and patent medicine business, but in 1898 he got his big inspiration on a trip to Cuba where he encountered a bottled carbonated pineapple drink called Pina Frio. Thinking that the new beverage Coca-Cola might also work well in bottles, Thomas made repeated futile trips to Atlanta to get a contract from Candler. He then enlisted Whitehead, and the contract was finally signed. The simple 600-word document was permanent (it could be passed on to whatever bottling companies Thomas and Whitehead established), and it did not allow for an increase in the price the bottlers paid Coke for the syrup. These two "jokers" in the contract ensured conflict and plagued the Coke family through the next century.

1900   Marcus Daly, creator of the gigantic Anaconda Copper Company, dies at age 58. A poor Irish immigrant at age 15, Daly developed expertise in mining practices and prospecting in the American West, and after several successful ventures, persuaded investors to purchase the Anaconda silver mine near Butte, Montana. The silver soon gave out, but Daly discovered a rich vein of copper underneath. It was a great stroke of luck, and Daly played it well, immediately closing the mine and buying up other mines in the area. He parlayed his mineral earnings by developing the community—making Butte a world center in copper production. Daly's final achievement was combining a number of mining and lumber companies into the Amalgamated Copper Company, capitalized at $75 million.

1983 Cabbage Patch dolls are launched in Hollywood, California, starting a marketing phenomenon. Created by Xavier Roberts and licensed for mass marketing to Coleco Industries, each doll was physically unique and came with its own birth certificate and adoption papers. The craze reached a peak in 1985, when retail sales hit $600 million.

1990 English computer scientist Tim Berners-Lee circulates a draft proposal for a "hypertext" interconnected computer system, which he calls the "World Wide Web."

NOVEMBER 13

1789 "But in this world nothing can be said to be certain, except death and taxes." —Benjamin Franklin, in a letter to Jean-Baptiste Le Roy

1877 George Eastman pays $54.58 on this day for his first photography equipment. The 1877 equipment was expensive, cumbersome, and dangerous, requiring a small chemical lab for film developing, and it was so difficult to use that $5 of Eastman's original purchase went for lessons.

1879 Telephone and telegraph lines are installed in the New York Stock Exchange.

1914 Socialite Mary Phelps Jacob patents the elasticized "backless brassiere." It was essentially the modern garment of today. She conceived the idea one night when dressing for a ball, facing the discomfort of trying to dance the night away in the prison of a whalebone corset. Within a half hour her French maid, Marie, had stitched together the prototype out of two handkerchiefs, some ribbon, and a cord. Jacob's friends started asking her for their own. A turning point came when she received a letter from a stranger enclosing a dollar bill and a request for one of "your contraptions." Realizing there might be a market for the item, she gathered a group of friends and hand-made several hundred. The venture soon collapsed without proper marketing muscle. By chance she was introduced socially to a designer for the Warner Corset Company of Bridgeport, Connecticut, to whom she eventually sold the patent rights for a one-time payment of $1,500. Had she opted for royalties instead, she would have earned at least a hundred times that. The patent has since been valued at $15 million.

1933   The nation's first modern sit-down strike is begun in the meat-packing plant of George A. Hormel & Co. in Austin, Minnesota, when striking employees cannot reach an agreement with management and seize control. The Industrial Commission of Minnesota held mediation hearings November 16–18 and rendered a decision on December 8.

NOVEMBER 14

1896   England repeals the Locomotive on the Highways Act, which had banned the use of motor vehicles in that country.

1960   "Like the wheel—which we have learned to make stronger and more cheaply, but which remains unaltered in concept—the book, we may hope, is a unique and lasting invention." —Dan Lacy, managing director, American Book Publishers Council, in *Newsweek*

1972   The Dow Jones Industrial Average closes above 1,000 for the first time. It rose 6.00 on the day, finally resting at 1003.16. In early December it hit 1,036, but then fell sharply at news of a breakdown in the Vietnam peace talks. By January 11 it closed back up at 1051.70, but that record would not be reached again until 1982. The oil embargo, recession, rising inflation and interest rates, and Watergate/Nixon resignation drove the Dow down to 577.60 on December 6, 1975.

1981   "We didn't actually overspend our budget. The Health Commission allocation simply fell short of our expenditure." —Dr. Keith Davis, Australian administrator and physician, in the *Sydney Morning Herald*

1986   On "Boesky Day," as it became known, the Securities and Exchange Commission announces that Ivan F. Boesky—Wall Street's most notorious arbitrageur—has confessed to insider trading offenses and is cooperating with investigators.

1994   At the Comdex computer exposition in Las Vegas, Microsoft announces that it will be entering cyberspace by beginning its own Internet online service. Called the Microsoft Network (now known as MSN), the software to run it was bundled in with the forthcoming Windows 95.

NOVEMBER 15

1620   The Pilgrim fathers at Plymouth Plantation in the New World buy out their London investors for £1,800.

1867   The stock ticker is introduced in New York City. Invented by Edward A. Calahan, the device provided a constant stream of business data. The ticker soon became an icon of market activity, and the reams of ticker tape that it produced later became a key part of important parades down Broadway. The first ticker-tape parade came 52 years and four days later, on November 19, 1919, for the Prince of Wales.

1969   The first Wendy's fast-food restaurant opens in Columbus, Ohio. It has three full-time employees, including Gloria Ward Soffe, who was the bookkeeper, chili maker, and cash register operator. Founder Dave Thomas explained his strategy: "The customer could come up with hundreds of combinations, but the menu itself was super narrow. The only item on the original menu that we got rid of was sugar cream pie at 40 cents a slice. Why? Because I kept on eating it all."

1977   The 100 millionth Ford automobile to be built in America rolls off the assembly line in Mahwah, New York. It was a 1978 Ford Fairmont four-door sedan.

NOVEMBER 16

1779   "Trade could not be managed by those who manage it if it had much difficulty." —Samuel Johnson, in a letter to Hester Thrale

1812   John Walter I, founder of one of the world's great newspapers, the *Times* of London, dies at age 73 in Teddington, England. His was a colorful, scandal-plagued life; he was never considered a particularly talented or honest journalist. Beginning his professional adventures as a coal dealer and then a marine-insurance underwriter, Walter acquired a patent in 1783 for a printing system. He took over an idle printing works in Blackfriars, London, intending to make a business out of publishing books and pamphlets. On January 1, 1785, he published the first edition of the *Daily Universal Register*, a newspaper intended mainly as publicity for his book business. When the book business failed, Walter was forced to concentrate on the newspaper, which he renamed the *Times* for the issue of January 1, 1788. In the early years much of his income was obtained from society figures wishing to suppress news. When he published criminal libels on the Prince of Wales and the Duke of York, Walter was imprisoned and had to edit the paper from behind bars for two years. In 1795 he turned management over to his two sons and thus began a publishing dynasty that lasted for 125 years.

1914   The nation's current central bank, the Federal Reserve System, begins operation. The 12 newly created Federal Reserve Banks were formally opened. A century-long continuous cycle of bank panics (the most serious recent one in 1907) prompted the formation of the National Monetary Commission, which concluded that the country's banks were so "unrelated and independent of each other that the majority of them had simultaneously engaged in a life and death contest with each other." The nation as a whole was vulnerable without a coordinated response to financial panic. The result was the Federal Reserve Act of 1913, which laid the groundwork for today's opening. The Fed was initially designed as a rather passive reserve fund for times of panic, to give the country "an elastic currency," but over the years has taken more of a proactive roll in guiding and stabilizing financial markets.

1989   "The roll of takeovers is to improve unsatisfactory companies and to allow healthy companies to grow strategically by acquisitions." —James Goldsmith, British entrepreneur/financier/politician, in the *International Herald Tribune*

NOVEMBER 17

1864   The banker who grew National City Bank to international prominence, Frank Arthur Vanderlip, is born on a farm near Aurora,

Illinois. Among Vanderlip's innovations were new means of soliciting accounts, entering the investment field, moving heavily into foreign banking, starting a program to select and train future bank officers, and instituting a monthly "bank letter" that became world famous. A falling out with the board of directors ended Vanderlip's tenure in 1919, the very year that his bank achieved a singular milestone (see below). Vanderlip died June 29, 1937.

1906   Soichiro Honda, maverick founder of the Honda Motor Company, is born the son of a blacksmith in Hamamatsu, Japan, 150 miles from Tokyo. Displaying unusual mechanical intuition as a child, Honda began working in an auto repair shop at age 15. He also began racing cars and was nearly killed in a crash in 1936 while setting a speed record. Just after World War II, with Japanese industry in ruins, Honda purchased a surplus of small generator engines from the military and attached them to bicycle frames. The fuel-efficient vehicles sold well, leading him in September 1948 to found the Honda Motor Company with just $1,500. A talented manager as well as a mechanic, Honda made his enterprise the country's largest producer of motorcycles by 1955 and the world's largest by the early 1960s. Car production began in 1962. His first vehicle, the pint-sized S-360, failed to dent the American market, but his Civic 1200 (introduced in 1972 just before the fuel crisis of 1973) was a huge seller. Honda retired in 1973, but a tradition had been started. The Honda Accord became the top-selling car in America in 1989. Honda died August 5, 1991, in Tokyo.

1919   National City Bank (later Citibank) of New York City becomes the first U.S. bank with assets to exceed $1 billion, reaching $1,027,938,114.31 on this day. It was largely the work of Frank Vanderlip, who was forced out of the bank's presidency this year.

1957   "It is one thing to be moved by events; it is another to be mastered by them." —Ralph W. Sockman, bulletin of the Fourth Presbyterian Church, Chicago

1969   Media mogul Rupert Murdoch publishes his first issue of the renovated London tabloid newspaper, the *Sun*. "Horse Dope Sensation/*Sun* Exclusive" read the front-page headline. Perhaps an odd choice of headline, but Murdoch loves horse racing and so does England. Murdoch introduces a new wrinkle to British journalism, soon to be called the "Page 3 girl"; on the third page of the issue was a large photograph of a pretty girl, a fully clothed Swedish model. Her picture was followed by an interview with the prime minister, Harold Wilson.

1970 Rupert Murdoch refines the now-popular tradition of the Page 3 girl. (These models had by now acquired the national nickname of "the Sunbirds" since their introduction exactly a year before.) In today's issue the pinup is naked from the waist up. Never again would the Page 3 girl wear a blouse. By the end of 1970 sales of the *Sun* had climbed to 1.7 million, second in Britain only to the *Daily Mail*.

NOVEMBER 18

1477 The first dated book to be printed in the English language, *Dictes and Sayenges of the Phylosophers*, is published in Westminster, England, by the first professional English printer, William Caxton.

1861 Josiah Kirby Lilly—the pharmacist/manager who took the Eli Lilly Company from a small producer of capsules and patent medicines to an international powerhouse in the invention, development, and manufacture of many pharmaceuticals—is born the son of Eli Lilly and Emily Lemon in Greencastle, Indiana.

1883 The railroad industry changes how the world keeps time. On this day at noon, standard time went into effect throughout the United States, when the daily telegraph signals sent from the Naval Observatory in Washington, D.C., first conformed to the new system of dividing the continent into four time zones. The main sponsor of the controversial system was the American Railway Association, in order to deal with the scheduling chaos of long-distance trains going through local communities that kept their own time, independent of other locales. To the confusion of everyone, timetables were printed with these idiosyncratic local times. In the following year, delegates from 27 nations adopted the modern system of worldwide time zones.

1906 "A camel is a horse invented by a committee" was one of the witticisms of engineer/car designer Sir Alec Issigonis, born on this day in Smyrna, Turkey. He created the Morris Minor and the Mini, Britain's most beloved cars of the 1950s and 1960s.

1928 The first cartoon with synchronized sound and action, *Steamboat Willie*, debuts on this Sunday evening at New York's Colonial Theater, as the opening short for the feature film *Gang War*. In addition to the new technology, *Steamboat Willie* introduced the world to two future giants in the entertainment industry: Walt Disney and Mickey Mouse. Mickey was conceived earlier in the year on a sad train ride back to California from New York, where Disney, 26, discovered that his successful character Oswald the Lucky Rabbit had been stolen from him. By the time he had reached California, Disney had a preliminary idea for his new character, which was designed with collaborator Ubbe Iwerks. "Slap a mortgage on everything we got and let's go after this thing in the right manner," said Disney's business manager, his brother Roy. Disney did just that; though just seven minutes long, *Steamboat Willie* was an elaborate production. An orchestra was hired for the musical portions, 20,000 hand-crafted frames were created, Disney licensed the new "cel" technology of J. R. Bray, and a press agent was hired. Disney himself provided the voice of Mickey. The cartoon was an immediate critical and financial success. Said Disney later of his entire empire, "I hope we never lose sight of one fact—that this was all started by a mouse."

NOVEMBER 19

1909 Three huge figures in 20th-century business management share a common birthday. The renowned business historian/theorist/consultant Peter Drucker is born in Vienna on this day. In **1935** Jack Welch ("Neutron Jack," who ran General Electric for 20 years and increased its stock valuation by over $450 billion with his "fix, sell, or close" strategy) was born in Peabody, Massachusetts. And in **1938** Ted Turner was born in Cincinnati; his legacy includes changing the way the world gets its news with his founding in June 1980 of the Cable News Network (CNN).

1916   Edgar Selwyn, Archibald Selwyn, and Samuel Goldfish form the Goldwyn Pictures Corporation. It initially produced films using famous names from the theater and opera (a concept introduced by Adolph Zukor), but that gradually changed when it was realized that established movie actors were better draws. Goldfish changed his name to Goldwyn in 1918. In 1922 he was removed as president of the company by a vote of the stockholders, and the company merged with Metro Pictures Corp. and the independent company of Louis B. Mayer to form Metro-Goldwyn-Mayer (MGM). Goldwyn's case was a unique one where the founder took his name from the company, rather than the other way around.

1959   The Ford Motor Company announces that it is halting production of the famous failure, the Edsel.

NOVEMBER 20

1811   Declaring to friends that he "had no further interest in spices," Friedrich Krupp founds the firm of Fried. Krupp of Essen "for the manufacture of English Cast Steel and all products made thereof." The firm begins its ascent to international prominence once its founder dies (see October 8).

1906   Rolls-Royce Ltd., the elite car and engine company, is founded by marketer Charles Stewart Rolls and engineer/designer Frederick Henry Royce.

1923   History's best-known case of hyperinflation (Germany in 1923; see November 6 and other references) comes to an abrupt halt. The government announced that the reichsmark was no longer legal tender and would be redeemed at the rate of 1 billion for each new rentenmark. Miraculously, the value of the rentenmark held. Why the economy quickly stabilized remains somewhat mysterious. The government announced that the new money was backed with government land, but the government had no new lands and apparently no one tried to redeem the notes for property. Circumstances must have helped. The government had virtually stopped making reparation payments to the Allies and in fact was being lent considerable sums. The industrial heartland of the Ruhr valley was humming again after the government abandoned passive resistance to French occupation there. New taxes had been levied, and easy government credit was no longer extended to industry. "Perhaps [the German hyperinflation] ended simply because it could not go on," suggested John Kenneth Galbraith. Another momentous event in German economic history occurred on this same day. Hjalmar Horace Greeley Schacht was made head of the Reichsbank. He was credited with being the "man behind the miracle of the rentenmark" and with creating the financial machine to fund Hitler's war and industrial machines. For that he was tried and acquitted at Nuremberg.

1986 "He who owns the most when he dies, wins." —Ivan Boesky, financier, in the *Times*

NOVEMBER 21

1787 Sir Samuel Cunard—shipping magnate and founder of the first regular Atlantic steamship line—is born in Halifax, Nova Scotia. Exactly 120 years after his birth (**1907**) the Cunard liner *Mauritania* traveled 624 nautical miles in one day, setting a speed record for steamship travel.

1834 The "witch of Wall Street," Henrietta Howland Green, is born in New Bedford, Massachusetts (see July 3).

1907 The first of the "Gary Dinners" is held at New York's Waldorf-Astoria hotel. Hosted by the chief executive of U.S. Steel, Elbert Gary, it was attended by 49 steel industry leaders. Steel pricing was the main topic of conversation, but Gary insisted it was not an attempt to fix prices, merely to come to "gentlemen's agreements" about them. To allay suspicions, Gary notified newspapers, steel trade journals, and government officials of the events. In the end, the price regulating tactic proved a failure because small, independent producers did cut prices, and the large companies had to follow. A price war ensued, and this did not end until World War I, when Gary instituted another famous program, the "umbrella concept," in which cutthroat competition was avoided by establishing a price umbrella over the industry's weaker firms that did not drive them out of business.

1945   The United Auto Workers union stages the first major strike in the post–World War II era. Labor-management disputes were postponed during the war and the national unity it brought. The gloves came off today. Two hundred thousand workers walked off their jobs at General Motors and stayed out until a settlement was reached the following May.

1985   "There are more pompous, arrogant, self-centered mediocre . . . people running corporate America . . . their judgments and misjudgments have made me rich." —Joseph D. Jamail, corporate lawyer, referring to the $10.5 billion settlement he had just won for Pennzoil against Texaco, in the *New York Times*

1990   The brilliant but crooked Michael Milken, "king of the junk bonds," is sentenced in New York by Judge Kimba Wood to 10 years in prison and fined more than $600 million for various securities and insider trading crimes. "Mr. Greed of an historically greedy epoch" was *Barron's* label for Milken.

1995   The Dow Jones Industrial Average closes above 5,000 for the first time.

NOVEMBER 22

643   The first worker's compensation law is issued by the Lombard king of Italy, Rothari. On this day he issued a famous law code in 388 articles which, among other things, established a money fine for serious offenses; the blood price of injured or murdered persons was to vary with social status. Also among the articles was the edict that bodily harm caused by accident to builder's laborers should be compensated.

1891   The "father of public relations," Edward L. Bernays, is born in Vienna, a nephew of Sigmund Freud. Bernays was a genius at molding public opinion, inventing new ways to exploit cultural tradition, conducting public opinion surveys, and providing expert testimony for the enhancement of his client's image. From 1913 to 1917, he worked for theater companies and the Metropolitan Opera. His first big splash involved the play *Damaged Goods*; the taboo theme of venereal disease was keeping audiences away in droves—until Bernays secured endorsements from civic leaders. It became a hit. During World War I he was a propaganda agent for the U.S. government (his most memorable campaign was the reemployment of returning veterans) and then opened his own firm with his future wife, Doris Fleischman. General Electric, General Motors, Time Inc., CBS, and NBC were among his foundation clientele. For Lucky Strike cigarettes, he helped gain acceptance for women to smoke in public. (In later years he created antismoking campaigns.) Bernays was a pathfinder in the commercialization of American culture; he not only changed business procedures, he changed society. He lived to be 103, dying on March 9, 1995.

1963   The assassination of President John F. Kennedy on this day comes amid a rising stock market. Kennedy's unbalanced budget and general uncertainties about his economic policies had caused wariness at first, but the markets soon barged ahead. Market response to the assassination itself followed a similar pattern: dip and recovery. News of Kennedy's shooting in Dallas caused an immediate and huge sell-off. In less than an hour the New York Stock Exchange had lost $13 billion of its total value, and trading was temporarily halted. Market indices in aggregate fell by about 3 percent, but that was recovered when it was apparent that Lyndon Johnson was in full control of the White House.

1999   "I'm not retiring because I'm old and tired. I'm retiring because an organization has had 20 years of me. My success will be determined by how well my successor grows it in the next 20 years." —Jack Welch, chairman and CEO, General Electric, referring to his planned retirement the following year, in *Fortune*

2001   Mary Kay Ash dies of natural causes in her home in Dallas at age 83. Her cosmetics empire boasted 850,000 salespeople in 37 countries, with wholesale revenue of $1.3 billion. Her legacy was the independence and strength her company gave to its employees. "My interest in starting Mary Kay Inc. was to offer women opportunities that didn't exist anywhere else," she said (see September 13).

NOVEMBER 23

1869   Elon Huntington Hooker, founder of the Hooker Chemical Company, is born in Rochester, New York, the son of an inventor and a dreamer. Hooker worked his way through college to a Ph.D. in civil engineering from Cornell in 1895. He was so outstanding that he was offered the deanship of the School of Civil Engineering but turned it down. After several appointments by Teddy Roosevelt and an unsuccessful bid for the New York governorship, Hooker entered private industry as the vice president of an entrepreneurial holding company that looked for new ventures to invest in. In 1903 Hooker launched his own company of a similar nature, the Development and Funding Company. After looking at some 250 projects, D&F decided to go into chemical manufacturing using the new Townsend electrochemical process. A plant was built at Niagara Falls to use the vast hydroelectric power, and the Hooker Electrochemical Company was formed from this successful venture. Decades after Hooker's death (May 10, 1938), the Love Canal disaster was splashed across the national headlines in 1979. From 1947 to 1953 the company had been secretly dumping highly toxic waste into Love Canal near Niagara Falls. Birth defects, miscarriages, and community-wide illnesses were all part of the Love Canal legacy.

1936   Henry Luce publishes the first issue of *Life* magazine, with Margaret Bourke-White's unforgettable cover photo of the Fort Peck Dam. The pictorial magazine was a great success and was continuously in publication until 1972.

1939   By proclamation of President Franklin Roosevelt, Thanksgiving is celebrated for the first time on the fourth Thursday of November, rather than the last Thursday. In this year, with merchants and the economy still mired in the Great Depression, the change meant an extra week of Christmas shopping. Fred Lazarus, Jr., chief of the Ohio-based Federated Department Stores, proposed the switch; the Ohio State Council of Retail Merchants and the Cincinnati *Enquirer* endorsed it; and Roosevelt loved it. Some said it was blaspheming some sort of divine order to change a holiday that had originated by proclamation of Abraham Lincoln.

1954   The Dow Jones Industrial Average finally makes up the ground it lost in the 1929 crash, passing that year's high of 381.17 for the first time. The Dow closed the year at 404, up from 280.

1997   "My philosophy is to stay as close as possible to what's happening. If I can't solve something, how the hell can I expect my managers to?" —Harold S. Geneen, telecommunications entrepreneur and CEO of ITT, in the *New York Times*

NOVEMBER 24

1863   The nation's second transcontinental railroad, the Atchison, Topeka and Santa Fe, is formed by abolitionist/entrepreneur Cyrus K. Holliday of Topeka and Senator S. C. Pomeroy of Atchison. In 1868 construction began after sufficient state and federal land grants and bond sales had been secured. The line opened in 1883 but kept expanding until, by 1887, its 7,373 miles of track made it one of the largest railway systems on earth. Its main line went from Kansas to California via the old Santa Fe Trail, with additional lines running to Denver, the Gulf of Mexico, and Lake Michigan. Holliday remained its director until his death in 1900.

1961   "Rumor, that most efficient of press agents . . . " —Bruce Barton, Jr., art editor for *Time* magazine, on behind-the-scenes talk in the galleries of Manhattan

1998   AOL's $4.2 billion acquisition of Netscape is confirmed. The former was the world's largest Internet access company; the latter pioneered the software used on the Internet, and its Navigator web browser was the world's most popular. The merger was both offensive in nature (aimed at creating an enormous source of both revenue and technological advance in a very fast-changing environment) and defensive (against the monopolistic 800-pound gorilla, Microsoft, which had just recently entered the market for Internet users). The strategy worked, sort of. In the following year, under the AOL banner, Netscape's web portal surpassed 13 million members for the first time, but in the same year the 800-pound gorilla really picked up steam, and Microsoft's Internet Explorer caught and overtook Navigator in market penetration.

NOVEMBER 25

1835   Andrew Morrison Carnegie is born in Dunfermline, Scotland, in a small cottage that serves as both home and workplace of his father, an artisan weaver of damask linen. Within several years the family was driven into poverty, and then into emigrating to America, by the Industrial Revolution. Ironically, the very qualities that made hand weaving so special a craft—the large amount of labor, time, and skill required to produce each piece—were the very qualities that made it particularly vulnerable to competition by machines.

1985   "The notion that by succeeding academically or later, by succeeding in any management, you therefore destroy your 'femininity' is the most pervasive threat against women." —Mary Warnock, British philosopher and author, in a speech to the Institute of Directors, London

1948   Commercial cable television is invented. Radio station operator Ed Parsons of Astoria, Oregon, detected a usable TV signal from a station 150 miles away. He ran a cable from the antenna on top of the hotel where he lived to his living room and got a picture. He then put a TV set in a store window and brought a signal to it through a coaxial cable; it was the first known time such a coaxial linkup was used. Astoria is surrounded by mountains and heretofore had been unable to get good reception. In the following year an enormous antenna was erected on high ground, and a cable network was established.

1994   The Sony board of directors in Tokyo formally accepts the resignation of Akio Morita as chairman. Morita's role was largely ceremonial at this point; he had essentially turned over the reigns of leadership in 1989 to president Norio Ohga and in 1993 had suffered a stroke. Morita cofounded the electronics giant in 1946 with $500, saw it rise to world leadership, and stayed just long enough to witness the ugly debacle of its first major step of diversification into the entertainment industry with the purchase of Columbia Pictures in 1989. Exactly one week before today's action, Sony announced a $2.7 billion write-off of its failed investment in Columbia. Sony nevertheless persisted in its efforts to become a media/ entertainment kingpin, and by century's end, it was just that.

NOVEMBER 26

1876   Willis Haviland Carrier, the inventor and industrialist who created the modern air conditioner, is born in Angola, New York. After he graduated from Cornell with a degree in electrical engineering in 1901, Carrier began work with the Buffalo Forge Company as a research engineer and soon had an assignment to control the temperature and humidity in a printing operation; it was there that Carrier developed the basic methods of modern air conditioning (see July 17). He then embarked on a series of experiments and inventions to refine the basic elements of his system. Carrier-designed units were selling so well that Buffalo Forge established a whole new subsidiary, the Carrier Air Conditioning Company, to engineer and market complete systems. A variety of industries began installing Carrier equipment—tobacco, rayon, rubber, paper, pharmaceuticals, and food processing. When Buffalo Forge decided to limit itself to manufacturing in 1914, thereby ending its engineering and developmental activities, Carrier formed the Carrier Engineering Corporation, through which he continued to experiment and invent. His focus turned to optimizing air conditioning methods for places of human use, like theaters, office buildings, and various residences. Carrier died October 7, 1950.

1948   The Polaroid Land Camera, which develops film within the camera body in 60 seconds, first goes on sale at Boston's Jordan Marsh department store.

1956   The most famous fraud in television history is created. Charles Van Doren—the tall, handsome professor at Columbia University—privately met with *Twenty-One*'s producer, Al Freedman, who told him that the game show would be rigged so that Van Doren would defeat the current champion Herb Stempel. Brilliant, but not tall or sexy, Stempel had to be defeated for the sake of ratings. Van Doren was seduced by the promise of cash and by the argument that he would improve public respect for teachers and intellectuals. Stempel also agreed. Van Doren became a rich celebrity, appearing on the cover of *Time* magazine and on NBC's *Today* show—until an angry Stempel blew the whistle. After fleeing once to avoid testifying before a congressional committee, Van Doren finally appeared on November 2, 1959. His contrite confession won approval and forgiveness from most of the committee, which further tormented Stempel. Van Doren was fired from Columbia and NBC and spent the rest of his days as an author and editor.

1990   The day before the 96th birth anniversary of founder Kenosuke Matsushita, the Matsushita Electronic Industrial Company announces that it is buying the American entertainment corporation MCA for $6.6 billion. It was the largest amount yet paid by a Japanese company for any American property. It was also the second time in a year that an enormous Japanese consumer electronics manufacturer had purchased an American provider of entertainment programming. In the previous year Sony had purchased Columbia Pictures.

NOVEMBER 27

1759   "They may be false who languish and complain, But they who sigh for money never feign." —Mary Wortley Montagu, in a letter to James Steuart

1924   The sales gimmick that became a national tradition: the Macy's Thanksgiving Day Parade is held for the first time, down a two-mile stretch of Broadway from Central Park West to Herald Square. The main attraction was large, decorated platforms mounted on hidden cars beneath, giving the illusion that the displays were "floating" down Broadway. The event was designed to boost sales at Macy's department store and to draw attention to its new flagship store at Herald Square. The audience was so large (estimated at 250,000) that the store decided to do it again the following year, and it has been going on ever since. In 1927 huge balloons of cartoon characters were added; Felix the Cat was the first. In 1950 the event was televised nationally for the first time.

1930   After 36 hours of nonstop negotiations in Room 1553 in the Baker Hotel, Dallas, Texas, Columbus "Dad" Joiner—the 71-year-old wildcatter who had recently discovered the largest oil field in America's history (see October 3)—signs over all his rights to the gambler-wildcatter H. L. Hunt. Hunt promised Joiner $1.33 million, $30,000 to be paid up front, and the rest to come from production. Once he cleared up the problems of title that Joiner had created for himself in trying to finance the exploration (like selling one lease to eleven different buyers), Hunt worked the field for decades, profiting an estimated $100 million and earning himself the crown (for a while) of the richest man in America. Joiner used his money to hunt for more oil strikes and to romance several more women, until he died at 87 with an estimated net worth equal to his house and his car.

1967 Herb Kelleher files the first application of Southwest Airlines for a flight route. He requested approval of the Texas Aeronautics Commission (TAC) to fly commercially between Dallas, Houston, and San Antonio. The day after approval was granted, Goliaths started attacking this David; Braniff, Texas International, and Continental all filed restraining orders to stop Southwest. To the detriment of their market share, they were unsuccessful. Started with a sketch on a cocktail napkin in 1966 with a vision of good service at the cheapest price, Southwest continued to grow for decades, while the established, bloated airlines shrank or disappeared completely.

1999 "We all of us, rich and poor, have to live with the insecurity caused by an out of control global casino with a built-in bias towards instability. Because it is instability that makes money for the money-traders." —Anita Roddick, founder, The Body Shop, in a speech to the International Forum on Globalization, Seattle

NOVEMBER 28

1905 Arm & Hammer baking soda is trademark registered.

1907 Russian immigrant scrap-metal dealer, Louis B. Mayer, opens a small theater in Haverhill, Massachusetts. Mayer acquired the old burlesque house for $600; in order to counter its unsavory reputation, his first presentation was a religious movie. Having won community approval, Mayer alternated films with stage shows. It wasn't long before he owned the other five theaters in Haverhill too. Mayer formed the Gordon-Mayer Circuit with another theater owner, Nat Gordon, and it was not long after that they controlled the largest chain of theaters in New England. In 1914 Mayer opened his own distribution company in Boston in order to ensure a steady supply of films. Soon he paid $25,000 for the exclusive rights to show D. W. Griffith's *Birth of a Nation* in New England. It was the most expensive licensing deal in history, but it netted Mayer over $100,000. In 1915 Mayer helped form the Metro Pictures Corporation of New York, and not long after that (1918) he moved to California to enter the production side of the industry. The Louis B. Mayer Pictures Corporation was headquartered in Culver City. His early efforts were undistinguished, until he hired the brilliant Irving Thalberg as his head of production. All this led up to a merger that was engineered by theater magnate Marcus Loew: the combination of Mayer's two companies with the Goldwyn Pictures Corporation to form the Metro-Goldwyn-Mayer Corporation (MGM). Mayer at 39 had now realized his dream of world-wide control of production, distribution, and exhibition—complete integration, from script to screening. He died October 29, 1957.

1922   The *Time* magazine venture is incorporated by Yale classmates Henry Luce and Briton Hadden, both 24. Their capitalization of $86,000 was raised from 72 investors. The first issue came out the following March. By 1929 their own stock made them both millionaires before the age of 30 (Hadden's goal). Hadden died in February of that year.

1929   Founder of Motown Records and essentially founder of the Motown genre of music, Berry Gordy, Jr., is born in Detroit, Michigan, the son of a plastering contractor. After stints as a soldier, a boxer, and a record store manager, Gordy began writing songs for local acts and quickly developed a reputation as a songwriter, producer, and hustler. His first major break came in 1957, when he sold the song *Reet Petite* to Brunswick Records for singer Jackie Wilson. Based in a Detroit house at 2648 West Grand Boulevard, which he dubbed "Hitsville U.S.A," Gordy established his own production company in 1959 called Tammie Records, which became Tamla, which became Tamla-Motown, and finally Motown. It was sold in 1988 after hundreds of hits and permanent marks on cultural and music industry history.

1988   "Money you haven't earned is not good for you." —Robert Maxwell, British-Slovak publishing magnate/entrepreneur/politician, in *Time*

NOVEMBER 29

1596   Once the richest and most formidable power on earth, Spain announces that it is virtually bankrupt. Official reasons cited by the government of Philip II included a never-ending series of wars, especially the futile effort to invade England. Bad weather, bad financial management, heavy domestic spending, and revolts against the Spanish empire in the New World had also contributed to the draining of the royal treasury. Despite its rather dire state, Spain launched another armada against England the following year. Once again, a storm scattered the ships, rendering the assault worthless.

1975   The name "Microsoft" (for microcomputer software) is used for the first time, in a letter from Bill Gates to Paul Allen.

1993   The shortest commercial in television history airs in the United States on King TV's *Evening Magazine*. The ad was for Bon Marche's Frango sweets and lasted a mere four frames (there are 30 frames in a second).

1994   In Moscow, officials of the Red October Candy Factory announce that it will be the first former Soviet state company to sell shares to the general public.

1995   Shares in Pixar Animation Studios go on sale to the public for the first time and double in value in the first hour of trading. Priced at $22 the day before, the shares burst to $45.50 shortly after trading began. The initial public offering came one week after the triumphant opening of Pixar's first feature-length animated film, *Toy Story*. Matching good old-fashioned drama and comedy with the most modern of computer technology, *Toy Story* was the top box-office draw over the weekend. It was the first of a three-picture distribution deal with the Walt Disney Company. Pixar's president, Steve Jobs, purchased the studio in 1986 from LucasFilm and invested millions to build its facilities. By the end of the day's trading, Jobs's personal stock in Pixar was worth $1.5 billion.

NOVEMBER 30

1871   John D. Rockefeller and partner Henry M. Flagler meet privately with railroad executive Peter Watson in the Saint Nicholas Hotel in New York City to discuss a secret cartel of the nation's three most powerful railroads allied to a growing cartel of oil companies that Rockefeller was creating. The meeting resulted in the formation of the South Improvement Company. On the same day, Rockefeller wrote to his wife, Cettie, "A man who succeeds in life must sometimes go against the current."

1982   The Associated Press called this one "an amazing statistical goof." At 10:00 A.M. the Commerce Department announces that the Index of Leading Economic Indicators has risen a hefty 0.6 percent, which in the current recessionary period could be called "whopping." The good news did not last for long. At 4:00 P.M. it was announced that the rise was just 0.2 percent. The size of the earlier figure was so suspicious that the numbers were rechecked, and a statistical error was found. Meanwhile, before the mistake was discovered and announced, the Dow Jones Industrial Average rose 36.43 points, at the time the fourth largest one-day advance in Wall Street history.

1985   The largest corporate takeover in history is settled. At a little before 9 P.M. this evening, the board of RJR Nabisco voted unanimously to accept the $108-per-share takeover bid ($24.88 billion) from the buyout firm of Kohlberg, Kravis, Roberts & Company.

1986   "There cannot be a situation where a businessman says, 'I base all my business on moral considerations.' Equally, you can't say you can run a business without morality."—Timothy Bevan, chairman, Barclays Bank Ltd., when asked about Barclays' withdrawal from South Africa, in the *Observer*

DECEMBER

DECEMBER 1

1925   Mr. Peanut, the tuxedo-wearing legume that represents Planters Peanuts, is trademark registered.

1929   Alfa Romeo racing driver Enzo Ferrari, 31, forms Scuderia Ferrari with several partners in Modena, Italy. It was mainly a racing organization, with plans to sell Alfas in three provinces. Not an especially good driver himself, Ferrari was able to build winning teams and winning cars. In 1947 he began to build cars under his own name and under the famous logo of a black prancing horse.

1948   The Scrabble board game is copyright registered.

1978   In Tokyo the Nikkei Dow Jones Industrial Average closes above 6,000 for the first time. It had reached 5,000 six years earlier, in 1972, but then swooned in the wake of the 1973 oil crisis (Japanese industry relies totally on imported oil) and did not reach 5,000 again until January 1978.

1985   "Management have been allowed to act like owners. But it is the stockholders who own companies, not managements and the stockholders are just beginning to realize it." — Boone Pickens, oil company executive/entrepreneur/corporate raider, in the *Sunday Times*

1985   "Everything [T. Boone Pickens] says is horse shit and hot air." —Armand Hammer, industrialist/philanthropist/oil company executive, in the *Sunday Times*

1999   Eleven letters and a dot are sold for millions of dollars. Texas entrepreneur Marc Ostrofsky sold business.com to the firm eCompanies for $7.5 million, a record-setting price for an Internet domain name.

Ostrofsky had purchased the name for $150,000 from an Internet service provider in London in 1996. Unlike many Internet properties that fetched enormous prices during this time, business.com survived into the next century.

DECEMBER 2

1816   In Pennsylvania, the first savings bank in America to actually receive money on deposit—the Philadelphia Saving Fund Society—opens for business. The idea had first been suggested a week before, on November 25, by Condy Raguet to four others.

1836   That famous phrase of misplaced reverence, "the almighty dollar," is coined by an anonymous author in today's *Philadelphia Star Ledger*: "The almighty dollar is the only object of worship." (Washington Irving is often mistakenly cited as the source of the phrase in *Wolfert's Roost*, but that book was published in 1855.) The earliest known similar phrase in English dates to 1616, in a couplet written by Ben Jonson in a letter to Elizabeth, Countess of Rutland: "Whilst that for which all virtue now is sold / And almost every vice—almighty gold."

1887   "All you need in this life is ignorance and confidence; then success is sure." —Mark Twain, in a letter to Mrs. Foote

1892   Two robber barons die on this day. In 1892 the villainous railroad speculator Jay Gould died of consumption at age 56 in New York City. In 1919 the Machiavellian steel executive Henry Clay Frick died at 69, also in New York City; his entire fortune was given to the public.

1901   King Gillette patents his safety razor, and a new industry is founded.

1984   History's largest industrial accident begins this evening in the Union Carbide plant in Bhopal, India. Water was leaking into a tank containing methyl isocyanate (MIC), a highly toxic pesticide component that reacts violently with water. By 12:40 A.M. workers were being choked by leaking gas, and by the time safety measures were initiated, the gas was already flooding the atmosphere. The only employee hurt was the plant supervisor, who broke his ankle climbing over a fence. Four thousand town residents died within the first 24 hours of the leak. It is estimated that between 6,500 and 16,000 lives were lost over the next 10 years (through 1994) due to the gas that descended on Bhopal, with 20,000 more permanently disabled, and 200,000 more suffering some kind of injury.

2001   Enron declares bankruptcy.

DECEMBER 3

1753   Samuel Crompton—inventor of the spinning mule, which made possible the large-scale manufacture of high-quality thread and yarn—is born in Firwood, near Bolton, England.

1842   The founder of the Pillsbury food company, Charles Alfred Pillsbury, is born in Warner, New Hampshire, the son of a grocer. At age 27, Pillsbury joined his uncle's small milling firm in Minneapolis and purchased a one-third stake in the business. Due to the civic and political activities of his uncle, Pillsbury was essentially left to manage operations on his own. Not only did he master the business, but he also came to be one of the industry's foremost executives, largely due to being one of the first to embrace new technologies. In 1880 the Pillsbury A mill was opened in Minneapolis, and it became the world's largest. Pillsbury died September 17, 1899.

1861   "Labor is prior to, and independent of, capital. Capital is only the fruit of labor, and could never have existed if labor had not first existed. Labor is the superior of capital, and deserves much the higher consideration. Capital has its rights, which are as worthy of protection as any other rights." —President Abraham Lincoln, in his first annual message to Congress

1879   Thomas Edison gives the first demonstration of his electric lightbulb in a private meeting with financial backers J. P. Morgan and members of the Vanderbilt family. Neon lighting (invented by French physicist Georges Claude) was given its first public demonstration exactly 31 years later (**1910**) at the Paris Motor Show.

1993 The Sony PlayStation is launched in Japan with eight game titles. Three hundred thousand units were sold in the first three months, three times the number Sony had made. By 1998, 50 million had been sold; it was history's best-selling game computer. Executive Teruo "Terry" Tokunaka later recalled how his hand trembled when he signed the purchase order for $50 million to pay for 1.3 million computer chips for the first batch of PlayStations.

DECEMBER 4

1871 Germany goes on the gold standard and adopts the mark as its unit of currency.

1928 The most infamous of the 1920s investment trust companies, Goldman Sachs Trading Corporation, is formed. It sold stock in itself, backed by its investments in other companies. This fairly new form of investment opportunity was supposed to stabilize the market and provide the benefits of professional management, but the greedy, ill-managed trusts artificially boosted profits by borrowing, lent their own surplus cash to the call loan market (thus destabilizing the market), were frequently diluted with "junk" securities from their parent investment banks which could not unload the junk elsewhere, and invested in affiliated trusts rather than in bona fide industrial companies. The Trading Corporation's initial stock offering was $100 million, 90 percent of which was sold to the public. In February it merged with another trust, and together they launched a new trust company, the Shenandoah Corporation. Stocks totaling $102.3 million were authorized for Shenandoah, but the offering was oversubscribed sevenfold, so more stock was issued and a new trust, Blue Ridge Corporation, was formed. This time $142 million in stock was issued. Shenandoah stock was first issued at $17.50, rose to $36, then fell to 50¢. Its parent, the Trading Corporation, did worse; in February (aided by the company pushing up the stock price by purchasing its own stock) its share price hit $222.50. Two years later it was selling at about $1. "He took my fortune," said one investor of his broker, "and ran it into a shoestring."

1991 The once-great airline Pan Am ceases operations. The doors opened for business in the morning and then shut almost immediately.

The death stroke had come the day before, on the day that the restructured Pan Am was supposed to emerge from Chapter 11 bankruptcy protection; lawyers for Delta Airlines had informed bankruptcy judge Cornelius Blackshear that no further money could be pumped into Pan Am to save it. Since September, Pan Am had burned through $115 million of Delta's cash "like a prairie fire" without making a dent in the continued decline of ticket sales. The mere hint of failure had driven customers and travel agents to other carriers. Recently giant airlines Eastern and Braniff had both suddenly failed, leaving travelers stranded around the globe.

1996   "Two things to help keep one's job. First, let the boss think he's having his own way. Second, let him have it." —Sam Ewing, author, in the *Wall Street Journal*

DECEMBER 5

1766   James Christie, founder of the famous London auction house that bears his name, holds his first auction under his own name. Christie's was eventually sold to the French businessman and art collector Francois Pinault in 1998, after which it suffered considerable scandal (see below).

1841   Marcus Daly—famous for creating the gigantic Anaconda Copper Company—is born into poverty in Ireland (see November 12).

1901   Walt Disney is born in Chicago. As a youth Disney produced a weekly sketch for a local barber in return for 25¢ or a free haircut.

1996   Chairman of the Federal Reserve Board Alan Greenspan coins the famous phrase "irrational exuberance" in a speech in Washington to the American Enterprise Institute. He was accepting the Francis Boyer Award. "How do we know when irrational exuberance has unduly escalated asset values. . . . And how do we factor that assessment into monetary policy?" The phrase seems to have come to him in the bathtub while contemplating his speech. He did not use it lightly. Greenspan correctly anticipated that the phrase could have market consequences because it would indicate that he felt the stock market was overvalued and possibly due for a fall. The fallout started immediately. The markets in Japan, which were still open, began to drop sharply. The Dow Jones Industrial Average fell 145 points in the first half hour of trading the next day. The markets in London, Hong Kong, and Frankfurt lost similar amounts.

2001   A. Alfred Taubman, the former head of Sotheby's auction house, is convicted by a federal jury of plotting with his counterpart at Christie's to fix the commissions paid by sellers of fine art. The two houses controlled about 90 percent of the world's art auctions, and this scandal sent that world spinning. Taubman and Anthony Tennant of Christie's allegedly stole as much as $400 million in commissions from 1993 to 1999.

DECEMBER 6

1745   The original Black Friday in financial history grips England, two days after Bonnie Prince Charlie led several thousand Highlander revolutionaries across the border to take over the major English town of Derby. (The three Black Fridays that history knows so well—1869, 1929, and 1987—were all due to a new phenomenon, unbridled financial speculation. If the present pattern continues, the next Black Friday is due sometime around 2049.)

1979   The television satellite Satcom-3 is launched into space. Owned by RCA, it contained the transponder that Ted Turner had leased for his new television network, CNN, which he had promised would be on the air in six months and 21 days. Within 72 hours Satcom-3 was lost. Turner hit the ceiling when RCA lied to him, saying that there was no room on the already-orbiting Satcom-1, but offering space on Comstar D-2 (which would not be usable by the cable operators that Turner had already lined up). "I'm going to sue your ass, buddy!" Turner bellowed in one of the negotiating meetings. "I've spent $35 million already, and I'll be damned if I'm going to let a punk like you stick me on some God-forsaken Comstar satellite. . . . I may lose this whole thing, but I'll bleed you guys to death." Turner got his satellite.

1989   "If we do not succeed, then we run the risk of failure." —Vice President Dan Quayle

1994   The largest municipal bankruptcy in history is filed by Orange County, California, declaring investment losses in the neighborhood of $2 billion. The county's investment portfolio contained a foundation of low-risk bonds, but its treasurer, the septuagenarian Bob Citron (reportedly with the math skills of a schoolboy), was seduced by aggressive salesmen and the promise of the new derivatives markets. Unfortunately, the investments were highly leveraged and essentially a bet that interest rates would fall. But the frenzy that drove the rush into derivatives was the same frenzy that drove the Federal Reserve to fear inflation, and it repeatedly hiked interest rates through the year. Many investors lost heavily.

DECEMBER 7

1854   "Chance favors the prepared mind." This famous observation on the relationship between luck and effort is coined on this day by Louis Pasteur in his inaugural lecture at the University of Lille, given at the Douai campus. As with the greatest quotes, it is forever misquoted. The correct version is "Remember that in the fields of observation chance favors only those minds which are prepared."

1863   Founder of Sears, Roebuck and Company, Richard Warren Sears, is born in Stewartville, Minnesota. In 1880, Sears took an office job with the Minneapolis and St. Paul Railroad. Believing that more money could be made in small towns, he had himself transferred to Redwood Falls as the station agent there. With the abundance of free time that the job afforded, Sears became a merchant, selling coal, lumber, and venison that he purchased from the Indians. An enormous break happened in 1886 when the town jeweler refused to accept a shipment of watches sent to him by a wholesaler and on which no freight had been paid. Sears obtained permission to dispose of the watches as he saw fit. He offered them to other agents along the line for $14 apiece, which still allowed the agents to resell the watches at a price below what local jewelers could. He shipped the watches COD, and because the agents were bonded, there was no risk to Sears. It spawned a flourishing business, with Sears purchasing other watch shipments and abandoning rail work entirely. In late 1886 he formed the R.W. Sears Watch Company, based in an office that rented for $10 a month and housed a kitchen table, a 50¢ chair, and some record books. In the next year he was advertising in national periodicals, had moved to Chicago, and had enlisted the collaboration of Alvah C. Roebuck, a watchmaker/repairman who also ran a printing business. Sears died September 28, 1914.

1944   R.H. Macy Co., New York City, becomes the first retail store whose one-day sales exceed $1 million. On December 14, 1957, they first exceeded $2 million; on December 18, 1965, they first exceeded $3 million; and on December 18, 1967, $4 million.

1957   "When you try to formalize or socialize creative activity, the only sure result is commercial constipation. . . . The good ideas are all hammered out in agony by individuals, not spewed out by groups."
—Charles Brower, president, Batten, Barton, Durstine & Osborne advertising agency, in *Editor & Publisher*

DECEMBER 8

1765   Eli Whitney—inventor of the cotton gin and one of the first to manufacture with interchangeable parts—is born the son of a successful farmer in Westboro, Massachusetts (see January 8).

1816   Investment banker August Belmont—famous for establishing the Rothschild presence in America and making the House of Rothschild the major creditor of the American government during the Civil War—is born as August Schonberg in Alzey, Germany.

1839   Alexander Johnston Cassatt—early railroad executive who helped build the Pennsylvania Railroad into one of the nation's largest—is born in Pittsburgh. After taking a degree in civil engineering, Cassatt joined the Pennsylvania, where he was mentored by Thomas Scott, eventually succeeding to its presidency in 1899. During his administration, earnings and traffic density nearly doubled, a pension fund was established, and the original Pennsylvania Station was constructed in New

York City (it was the most gigantic railroad enterprise ever undertaken at that time). Cassatt also solved the rebate problem (whereby the railroads would essentially dissolve their own profits by giving fare rebates to industrial shippers in order to outcompete other railroads for the business). Cassatt created a "community of interest" by purchasing enough stock in competing railroads to influence their management and thus present a united, coordinated front to the industrial shippers. This enraged the industrialists, especially Andrew Carnegie. The community of interest was eventually struck down by the Supreme Court, but by that time rebates had been made illegal, largely at the insistence of the Pennsylvania Railroad and Cassatt. Cassatt died December 28, 1906.

1886 Delegates from 25 labor unions and organizations found the American Federation of Labor (AFL) at a convention in Columbus, Ohio. English immigrant and cigar-maker, Samuel Gompers was its first president from 1886 to 1924 (except for 1895).

1995 Do you know what DVD stands for? You're wrong, it's "digital versatile disk." In Tokyo on this day, representatives from "the Big Nine" in the computer/entertainment industry decide that digital versatile disk will be the name of the next big thing in computer/entertainment disks. "Digital video disk" had been the favored name, but marketers changed it to be more inclusive of music and computers.

1995 The Grateful Dead announce their breakup in San Francisco, California, after the death of cofounder Jerry Garcia. It is impossible to accurately gauge the net value of the Grateful Dead as a business enterprise. Start-up costs were virtually nothing. (Formed as the Warlocks in 1964, the band changed its name when members discovered that their choice was already taken.) Future profit predictions were all but meaningless because of the band's enormous output, its spread into nonmusic products (foods, literature, clothing), its semireligious cult status, and its continuing brisk sales well beyond its breakup. Some things are known. For years it was one of the world's most popular concert draws, grossing tens of millions of dollars annually. While Garcia was alive, the band had one multiplatinum record of more than 3 million sales, three platinum albums of at least 1 million sales, and six gold albums of at least

500,000 sales. They're still selling, as are spin-off items. For example, Cherry Garcia continues to be a best-selling ice cream for Ben & Jerry's.

2001   One of the unsung heroes in modern advertising, Don Tennant, dies at age 79 in Los Angeles. Tony the Tiger, the Jolly Green Giant, and the Coppertone girl were among Tennant's creations. Other memorable campaigns and slogans he created were "Fly the friendly skies of United," "Put a tiger in your tank" (for Exxon), "Nothin' says lovin' like something from the oven" (for Pillsbury), and "Come to Marlboro Country." That last campaign, in 1955, was credited with changing Marlboro from a women's cigarette to a masculine-oriented brand, which it firmly remains.

DECEMBER 9

1878   Joseph Pulitzer, 31, purchases the St. Louis *Dispatch*, a shattered daily newspaper, for $2,500. He was left with $2,700. The one thing the *Dispatch* did have was Associated Press membership, and Pulitzer used this as leverage to form a merger with the St. Louis *Post*. The *Post-Dispatch* showed profits immediately, Pulitzer gained complete control, and circulation doubled within a year. Pulitzer suffers ill health, and when his chief editorial writer shot a political opponent to death, Pulitzer went on an extended vacation. While passing through New York City, he decided to purchase the New York *World* from Jay Gould, and it was with the *World* that Pulitzer established his reputation as a great media executive.

1886   Creator of the frozen foods industry, Clarence Birdseye, is born the son of a lawyer in Brooklyn, New York. During and after his two years in college Birdseye worked as a field naturalist, office boy in an insurance agency, and snow checker for the New York Street Cleaner Department. Apparently, cold temperatures agreed with him, because in 1912 he went to Labrador and worked for four years as a fur trader, traveling by boat and dog sled for thousands of miles. It was during these years that he did his first experiments in quick-freezing foods, following his observation that fish caught through the ice froze immediately and retained good taste when defrosted and eaten later. He also noticed that Inuits successfully quick-froze caribou, and it too retained flavor for months. (Industrial freezing methods of the time all used slow, higher temperature freezing, which degrades tissue and flavor.) By 1923 he had secured several patents on a process that essentially duplicated the ancient processes of the Inuits, had formed Birdseye Seafoods in New York, and was getting well acquainted with the condition called bankruptcy. He barely managed to stay afloat, continued to perfect his freezing methods (partially in collaboration with Charles Seabrook), and in 1926 had established a small plant and company called General Seafoods Company in Gloucester, Massachusetts. In that year Marjorie Merriweather Post of the Postum Company happened to dock her yacht for provisioning in Gloucester and encountered Birdseye's products. The following year she finally convinced her board of directors to purchase the company, and the nucleus of the food conglomerate General Foods was formed. Birds Eye Frosted Foods were introduced in 1930 and given national distribution in 1931. Birdseye went on to other inventions and suffered a fatal heart attack in the high altitude of Peru while trying to turn the agave plant into paper.

1924   Wrigley's chewing gum is trademark registered.

1996   "More and more CEOs have become conscious that they are the CEO of marketing. You're selling trust." —Philip Kotler, marketing management thinker and academic, in *BusinessWeek*

DECEMBER 10

1792   The nation's first general insurance company to offer life insurance was the Insurance Company of North America, which is organized on this day in Philadelphia, capitalized at $600,000. Its first policy was issued five days later, but after five years only six life insurance policies had been written, and the life insurance feature was canceled in 1804.

1953   Hugh Hefner, 27, publishes the first issue of *Playboy* magazine. He'd invested $7,600 and did the editing on a kitchen table in an apartment that he shared with wife Mildred and their infant daughter,

Christie. The historic issue has no date because Hefner doubted a second issue would ever be printed. A year later he had a staff of 30 (two of whom he was dating), who occupied a four-story building in downtown Chicago. He slept in a small bedroom behind his office on the top floor, working all hours of the day and night.

1962   "The only real elegance is in the mind; if you've got that, the rest really comes from it." —Diana Vreeland, on becoming editor-in-chief of *Vogue* magazine, in *Newsweek*

DECEMBER 11

1849   The rapid movement of information—specifically, mail and newspapers—was one of the earliest clear advantages of the railroad over traditional forms of land travel. On this day, in order to publicize their joint route between London and Paris, the South Eastern and Nord railways of Britain and France dispatch copies of the morning *Times* in London at 7 A.M. and have them in Paris at 1:30 P.M.

1972   "Government does not solve problems; it subsidizes them." —Ronald Reagan, in a speech as governor of California

1987   Oliver Stone's film *Wall Street* premieres. Michael Douglas won the year's best actor Oscar for his portrayal of the reptilian wheeler-dealer Gordon Gecko, who delivered the movie's banner speech: "The point is, ladies and gentlemen, that greed, for lack of a better word, is good. Greed is right. Greed works. Greed clarifies, cuts through and captures the essence of the evolutionary spirit. Greed, in all of its forms—greed for life, for money, knowledge—has marked the upward surge of mankind and greed—you mark my words—will not only save Teldar Paper but that other malfunctioning corporation called the USA." The speech and character were based on that of real-life arbitrager Ivan F. Boesky. It is unknown whether Boesky attended today's premiere; exactly one week later he was sentenced to three years in prison and fined $100 million for exercising his greed.

1995   Malden Mills burns to the ground in Lawrence, Massachusetts, after a celebration of the 70th birthday of CEO Aaron Feuerstein.

Founded in 1906 by Feuerstein's grandfather, Malden Mills already had a reputation for solid corporate ethics; employees worked alongside trusted managers, retention of both employees and customers was an eye-popping 95 percent, and the company steadfastly refused to join other textile firms in the migration south. But none of these stellar landmarks could prepare the staff for Feuerstein's announcement a few days after the fire, when he pledged to pay the salaries and health insurance of all 2,400 workers for the foreseeable future, even though there would be no work. Full capacity was established within three months, by which time Feuerstein's generosity and loyalty cost nearly $10 million. But Feuerstein felt that he had been paid back "tenfold." For one thing, worker productivity and quality shot up, from 6–7 percent "off quality" production before the fire, dropping to 2 percent afterward. Economic downtrends in the late 1990s forced layoffs and division closures at Malden, but Feuerstein's robust morality had created a new star in the business heavens by then.

DECEMBER 12

1805   Henry Wells—a founder of both American Express and Wells Fargo—is born in Thetford, Vermont, the son of a Presbyterian clergyman. After working on a farm and spending several years as a tanner and shoemaker, Wells entered the express delivery field as an agent in Albany, New York, around 1841. Two years later he founded his own firm, the Livingston, Wells and Pomeroy Company, in which he was also a messenger. He made a weekly trip using two stages and five or six railroads between Albany and Buffalo. Wells charged 6¢ a letter, or $1 for 20 letters, while the government charged two to four times that amount. He soon cut his expenses in half (by establishing a commutation system in which he no longer had to pay separate fares for a person and a trunk) and began deliveries to other stations in New England. His service was hotly opposed by the U.S. Post Office, but public support kept it open. In 1844 Wells established a line between Buffalo and Detroit, and future partner William G. Fargo was hired as a messenger. In 1852 Wells Fargo was established to service the California gold fields, making the company transcontinental and a key accessory to the opening of the West. He died December 10, 1878.

1900   The most famous banquet in industrial history is held at the University Club in Manhattan, attended by 80 bankers and manufacturing executives. The stated reason for the gathering was to thank Charles Schwab (president of Carnegie Steel) for being such a good host at a recent tour for bankers of the Carnegie steel works around Pittsburgh. The real reason was to bring together various steel interests, most importantly those of Carnegie and J. P. Morgan, with a view toward forming an enormous trust. At the end of the meal, Schwab rose to speak, glorifying the American ore resources and manufacturing methods and saying that there was only one path toward lowering prices: consolidation followed by specialization. Schwab concluded altruistically: monopolistic control should only be used to lower prices, not to restrict output and raise prices. At the end of the evening, Morgan pulled Schwab aside for a half-hour chat. Their next meeting was an all-night conference in early January in Morgan's "black library" in Manhattan, with just the two of them and steelman John "Bet-a-Million" Gates and Morgan lieutenant Robert Bacon. Morgan famously concluded that meeting in the dawn light by saying to Schwab, "If Andy wants to sell, I'll buy. Go find his price." It was the birth of U.S. Steel.

1927   Coinventor of the microchip, cofounder of Intel, and one of the first technologists into Silicon Valley, Robert Noyce is born in either Burlington or Denmark, Iowa (sources differ).

1971   "Competition brings out the best in products and the worst in people" was one of the witticisms of David Sarnoff, the great media executive, who dies in New York City at age 80 (see February 27).

2002   "We made a professional judgment about the appropriate accounting treatment that turned out to be wrong," admits Joseph Berardino, Arthur Andersen CEO, in a government hearing on Enron. Berardino resigned in disgrace in March 2002. He had presided over the complete self-destruction of the venerable firm.

DECEMBER 13

1621   Furs are first exported from North America for England aboard the *Fortune*. The ship had arrived at Plymouth Colony, Massachusetts, just one month before with new colonists who anticipated making a living through cod fishing. Within several years, however, fur trading dominated the colonial economy. Also aboard the *Fortune* on today's launch were sassafras, clapboards, and wainscot. The entire cargo was valued at $2,450. The boat was captured by the French and the cargo seized.

1790   Alexander Hamilton submits the second *Report on the Public Credit* to Congress. It was the second of four famous reports that Hamilton wrote while secretary of the treasury, which essentially formed the blueprint for the modern American economy. The first *Report on the Public Credit* had been submitted 11 months before, and together the two documents recommended that (a) the federal government fund and pay off in full the national debt from the Revolutionary War; (b) the federal government pay off the debts incurred by individual states during the war; and (c) a system of taxation be established to fund these obligations. Hamilton clearly wanted to establish good credit with the rest of the world, and he also aimed in these measures to bind men of wealth and influence (who held most of the government bonds issued domestically) to the fate of the federal government. Opposition to Hamilton's plan was staunch, and Congress accepted it only after Hamilton cut a deal with Secretary of State Thomas Jefferson, in which Jefferson would deliver the necessary votes if Hamilton agreed to establish the national capitol on the banks of the Potomac, in Jefferson's backyard. Hamilton submitted his third report on the following day (see December 14).

1816   Werner von Siemens—the eldest of four brothers who founded the Siemens business empire based on their scientific discoveries and inventions—is born in Lenthe, Germany. Werner's first important chemistry experiments were conducted in prison (where he was serving a brief sentence for acting as a second in a duel between fellow army officers). From these experiments he invented the electroplating process. This later was a moneymaker, but the first Siemens companies dealt with the manufacture of telegraph equipment. Werner died December 6, 1892, in Berlin.

1934   The first person ever to receive a telephone call—Thomas A. Watson, who was Alexander Graham Bell's assistant and later became an important shipbuilder—dies at 80 in Passagrille Key, Florida.

2002   Coca-Cola announces that it will no longer release quarterly and annual earnings forecasts. Coke was one of just a few major companies that now had this no-forecast policy; the Washington Post Co. and Gillette were two others. Ace investor Warren Buffett was on the board of all three, and one of his strongest tenets was investing for the long term and not reacting to short-term developments. Forecasts cater to those looking short-term. Coincidentally, on this same day, the stock price of PepsiAmericas Inc. dropped dramatically (26 percent) on the New York Stock Exchange after the company admitted that after poor forecasting it would have to revise earnings predictions downward.

DECEMBER 14

1720   The colorful John Law—once a French national hero for his financial acumen, but now seen as a huckster because his "Mississippi Bubble" has burst—flees France with his son, a few mediocre gems, and just 2,000 livres (at the height of the bubble, a single share in the Mississippi Company cost six times that amount). Law had indeed created the bubble, but he profited little from it: he invested heavily in it and lost everything, he deposited no funds abroad, and he directed funds to the public good when the bubble was sucking money into the royal coffers. Under his two-year regime as France's chief financial officer (1719–1720) taxes were reduced; corrupt tax agencies were abolished; tariffs on imported foods and other goods were abolished; roads, canals, and bridges were built; artisans were imported to start industries; the merchant marine was expanded; trade in Africa, America, and Asia was expanded; and French enterprises were increased by 60 percent. Law is often vilified in history, but his sour reputation rests partially on the fact that the bubble caused so much public misery and partially because corruption surrounded him. Following today's flight, Law, 49, went to Brussels. There he received an invitation from Peter the Great to come and take control of Russia's finances. Law refused, went to Venice, was joined by his wife and daughter, and lived in obscurity and poverty until he died in 1729 (see January 5).

1790   Alexander Hamilton submits *Report on a National Bank* to Congress. It was the third of the four famous reports that Hamilton wrote while secretary of the treasury, outlining the future American economy. In this document, Hamilton advocated a national bank called the Bank of the United States, which was to be modeled after the Bank of England. It would serve as the repository for national funds, would serve as a lending institution, and would cement the partnership between the government and business classes, which would benefit most from it. As with previous reports, there was stiff opposition to his plans (see December 13). President Washington signed the bill for the bank on February 25, 1791, but Hamilton's vision of a strong central bank was not realized until 1913, with the creation of the Federal Reserve System.

1943   John Harvey Kellogg—physician and health food pioneer whose chance discovery of cornflakes was largely responsible for the birth of the flaked-cereal industry—dies at age 91 in Battle Creek, Michigan.

DECEMBER 15

1668   Louis XIV, chairman of the board of directors of the new French East India Company, hosts a meeting of disgruntled shareholders at the Tuileries. Instead of sending a fleet to India for merchandise as he'd promised, the Sun King, 30, had ordered the ships to Madagascar to expand his empire and his glory. Finance minister Jean-Baptiste Colbert tried to mollify the angry investors, promising a concentration in the future on economic returns. When it was Louis's turn to speak, he said nothing of the sort, instead reminding the investors of their obligations to pay up on their pledges. Things got worse for the company. Traded goods brought no profit. Ships got into difficulties with accidents and pirates. Dutch employees cheated their French employers. In 1675 the company folded, and the investors lost everything.

1886   More than a million shares of stock are traded for the first time on one stock exchange. On this day, 1,096,509 shares changed hands on the New York Stock Exchange.

1892   Destined to be the world's richest man for a while, Jean Paul Getty is born in Minneapolis. His father was a lawyer and successful oil-man. At age 21, after graduating from the University of California and doing graduate work in economics at Oxford, Getty went into the oil business with a vow to earn a million dollars within two years. He bought and sold oil leases with great success and earned his first million on time. He then took a few years off to enjoy his money, spending it largely on women. His most daring and most profitable business venture began in 1949, when he paid Ibn-Saud $9.5 million in cash and $1 million a year for a 60-year concession to a tract of barren land near the border of Kuwait and Saudi Arabia. No oil had ever been discovered there, and none was discovered for the first four years of Getty's contract. From 1953 onward, however, Getty's gamble produced over 16 million barrels a year and earned Getty his first billion. "I'm a bad boss," he once confessed. "A good boss develops successors. There is nobody to step into my shoes." (See June 6.)

1966   Walt Disney dies at age 65 in Los Angeles. "You may not realize it when it happens, but a kick in the teeth may be the best thing in the world for you," he once said (see December 5).

1995   On the 109th anniversary of first trading one million shares of stock in a single day (see above), the New York Stock Exchange sets another trading volume record: 652.8 million shares. The old record was 608.2 million shares traded on October 20, 1987. Kmart Corporation spurred today's charge, with 24.3 million of its shares traded. Today was not a good day for investors; Kmart's stock price sank to its lowest level in thirteen years, and the market suffered a modest overall loss.

1999   "The market economy succeeds not because some people's interests are suppressed and other people are kept out of the market, but because people gain individual advantage from it." —Amartya Sen, Indian economist and winner of the 1998 Nobel Prize in Economics, in the *Atlantic Monthly*

DECEMBER 16

1774   Two important economists—Francois Quesnay and Leon Walras—share passings on this day. One helped create the "classical" school of economics, the other helped kill it. Quesnay dies at Versailles at age 80 on this day in 1774. An important influence on Adam Smith, Quesnay was the intellectual leader of the physiocrats, the first systematic school of economics (see June 4). In **1834** Walras was born in Evreux, France. He independently discovered the marginal utility theory of value, and his *Elements d'economie politique pure* (two volumes, 1874 and 1877) was one of the first comprehensive mathematical analyses of economic equilibrium; it tied together theories of production, exchange, money, and capital for the first time. Valuation is a cornerstone of any economic system. Walras's marginal utility theory of value stated that the value of anything depends on the satisfaction that the next unit will provide. The theory marked the boundary between "classical" and "neoclassical" economics because it rejected objective cost-of-production theories of value and replaced them with a focus on subjective/psychological principles of utility and consumer demand.

1945   Founder of Fiat (Fabrica Italiana Automobili Torino), Giovanni Agnelli, is born in Villa Perosa, Piedmont, now Italy.

1949   The Swedish airplane company Svenska Aeroplan Aktiebolagat (renamed Saab in the 1960s) produces its first automobile. Intended to diversify its product line and compete with the successful 22-year-old Swedish company Volvo, Saab cars were engineered with the precision of fighter planes, which happened to be the company's other main product. Safety, reliability, and high performance became the hallmarks of Saab vehicles. By 1990 General Motors owned a large portion of the company, and 10 years later it owned all of the automotive operations.

1954   The Federal Communications Commission reports for the first time that television industry profits exceed those of radio. For the year 1953, television and network profits were $68 million, as opposed to $55 million for radio and its networks.

1983   "The two sides of industry have traditionally always regarded each other in Britain with the greatest possible loathing, mistrust and contempt. They are both absolutely right." —Auberon Waugh, British writer and journalist, in *Private Eye*

DECEMBER 17

1679   A group of manufacturers sign the first pricing agreement—the essence of a monopolistic trust—in U.S. history. Twenty-one coopers in New York City agreed upon "ye Rate and Prizes of Caske, this is to Say, for euery Dry halfe Baril one shilling Six Pence . . . " The pact concluded, "And Wee, ye Under Written, Doo Joyntly and Seavorally Bind ourselves, that for Euery one that shall sell any cask Beefore mentioned under the Rate or Prizes aboue, Sd., that for euery Such Default ffiuety Shillinges he or they shall pay for vse of the poore, as Wittnes our hands, this 17th Day of December, 1679." (See January 8 for the fate of the 21 coopers.)

1860   James Herbert McGraw—who started the McGraw-Hill publishing empire with the purchase of a broken magazine about railroad appliances—is born in Panama, Chautauqua County, New York, the son of Irish immigrant dairy farmers. McGraw was a teacher and school principal in upstate New York who sold magazine subscriptions on the side. In 1886, while trying to collect $1,500 owed to him from the *American Journal of Railway Appliances*, he was given the opportunity to buy the magazine. Borrowing $1,000 from a wealthy Chautauqua farmer, McGraw made the purchase, moved to New York City, and immediately switched the magazine's focus from horsecars to electrification. He also dealt with competitors by buying them out and consolidating. At about the same time, his future partner, John Alexander Hill, was establishing his own career in publishing. A locomotive engineer who began writing articles for *American Machinist* and *Locomotive Engineer*, Hill came to own both. Both McGraw and Hill specialized in technical trade magazines, and both were innovators in similar fashion: (a) they drew clear distinctions between advertising and editorial material (uncommon in the day's trade publications); and (b) they reported circulation figures honestly (also rare). In 1909 they formed McGraw-Hill Book Company and soon became a major force in both books and periodicals on technical subjects. McGraw died February 21, 1948.

1875   H. J. Heinz declares bankruptcy. "I have two thousand dollars to meet tomorrow, and not a penny to meet it with," he had written in his diary in late November. Creditors accused him of fraud and had him arrested twice. He broke out in boils. The 31-year-old was years from becoming a successful food processor. Another diary entry recorded his personal misery: "No Christmas gifts to exchange. Sallie [his wife] seemed grieved, and cried, yet said it was not about our troubles; only she did not feel well. It is grief. I wish no one such trials. . . . I feel as though people are all pushing us down because we are bankrupt. Such is the world."

1963   "A man who trusts nobody is apt to be the kind of man whom nobody trusts." —Harold Macmillan, British prime minister and statesman, in the *New York Herald Tribune*

1974   The 1 millionth U.S. trademark is registered to the Cumberland Packing Corporation for a simple G clef and staff design used on Sweet 'N Low packets.

1977   Ben & Jerry's Homemade Inc.—famous for its distinctive ice creams and its social activism—incorporates in the state of New Hampshire. Ben's name was listed first because Jerry was listed as president. In February Cohen and Greenfield set up shop in an abandoned gas station in Burlington. There was no heat and four inches of ice on the floor when they first opened the door. The place was a mess: no drywall, debris everywhere, a roof that was essentially plastic sheeting over insulation. To accommodate their limited construction skills and a hardly there budget, they made a deal with handyman Darrell Mullis; in exchange for his services, he would get an unlimited supply of ice cream for as long as the boys managed to stay in business. Darrell was the charter member of the Ice Cream for Life Club. That was the first of many creative promotions from their fertile minds.

DECEMBER 18

1972   The term *junk food* first appears in print, in *Time* magazine.

1984   The Chevy Nova automobile is introduced by New United Motor Manufacturing, Inc. (a joint venture between Toyota and General Motors). The Nova became a fixture in the literature on what *not* to do in marketing when it was introduced in Spanish-speaking South

America. In English *nova* refers to a celestial body, but in Spanish *no va* translates as "no go" or "does not move."

1987   Ivan Boesky is sentenced by Federal Judge Morris E. Lasker to three years in light security prison and fined $100 million (half of which is tax deductible) for insider trading fraud that the *Wall Street Journal* called the "largest scandal in Wall Street history." Many criticized the leniency of the sentence, but Boesky was granted the leniency because he provided evidence against his coconspirators.

1991   General Motors announces it will close 21 North American plants over the next four years and slash tens of thousands of jobs in a sweeping restructuring of the world's largest company.

1994   "Only the paranoid survive." —Andrew S. Grove, entrepreneur and chairman of Intel Corporation, on the philosophy by which he ran Intel

DECEMBER 19

1903   "Do not think a man has done his full duty when he has performed the work assigned him. A man will never rise if he does only this. Promotion comes from exceptional work." —Andrew Carnegie, stating the fourth of his rules of business success in the *Pittsburgh Bulletin*

1936   Parker Brothers president George Parker sends a memo to the manufacturing plant ordering it to "cease absolutely to make any more boards or utensil boxes. We will stop making Monopoly against the possibility of a very early slump." Decades later the game continues to be a top seller in dozens of countries.

1974   The personal computer revolution begins. The Altair 8800, a do-it-yourself minicomputer kit, goes on sale for $397. It was produced by the MITS company in Albuquerque, New Mexico. The Altair was named after a fictional planet on the TV series *Star Trek*. It had no screen or keyboard: rows of toggle switches were used for inputs, and flashing lights were the output display. Two young computer geeks in Cambridge, Massachusetts, saw the Altair advertised in the January issue of *Popular Electronics*. One was Bill Gates, a student at Harvard who would soon drop out. The other was a high school classmate, Paul Allen, who had already dropped out of the University of Washington to pursue a career in computers and had recently taken a job with Honeywell. The pair concluded that the Altair would not be a practical success without an operating language, and that they were just the pair to produce that language, based on their mastery of the computer language BASIC. They immediately started to work on the BASIC adaptation for the Altair, and Gates wrote to MITS saying they had already produced the adaptation. Ed Roberts, inventor of the Altair, liked what he heard and invited the boys to New Mexico. Gates and Allen had never seen a real Altair, but they rigged up another computer to simulate one, and in eight feverish weeks produced a code they hoped would work. In February a nervous Paul Allen flew to New Mexico, still never having seen an Altair. He entered the code (most of which was on paper tape; some last-minute commands were entered by hand) and was asked at the teletype for some specifications. When these were entered, the Altair sent back the message, "Ready." With that word, a new computer software industry was born. Roberts decided on the spot to offer BASIC with the Altair. In the summer of 1975, with a contract from MITS in hand, Gates and Allen formed Microsoft (the name of the company was originally hyphenated as Micro-Soft).

1997   Cofounder of Sony, Masaru Ibuka, dies of heart failure at 89 in Tokyo. In 1945 he started his own radio repair shop in a bombed-out Tokyo building. Although the company developed several new products, its great breakthrough did not happen until the early 1950s, when it purchased the Japanese rights to the American invention, the transistor. "At the time, research and development of transistor [technology] was largely aimed at industrial and military use," Ibuka said in a 1992 government ceremony honoring his invention of the transistor radio. "Nobody was thinking about making use of it in commercial products."

DECEMBER 20

1790   The nation's first mill to successfully spin cotton yarn is begun in Pawtucket, Rhode Island, by 22-year-old British immigrant Samuel Slater and wealthy 52-year-old merchant Moses Brown. The mill was 40 feet long, 26 feet wide, and two stories high, with an attic as well. Power was obtained from an old fulling mill waterwheel on the Blackstone River. It required nine *children*, supervised by Slater, to operate. Credited with establishing the textile industry and the factory system in America, Slater's mill gained immediate recognition; in his report to Congress on December 5, 1791, Secretary of the Treasury Alexander Hamilton said, "The manufactory at Providence has the merit of being the first in introducing into the United States the celebrated cotton mill, which not only furnishes materials for the manufactory itself but for the supply of private families, for household manufacturing."

1820   A tax on bachelorhood is first levied in the United States by the state of Missouri. Taking effect the following January 1, the tax of $1 was levied "on every unmarried free white male, above the age of 21 years and under 50 years."

1973   "But I'm merely a simple Bedouin." —Sheik Ahmed Zaki Yamani, Saudi Arabian statesman who masterminded the OPEC pricing strategy that brought huge returns to producers but ultimately precipitated the oil crisis of the 1970s, in *Newsweek*

1995   The record for most shoppers to visit a department store in a single day is set in Shanghai, China, at the Nextage store, when an estimated 1.07 million customers walked into the establishment.

DECEMBER 21

1844   The cooperative movement is born when Charles Haworth and 27 poverty-stricken English weavers in Rochdale, Lancashire, form the Rochdale Society of Equitable Partners. They established a tiny food store on Toad Lane, sold strictly for cash at local retail prices, and at year's end divided all profits among the members. Flour, oatmeal, butter, and sugar were the initial offerings, but tea, coal, clothing, and furniture were soon added. Cooperatives—organizations owned by and operated for the benefit of their members—spread rapidly across Europe, America, and Latin America, and now have been established in various industries, including farming, wholesaling, power, credit and banking, and housing.

1929   America's first group hospital insurance plan is effected on this day by Baylor University Hospital, Dallas, Texas, for Dallas public school teachers.

1937   Walt Disney's *Snow White and the Seven Dwarfs* premieres at the Carthay Circle Theater in Hollywood. Based on the Grimms' fairy tale, it was the first full-length animated feature film, and the first feature in Technicolor. The budgeted $1 million production cost swelled to $1.5 million (making Disney's chief creditor, the Bank of America, jittery and earning the project the nickname of "Disney's folly"), but that was soon recouped. The film grossed $8.5 million on the first of several releases. "All the Hollywood brass turned out for my cartoon!" exulted Disney at today's opening. He was to receive a special Oscar for his achievement, and on the strength of the film's success, Walt and his brother Roy (the studio's business manager) purchased 51 acres in Burbank, California, and erected a state-of-the-art animation facility. "The house that Snow White built" was Disney's name for it.

1979   Early in the morning, the U.S. Congress approves a $1.5 billion loan guarantee to aid the sinking Chrysler Corporation. It was the largest federal rescue plan ever for a U.S. company. To the surprise of many, the plan worked. Under the stewardship of Lee Iacocca, Chrysler developed new cars that sold well, union wages and benefits were reduced, and thousands of workers were laid off. All the loans that were guaranteed by today's vote were paid back—early. By the late 1980s the company was posting record profits. The government actually made money, $311 million, when it sold back to Chrysler its right to buy shares in Chrysler at a set price. The government's stake would have been worth $2.9 billion if it had held out until 1998, however, when Chrysler merged with Daimler-Benz to form Daimler Chrysler.

1993   Founder of Domino's Pizza Inc., Thomas Monaghan, announces in Detroit that his company is ending its famous and successful guarantee of delivering its pies in 30 minutes or less. The announcement came four days after a St. Louis jury awarded $78 million in punitive damages to a woman struck by a Domino's driver who ran a red light in 1989.

DECEMBER 22

1650   New England colonists pass a law requiring bakers to make standard-weight loaves and to use only pure wheat or rye flour. The action came amid growing complaints about the leanness of the common loaf of bread. In this same year, bakers in Stockholm fought at the town gates for flour following the worst harvest of the century. The clergy and the burghers sided with the bakers, but the threatened revolution never materialized.

1882   The first string of Christmas tree lights is created by Edward H. Johnson, an associate of Thomas Alva Edison. The dangerous custom of decorating Christmas trees with burning candles was soon obsolete.

1900   A new 35-horsepower car built by Gottlieb Daimler from a design by investor Emil Jellinek is completed. The auto was named for Jellinek's daughter, Mercedes.

1913   Shortly before 11:00 P.M., by an overwhelming vote of 298 to 60, the House of Representatives adopts the conference agreement on the Currency Act (also called the Glass-Owen Federal Reserve Act). The law was approved by the Senate the following day and quickly signed by President Woodrow Wilson, who had pushed it through Congress. The act made possible the issuance of more currency and—more important to posterity and the world's financial security—established the Federal Reserve system. Not since Andrew Jackson's time had the United States had a central bank. Then, as now, there was a public fear over the concentration of the nation's wealth, which is why the Federal Reserve was divided into regional banks. The need for a central bank became clear with the panic of 1907, which the government was unable to stem, but which J. P. Morgan stopped abruptly by organizing several bankers' alliances.

1987   "It would have been cheaper to lower the Atlantic." —Lew Grade, British entertainment entrepreneur, on the failure of his movie *Raise the Titanic*, in the *Sun*

DECEMBER 23

1732   "Father of the factory system," Sir Richard Arkwright is born in Preston, England.

1867   Cosmetics manufacturer and developer, as well as the first black female millionaire, Madame C. J. Walker is born as Sarah Breedlove near Delta, Louisiana. Her parents were poor farmers, and Sarah was orphaned at age six. She was raised by her older married sister, married at 14, delivered a child, and was widowed at 20. She then moved to St. Louis and for 18 years supported herself and her daughter, A'Lelia, as a washerwoman. She experimented with hair treatments using washtubs and kitchen utensils and in 1905 hit upon a formula—later to be called the Walker method, or Walker system—that could straighten, smooth, and shine the hair of black women. It involved shampoo, a pomade "hair grower," heated combs, and vigorous brushing. She quickly achieved local success, initially through door-to-door sales and demonstrations. She then moved to Denver to join her brother, and it was there that she met and married newspaperman Charles J. Walker. Henceforth she was known as Madame C. J. Walker. She devoted herself to developing and manufacturing her products, which were marketed through a fast-growing corps of "Walker agents." A second office was opened in Pittsburgh, but then in 1910 the headquarters was moved to Indianapolis, where she established a manufacturing plant and laboratory. At its peak, her enterprise employed 3,000 people, by far the nation's largest black-owned business. "I am a woman who came from the cotton fields of the South. From there I was promoted to the washtub," she told a black business convention in 1912. "From there I was promoted to the cook kitchen. And from there I promoted myself into the business of manufacturing hair goods and preparations. . . . I have built my own factory on my own ground."

1928   NBC establishes a permanent coast-to-coast radio network, the first in the country. The glory was short-lived; earlier in the year, William Paley had founded CBS and soon would be breathing down the neck of David Sarnoff's NBC. A football game was televised coast-to-coast for the first time on this day in 1951; the Dumont Network broadcast the NFL championship game in which the Los Angeles Rams defeated the Cleveland Browns, 24–17.

DECEMBER 24

1814   On this day the Treaty of Ghent is signed, officially ending the War of 1812. Like other threatened cities, New York had built fortifications against invasion during the war. Because the federal government was bankrupt, New York spent its own funds, a total outlay of $933,007.90. In February 1815, Secretary of the Treasury Alexander Dallas notified New York officials that President James Madison had authorized him to repay the debt in "stock and Treasury notes," rather than in cash. The city fathers rejected the offer. In March 1818 Secretary of War William H. Crawford rejected the city's entire claim for reimbursement on the grounds that there was no valid documentation of the loan. The War Department, he said, had no record of authorizing New York to construct the ramparts. And that's where the matter sits today. With the original principle of nearly $1 million, plus 5 percent interest compounded annually, the Big Apple has a claim of well over $12 billion.

1867   On this day, R. H. Macy's department store in New York City stays open on Christmas Eve until midnight for the first time and sets a record for one-day receipts of $6,000.

1905   Howard Hughes is born in Houston, Texas, the only child of the machine tool industrialist Howard Hughes, Sr. Howard Jr. lost his mother when he was 16 and lost his father three years later. While a freshman at Cal Tech, he took over his father's business and began to run it. He was offered $7.5 million for the business but refused, and within a year he was making over $2 million per annum from it. It was the basis of a fortune he grew to enormous size.

1988   "I sell enthusiasm." —Silvio Berlusconi, Italian media entrepreneur and prime minister, in the *Financial Times*

1997   Jerry Seinfeld turns down $100 million. On this day the comedian telephoned the chairman of GE/NBC, Jack Welch, who 10 days before had offered him $100 million in GE stock to keep his top-ranked, award-winning TV show on the air just one more year. "Jack, this is a very hard decision for me, and I hate to disappoint you," said Seinfeld from Burbank, California. "Jack, it's Christmas Eve and I'm in my cubicle. Everyone else has gone off to their families, and I'm here writing a show. I can't do it another year, Jack. I can't."

DECEMBER 25

1863   Charles Pathé—pioneer motion picture executive whose vast network of production and distribution facilities dominated the world film market in the early 20th century—is born in Paris. At age 33 he founded Pathé Freres (Pathé Brothers, 1896) with brother Emile in Paris; the company manufactured and sold phonographs and phonograph cylinders. They quickly adopted the new technologies created by Edison and the Lumiere brothers and began making their own short films, most of which involved sensational crimes, melodramatic love affairs, or comic anecdotes. In 1909 Pathé produced his first feature-length movie, *Les Miserables*, and also created the newsreel (with its distinctive crowing rooster, the newsreel was an international fixture in cinemas until 1956). In 1914 Pathé Freres released *The Perils of Pauline* in the United States, one of the earliest and best remembered screen serials. With production facilities in France, Britain, and America, and a worldwide distribution network, Pathé Freres was enormously lucrative. Some of its productions yielded profits 50 to 100 times their cost. Pathé retired in 1929; by that time he had already started to sell off production facilities. Pathé Freres continued as a major film distributor. Pathé died December 26, 1957.

1865   The Union Stock Yards open in Chicago, making that city the hub of transcontinental commerce. The land itself was a 345-acre tract of reclaimed swampland southwest of the city limits. With the Mississippi River virtually shut down by the Civil War, Chicago replaced Cincinnati, Louisville, and St. Louis as the nation's meatpacking center. The city doubled its packing capacity in a single year of the war with eight new large packing plants and many small ones to serve the nine railroads that converged on Chicago. The city had spent $1.5 million to build the Union Stock Yards, with pens that could hold 10,000 head of cattle and 100,000 hogs at any given time.

1870   Cosmetics queen Helena Rubinstein is born in Krakow, Poland, the daughter of a merchant. She studied medicine briefly in Switzerland before a visit to relatives in Australia in 1891 changed her life. To treat their skin which had been dried and roughened by the climate "down under," her female relatives borrowed the skin cream she had brought from Poland. Her eyes were opened to the shortage of cosmetics there, and soon she had established an importing and consulting business. The concept of a salon where women could buy products as well as receive free consultations was an independent discovery of her own. After studying dermatology with several leading authorities in Europe, she opened her first salon in Melbourne in 1902. A newspaper article about her night cream brought 15,000 orders by mail, with every woman sending cash for her order. In 1904 she left the Australian operation in the care of two sisters and took $100,000 in profits to establish other salons in Europe (and later in America, where she ended up focusing most of her time). During these years her line of trademarked beauty products grew steadily and was mainly marketed through retail shops and department stores. Her clientele was upscale. The salons themselves existed largely for the social caché they provided, and frequently showed net losses. Overall, however, the business was very lucrative, and Rubinstein became one of the richest women in the world.

1887   Hotel entrepreneur Conrad Nicholson Hilton is born the son of a Norwegian immigrant in San Antonio, New Mexico (see January 3).

1925   The great financial powerhouse, Nomura Securities Company Ltd, is formed in Osaka (see January 4).

1953   Theater chain owner Lee Schubert dies at about age 80, and exactly 10 years and one day later (1963) his younger brother and partner, Jacob J. ("J.J.") Schubert, dies at age 83 in New York City, where the duo had controlled 35 theaters. They established the most successful theater chain in history but were hard hit by the Great Depression and then by antitrust prosecution after they had reorganized. In the 1920s, in collaboration with Abraham Erlanger, the Schubert Brothers controlled 75 percent of all theater tickets sold in the United States.

DECEMBER 26

1852 "An error is the more dangerous in proportion to the degree of truth which it contains." —Henri Amiel

1854 Two office mainstays—wood-pulp paper and the coffeemaker—are patented. In 1854 Hugh Burgess and Charles Watt patented the first useful process for making paper from wood fiber in the United States (eventually replacing the more expensive rag-pulp preparation). On this day in 1865 a coffee percolator was first patented in the United States by James H. Nason of Franklin, Massachusetts.

1880 Industrial psychologist George Elton Mayo is born the second of seven siblings in Adelaide, Australia (see September 7).

1904 Pioneer of the "takeover bid," financier Sir Charles Clore is born the son of a Russian immigrant in London.

1946 The glamorous Flamingo Hotel opens in Las Vegas, beginning that town's transformation into a resort of grandiose hotel-casinos. Jimmy Durante, Rose Marie, and Xavier Cugat were the entertainment headliners on opening night. The project was the vision—and downfall—of mobster "Bugsy" Siegel. A murderer and rapist he may have been, a building contractor he was not. He paid premium prices for building materials, which the war had made scarce. Other suppliers stole him blind; one story tells of expensive palm trees being driven in during the day and driven out at night; Siegel seems to have purchased the same trees several times. The $1 million projected cost ballooned to $6 million, and Siegel borrowed the money from gangsters Meyer Lansky and Lucky Luciano. Siegel was gunned down on June 20, 1947; his creditors immediately took possession of the Flamingo.

DECEMBER 27

1703 The far-reaching Methuen Treaty is signed between Portugal and England. It was named for the English envoy John Methuen, who got the better of the deal. Portugal agreed to admit English textiles (previously banned), and England agreed to import Portuguese wines at a duty rate one-third lower than that imposed on French wines. In combination with another treaty signed earlier in the year, Portugal was now freed of Franco-Spanish domination, only to have it replaced with economic dependence on England. The pact undercut the Portuguese economy and boosted the British in several other ways. Much of Portugal's wine-growing region was owned by English capitalists, and soon vast fields of grain were converted into vineyards. Thus, Portuguese bread was sacrificed for English wine. Furthermore, Portugal continued to be an agricultural country, a producer of raw materials, and an importer of manufactured goods; as a result, nascent industry in Portugal was deterred for well over a century. The treaty was finally revoked in 1842.

1848   Giovanni Battista Pirelli—founder of Italy's first rubber factory and a pioneer in the manufacture of automobile tires—is born in Varenna, Italy.

1898   Uneeda Biscuit—one of the first foods to be given a nationwide advertising campaign and established as a national brand (see February 4)—is trademark registered.

1945   Twenty-eight nations sign an agreement in Washington, D.C., that creates the International Monetary Fund and the World Bank.

DECEMBER 28

1895   The first screening of a movie for a paying audience takes place in the basement of the Grand Café on the Boulevard des Capucines in Paris. Thirty-three people were in the audience, watching several short films showing scenes from normal French life. The event has been referred to as "the birth of the film industry." The camera and projector were invented by the Lumiere brothers, and their *Lunch Break at the Lumiere Factory*, shown today, is considered history's first movie. The Lumieres called their projector/camera the *cinematographe*, which gave rise to the word *cinema* and its derivatives.

1967   Muriel ("Mickie") Siebert becomes the first woman to be a member of the New York Stock Exchange. Her seat cost $445,000 plus a $7,515 initiation fee.

2000   Montgomery Ward announces it will refile for bankruptcy and is closing its doors forever, after 128 years in business. Holiday sales had been sluggish, and GE's Capital Unit (the current owner) had decided to pull the plug; 250 stores in 31 states closed. Founded in 1872, Wards pioneered mail-order catalogs when it came out with a single sheet of drygood items. It was the nation's first mail-order house to sell general merchandise. (Sears Roebuck was not founded until 1886, and its first catalog appeared a decade later.) The first Wards store opened in Plymouth, Indiana, in 1926.

DECEMBER 29

1800   The inventor of vulcanized rubber, Charles Goodyear, is born in New Haven, Connecticut, and the inventor of celluloid, Alexander Parkes, is born thirteen years later (**1813**) in Birmingham, England. Goodyear's process, discovered when he accidentally dropped a chemical solution on a hot stove, made rubber commercially viable. Parkes' material was the first plastic.

1867   The first telegraph ticker to be used in a brokerage concern is installed on this day in the office of David Groesbeck & Company, a member of the New York Stock Exchange, by the Gold and Stock Company of New York City. A rental of $6 a week was charged for the service, which was operated by that clever rascal Daniel Drew.

1891   Founder of Hallmark Cards, Joyce Clyde Hall is born the fifth son of a minister in David City, Nebraska. From the age of nine he worked after school and on the weekends in a stationery store owned by brothers William and Rollie. At 14, pooling his savings of $158 with equal amounts from his brothers, he opened his first business, an agency for selling cards. He began going on the road as a salesman of scenic postcards (and also selling a sawdust sweeping compound to pad his income). In 1910, having quit school at 15, he took his savings of $3,500 and established himself as a jobber of postcards while attending business college at night. His first inventory was two shoeboxes of imported postal cards. The Hallmark label was born in 1913 when he went into partnership with Rollie to sell their own Christmas cards as well as cards manufactured by others. An early fire left them without an inventory, without a plant, and with a debt of $7,000, but they rebounded. Hall was a gifted and pioneering marketer. He developed the Eye Vision Display Fixture; he went big into radio and television advertising (developing several showcase programs like the "Hallmark Hall of Fame" television series); he was one of the first to use Walt Disney characters on cards and to use the works of noted artists like Norman Rockwell and Grandma Moses; and he created unfolding cards that told a story. A brand that meant quality was a main marketing objective. "When you care enough to send the very best" was the company's brilliant slogan. By 1953 Hallmark was the largest greeting card firm in the world, producing more than 1,500,000 cards a day. His business really boomed after World War II, producing 8 million cards a day at the time of his death on October 29, 1982.

2000   Europe's oldest currency, the 2,650-year-old Greek drachma, endured war and turmoil. It finally met its match in the euro, and on this Friday drachmas are traded for the last time on the international market. Greece officially joined the European Union's single currency on January 1, and financial institutions began trading in the euro on the next business day. The drachma—meaning "handful" in ancient Greek—was the standard silver coin of Greek antiquity. Believed to have first been minted in about 650 B.C. in what is now western Turkey, it was originally worth a handful of arrows. It was produced separately by different city-states and was widely spread across Europe and Asia by trade and by conquest. It was the coin of Alexander the Great. It also served as the model for another ancient coin, the dirham, which is still used in the Islamic world today.

DECEMBER 30

1525   Jakob Fugger II—the "culminating genius of the family" that became Europe's wealthiest through its activities in mining, trading, banking, and manufacturing, not to mention the financing of emperors, popes, and kings—dies at age 66 in Augsburg, Germany, the city he made the financial capital of Christendom at the end of the 15th century. Jakob's career is seen as a watershed between the primitive commercial practices of the Middle Ages and the dawning of modern capitalism (marked by the growth of private monopolies, the formation of public companies, and the dominance of businessmen controlling money over feudal lords owning land). Originally destined for a career in the church, Jakob took to studying the latest methods in bookkeeping from an early age, and his career was marked by intense study of all aspects of business, trade, and production. "I want to gain while I can" was his stated motto. His management was phenomenal: Jakob became sole head of the firm in 1511, when its assets were 196,791guilders; in 1527 the Fugger assets were estimated at 2,021,202 guilders. That is a 50 percent profit per year through 16 years.

1844   A founding father of General Electric, Charles Albert Coffin, is born in Somerset, Massachusetts, and a founding father of Coca-Cola, Asa Candler, is born near Villa Rica, Georgia on this day in **1851**. Coffin was the first president of General Electric after it was formed by the merger of Thomson-Houston with Edison General Electric in 1892. Candler was the first president of Coca-Cola after it incorporated in 1892.

1854   The nation's first oil company, Pennsylvania Rock Oil Company, incorporates in New York City with a capital stock of $250,000 (10,000 shares at $25 each). Its principal trustees were George Henry Bissell and Jonathan G. Eveleth, each of whom owned 1,250 shares. The company controlled 200 acres in western Pennsylvania and initially gathered surface oil using shallow wells and trenching. The oil was used for health purposes in salves and medicines. Bissell had a hunch that it could also be used as a fuel/illuminant and as a lubricant, and he sent a sample to Yale professor Benjamin Silliman, Jr., for analysis of its properties and potential. Silliman's glowing report caused Bissell and Eveleth to reorganize and refinance their company, with Silliman as its president. They continued to harvest only surface oil until 1859 when a field agent in their employ, Edwin Drake, struck a deep vein in Titusville using an entirely new method, drilling. It was the world's first oil strike, and it would have enormous industrial and environmental ramifications.

1953   The first color television sets go on sale to the public for about $1,175. Exactly six years later, in **1959**, the *New York Times* reported an announcement by RCA chairman David Sarnoff that their color televisions were profitable for the first time since their introduction in 1955. "Color TV in Black for First Time" read the *Times* headline.

1989   "An overburdened, stretched executive is the best executive, because he or she doesn't have time to meddle, to deal in trivia, to bother people." —Jack Welch, former chairman and CEO, General Electric, in the *Financial Times*

DECEMBER 31

1600   The British East India Company is granted a charter by Queen Elizabeth I. Organized as a joint stock company and initially capitalized at £70,000 through the sale of shares, its proper name was The Honourable East India Company, the Governor and Merchants of London Trading into the East Indies. Its aim was to break the Dutch monopoly on the lucrative spice trade in what is now Indonesia, but it soon discovered more profit coming out of other locations, and by the 1630s the company was concentrating on Indian textiles and Chinese tea. The very first expedition of the East India Company netted a profit of 87.5 percent.

1860   Founder of Texaco, Joseph Cullinan is born to Irish immigrants in Sharon, Pennsylvania (see April 7). He is remembered for his skill in the field, for establishing Texas's first pipeline and refining company (in 1897), and for ruthless management. Cullinan once accepted leadership of an oil field firefighting crew on Spindletop on the condition that he could shoot disobedient workers.

1884   Florence Nightingale Graham—known to the world as Elizabeth Arden, "the mother of the treatment business" and creator of a beauty empire in cosmetics, salons, and clothes—is born in Woodbridge, Ontario. After a variety of jobs, she moved to New York City and took a job as a secretary for a cosmetics firm where she learned the rudiments of the beauty business. In 1910 she opened a salon on Fifth Avenue with Elizabeth Hubbard. The business and the partnership flopped, but she kept Elizabeth's name; the "Arden" came from Tennyson's "Enoch Arden," her favorite poem at the time. With $6,000 borrowed from a relative, she hired chemists to produce two original products (the first of 300 that would be in her line) and sank most of the rest into fancy decor for her new salon. The business was so successful that she repaid the loan in several months. Through the wholesaling of her expanding line of products, clever advertising, and the addition of new salons over several continents, she was rich and world famous by 1929. Some of her money was spent on two Maine Chance Farms (stables in Maine and Arizona); she became one of the nation's foremost racehorse owners and produced Jet Pilot, winner of the 1947 Kentucky Derby. "Treat a horse like a woman and a woman like a horse," she once said, "and they'll both win for you."

1955   General Motors ends the year as the first American company with a net income of more than $1 billion in one year. Its profit this year was $1,189,477,082 (9.6 percent earnings on sales of $12,443,277,420). GM exceeded $1.5 billion profits in 1963 and $2 billion in 1965.

1993   "Look, you can take anything away from IBM . . . but leave our people and this business will re-create itself overnight." Thus wrote the great executive and key figure in the computer revolution, Thomas J. Watson, Jr., in 1990, several years before his death on this day in New Haven, Connecticut, at the age of 79 (see January 8). "I never hesitated to promote someone I didn't like."

INDEX

AARP: May 16
ABB company: Aug 10
Abbott, Robert S.: May 5
Abbott Laboratories: Mar 15
ABC: Feb 2; Apr 14; May 3; Aug 8; Oct 14
Abney, James: Oct 11
Abolitionists: July 4; Aug 1
AC Milan soccer team: May 26
Accident insurance, first: Mar 15
Acheson, Dean: May 26
Acme Corp.: Sep 17
Act of Multipliers: Jan 13
Acton, John Emerich, Lord: Apr 5
Actors' Equity Association: Jan 4
Actors' National Protective Union: Jan 4
Actuarial tables, development of: Jan 27; Nov 8
Adair, John George: Mar 5
Adam and Eve: Apr 19; June 9
Adams, John Quincy: May 19; July 4
Adams, Thomas, Jr.: Apr 11
Adelphia: June 25
Adventures in Good Eating (Hines): Sep 9
Advertising and public relations
    historic developments in the industry: Feb 4;
        Mar 12, 25; Apr 8, 30; May 1; June 11;
        July 1, 11, 16, 27; Aug 6, 28; Sep 26;
        Oct 28; Nov 11, 22, 29; Dec 8
    quotes on: Jan 6; Feb 14, 15; Mar 12, 20;
        May 20; Aug 28; Sep 8, 16; Oct 18,
        30; Nov 24
AFL (American Federation of Labor): Jan 4, 8,
    25; Feb 9; May 4; June 27; Aug 2; Sep 6;
    Dec 8
AFL-CIO: Feb 9
Agate, James: July 19
Agnelli, Giovanni: July 1; Aug 13; Dec 16
Agricultural Department, U.S.: June 23
Agriculture Labor Relations Act: Feb 14
Air conditioning, development of: July 17;
    Nov 26
Air France: Aug 30
Air transport industry: Feb 20; Mar 22; June 28;
    Aug 10, 30; Oct 24. *See also* Wright
    Brothers; Zeppelin; *and names of specific
    companies*
Airmail Act of 1925: Oct 7
Aislabie, John: Jan 21
AK-47 rifle: Jan 24
Akron Beacon Journal: Feb 5
Al Qaeda: Sep 11

Albert, Stew: Aug 24
Alchemy: Jan 13
Aldrich, Nelson W.: June 23
Aldus company: July 15
Alexander III, Czar: May 30
Alexander the Great: Dec 29
Alfa Romeo automobiles: Dec 1
Alfonso, Juan Pablo Perez: Aug 9; Sep 10
Alison, Francis: Jan 10
Alka-Seltzer: Feb 21
"All The News That's Fit To Print" business
    slogan first used: Feb 10
Allen, Fred: Jan 25
Allen, Paul: Oct 28; Nov 29; Dec 19
Allen, Woody: Oct 25
Allied Chemical Corporation: July 17
Allis-Chalmers: Feb 16
"Almighty dollar," origin of phrase: Dec 2
Alsop, Stewart: Aug 24
Altair 8800 computer: Dec 19
Amalgamated Copper Company: Nov 12
Amazon.com: Jan 12, 22; July 16
American Can company: Aug 13
American Express: May 20; July 7; Aug 5; Oct 1;
    Dec 12
American Fur Company: Mar 29; Apr 6;
    June 23
American Ice Company: Oct 21
American Journal of Railway Appliances: Dec 17
American Medical Association: May 7
American Motors: June 6
American Mutual Liability Insurance Company:
    Mar 30
American National Resources (ANR): Feb 4
American Newspaper Annual, The: Feb 4
American Railway Association: Nov 18
American Railway Union: June 26
American Revolutionary War. *See* Revolutionary
    War, U.S.
American Stock Exchange: Oct 28
American Tobacco Co.: Jan 31; Apr 14; May 1;
    Oct 10
Amiel, Henri: Dec 26
Amos and Andy comedy team: Oct 5
Anaconda Copper Company: July 26; Nov 12;
    Dec 5
Anarchists: Apr 18; May 3, 4; July 23; Sep 16;
    Nov 4
Anderson, Jack: Sep 26
Anderson, Richard W.: Mar 28

"Anderson Bombshell" in the microchip industry: Mar 28
Anglo-Chinese War, 1856: Aug 26
Anglo-Persian Oil Company: Apr 19; Sep 17
Animal testing of products: June 30
Annenberg, Moses: Feb 11
Annenberg, Walter: Feb 11
Anthracite Coal Commission: Sep 14
AOL: Jan 6, 12; Apr 24; Nov 24
AOL Time Warner: Jan 6; Apr 24; July 18
A&P food retailer: Feb 10
Apple Computers: Jan 24; Feb 24; May 31; June 5, 25; Aug 11; Sep 17
Apple Records: Aug 11
Arbitration, industrial: May 3
Archnacarry Agreement: Sep 17
Arden, Elizabeth: Dec 31
Argentina, hyperinflation in: Apr 26
Arkwright, Richard: June 9; Dec 23
Arm & Hammer baking soda: Nov 28
Armas, Carlos Castillo, Colonel: June 17
Armour, Jonathan Ogden: Nov 11
Armour, Philip Danforth: May 16; Nov 11
Armour meat companies: Jan 20; May 16; Nov 11
Armstrong, Louis "Satchmo": July 5
ARPANET: Aug 30
Arps, Leslie: Apr 1
Arrow shirts: Oct 18
Arthur Andersen accounting firm: Mar 14, 15; Dec 12
Arthur Guinness and Sons brewers. *See* Guinness breweries
Asbestos: Apr 29
ASCAP: Oct 14
ASEA company: Aug 10
Ash, Mary Kay. *See* Mary Kay
Ash, Roy Lawrence: Oct 20
Ashcroft, Lord: Jan 16
Ashley, William H.: Sep 8
Asian financial panic, 1990s: July 2, 28
Asimov, Isaac: Jan 19
Aspirin created: Mar 6
Assembly line, moving: Jan 5, 23
Associated Actors and Artists of America: Jan 4; Sep 6
Association of American Advertisers: Aug 21
Astor, John Jacob: Mar 29; Apr 6; June 23; July 17
Astoria (fur-trading town): June 23
Atchison, Topeka and Santa Fe Railroad: Apr 4; May 31; Nov 24
Atlas Tack Company: May 19
ATM cash machine: Apr 27; May 13
Atomic Trades and Labor Council: Mar 19
AT&T: Jan 7, 13, 14, 30; Feb 6, 11; Mar 2; Apr 25, 26; June 25; July 9; Aug 16, 28; Sep 5; Oct 17; *See also* Bell Telephone companies
AT&T Wireless Group: Apr 26
Audit Bureau of Circulations: Aug 21; Nov 1
Auschwitz concentration camp: May 21
Austrian National Bank: May 11
Autobiography (Gibbon): Jan 15

Automobile, first use of word: Jan 3
Automobile industry: Feb 5, 16; Mar 1, 20, 30; June 1, 3, 4, 10; Aug 17; Sep 21, 25; Nov 2, 14, 18; Dec 22. *See also* Chrysler; Ford; GM; Internal combustion engine; Lincoln; Packard; Studebaker; Used car dealership; Volkswagen
Automobile insurance, first policy issued for: Feb 1
Automobile tire industry: Jan 16; July 23; Aug 29; Dec 27. *See also* Firestone tire companies
Averill Chemical Paint Company: Oct 25
Aviso Relation oder Zeitung (newspaper) Jan 15
Avon cosmetics company: July 18
Ayer, Francis Wayland: Feb 4

Babbage, Charles: June 5
Babson, Roger: Sep 5
"Babson Break": Sep 5
Baby boomers: Nov 2
Baby food industry, founding of: Jan 12; Oct 7
Bache Halsey Stuart Shields: Mar 27
Bachelorhood, tax on: Dec 20
Bacon, Robert: Dec 12
Baer, George F.: July 17
Bagehot, Walter: Feb 3
Baird, John Logie: Jan 27; Feb 8; Aug 13
Baird Television Development Company: Feb 8
Baker, George Ellis: Mar 27
Baker, George Fisher: Mar 27; May 2
Baker, Samuel: Mar 11
Balderston, C. Canby: Apr 17
Ballmer, Steve: July 8
Ball-point pen industry: June 10; Oct 5, 6
Baltimore and Ohio Railroad Company (the B&O): Jan 7; Feb 28; July 4; Aug 30
Banca Nazionale del Lavoro: Sep 6
Bank for Savings in the City of New York: July 3
Bank of America: May 6; June 3; Oct 17; Dec 21
Bank of England: Jan 22; July 27; Nov 4; Dec 14
Bank of Italy: Oct 17
Bank of Japan: June 27
Bank of Manhattan: Apr 2; Sep 12
Bank of North America: Jan 7
Bank of Scotland: Apr 19
Bank of the United States: July 10
Bank One: July 14
Bank robbery, first U.S.: Mar 19
Bankers Trust Company: Jan 12; Mar 24; Nov 3
Bankruptcy law, first U.S.: Apr 4
Banks and bankers, quotes on: Jan 18, 26; May 28; June 20; Oct 31
Bannister, Michael: Oct 24
Banque de France: Feb 13
Bao, Zhenan: Nov 8
Barber, Ohio Columbus: Apr 20
Barbie doll: Feb 13; Mar 9; Apr 27; July 24; Sep 6
Barclays Bank Ltd.: Nov 30
Bar-code reader first used: June 26
Barings Brothers (Barings PLC) merchant bank: Feb 23, 26; Mar 2

Barnard, Chester I.: Nov 7
Barnevik, Percy: Aug 10
Barney, Charles: Oct 21
Barnum, P. T.: Feb 22; Apr 28; June 2
Barron, Clarence: Nov 6
Barrow, Clyde: Apr 10
Barry, Dave: July 7
Barrymore, John: Aug 6
Bartholdi, Frederic-Auguste: Feb 18
Barton, Bruce, Jr.: Nov 24
Barton, Bruce, Sr.: Aug 5
Baruch, Bernard: May 9; June 20; Aug 19
Baseball: May 18, 29; June 5; July 6, 12, 20. *See also* New York Yankees
Baths of Caracalla: Feb 4
Battelle Memorial Institute: Feb 8
Batten, Barton, Durstine & Osborn advertising agency: May 20; Aug 5; Dec 7
Battle Creek Sanitarium: Feb 19
Battle Creek Toasted Cornflake Company: Feb 19
Battle of the Overpass (Ford labor dispute): May 26
Bayer company: Mar 6
BBC (British Broadcasting Company): July 7; Aug 13
BBN company: Aug 30
BCCI (Bank of Commerce and Credit International): July 5
Be My Guest (Hilton): Jan 3
Bear Stearns company: Sep 2; Oct 2
Beards, tax on: Sep 1
Beardsley, Hub: Feb 21
Beatles (music group): May 9; Aug 11; Nov 9
Beecham's Pills: Aug 6
Beef Trust: Jan 20
Beer industry: July 13. *See also* Busch; Pabst
Behn, Hernand: Jan 30
Behn, Sosthenes: Jan 30
Bell, Alexander Graham: Jan 14, 18, 30; Feb 14; July 9; Aug 15, 25; Dec 13
Bell, Elliot V.: Oct 29
Bell, Mabel Hubbard: Aug 25
Bell, Roger, Justice: June 19
Bell Atlantic Corporation: Aug 1
Bell Telephone Labs/companies: Jan 14; Feb 6, 8, 19; Mar 2; June 30; July 9; Aug 6, 28; Sep 29; Oct 10, 17; Nov 8. *See also* AT&T
Bellanca Aircraft Corporation: Aug 2
Belmont, August: Dec 8
Ben and Jerry's ice cream company: Dec 8, 17
Benn, Tony: Apr 18; Oct 6
Bennett, Harry: May 18; June 18; Sep 21
Bennett, James Gordon: May 6; June 13; Aug 19; Sep 1
Bennis, Warren: Sep 3
Benny, Jack: Jan 2
Benz, Karl-Friedrich: June 4
Berardino, Joseph: Dec 12
Berbaum, Francois: May 30
Bergstresser, Charles: Nov 6
Bergstrom, George Edwin: Jan 15
Berkman, Alexander: July 23
Berkshire Hathaway. *See* Buffett, Warren

Berlusconi, Silvio: Dec 24
Bernays, Doris: Nov 22
Bernays, Edward L.: Nov 22
Bernbach, William: Aug 13
Berners-Lee, Tim: Jan 15; Nov 12
Bessemer, Henry: Aug 14; Oct 17
Bessemer steel-making process: Aug 14; Sep 14; Oct 17
Bestfoods company: June 6
Bethlehem Steel Company: Mar 3; June 11; Sep 28
Betty Crocker products: Sep 11
Beuthien, Reinhard: July 24
Bevan, Timothy: Nov 30
Beveridge, Albert J.: Apr 27
Bezos, Jeff: Jan 12; July 16
Bhopal chemical spill: Dec 2
Billington, George: Feb 25
Binnie, Brian: Oct 4
Biograph Pictures: Apr 20
Birch, John: Jan 30
Birds Eye Frosted Foods company: Mar 6; Dec 9
Birdseye, Clarence: Mar 6; Oct 7; Dec 9
Biro, Laszlo: June 10; Oct 6
Birth of a Nation: Nov 28
Bismarck, Otto von: Mar 15
Bissell, George Henry: Dec 30
Black, Eli, M.: Feb 3
Black, Fisher: Oct 14
Black, Joseph: July 10, 17
Black Friday
    of 1745: Dec 6
    of 1869: Feb 25; Sep 24
Black Hole of Calcutta: June 20
Black Thursday
    of 1873: Sep 18, 20
    of 1929: Oct 23
Black Tuesday of 1929: Oct 29
Black-Scholes model: Oct 14
Blackshear, Cornelius: Dec 4
Blank, Arthur M.: Aug 26
Blockbuster Video: Oct 19
Blood, Brains and Beer (Ogilvy): June 23
Bloody Sunday, Russia: June 27
Bludhorn, Charles G.: Sep 20
Blue, Monte: July 31
Blue Ridge Corporation: Dec 4
"Blue sky" laws: Mar 10
BMI (Broadcast Music, Inc.): Oct 14
BMW automobile company: July 3
BOAC airlines: Oct 4
Bobst, Elmer Holmes: May 15
Body Shop, The: Aug 22; Nov 27
Boeing, William E.: June 29; July 15; Oct 1
Boeing aircraft company: Apr 28; June 29; July 15; Sep 6; Oct 1
Boesky, Ivan: Feb 4; Mar 6, 21; May 4, 18; Sep 17; Nov 14, 20; Dec 11, 18
Bohan, Owen W., Judge: Apr 11
Bok, Edward: May 29; Oct 9
Bon Marche company: Nov 29
Bond, Alan: Feb 12
Bonds, first U.S. government: Aug 4

Bonnie and Clyde: Apr 10
Bonnie Prince Charlie: Dec 6
Boo.com: May 17
Booth, Mary Louise: Nov 2
Booth Newspapers Inc.: May 24
Bootleggers, income tax and: May 16. *See also*
    Capone, Al
Borden, Gail: Nov 9
Borman, Frank: Apr 21
Boston News-Letter (first successful U.S.
    newspaper): Apr 17
Boulton, Matthew: Aug 17; Sep 3
Bourke-White, Margaret: Nov 23
Boussac, Marcel: Jan 21
Boutwell, George S.: Sep 24
Boycott, Charles Cunningham: Mar 12; Sep 23
Boycott, economic, origin of term: Sep 23
Bra invented: Nov 13
Bradley, Henry W.: Jan 3
Bradley, Milton: Nov 8
Brady, "Diamond" Jim: Jan 1
Bragg, Melvyn: Sep 23
Brainard, Paul: July 15
Brainstorming, origin of term: May 5
Bran Flakes: Oct 26
Brand imaging and creation: Feb 4; Apr 2, 21;
    May 7; June 5; Aug 20, 21; Oct 1. *See
    also* Advertising; Rolls-Royce;
    Wedgwood pottery
Brandeis, Louis: June 30
Brandywine Rolling Mill: Jan 6
Braniff airlines: Feb 20; Nov 27; Dec 4
Bray, J. R.: Nov 18
Bread, marketing of: Jan 16; Aug 17; Dec 22
Breech, Ernest: Nov 8
Bretton Woods conference: July 3
British Air company: Oct 4
British East India Company: June 20; July 1; Aug
    24; Sep 4; Dec 31
Britt, Steuart Henderson: Oct 30
BroadVision Inc.: July 29
Brolin, Charles D.: Feb 19
Brooklyn Dodgers: July 6
Brooks, Garth: Jan 30
"Brother, Can You Spare a Dime?" song
    introduced: Oct 5
Broun, Heywood Hale: July 21
Brower, Charles: May 20; Aug 10; Dec 7
Brown, George Rufus: May 12
Brown, John: Sep 9
Brown, Moses: June 9; Dec 20
Brown, Nancy: July 8
Brown Boveri company: Aug 10
Brown & Root construction company: May 12
Brown & Williamson Tobacco Corporation: Mar
    8; Apr 14
Brunswick Corp.: Mar 15
Brunswick Records: Nov 28
Bryan, Arthur: Mar 30
"Bubble blowers": Apr 18
"Bubbles," economic. *See specific names* (Asian,
    Dot.com, Florida real estate, Japanese,
    Mississippi, South Sea, "Tulipmania")

Buena Vista Hills oil reserve: Apr 7
Buffett, Warren: Feb 27, 28; Mar 7; May 3; July
    14; Aug 30; Sep 23; Dec 13
Bugas, John: Sep 21
Buick (the automobile and the company): Sep 16
Bukanin, Mikhail A.: Nov 4
Bulova Watch Company: July 1
Bunk, origin of term: Feb 25
Bunker-Ramo Corp.: May 21
Bunyan, John: Mar 17
Bureau d'Adresse: July 4
Burgess, Hugh: Dec 26
Burke, Edmund: Jan 19; Feb 7
Burmah Oil Company: May 26
Burnham, Daniel: Sep 3
Burnham, Kate: Feb 17
Burpee, David: Apr 5
Burpee, Washington Atlee: Apr 5
Burr, Aaron: Apr 2; Sep 12
Burr, Donald: Apr 30
Busch, Anheuser, Jr.: Mar 28
Bush, George: Jan 2
Business.com: Dec 1
Business consulting: Jan 22; Oct 19
Business failure, causes of: Aug 25
Business letter, ideal: Apr 6
Business magazine, first: July 30
BusinessWeek: Sep 7
Butler, R. A.: Jan 29
Buttonwood Agreement: May 17
Byrn, M. L.: Mar 27
Byron, Lord: June 5

Cabbage Patch dolls: Nov 12
Cadell, Thomas: Mar 9
Cadillac, Antoine de la Mothe: Aug 22
Cadillac (the automobile and the company):
    Feb 16, 29; Aug 17, 22; Sep 13, 16
Cadman, John: Sep 17
Calahan, Edward A.: Nov 15
Calculator, origin of term: Feb 5
Calcutta founded: Aug 24
California gold rush: Feb 26; May 20; Aug 8,
    24; Oct 27
Calloway, Wayne: Mar 11
Camel cigarettes: July 20
Campbell, John: Apr 17
Campbell, William I.: Apr 14
Campbell Soup Company: Sep 21; Nov 11
Canada, first railway in: July 21
Canarsee Indians: May 24
Candler, Asa: Nov 12; Dec 30
Cantor, Eddie: Oct 20
Capital Brush Company: Jan 13
Capitalism
    origin of term: Mar 17
    quotes on: Apr 21; Nov 8
Caplan, Mortimer: Feb 1
Capon, Robert F.: Aug 5
Capone, Al: June 12
Caracalla, Emperor: Feb 4
Caravan automobile (first minivan):
    Nov 2

Carbon paper: Oct 7
Carlson, Chester F.: Feb 8; Oct 22
Carlton, William J.: Oct 28
Carlyle, Thomas: Apr 2
Carnegie, Andrew (including Carnegie steel
    companies/factories): Feb 25; Mar 3, 28;
    May 17; June 23; July 6; Aug 11; Sep 28;
    Nov 25; Dec 8, 12, 19
Carnegie, William: May 17
Carpentier, Georges: July 2
Carrier, Willis H.: July 17; Nov 26
Carrier Air Conditioning Company: Nov 26
Carrier pigeons as business tools: Feb 23; Apr 17;
    July 21
Carroll, Charles: July 4
Carte Blanche credit card company: Jan 3
Carter, Grady: Mar 8
Carter, Jimmy: Jan 6; June 1
Carty, John Joseph: Feb 8
Case, Steve: Jan 6, 12
Casey, Jim: Aug 28
Cash register patented: Jan 30
Casket industry: Aug 16
Caslon, William: Jan 23
Caslon typeface: Jan 23
Cass, Lewis: Jan 29
Cassatt, Alexander J.: Dec 8
Cassell, Ernest: June 20
Castro, Fidel: Nov 8
Catherine the Great: Aug 23
Caxton, William: Nov 18
CBS: Jan 2; Apr 18; June 25; Sep 19, 26; Oct 11;
    Nov 22; Dec 23
CD (compact disk): July 7
"Cel" animation technology: Nov 18
Celera Genomics: June 26
Celluloid created: Dec 29
Center for Reflection, Education and Action:
    Sep 15
Chamber of Commerce, first U.S.: Mar 13
Chambers, Ray: May 19
Champy, James: Jan 7
"Chance favors the prepared mind," origin of
    phrase: Dec 7
Chanel, "Coco": May 5; Aug 19
Chanel No. 5 perfume: May 5
Chapin, Roy D.: Sep 6
Chaplin, Charlie: Apr 9
Chappe, Claude and Ignace, (system of
    telegraphy): July 12
Charlemagne: Jan 28
Charles II, king of England: May 2
Charnock, Job: Aug 24
Chase, Salmon P.: Feb 18; Apr 8; Sep 12
Chase Manhattan Bank: Sep 12
Chase National Bank: Sep 12
Chattanooga Times: Aug 18
Chautemps, Camille: Feb 6
Chavez, Cesar: Feb 14
Check, first known: Feb 6
Cheek, Joel: May 11
Cheerios introduced: May 1
Cheese factory, first commercial: Feb 3

Chesapeake and Ohio (C&O) Canal: Jan 29;
    July 4
Chesebrough, Robert A.: Jan 9; Sep 8
Chesebrough-Ponds Inc.: Jan 9; Sep 8
Chesterfield, Earl of: Feb 5; Mar 10; Aug 7;
    Oct 9
Chevins, Anthony: Apr 27
Chevrolet, Louis: June 6
Chevrolet Motor Car Company: Sep 16
Chevron: Oct 26
Chewing gum: Sep 23. *See also* Wrigley's chewing
    gum
Chicago, Burlington and Quincy Railroad:
    July 26
Chicago and Alton Railroad: Aug 3
Chicago & Milwaukee Railroad: Aug 4
Chicago Board of Trade: Feb 20
Chicago Defender: May 5
Chicago fire of 1871: Jan 5; Feb 8
Chicago riots of 1919: May 5
Chicago White Sox (Disco Demolition Night):
    July 12
Child & Co., Mssrs: Feb 6
Child labor laws: Aug 29
China
    economic expansion of: Oct 8
    westernization of economy: Oct 20
Chinese laundry, quote on: Oct 23
Chippendale, Thomas: June 5
Christie, James: Dec 5
Christie's auction house: May 2; Dec 5
Christmas tree lighting: Dec 22
Christy, David: Mar 4
Chrysler, Walter Percy: June 6
Chrysler Corporation: Jan 6; Mar 20; May 13;
    June 6; July 7; Nov 2; Dec 21
Ciardi, John
Ciena company: Sep 18
Cinema, origin of term: Dec 28
CIO (Congress of Industrial Organizations): Feb
    9, 11
Cipollone, Rose: Mar 8
"Circuit-breaker rules," Wall Street: Oct 27
CIT Group: June 2, 10
Citibank: Jan 20; Mar 1; June 16; Nov 17
Citicorp: Mar 1; Apr 6
Citigroup: Jan 13; Apr 6; June 16; July 28
Citizens Loan Corporation: Nov 1
Citroën, Andre-Gustave: Feb 5; Mar 1
Citron, Bob: Dec 6
City Bank of New York: Mar 1; June 16
Civil War, American: Feb 1, 18; Apr 8; May 16;
    July 10, 11; Aug 7, 14; Nov 9; Dec 8, 25
Civil Works Administration: Nov 9
Claflin, Tennessee Celeste: Jan 20
Clark, Alan: June 25
Clark, Edward: Aug 12
Clark, Maurice: Feb 2
Clark, William (of Lewis and Clark expedition):
    Sep 8
Clark, William F. (photographer): July 17
Claude, Georges: Dec 3
Claypoole, David C.: Sep 21

Clayson, Jane: June 25
Clayton, Henry De Lamar: Oct 15
Clayton Anti-Trust Act: Oct 15
Clearinghouse (banking institution), first U.S.:
    Aug 23
Cleese, John: June 15
Clerical/computer errors, massive: Apr 5; May 8;
    Sep 13; Oct 2; Nov 5, 30
Cleveland, Grover: Oct 23
Cleveland Browns: Dec 23
Cleveland Cavaliers: May 22
Clews, Henry: Aug 14
Clinton, Bill: June 26
Clore, Charles: Dec 26
Close Encounters of the Third Kind: Oct 31
CNN: June 1; Nov 19; Dec 6
Coal strike of 1902: May 12; Oct 13
Coastal Corporation: Feb 4
Cobb, Ty: May 18
Coca-Cola: Jan 31; Feb 28; Mar 13, 29; Apr 22,
    23; May 8, 10, 19; June 10, 19; July 11,
    14; Aug 6, 26; Nov 12; Dec 13, 30. *See
    also* New Coke; Pepsi-Cola company
Coffee industry: Sep 15; Dec 26
Coffin, Charles A.: Apr 15; June 1; Dec 30
Cohen, Ben: Dec 17
Colbert, Jean-Baptiste: Mar 23; Aug 29; Sep 6;
    Dec 15
Colebrooke, Sir George: May 1
Coleco Industries: Nov 12
Collins, Francis: June 26
Colombia: Jan 22
Colonial Air Transport: Oct 7
Colony, George: Aug 4
Colt, Samuel: July 19
Columbia Exposition: Aug 6
Columbia Pictures: Sep 27; Oct 31; Nov 25, 26
Columbus, Christopher: Jan 20; Apr 17
Combination Acts, British: June 21
Commercial Company: May 20
Commission rates, stockbrokers' fixed, end of:
    May 1
Communism: July 23; Sep 2; Nov 10. *See also*
    Lenin; Marx, Karl; Socialism
Company of Scotland: Nov 4
Company of the Hundred Associates: Apr 25
Competition, quotes on: Mar 11; Apr 9, 15; June
    12; June 16; Oct 27; Nov 1, 7, 20; Dec
    12, 18
Computer hacking: Feb 18
Computer industry, development of: Apr 9; Aug
    7. *See also* Babbage, Charles; ENIAC; IBM;
    Jacquard; Laptop computer; Microsoft;
    Mouse; SSEC; Transistors and chips;
    UNIVAC
Computer viruses: Aug 31
Computing-Tabulating-Recording Company (C-
    T-R): Jan 8; Feb 14; June 8, 16
Comsat satellite company: June 2
Comstar satellite: Dec 6
Con Ed (Consolidated Edison power company):
    Sep 4; Oct 23
Concorde aircraft: Oct 23

Condé Nast Publications: May 24
Cone, Fairfax: Mar 20
Conglomerates: Jan 9; Feb 3. *See also* ITT; Gulf
    & Western; Litton Industries
Connor, Jean: May 5
Conran, Terence: Feb 21; Oct 5
Consolidated Bank and Trust Company: July 15
Consumer protection law, first: June 13
Consumer Reports: July 24
Containerships: Aug 15
Continental Airlines: Feb 20; Nov 27
Continental Baking Company: Aug 2
Continental Can company: Aug 13
Cook, Thomas: July 5
Cooke, Jay (includes Jay Cooke & Co.): Feb 18;
    Apr 8; Aug 10, 14; Sep 18, 20
Coolidge, Calvin: Jan 17
Cooper, Art: June 9
Cooper, Daniel M.: Oct 30
Cooperatives, founding of: Dec 21
Coppertone girl (advertising symbol): Dec 8
Copyright Act of 1709, England: Apr 10
Corante: Sep 24
Corbin, Abel: Sep 24
Cordwainers, Federal Society of Journeymen:
    May 1, 25
Corkscrew patented: Mar 27
Corn Laws: Mar 23; Aug 16
Cornflakes: Feb 19, 26; Mar 7; May 31
Cornwallis, Charles, Lord: Jan 7
Corporate governance, study of: Feb 22
Corporate raiding: Apr 18. *See also* Icahn, Carl
    C.; Pickens, T. Boone; Goldsmith, James
Corporation for the Relief of Poor and Distressed
    Presbyterian Ministers and of the Poor and
    Distressed Widows and Children of
    Presbyterian Ministers: Jan 11
Cortelyou, George B.: Oct 23
Costa Rica, first railroad in: Aug 18
Costco Wholesale Corp.: Aug 16
Cotton gin: Jan 8; Mar 14; Dec 8
"Cotton is king," origin of phrase: Mar 4
Country Club Plaza: Apr 22
Couzens, James: Jan 5
Coward, Noel: June 21
Coxe, Trench: May 22; Sep 11
Crawford, William H.: Dec 24
Creative destruction
    origin of term: Feb 8
    quotes on: July 3; Sep 22; Oct 26
Creative thinking, origin of term: May 5
Creativity, quotes on: Jan 4, 6, 16; Apr 27; Aug
    10, 12, 13, 19, 24; Sep 18, 29; Oct 6;
    Dec 7
Credit Ansalt (Austrian bank) May 11
Credit card industry: Sep 26; Oct 1
Credit rating industry, history of: May 23;
    Aug 1, 7
Credit reports, errors in: June 17
Cringley, Robert X.: Mar 6
Crocker, Charles: Apr 21
Crompton, Samuel: Dec 3
Cromwell, Oliver: Sep 1

Cronk, Harriman: June 25
Cross, Alonzo (and the Cross pen company):
    Oct 5
Crowe, Pat: Jan 20
Crowell, Henry P.: Jan 27
Cudahy, Eddie: Jan 20
Cudahy meat company: Jan 20
Cugat, Xavier: Dec 26
Cugnot, Nicholas Joseph: Sep 25
Cullinan, Joseph: Apr 7; Dec 31
Cumberland Packing Corporation: Dec 17
Cunard, Samuel: Nov 21
Cunard ship company: Sep 27
Cunningham & Walsh advertising agency: Apr 27
Currency Act of 1913: Dec 22
Curtis, John: Sep 23
Curtis Publishing Company: May 29
"Customer is always right" business slogan
    coined: Jan 11
Cutler, Carol: Jan 13

Dacre, Lord: Apr 23
Daimler, Gottlieb: Dec 22
Daimler Chrysler: Dec 21
Daimler-Benz: Dec 21
Dale, David: May 14
Daley, Marcus: Nov 12; Dec 5
Daley, William: Feb 5
Dallas, Alexander: Dec 24
Damaged Goods (play): Nov 22
Dane, Maxwell: Aug 13
Danton, Georges Jacques: Sep 2
Das Kapital (Marx): Sep 14
Dateline: Feb 9
David, Michelangelo's statue of: June 10
David Groesbeck & Company: Dec 29
Davis, Jacob: Feb 26
Davis, Keith: Nov 14
Davison, Henry P.: Mar 24
De Beers diamond company: June 26
De Forest, Lee: Aug 28
De Leon, Daniel: June 27
Dean Witter Discover: Feb 6
Debs, Eugene: May 23; June 26, 27; Nov 5
Debtors, imprisonment of: Feb 9; Mar 9; May 28;
    June 6
DeButts, John: Mar 2
Decentralized corporate structure: May 23; Aug
    10; Sep 15
Decker, Andrew: May 2
Deeds, Edward A.: Aug 17
Deere, John: Feb 7; May 17
Def Jam records: Oct 4
Del Monte foods company: Apr 21
Delco company: Aug 17
Delk, Edward Buehler: Apr 22
Dell, Michael: Aug 25; Sep 10
Dell Computer Corporation: Aug 25; Sep 10
Delors, Jacques: Sep 14
Delta Airlines: Dec 4
Delta Faucet Company: Oct 11
DeMille, Cecil B.: May 8; Aug 12
Deming, W. Edwards: June 16; Oct 14

Demographics, science of, founded: Apr 24
Dempsey, Jack: July 2
Denham Studios: Sep 16
Dennison, Aaron Lufkin: Mar 4
Dennison, Henry Sturgis: Mar 4; Sep 3
Dennison Manufacturing Company: Mar 4
Department of Commerce and Labor, U.S.: Sep
    14, 16; Oct 23
Department store record attendance: Dec 20
Depressions, economic. *See* Great Depression;
    Panics, financial
Deterding, Henri: Sep 17
Detroit Automobile Company: Aug 5
Detroit Tigers: May 18; July 12
Dewar, James: Apr 6
Dey, Alexander: Sep 24
Diamond Match Company: Apr 20
Diamond v. Chakrabarty: June 16
Dickens, Charles: Feb 9
Dictes and Sayenges of the Phylosophers (Caxton):
    Nov 18
Diet Coke: Aug 6
Diller, Barry: Feb 2
"Dime novel," first: June 7
Dior, Christian: Jan 21
Discover credit card: Feb 6
Disney, Roy: Nov 18; Dec 21
Disney, Walt: Jan 13; Aug 9; Nov 18; Dec 5,
    15, 21
Disney Corporation: Apr 19; Nov 29; Dec 29
Disposable razor: Jan 5. *See also* Gillette
Disraeli, Benjamin: Apr 3; May 15; June 24
Dodd, Samuel C. T.: Jan 2
Dodge automobile company: July 7; Nov 2
Dodge brothers: June 16
Doheny, Edward L.: Apr 7; May 31
Dolan, Thomas P.: Jan 22
Dollar established as U.S. currency: July 6
Dollar sign created: Apr 1
Domino's Pizza Inc.: Dec 21
Don Juan: Aug 6
Dorrance, Arthur and John Thomas: Sep 21;
    Nov 11
Dos Passos, John: Oct 25
Dot.com bubble (tech/Internet bubble): Feb 13;
    Mar 10; Apr 14; May 17; Dec 1
Douglas, Michael: Dec 11
Douglas, William O.: Aug 11
Douglas Aircraft company: Apr 28
Douglass, Frederick: May 10
Dow, Charles Henry: July 8; Nov 6
Dow Jones & Co.: July 8; Nov 6
Dow Jones Industrial Average (milestones,
    records, key events): Jan 5, 8, 12, 14; Feb
    13; Mar 5, 16, 29; Apr 6, 14, 17; May 27,
    28; July 8, 16; Aug 25; Sep 3; Oct 8, 19,
    26, 27, 28, 29; Nov 6, 14, 21, 23, 30
Doyle, Ned: Aug 13
Doyle Dane Bernbach advertising agency: Aug 13
Dr. Seuss: Oct 24
Drake, Edwin L. "Colonel": Jan 9; Aug 27;
    Dec 30
Drake, Francis: Apr 11

Dreft detergent: Oct 10
Dresser, Clarence: Oct 8
Drew, Daniel: May 20; Dec 29
Drexel, Anthony Joseph: Jan 24
Drexel, Joseph William: Jan 24
Drexel Burnham Lambert Inc.: Feb 4, 13; Mar 21; May 4
Dreyfuss, Henry: Mar 2
Drucker, Peter: May 15; Oct 27; Nov 19
Du Pont de Nemours, E. I.: Jan 3; July 19
Du Pont de Nemours, Pierre Samuel: Jan 3
Du Pont de Nemours, Victor: Jan 3
Du Pont, Pierre Samuel: Jan 15; May 18, 23; June 7
Dublin Stock Exchange: July 9
Dudley, Henry Bate: Sep 13
Duer, William: Mar 18; May 17
Duke, Doris: Oct 10
Duke, James Buchanan "Buck": Jan 31; Oct 10
Duke University: Oct 10
Dumont (Television) Network: Dec 23
Dun, (Robert) Graham: Aug 1, 7
Dun & Bradstreet: Aug 1, 7
Dunlop, John Boyd: July 23
Dunlop tire company: July 23
Dunning, Daniel: May 20
DuPont chemical corporation: Jan 3, 15; Apr 6; May 11, 21; June 4; July 28
Durant, William Crapo: Feb 2; Sep 16
Durante, Jimmy: Dec 26
Durocher, Leo: July 6
Duryea (Charles, J. Frank, and Motor Wagon Company): Sep 21
Dutch West India Company: May 24; June 3
DuVall, K. K.: Sep 10
DVD: Dec 8
Dynamite invented: Apr 12

E. F. Hutton brokerage: May 2
Eames, Charles: May 3
Earhart, Amelia: July 7
Earl, Harley: May 16
Earnhardt, Dale: Oct 24
East Texas oil strike: Oct 3; Nov 27
Eastern Airlines: Dec 4
Eastern and General Syndicate: Sep 9
Eastman, George: Mar 14; May 7; July 12; Nov 13
Eastman Kodak company: Mar 1; Oct 28
Eaton, Robert J.: Mar 18
EBay: Sep 24
Ebbers, Bernard: Feb 7; Mar 2
Ebony: Nov 1
Eckert, John Presper, Jr.: Apr 9
Ecological problems. *See* Environmental disasters/endangerment
ECompanies: Dec 1
Econometric Society: Jan 31
Econometrics, origin of term: Jan 31
Economic Consequences of the Peace, The (Keynes): Feb 29

Economics: Jan 31. *See also* Capitalism; Communism; Economics and economists, quotes on; National debt; Physiocrats; Value; *and specific economists, concepts, works, etc.*
Economics and economists, quotes on: Jan 13, 26, 28, 30; Feb 9, 23; Mar 3, 18, 22; Apr 8, 17, 18; May 8, 15; June 2; July 28; Aug 16, 27; Sep 13, 19; Oct 19; Nov 14; Dec 3, 11
Economist: Feb 3
Edison, Thomas Alva: Jan 27; Feb 19; June 28; Aug 15; Sep 4; Oct 15; Dec 3, 22, 25
Edison electric lighting companies: Sep 4; Oct 15
Edison General Electric Company: Apr 15; June 1, 28; Dec 30
Edison Motion Picture Patent Company: June 8
Edmunds, Gladys E.: Aug 9
Edward I, king of England: Oct 3
Edwardes, Michael Owen: Oct 27
Eight-hour workday, early developments of: June 25; Sep 5
Eisenhower, Dwight D.: Jan 17; Feb 9; Apr 3; June 19; Sep 25
Eisenhower dollar: Sep 26
Eisner, Michael: Apr 19
El Redactor (New York newspaper): July 1
Electric lighting, commercial history of: Sep 4; Oct 15; Dec 3
Eli Lilly Company: Nov 18
Eliasberg, Louis: Apr 8
Eliot, T. S.: Sep 22
Elizabeth I, queen of England: Mar 25; Apr 11; Sep 27; Dec 31
Elizabeth II, queen of England: Apr 29; Sep 27
Elkins Act: Sep 14
Elks Hills oil reserve: Apr 7
Elmira Gazette: Sep 15
Emergency Price Control Act: Jan 30
Emerson, Ralph Waldo: Aug 31
EMI Parlophone music company: Jan 30; May 9
Employment agency, first: July 4
ENEL electricity company: Oct 31
Engels, Friedrich: Sep 18
ENIAC computer: Apr 9; Aug 30
Enrico, Roger: Apr 22
Enron: Feb 7; Mar 14, 15; June 5; July 28; Aug 14; Oct 16; Dec 2, 12
Entrepreneurs, quotes on: May 27; Aug 9
Envelope-folding machine patented: Jan 21
Environmental disasters/endangerment: Aug 26. *See also* Bhopal; *Exxon Valdez*; Love Canal
Epstein, Brian: Nov 9
Equitable Trust Company: Sep 12
Erbitux: Feb 12
Erie Canal: July 4
Erie Railroad: Jan 6; Sep 30
Erlanger, Abraham: Dec 25
Errors, massive clerical/computer. *See* Clerical/computer errors, massive
Eskimos. *See* Inuit Eskimos
Etch-A-Sketch: Oct 6

Ethics
 in business decisions: Feb 23; Sep 22
 quotes on: Jan 21; Feb 20, 23; Oct 17; Nov
  30. *See also* Malden Mills; Merrill,
  Charles E.
Euclid Avenue Baptist Church: May 23
Euro currency: May 11; Dec 29
Euronext stock exchange: Mar 20
European Commission: Sep 14
European Union: Mar 24
Evans, Joni: July 22
Eveleth, Jonathan G.: Dec 30
Evening Magazine: Nov 29
Everleigh, Ada: Jan 3
Everleigh, Minna: Jan 3
Everleigh Club: Jan 3
Ewing, Sam: May 22; Dec 4
Examiner: Feb 11
Exchange Buffet: Sep 4
Exxon corporation: Dec 8
Exxon Valdez (oil tanker and ecological disaster):
  Apr 29
Eye scanning, ATM machines and: May 13

FAA (Federal Aviation Authority): Oct 4
Fabergé, Peter Carl: May 30
Fabergé eggs: May 30
Factory accident, the first: Jan 10
Fair Labor Standards Act of 1938: Oct 24
Fair Packaging and Labeling Act of 1966:
  Nov 3
"Fair trade" marketing movement: Sep 15
Fairbanks, Douglas, Sr.: Apr 9
Fairchild Semiconductor company: Apr 25;
  Sep 12
Fall, Albert B.: Apr 7; May 31
Fannie Mae: Jan 14
Faraday, Michael: Sep 22
Fargo, William George: May 20; Dec 12
Farming: Feb 7
  quotes on: Jan 13; Apr 23; Sep 25. *See also*
  McCormick, Cyrus Hall
Farnsworth, Philo: Aug 19
FASB (Financial Accounting Standards Board):
  June 8
FCC (Federal Communications Commission):
  Mar 2; Apr 3, 18; May 3, 9; July 1; Oct
  11, 14; Nov 11; Dec 16
FDA (Food and Drug Administration): Feb 12;
  Mar 27; Sep 22; Oct 15
FDIC (Federal Deposit Insurance Corporation):
  Mar 23
Feather, Vic: Aug 8
Federal Express: Mar 12
Federal Pacific Electrical: Feb 16
Federal Reserve Act of 1913: Nov 16
Federal Reserve Board/System: Jan 16; Apr 17;
  June 2, 12; July 17; Sep 2, 23; Oct 19;
  Dec 14, 22
Federal Trade Commission: Feb 5; Sep 26
Federated Department Stores: Nov 23

Federation of Organized Trades and Labor
  Unions, The: Aug 2
Ferdinand, king of Spain: Apr 17
Ferrari, Enzo: Dec 1
Feuerstein, Aaron: Dec 11
Fiat automobile company: July 1; Aug 13; Dec 16
Fifth Avenue, New York, groundbreaking for:
  Aug 2
Figaro Illustre: Jan 21
Filene, Edward: Sep 3
Filene's department store: Sep 3
Firestone, Harvey: May 21; June 8; Aug 3
Firestone tire companies (including
  Firestone/Bridgestone company): May 21;
  June 8; Aug 3
First Internet Bank of Indiana: Feb 22
First National City Bank of New York: Mar 1;
  May 2
Fischbach Corporation: May 4
Fisher, Fred: May 18
Fisher, Irving: Feb 27; Oct 16
Fisher, Richard: Feb 6
Fisk, "Jubilee" Jim: Jan 6, 7; Aug 4; Sep 24
Fisk, Lucy: Jan 7
Flagler, Henry Morrison: Jan 2; Nov 30
Flamingo Hotel, Las Vegas: Dec 26
Flanagan, William: Oct 31
Flint, Charles R.: June 8
Florida East Coast Railway: Sep 19
Florida real estate boom/bubble: Sep 19
Flour mill patented: Mar 23
Follett, Mary Parker: Sep 3
Foote, Cone and Belding advertising agency:
  May 1
Ford, Clara: June 18
Ford, Edsel (Bryant): Jan 1; May 18, 26; June 18;
  Aug 27; Nov 6
Ford, Henry: Jan 23; Feb 16, 28; Apr 7, 10; May
  18, 21, 25; June 4, 14, 16, 18; July 30;
  Aug 5, 22; Sep 21; Nov 1, 8
Ford, Henry, II: June 13; July 13, 30; Sep 21, 29;
  Oct 1; Nov 8
Ford Motor Company: Jan 1, 5; Mar 16; May 18,
  21; June 13, 16; July 7, 22; Sep 5, 16; Oct
  12; Nov 15, 19
  Edsel: Aug 27; Nov 8, 19
  Explorer: May 21
  Fairlane: Nov 15
  Model A: June 16; July 15; Nov 1
  Model T: May 21; June 4; Aug 12; Sep 24;
   Nov 1
  Pinto: June 10; Sep 11
  Thunderbird: Mar 16
"Ford stomach": May 18, 26
Forepaugh, Adam: Apr 28
Forrister Research: Aug 4
Fouquet, Nicolas: Mar 23
Fox network: Feb 2
Franco-Prussian War: Mar 30; Apr 13
Frankel, Martin: May 5, 15
Frankensteen, Richard: May 26

Franklin, Benjamin: Apr 6, 22; July 11, 21; Nov 13
Franklin National Bank: Sep 8
Franklin Simon Company: Sep 26
Fraser, Douglas A.: May 13
Frauds and swindles: Feb 1, 3, 6, 16, 26 (a quote): Mar 8, 18; Apr 18; May 2, 6, 23; Aug 2; Sep 6, 8; Oct 4, 15, 21; Nov 11, 26; Dec 4, 5. *See also specific cases/ individuals* (Boesky, Capone, Duer, Enron, Fisk, Frankel, Gould, Grubman, Handler, Milken, Ponzi, Teapot Dome, Tyco, Waksal, WorldCom)
Fraunces Tavern: Mar 13
Freedman, Al: Nov 26
Freeman's Journal: July 1
Fremont Canning Company: Jan 12
French East India Company: Dec 15
French franc adopted: Aug 15
French Revolution: Jan 3; Feb 13; Mar 19; July 7, 17; Aug 15; Sep 2; Oct 12. *See also* Louis XIV; Turgot
Freud, Sigmund: Nov 22
Frick, Henry Clay: July 6, 23; Nov 4; Dec 2
Friedman, Milton: Jan 30
Frisch, Ragnar: Jan 31
Frito-Lay: Feb 10
Fugger, Jakob, II: Dec 30
Fuller, Alfred Carl: Jan 13
Fuller Brush Company: Jan 13
Functions of the Executive (Barnard): Nov 7
Fur trade/industry: Mar 29; Apr 6; Sep 8; Dec 13. *See also* Astor, John Jacob
Fust, Johann: Aug 22; Sep 30

Galbraith, John Kenneth: Mar 3; June 19; Nov 20
Gambling industry: Sep 25
Gandhi, Indira: Feb 10; Apr 13
Gandhi, Mahatma: Sep 17
Gannett, Frank Ernest: Sep 15
Gannett Company: Sep 15
Garcia, Jerry: Dec 8
Garner, John Nance: Feb 15
Garrick, David: Sep 13
Garth–St. Germain Depository Institutions Act of 1982: Oct 15
Gartner, Michael: Feb 9
Gary, Elbert: Nov 4, 21
"Gary Dinners": Nov 21
Gasoline, first tax on: June 6
Gassee, Jean Louis: June 25
Gates, Bill: Mar 3; Apr 7, 8; May 28; June 25; July 20; Aug 24; Oct 28; Nov 5, 29; Dec 19
Gates, John "Bet-a-Million": Apr 7; Dec 12
Gauss, Carl Friedrich: July 21
Gay, Edwin F.: Sep 30
Gecko, Gordon: Dec 11
Geisst, Charles R.: May 28
Geneen, Harold S.: Jan 22; June 4, 19; Nov 23

General Electric (GE): Feb 16; Apr 1, 15; May 11, 30; June 1, 28; July 11; Aug 6; Oct 2, 17; Nov 6, 19, 22; Dec 24, 28, 30
General Foods: Mar 6; May 9, 14; July 11; Oct 26; Dec 9
General Mills food company: May 1; Sep 11
General Motors (GM): Jan 11, 15; Feb 2, 9, 11, 17; Mar 16; Apr 16; May 16, 18, 23; June 7; July 7; Aug 17, 22, 27; Sep 16; Oct 17; Nov 21, 22; Dec 16, 18, 31
    GM Technical Center: May 16
Generation X: Nov 2
Geohagan, Tony: Sep 19
George, David Lloyd: Feb 20
George, Eddie: Feb 26
George III, king of England: Mar 13
George Peabody & Co.: Apr 13
Gerba, Chuck: June 3
Gerber, Daniel Frank, Sr.: Jan 12; Oct 7
Gerhardt, Charles F. von: Mar 6
German mark adopted: Dec 4
German war reparations: Feb 29; Aug 27; Oct 29; Nov 20
Gerry, Elbridge: Jan 26
Gerstner, Louis V., Jr.: Feb 3
"Get A Job" (song): Jan 29
Geta (son of Septimus Severus): Feb 4
Getty, J. Paul: Jan 10; Feb 11, 24; June 6; Dec 15
Getty, J. Paul, Jr.: Sep 7
Ghent, Treaty of: Dec 24
Giacalone, "Tony Jack": July 30
Giannini, Amadeo Peter: May 6; June 3; Oct 17
Gibbon, Edward: Jan 15
Gibson Greeting Card Inc.: May 19
Gifford, Walter S.: Jan 7; Apr 25
Gilbert, Cass: Apr 24
Gilbreth, Lillian and Frank: May 24; Oct 19
Gillette, King Camp: Jan 5; Sep 28; Dec 2
Gillette Safety Razor Company: July 14; Sep 28; Dec 13
Gimbel, Isaac: Apr 24
Gimbel Brothers department store: Oct 6
Glass-Owen Federal Reserve Act of 1913: Dec 22
Glass-Steagall Act of 1933: Apr 6, 11; Sep 5
Glickman, Louis: Sep 3
Goebbels, Joseph: Jan 17
"Going postal": Apr 18
Goizueta, Roberto: July 11; Aug 6
Gold and Stock Telegraph Company: May 20; Dec 29
Gold Record, first: Feb 10
Gold rush. *See* California gold rush
Gold standard: June 5; Dec 4
Goldman, Emma: July 23
Goldman, Henry: July 28
Goldman, Marcus: July 28
Goldman, Sachs and Company: July 28; Oct 12
Goldman, Sylvan N.: June 4
Goldman Sachs Trading Corporation: Dec 4
Goldsmith, James: Mar 21; Nov 16
Goldwyn, Sam: Aug 27; Sep 9; Nov 19
Goldwyn Pictures Corporation: Nov 19, 28

Golf: July 7
Gompers, Samuel: Dec 8
Good Housekeeping: Sep 21
Goodnight, Charles: Mar 5
Goodnight-Loving Trail: Mar 5
Goodrich, B. F.: Aug 3; Nov 4
Goodyear, Charles: Dec 29
Goodyear Tire and Rubber Company: Aug 29;
    Oct 26
Google.com: Sep 7
Gorbachev, Mikhail: Sep 25
Gordon, Nat: Nov 28
Gordy, Berry, Jr.: Nov 28
Göring, Hermann: Feb 20
Gorney, Jay: Oct 5
Gould, Jay: Jan 6; Feb 1; Aug 4; Sep 24; Dec 2, 9
Government of Singapore Investment
    Corporation: Jan 13
GQ: June 9
Grable, Betty, legs insured: Apr 29
Grade, Lew: Dec 22
Graham, Katharine M.: July 17; Oct 31
Gramophone Company: Apr 25
Grandma Moses: Dec 29
Grant, Ulysses S.: May 6; Sep 24
Grant, Ulysses, Jr.: May 6
Grant, W. T.: Oct 2
Grant & Ward investment firm: May 6
Granville, Joseph: Jan 5
Grape boycott, U.S.: Feb 14
Grape-Nuts cereal: Oct 26
Grasso, Richard: May 20
Grateful Dead (music band): Dec 8
Graunt, John: Apr 24
Gray, Elisha: Feb 14
"Great Coal Strike," British: Mar 31
Great Depression: Jan 21; Feb 2, 5, 7; Mar 4, 5,
    7, 24; Apr 6; May 21, 30; June 9; July 7, 8,
    17; Sep 3; Oct 3, 5, 15, 24, 29; Nov 9, 23;
    Dec 25
Great Wish Book, The (Montgomery Ward
    catalog): Feb 17
"Greed is good," origins of phrase: May 18;
    Dec 11
Greek drachma: Dec 29
Greeley, Horace: July 13
Green, Adolphus W.: Nov 11
Green, Bartholomew: Apr 17
Green, Henrietta Howland: July 3; Nov 21
Greene, R. Hunt: May 27
Greenfield, Jerry: Dec 17
Greenspan, Alan: June 2; July 11; Dec 5
Greenway, Charles: Sep 9
Gresham, Thomas: June 7
Greyhound bus company: Aug 13
Griffith, D. W.: Apr 9; Nov 28
Grove, Andrew S.: Sep 2; Oct 10; Dec 18
Grubman, Jack: Jan 13
Guaranty Trust Company: Oct 2
Guardia, Tomas: Aug 18
Guatemala land reform: June 17
Gucci, Aida Calvelli: Oct 20

Gucci, Guccio: Oct 20
Gucci, House of: Mar 27; Oct 20
Gucci, Maurizio: Mar 27
Guggenheim, Meyer: Feb 1
Guinness, Benjamin Lee: Nov 1
Guinness breweries: Nov 1
Gulf & Western: May 8; Sep 20
"Guns or butter," origin of phrase: Jan 17
Gupta, Sanjeev: Feb 28
Gurney, Goldsworthy: Feb 27
Gutenberg, Johann: Jan 17; June 23; Sep 30
Gutenberg Bible: Sep 30
Guy, Thomas: Apr 22
Guzman, Jacobo Arbenz: June 17

H. J. Heinz food company: Mar 7; Apr 9; July
    14, 27
Haack, Robert W.: Oct 17
Habitat company: Feb 21
Hadden, Briton: Mar 3; Apr 3; Nov 28
Hain, Peter: Sep 13
Halberstam, David: July 26
Hall, Joyce Clyde: Oct 29; Dec 29
Hallenbeck, George: Sep 13
Halley, Edmond: Jan 27; Nov 8
Hallmark Cards: Oct 29; Dec 29
Haloid Company: Feb 8; Oct 22
Hamel, Gary: Oct 26
Hamilton, Alexander: Jan 31; Mar 18; Apr 2;
    May 22; Sep 11; Dec 13, 14, 20
Hamilton, Tom: Apr 13
Hammer, Armand: Dec 1
Hammond, James Henry: Mar 4
Hand, Learned, Judge: Mar 6
Handler, Barbara: Feb 13
Handler, Ruth: Feb 13; July 24; Sep 6
Handy, Charles: Apr 12
Hanseatic League: Feb 24
Happiness (failed board game): Nov 8
"Happy Birthday to You" song copyrighted:
    Oct 13
Harburg, E. Y.: Oct 5
Harding, Warren G.: May 31
Hargreaves, James: Apr 22
Harkness, Richard: June 15
Harley-Davidson company: Mar 17
Harper, Marion, Jr.: Sep 16
Harper & Bros. publishing company: Nov 2
Harper's Bazaar: Nov 2
Harriman, Edward H.: Feb 25; May 9; Sep 30
Harris, Sydney J.: Jan 9
Harrison, George: Oct 24
Harry Potter and the Order of the Phoenix
    (Rowling): June 21
Hart, Robert M.: Feb 8
Hartford, George Huntington: Feb 10
Hartford, John Augustine: Feb 10
Harvard Business School: May 2; Sep 30
Harvard Mark I computer: Aug 7
Hathaway, James: June 24
Hathaway shirt company: Oct 18
Havas news agency: Feb 2

Havenstein, Rudolf: Aug 27
Hawes, Russell L.: Jan 21
Haworth, Charles: Dec 21
Hawthorne experiments: Sep 6
Hay-Herran Treaty: Jan 22
Haymarket Square bombing: May 3, 4
Haynes-Duryea automobile: Sep 21
Haywood, "Big Bill": June 27
Hazen, Charles Downer: Feb 29
HBO: May 22
Healy, Robert: June 30
Hearn, Barry: Apr 10, 15
Hearst, George: Apr 29
Hearst, William Randolph: Feb 11; Apr 29;
   Aug 14
Heathcoat, John: Jan 18; Aug 7
Hedges, William S.: Aug 28
Hedi (Han emperor): Mar 11
Hefner (Christie, Hugh and Mildred): Dec 10
Heinz, Henry John (H. J.): July 27; Oct 11;
   Dec 17
Heinz, Sallie: Dec 17
Heinz food company. *See* H. J. Heinz food
   company
Heinze, F. Augustus: Oct 21
"Hello" adopted as telephone greeting: Aug 15
Henry IV, king of France: Mar 22
Henry VIII, king of England: Sep 27
Henson, Jim: Nov 2
Hepburn Act: Sep 14
Hershey, Lewis: June 18
Hershey, Milton S.: Sep 13
Hershey candy companies: Sep 13
Heth, Joice: Feb 22; June 2
Heublein Corp.: Sep 9
Hewitt, Isaac: Sep 26
Hewitt and Tuttle: Sep 26
Hewlett, Bill: Jan 1; Aug 23
Hewlett-Packard (HP): Jan 1; Feb 24; Mar 24,
   28; Aug 18, 23
Higginson, Henry L.: June 1
High Price of Bullion, The (Ricardo): Apr 19
Hill, George Washington: May 1
Hill, James J.: May 9
Hill, John Alexander: Dec 17
Hill, Mildred and Patty: Oct 13
Hill & Knowlton public relations company:
   June 11
Hilton, Barron: Jan 3
Hilton, Conrad: Jan 3; Dec 25
Hilton Hotel Corp.: Jan 3
Hilton International: Jan 3
Hindenberg zeppelin: July 8
Hindustan Coca-Cola Beverages: Feb 28
Hines, Duncan: May 27; Sep 9
Hires, Charles Elmer: Aug 19
Hirshorn, Jeremy: July 25
"His Master's Voice" (advertising slogan and
   painting): Apr 25
"History is bunk," origin of quip: May 25
Hitler, Adolph: Jan 17; Feb 20, 29; May 26; July
   29; Nov 20
Hitler Diaries (forged documents): Apr 23

Hobie surfboards: Feb 26
Hodkinson, W. W.: May 8
Hoe, Richard: Apr 17; Sep 12
Hoe, Robert: Sep 12
Hoffa, Jimmy: July 7, 30
Hoffa, Josephine: July 30
Hoffman, Abie: Aug 24
Hoffman, Felix: Mar 6
Hoffmann, John: Jan 29
Holiday Inn: Jan 5; Aug 1
Hollerith, Herman: Jan 8; June 8; July 7
Holliday, Cyrus K.: Nov 24
Holmes, Oliver Wendell, Justice: May 29
Home Depot: May 20; Aug 26; Oct 26
Homestead steel strike: July 6
Honda Motor Company: Sep 10, 24; Nov 17
Honda Soichiro: Sep 24; Nov 17
Hone, Philip: May 22
Honeywell corporation: Dec 19
Hong Kong stock exchange: Oct 27
Hook, Albert: Nov 7
Hooker, Elon Huntington: Nov 23
Hooker Chemical Company: Nov 23
Hoover, Herbert (president) Mar 7, 24;
   Oct 29
Hoover, Herbert William (vacuum cleaner
   entrepreneur): Oct 30
Hoover, J. Edgar: Oct 22
Hoover Vacuum Company: Oct 30
Hopkins, Harry: Nov 9
Hormel, Jay Catherwood: Aug 30
Hormel Foods Corporation: June 26; Aug 30;
   Nov 13
Horne, Lena: Nov 1
Horrigan, Edward A.: Apr 14
Hostess Twinkies created: Apr 6
Hough, Charles Merrill, Judge: June 14
Houston Astros: June 5
Howe, Elias: Aug 12
Howe, Mia: Feb 8
Hubbard, Elizabeth: Dec 31
Hubbard, Gardiner: Jan 14; July 9; Aug 25
Hudson, Frederick: Mar 20
Hudson, Henry: Sep 4
Hudson Bay Company: May 2
Hudson Motor Car Company: Sep 6
Hudson River Railroad: Jan 17
Hughes, David Edward: May 20
Hughes, Howard: Mar 18; Dec 24
Hughes, Howard, Sr. (father of Howard Hughes):
   Dec 24
Human engineering, origin of term: Oct 19
Human genome mapping announced: June 26
Human Resources Administration of New York
   City: Jan 28
Hume, Joseph: June 21
Humphrey, George: Jan 26, 28; Feb 23
Humphreys, Joshua: June 28
Humpty Dumpty stores: June 4
Hungary, hyperinflation in: June 3
Hunt, H. L.: Nov 27
Hunt, Henry: Aug 16
Hunt, Nelson Bunker: Mar 26, 27

Hunt, W. Herbert: Mar 26, 27
Huntington, Collis P.: May 31
Hupmobile: Aug 13
Hurricane Ivan: Oct 11
Huskisson, William: Sep 15
Hussey, Obed: July 24
Hutchinson, William: May 13
Hutton, Edward Francis (E. F.): July 11
Hutton, James: July 10, 17
Hyatt Roller Bearing company: May 23

Iacocca, Lee: Jan 6; Mar 21; June 13; July 13; Sep 29; Dec 21
IBM (the company and its products): Jan 8, 23, 24; Feb 14; Apr 3, 7; June 1, 8, 16, 19, 25; July 7; Aug 4, 7, 12; Dec 31
Ibn-Saud: Dec 15
Ibuka, Masaru: Feb 19; May 7; Dec 19
Icahn, Carl C.: Feb 29; Nov 5
Ice Trust: Oct 21
ICI: Mar 24
Idemitsu maru (oil tanker): Aug 4
IG Farben company: May 21
Ihry, Dale: May 8
Il Milione (Polo): Jan 9
ILGWU (International Ladies' Garment Workers Union): June 3
ImClone: Feb 12; June 25; Oct 15
IMF (International Monetary Fund): July 2, 3, 28; Dec 27
Incubus running shoe: Feb 17
Index of Leading Economic Indicators: Nov 30
Indianapolis 500 auto race: June 8
Industrial design: Mar 2; May 3; May 16. *See also* Chippendale; Mies van der Rohe
Industrial psychology/sociology: May 24; June 1; Sep 7. *See also* Mayo, Elton
Industrial Revolution: Jan 19; Feb 9; Mar 8; Apr 22; July 7; Aug 17, 25; Nov 25
origin of term: Aug 23
Inflation, extreme cases of (hyperinflation): Apr 26; June 3; July 22, 28; Aug 27; Oct 29; Nov 6, 20
ING company: Mar 2
Ingersoll, Robert Green: Oct 29
Insull, Martin: Oct 4
Insull, Samuel: Oct 4
Insurance Company of North America: Dec 10
Insurance industry, development of: Feb 1; Mar 15, 30; Apr 4, 6, 24; Sep 25; Dec 10, 21. *See also* Lloyd's of London
Intel: Mar 28; Apr 25; Sep 2; Oct 10, 26; Dec 12, 18
Interchangeable parts, development of: Jan 8; Apr 16; July 19; Dec 8
Interest on loans, historic development of: Mar 22; Oct 12
Internal combustion engine patented: Jan 24
International Harvester Company: Feb 8; May 13
International Monetary Fund: Mar 1
International Working People's Association: May 3

Internet, development of: Jan 15; Feb 5, 22; May 13; June 1, 18; Aug 30; Sep 7; Oct 21; Nov 24; Dec 1
Inuit Eskimos: Dec 9
Investment and speculation, quotes and slogans on: Feb 28; Mar 7, 18; Apr 1; May 4; June 20; Sep 3, 28; Oct 25, 26; Nov 9, 10
Iraq Petroleum company: June 1
"Irrational exuberance," origin of phrase: Dec 5
Irving, Washington: Dec 2
Ishizaka, Fumito: Apr 5
Issigonis, Alec: Nov 18
I-T-E Circuit Breaker company: Feb 16
ITT: Jan 22, 30; June 4, 19
Iverson, Kenneth: Feb 5
Iwama, Kazuo: Feb 19
Iwama Reports: Feb 19
Iwerks, Ubbe: Nov 18
IWW (International Workers of the World; "Wobblies"): June 27

J. C. Penney store chain: Apr 14; May 30
J. P. Morgan & Co.: Mar 24; Sep 5
J. P. Morgan Bank, bombing of: Sep 16
J. P. Morgan Chase corporation: July 28
J. S. Morgan & Co.: Apr 13
J. Walter Thompson advertising agency: Apr 30; June 11; Aug 20; Oct 28
JA Ranch: Mar 5
Jackson, Andrew: Jan 29; May 19; July 10; Dec 22
Jackson, Thomas Penfield: Nov 5
Jacob, Mary Phelps: Nov 13
Jacquard, Joseph-Marie (and Jacquard loom): July 7
Jamail, Joseph D.: Nov 21
James, Duke of York: Jan 8
James, LeBron: May 22
James I, king of England: June 29
Jamestown colony: July 21
Janowitz, Tama: Sep 8
Japan, economy/businesses of. *See* Bank of Japan; Nikkei Average; Tokyo Stock Exchange; *and specific companies* (Honda, Matsushita, Mitsubishi, Mizuho, Nissan, Sony, Toyota)
Japan "opened" to Western countries: July 9
Japanese economic bubble: June 2; Sep 27
Japanese postwar recovery: June 16; Aug 4; Oct 14; Nov 17
Japanese yen adopted as currency: June 27
Jay Treaty of 1794: Mar 29
Jazz Singer, The: Oct 6, 7
Jefferson, Thomas: Jan 3, 26; Feb 21; Mar 17; Apr 10; May 16, 28; June 22; Sep 11; Dec 13
Jellinek, Emil and Mercedes: Dec 22
Jennings, Hugh, A.: May 18
Jersey Standard oil company: Sep 17
Jesus Christ: Aug 5
Jet: Nov 1
Jevons, William Stanley: June 1
Jobs, Steve: Feb 24; May 31; Aug 11; Sep 17; Nov 29

John XXIII, Pope: Apr 23
John Deere farm equipment companies: Feb 7
Johnson, Andrew: June 25
Johnson, Bryan: May 18
Johnson, Edward H.: Dec 22
Johnson, Edward Mead: Feb 15
Johnson, Harlan: May 8
Johnson, James Wood: Feb 15
Johnson, John H.: Jan 19; Nov 1
Johnson, Lyndon: Oct 12; Nov 3, 22
Johnson, Robert Wood: Feb 15
Johnson, Ross: Aug 21
Johnson, Samuel: Jan 27; Mar 27; Apr 14; May
    24; Oct 6, 18; Nov 16
Johnson & Johnson healthcare company: Feb 15;
    Oct 5
Johnston, Don (advertising executive): June 11
Johnston, Donald S. (tobacco executive): Apr 14
Johnston, Eric: Feb 23
Johnston, James W.: Apr 14
Joiner, Columbus M. "Dad": Oct 3; Nov 27
Jolly Green Giant: Dec 8
Jolson, Al: Oct 6
Jones, Barry Owen: July 12
Jones, Chuck: Sep 17
Jones, Clive: Oct 16
Jones, Edward D.: July 8; Nov 6
Jones, Ernest A.: Jan 16
Jones, George: Sep 18
Jones, John Harvey: Mar 24
Jones, Quincy: Jan 30
Jones, William: Sep 28
Jonson, Ben: Dec 2
Jordan Marsh department store: Nov 26
Joseph, Keith: Feb 19
Josiah Wedgwood & Sons Ltd: Mar 30
Journal of the American Medical Association:
    Feb 10
Jumbo the Elephant: Apr 28
Jungle, The (Sinclair): June 23
Jungrungraungkit, Suriya: Aug 11
Junk food: Apr 6; Dec 18
Just-in-time inventory control (JIT): May 28
JWT Group advertising company: June 11

Kaiser, Henry J.: May 9
Kalashnikov, Mikhail: Jan 24
Kalashnikov Vodka: Jan 24
Kamehameha III: Jan 14
Kanawha Salt Company: Nov 10
Kappel, Frederick: Aug 28
Kassem, Kerim: Sep 10
Kataoka, Otogo: Jan 4
Katona, George: Apr 9
Kearns, Robert W.: Mar 20
Keating, Paul: Aug 27
Keidanren (Japanese business organization):
    Aug 4
Keith, Minor Cooper: Aug 18
Keith-Albee United Booking Office: Nov 2
Kelleher, Herb: Nov 27
Keller, Helen: Jan 29
Kellogg, John Harvey: Feb 19, 28; Mar 7; May
    31; Oct 26; Dec 14

Kellogg, Will Keith (W. K.): Feb 19; Mar 7;
    Oct 26
Kellogg cereal company: July 21
Kemmler, William: Aug 6
Kendall, William M.: Sep 7
Kenealy, Alexander: Apr 28
Kennedy, John: Mar 3; Apr 11; Nov 22
Kennedy, Joseph P.: June 30; Sep 16
Kennedy, N. William: June 5
Kennedy, Robert: Feb 14
Kennedy half-dollar: Sep 26
Kentucky Fried Chicken company: Sep 9
Keogh, Donald: July 11
Keogh, Oonagh: July 9
Kerosene: June 27
Kermit the Frog copyrighted: Nov 2
Kettering, Charles F.: May 18; June 7; Aug 17
Keynes, John Maynard: Feb 29; Apr 19, 21; June
    5; July 3, 15
Khan of Cathay, 1400s: Apr 17
Khrushchev, Nikita: June 26
Kiam, Victor: June 12
Kidd, Captain William: Jan 26
Kiernan News Agency: Nov 6
Kilby, Jack: Sep 12
King, Edward: Nov 3
King, Martin Luther, Jr.: Apr 3
King, Richard: July 10
King, Stephen: Mar 10
King, W. L. Mackenzie: Mar 17
King Lear (Shakespeare play): Apr 12
King Ranch: July 10
Kirk, Paul: Feb 26
Klaw and Erlanger: Nov 2
Klein, Julius: June 9
Kmart: Jan 22; Dec 15
Knickerbocker Trust Company: Oct 21, 23
Knight, James L.: Feb 5
Knight-Ridder Inc.: Feb 5
Knights of Labor: May 4; Aug 2
"Know Your Customer" regulations: Mar 23
Knox, Henry: Apr 10; June 28
Knudsen, William S.: Feb 11; May 18
Kodak cameras: May 7; July 5. *See also* Eastman,
    George
Kohlberg Kravis Roberts & Company: June 2;
    Nov 30
Komansky, David: June 1
Korda, Alexander: Sep 16
Korean War: July 6; Aug 4
Kotler, Philip: Dec 9
Koyanagi, Kenichi: June 16
Kozlowski, Dennis: Jan 16; June 2, 10
Kresge, S. S.: July 31
Kroc, Ray: Apr 15; Oct 5
Krugman, Paul R.: Sep 30
Krupp, Alfred: Apr 26; Oct 8
Krupp, Alfried: July 31
Krupp, Friedrich: July 17; Oct 8; Nov 20
Krupp, Gustav: Feb 20
Kublai Khan: Feb 12
Kuhn, Loeb & Co.: May 9; June 12
Kuwait, first stock exchange for women in:
    Jan 28

La Gazette (first French newspaper): May 16
La Guardia, Fiorello: Mar 23
La Vita Inn: Oct 26
Labor unions. *See* Unions, labor
Lacy, Charles: Jan 18
Lacy, Dan: Nov 14
Ladies' Home Journal: May 29; Oct 9
Laemmle, Carl: June 8
Laissez-faire, origin of term: Aug 29
Lamont, Robert P.: Mar 22
Lamont, Thomas: Mar 24
Lampe, John: May 21
Landis, James M.: June 30
Landis, Kensesaw Mountain: Aug 3
Lanham Act of 1946: Oct 25
Lansky, Meyer: Dec 26
Laptop computer introduced: Apr 3
Las Vegas developed: Dec 26
LaSalle automobile: May 16
Lasker, Albert Davis: May 1
Lasker, Morris E., Judge: Dec 18
Lasky, Jesse L.: May 8; Aug 27
Lauder, Estee: Apr 24; July 1
Lauder, Harry: Nov 2
Laughton, Charles: Sep 16
Lavagna, Robert: Apr 26
Law, John: Jan 5; Dec 14
Law, Vernon: Aug 14
Lawrence, Charles: Mar 14
Lay, Kenneth: Oct 16
Lazarus, Fred, Jr.: Nov 23
Leander, Kajsa: May 17
Lee, Ivy Ledbetter: July 16
Lee, Robert E.: July 10
Leeson, Nick: Feb 23; Mar 2
Lefebvre, Andre: Mar 1
Lehman Brothers company: July 28
Leland, Henry Martyn: Feb 16, 29; Aug 22
Lenin: June 27
Lennon, J. P.: May 15
Lennon, John: Oct 24
Leno, Jay: Aug 24
Lenoir, Etienne: Jan 24
Lerena, Juan Jose de: July 1
Les Miserables: Dec 25
Leslie's Weekly: Aug 20
"Less is more," origin of phrase: July 28
Levin, Gerald: Jan 6
Levine, Dennis B.: Feb 4
Levi Strauss & Co.: June 20
Levis (the garment): Feb 26
Levitt, Arthur, Jr.: May 4; June 29; Sep 28; Nov 6
Levitt, William J.: Mar 7
Levitt and Sons, Inc.: Mar 7
Levittown housing development: Mar 7
Levy, Joseph: Nov 1
Lewis and Clark expedition: Sep 8
License plate auction, Thailand: Aug 11
Lick Observatory: Aug 23
Life: Aug 21; Oct 1; Nov 23
Life Savers candy: Aug 8; Oct 14
Liggett tobacco company: Apr 14
Lightbulb patented: Jan 27

Lilli doll: July 24
Lilly, Eli: Nov 18
Lilly, Emily Lemon: Nov 18
Lilly, Josiah Kirby: Nov 18
Lily-Tulip Cup Company: Oct 5
Limited liability partnership, first known: May 8
Lin Tse-hsu: Mar 23
Lincoln, Abraham: Sep 8, 12; Nov 23; Dec 3
Lincoln (automobile): Feb 16
Lincoln Motor Company: Feb 16
Lincoln Trust: Nov 3
Lindahl, Goran: Aug 10
Lindbergh, Charles: Mar 14; Oct 17
Linux software: Mar 24; Nov 5
Lipman, Hyman L.: Mar 30
Lisa, Manuel: Sep 8
Lister, Joseph: Feb 15
Listerine mouthwash: May 15
Litton Industries: July 22; Oct 20
Livermore, Jesse L.: July 26
Liverpool soccer team: May 26
Liverpool-Manchester railroad: Sep 15
Living organisms, patentability of: June 16
Ljungstrom, Gunnar: June 10
Lloyd's of London: Apr 29; June 22
Lockheed Tri-Star Airbus: Feb 4
Locomotive on the Highways Act: Nov 14
Lodbrok, Ragnar: Mar 28
Loew, Marcus: Nov 28
Loews Corporation: Apr 18
Lomenie de Brienne: July 19
London Company: July 21
London Daily Mail: Nov 17
London Daily Telegraph: June 29
London Evening Standard: July 1
London Exposition of 1851: July 24
London Film Productions: Sep 16
London School of Economics: May 29
London Stock Exchange: Apr 19; June 7
London Sun: Nov 17
London Times: June 29; Nov 16; Dec 11
Lorillard Tobacco Co.: Apr 14; June 28
Lorsch, Jay W.: Oct 1
Los Angeles, founded: Sep 4
Los Angeles and San Gabriel Valley Railroad: May 31
Los Angeles Rams: Dec 23
Louchheim, Frank P.: July 16
Louis XIII: Mar 22
Louis XIV: Jan 5, 22; Mar 23; Aug 29; Sep 6; Dec 15
Louis XV: June 4
Louis XVI: Mar 9; May 10, 30; July 19
Love Canal: Nov 22
Lovelace, Ada: June 5
Lovett, Robert: July 22
Loving, Oliver: Mar 5
LTCM (Long-Term Capital Management): Sep 2, 18, 23; Oct 14
LucasFilm: Nov 29
Luce, Henry: Feb 28; Mar 3; Apr 3; Aug 21; Nov 23, 28
Lucent Technologies: Jan 7; Apr 4; Oct 17
Luciano, Lucky: Dec 26

Lucite plastic, first production of: May 21
Lucky Strike cigarettes: Nov 22
Luddites: Jan 18; Aug 7; Oct 9
Ludlow Massacre: Apr 20
Lukens, Rebecca: Jan 6
Lukens Steel Company: Jan 6
Lumiere brothers: Dec 25, 28
Lunch Break at the Lumiere Factory: Dec 28
Lydia E. Pinkham's Vegetable Compound: Feb 9
Lynch, Edmund C.: Oct 19
Lynch, Michael C.: Nov 3
Lynch, R. L.: Jan 16

MacDonald, Ramsey: Oct 7
Machiavelli: May 3; June 21
Macintosh personal computer: Jan 24; June 25;
    July 15
Mack, John: Feb 6
MacManus, John & Adams, Inc.: Jan 16
Macmillan, Harold: June 9; Aug 13; Dec 17
Macmillan Cancer Relief charity: Oct 4
Macy's. *See* R. H. Macy Company
Madonna: Jan 30
Madison, James: Dec 24
Maillotins, tax revolt of: Mar 1
Mail-order industry: Feb 17; Apr 5; Aug 2;
    Dec 28
Malaeska, the Indian Wife of the White Hunter
    (Stevens): June 7
Malden Mills: Dec 11
"Malefactors of great wealth," origin of phrase:
    Aug 20
Malmsten, Ernst: May 17
Mammoth Oil Company: Apr 7
Man Nobody Knows, The (Barton): Aug 5
Management and decisions, quotes on: Jan 16,
    22; Feb 25, 27, 29; Mar 17, 24, 28; Apr
    14, 25, 29; May 16; June 4; July 13, 17;
    Aug 1, 11, 22, 23; Sep 2, 28, 30; Oct 26;
    Nov 16, 21, 23, 25; Dec 1, 9, 15, 30, 31
Manhattan (Island): May 24; June 3; Sep 4. *See
    also* New York City
Manhattan Company: Apr 2
Manhattan Elevated Railroad Company: Aug 4
Marconi, Guglielmo: June 2
Marconi telegraph and electrical companies: Feb
    27; Aug 13; Oct 17
Marcus, Herbert: Sep 10
Margarine patented: Jan 3
Marginal utility theory of value. *See* Value
MarketPerform.com: Aug 8
Markets and marketing, quotes on: Mar 17; Apr
    24; May 3, 11, 19; Aug 29; Sep 11; Oct
    16, 18; Nov 6, 27; Dec 15, 24
Markkula, A. C. "Mike": Sep 17
Markoe, James: Apr 18
Marlboro cigarettes: Apr 2; Dec 8
"Marlboro Friday" (sales promotion): Apr 2
Marley, Bob: Oct 24
Marshall, Alfred: July 26
Marshall, John, Justice: Mar 6
Marshall Field's department store: Jan 11; Feb 17;
    Mar 15

Martin, Glenn L.: June 29
Martin, Truman J.: Feb 1
Martin, William McChesney: Jan 25
Martinique, ice industry of: Sep 4
Marx, Jenny von Westphalen: June 19
Marx, Karl: Mar 17; June 19; Aug 24; Sep 14,
    18; Nov 4
"Mary Had a Little Lamb": Feb 19
Mary Kay (the woman and the cosmetics
    company): Sep 13; Nov 22
Marysville, Ohio, vehicle plant: Sep 10
Masjid-i-Suleiman oil strike: Apr 19; May 26
Massachusetts Bay Colony: Aug 23
Massachusetts Investors Trust: Mar 21
Massey, Jack: Sep 9
Matsushita, Kenosuke: Nov 26
Matsushita Electronic Industrial Company:
    Nov 26
Mastercard: Feb 18
Mattel toy company: Feb 13; Apr 27; Sep 6
Matthews, George: June 30
Mauchly, John W.: Apr 9; Aug 30
Mauritania (Cunard ocean liner): Nov 21
Maxwell, Robert: June 24; July 13; Nov 5, 28
Maxwell House Coffee: May 11
Maybury, William: Aug 5
Mayer, Gottfried: Mar 29
Mayer, Louis B.: July 4; Nov 19, 28
Mayer, Max: Mar 29
Mayer, Oscar: Mar 29
Mayo, George Elton: Sep 7; Dec 26
Mayo, Karen Lee: June 10
Maytag, Frederick Lewis: Mar 26; July 14
Maytag washing machine company: Mar 26;
    July 14
Mazarin, Jules, Cardinal: Aug 29
MCA entertainment corporation: Nov 26
McCann-Erickson advertising agency: Apr 21;
    Sep 16
McCaw Cellular Communications: Aug 16
McClean, John: Oct 23
McClellan, George B.: Oct 28
McConnell, David Hall: July 18
McCormick, Cyrus Hall: Feb 8; May 13; July 24
McCormick Harvester (the factory and
    company): May 3, 4. *See also* International
    Harvester Company
McCormick, Nettie Fowler: Feb 8
McCrory Stores: Oct 19
McCulloch v. Maryland: Mar 6
McDonald, Maurice (Mac) and Richard: Apr 15;
    Oct 5
McDonald's food company: Jan 31; Apr 15; June
    19; Sep 4; Oct 5
McDonnell Aircraft Corporation: Apr 28
McDonnell-Douglas Corporation: Apr 28
McGowan, Bill: Mar 2
McGraw, James Herbert: Dec 17
McGraw-Hill publishing company: Sep 7; Dec 17
McGregor, Douglas: Sep 16; Oct 13
MCI company: Mar 2
McKinley, William: Sep 14
McNamara, Robert: Oct 1

Means, Howard: Mar 8
Meany, George: Jan 8; Feb 9
Mecherle, George J.: June 7
Medici, Cosimo de: Jan 1; Aug 1
Medici, Giovanni di Bicci de: Aug 1
Medici, Giuliano de: Apr 26
Medici, Lorenzo "the Magnificent" de: Jan 1; Apr 9, 26
Medici, Piero "the Gouty" de: Jan 1; Aug 1
Medici family (banking/political dynasty): Jan 18; Apr 9, 26; June 21
Medicus, Heinrich: June 5
Meehan, Michael: Aug 2
Meese, Edwin, III: May 2
Meetings and conferences, quotes on: Jan 25; Apr 27; June 15; Sep 18
Meiggs, Henry: Aug 18; Oct 16
Mellon, Andrew William: Mar 24
Mellon, Richard: Mar 24
Mellon Plan: Mar 24
Mencken, H. L.: Sep 19
Meng, Hong: Nov 8
Mennen Talcum Powder: Oct 28
Mercantile Service (Agency): Aug 1, 7
Mercedes automobile named: Dec 22
Merchant Shipping Act: Feb 10
Mergers and acquisitions: Jan 30; Feb 6, 9, 14; Mar 20, 21; Apr 1, 2, 16, 28; Nov 16
    quotes on: Feb 27. *See also* AOL Time Warner; Citigroup; Clore; Edison General Electric Company; Time Warner
Mericantante, John, III: Sep 29
Meriwether, John: Sep 2
Merrill, Charles E.: Mar 31; Apr 1; Oct 6, 19
Merrill Lynch brokerages (various partnerships and names): Mar 31; Apr 1; June 1; July 27, 28; Oct 6, 19
Merton, Robert C.: Oct 14
Mesa Petroleum: May 22
Mestral, Georges de: May 12
Metal Management company: Oct 8
Methuen, John: Dec 27
Methuen Treaty: Dec 27
MetLife (Metropolitan Life) insurance company: Mar 20; Apr 4
Metric currency adopted by Britain: Feb 15
Metro Pictures Corp.: Nov 19, 28
Mexican War: July 19
Meyer, Eugene, Jr.: July 17; Oct 31
Mezidi, Faisal: Sep 10
MGM (Metro-Goldwyn-Mayer): Apr 16; July 20, 31; Aug 27; Nov 19, 28
Michelin, Andre: Jan 16
Michelin, Edouard: Jan 16
Michigan Southern Railway: Feb 20
Mickey Mouse: Nov 18
Mickey Mouse watch: Aug 3
Microchips. *See* Intel; Transistors and chips
Microsoft (the company and its products): Mar 3, 13, 24; Apr 8; May 28; June 25; July 8, 20; Aug 4, 12, 24, 31; Oct 26, 28; Nov 5, 14, 24, 29; Dec 19
Midlands County Railroad: July 5

Midvale Steel Company: Mar 20
Mies van der Rohe: June 5; July 28
Miles, Michael: Apr 2
Miles Laboratories: Feb 21
"Military-industrial complex," origin of phrase: Jan 17
Milken, Michael: Feb 4, 13; Mar 21; May 4; Sep 17; Nov 21
Miller, Arjay: Oct 1
Miller, Glenn: Feb 10
Miller, Phineas: Jan 8
Miller, Thomas G.: Apr 25
Mills, C. Wright: Jan 12
Milton Bradley & Co.: Nov 8
Minimum wage: Feb 17; Aug 23
Ministry of Defense, British: June 20
Minivan, first: Nov 2
Minow, Newton: May 9
Minuit, Peter: May 24
"Miracle of the rentenmark": Nov 20
Mississippi Bubble: Jan 5; Dec 14
Missouri Fur Company: Sep 8
MITS company: Dec 19
Mitsubishi Corporation: Sep 12
Mizuho Financial Holdings of Tokyo: Apr 5
Model Parliament: Oct 3
Mohawk and Hudson Railroad: Aug 9
Mohole Project: May 12
Molly Maguires: June 21
Monaghan, Tom: Dec 21
Money Trust: Feb 28; Mar 13
Monks Brew (Postum): Jan 1; Oct 26
Monopolies, economic: Mar 29; Apr 6, 20; May 29. *See also* Trusts, economic
Monopoly board game: Feb 7; Dec 19
Monroe, Marilyn: Oct 24
Monroe, Rose Will: May 31
Montagu, Mary Wortley: Nov 27
Montgomery Ward stores: Dec 28
Monti, Mario: Mar 24
Moore, Gordon: Apr 25
Moore, Marianne: Nov 8
Moore & Schley: Nov 3, 4
Morgan banking companies. *See* Morgan Stanley; J. P. Morgan & Co.; J. S. Morgan companies
Morgan, John Pierpont (J. P.): Feb 25, 28; Mar 31; Apr 11, 15, 17, 18; May 2, 9; June 1; July 17; Aug 20; Sep 4; Oct 13, 15, 21, 23, 24, 25, 28; Nov 3, 4; Dec 3, 12, 22
Morgan, John Pierpont, Jr. (Jack): Apr 18; Sep 7; Oct 2
Morgan, Joseph: Apr 13
Morgan, Junius (grandson of J. P. Morgan): Sep 16
Morgan, Junius S. (father of J. P. Morgan): Apr 13
Morgan Stanley company: Feb 6; Aug 8; Sep 5; Oct 2
Morita, Akio: Jan 26; Feb 19; June 15; Nov 25
Morita, Yoshiko: June 15
Morris, Dave: June 19
Morris, Robert: Jan 7; Aug 26
Morris, William: Nov 2

Morris automobiles (the Minor and the Mini):
    Nov 18
Morse, Anthony: Apr 18
Morse, Charles Wyman: Oct 21
Morse, Samuel F. B.: Jan 6; Feb 6
Mortimer, Charles: May 14
Morton, Joy: Sep 27
Morton, Julius Sterling: Sep 27
Morton Salt Company: Sep 27
Motley Fool Inc.: Feb 8
Motown Records: Nov 28
Mott, Charles Stewart: May 18
Mougayer, William: Aug 10
Mouse (computer device) introduced: Apr 27
Mr. Peanut: Dec 1
Mr. Potato Head: Apr 30
MSN (Microsoft Network): Nov 14
MTV: May 22
Muckrakers: Mar 17; Nov 5. *See also* Tarbell, Ida
Mullis, Darrell: Dec 17
Munsey, Frank: Mar 13
Munsterberg, Hugo: June 1
Muppets: Nov 2
Murdoch, Keith: Mar 11
Murdoch, Rupert: Feb 2, 11; Mar 11; Apr 23;
    July 14; Nov 17
Murray, Sir George Evelyn: Jan 7
Mutual Broadcast System: May 3
Mutual fund, first U.S.: Mar 21
Myers, Henry: May 31

Nabisco food company (National Biscuit
    Company): June 2; Nov 11. *See also* RJR
    Nabisco
Napoleon: Feb 13, 23; Mar 30; Aug 15
Napoleon III: May 13
NASDAQ: Mar 10; Apr 14; Oct 26; Nov 5
Nash, Charles: June 6
Nason, James H.: Dec 26
Nasser, Gamal Abdel: July 26
Nasser, Jacques: May 21
Nasr Farid Wasel, Mufti: May 10
Nation, Carrie: June 7
National Airlines: Aug 8
National Association of Manufacturers of the
    United States: Jan 22
National Bank Act of 1863: June 6; Sep 12
National Bank of Davenport, Iowa: June 6
National Cash Register Company (NCR): Jan 30
National Child Labor Committee: July 25
National City Bank: Nov 17
National debt, U.S.: Jan 8; Sep 16; Oct 3;
    Dec 13
National Grange: Feb 17
National Woman Suffrage Association: May 10
Nazis: Feb 20; May 21; June 10, 22; Sep 2
NBA basketball league: May 22
NBC: Jan 2; Feb 9, 27; May 3; July 1; Aug 28;
    Sep 9; Oct 11; Nov 11, 22, 26; Dec 23, 24
Nearly Me breast prosthesis: Apr 27
NEC Corp.: Nov 3
Necker, Jacques: July 19
Negro Digest: Nov 1

Negroponte, Nicholas: Jan 4
Neon lighting: Dec 3
Nesi, Nerio: Sep 6
Netscape: Aug 9; Nov 24
New Amsterdam: May 24
New Coke: Apr 22, 23; June 10; July 11
New Deal (Roosevelt economic plan): June 3;
    Aug 5
New Lanark (industrial community): May 14
New York (magazine): Oct 31
New York Central Railroad: Jan 17, 25; Feb 14;
    Apr 2; June 14, 15; July 3; Aug 9; Oct 8
New York City: Mar 21; Oct 28; Dec 24. *See also*
    Manhattan (Island)
New York Clearing House: June 6; Aug 23;
    Oct 25
New York Commercial Advertiser: Mar 10
New York Daily News: Nov 5
New York Daily Times: Sep 18
New York Fishing Company: Jan 8
New York Giants: July 6
New York Herald: May 6; June 13
New York Herald-Tribune: Mar 21; Sep 1
New York Journal: Apr 29
New York Journal-American: Mar 21
New York Post and Daily Advertiser: June 12
New York Recorder: Mar 25
New York Stock Exchange, development/key
    events of: Jan 19; Feb 12; Mar 5, 8, 10,
    16; May 17, 21; June 5, 11, 28; July 27,
    31; Aug 4, 24; Sep 13, 20, 24; Oct 24, 27,
    31; Nov 4, 13, 22; Dec 15, 28. *See also*
    Stock ticker
New York Sun: Aug 26
New York Times, development of: Feb 10; Aug 18;
    Sep 18
New York Tribune: Sep 12
New York World: Apr 29; Dec 9
New York World-Journal & Tribune: Mar 21
New York World-Telegram & Sun: Mar 21
New York Yankees: Apr 7
Newburger, Loeb and Company: Feb 12
Newcomen, Thomas: Sep 25
Newhouse, Samuel Irving: May 24; Aug 29
Newspaper and publishing industry, key events:
    Feb 2, 5, 11; Apr 1, 16, 17; May 5, 6; July
    21; Sep 21, 24. *See also* Printing industry,
    development of; *and specific publications,
    organizations, and people*
Newspaper Guild: Mar 21
Newton, Isaac: Apr 22
NeXT software: Feb 24
Nextage store: Dec 20
Niagara Falls: Nov 23
Niarchos, Christina (Tina): Oct 22
Niarchos, Stavros: Oct 22
"Nice guys finish last," origin of phrase: July 6
Nicholas II, Czar: May 30
Nielsen, Arthur Charles: Sep 5
Nielsen television rating service: Sep 5
Nieman, A. L.: Sep 10
Nieman, Carrie: Sep 10
Nieman-Marcus stores: Sep 10

Nike shoe company: May 22
Nikkei Average/Index: July 6; Dec 1
"9 to 5" (song): Jan 29
Nipper the dog (advertising icon): Apr 25
Nissan automobile company: July 27
Nix, John: May 10
Nobel, Alfred: Apr 12
Nobel, Ludwig: Apr 12
Nobel Prizes, origin of: Apr 12
Noble, Edward John: Aug 8; Oct 14
Nomura, Motogoro: Jan 4
Nomura, Tokushichi, II: Jan 4
Nomura Securities: Jan 4; June 7; Dec 25
Nord railroad: Dec 11
Norris, George William: Mar 23
Norris-LaGuardia Act: Mar 23
North, Simeon: Apr 16
North Sea oil strike: June 1
Northeast Utilities: Mar 15
Northern Pacific Railroad: Feb 18, 25; May 9;
    Sep 18
"Not worth a Continental," origin of phrase:
    Apr 22
"Nothing is certain except death and taxes,"
    origin of expression: Nov 13
Nova (Chevrolet automobile): Dec 18
Nowell, Alexander: July 13
Noyce, Robert: Apr 25; Sep 12; Dec 12
Nucor Corporation: Feb 5

Oak Ridge National Laboratory: Mar 19
OAS (Organization of American States): June 17
Ochs, Adolph S.: Aug 18
Office of Price Administration: Jan 30
Ogilvy, David: Apr 29; June 23; Aug 29
Ogilvy & Mather advertising agency: Apr 29
Ohga, Norio: Nov 25
Ohio Art Company: Oct 6
Ohio Life Insurance and Trust Company: Aug 24
Ohno, Taiichi: May 28
Oil embargo/crisis of 1973: Nov 14, 17; Dec 1, 20
Oil industry: Apr 7, 19; June 6; Sep 9, 17; Nov 3,
    14; Dec 15
    oil strikes. *See* Oil embargo/crisis; OPEC;
        Rockefeller, John, D.; *and specific strikes*
        (East Texas, Masjid-i-Suleiman, North
        Sea, Titusville, Spindletop)
Olds, Ransom: June 3; Sep 16
Oldsmobile (the automobile and the company):
    Mar 16; June 3; Aug 27; Sep 16
Olestra fat substitute: Feb 10
Omidyar, Pierre: Sep 24
Onassis, Aristotle: Mar 15; Aug 20; Oct 22
Onassis, Christina (Tina): Mar 15; Oct 22
Onassis, Jacqueline Kennedy: Mar 15
OPEC: June 1; Aug 9; Sep 10; Dec 20
Opium trade/War: Mar 23
Oppenheim (Warburg), Charlotte: June 12
Oppenheimer, Nicky: June 26
Orange County, California, bankruptcy of: Dec 6
Ordinances of Justice of Florence: Jan 18
O'Reilly, Tony: Apr 9
Organization Man, The (Whyte): Jan 12

Organizations, quotes on: Jan 4, 7, 12; Feb 5;
    May 28; June 29; July 10; Aug 28; Oct 26;
    Nov 18
Orient Trader, SS: June 5
Orlowsky, Martin: June 28
Orton, William: Jan 14
Osborn, Alex F.: May 5
Oscar Meyer meat company: Mar 29
Ostrofsky, Marc: Dec 1
Oswald the Lucky Rabbit (Disney character):
    Nov 18
Otis, Elisha Graves: Sep 20
Owen, Robert: May 14
Oxnam, Garfield Bromley: Feb 20

Pabst, Frederick: Mar 28
Pacific Fur Company: June 23
Pacific Mail Steamship Company: Aug 4
Package tour, first: July 5
Packard, Dave: Jan 1; Aug 23
Packard Bell company: Nov 3
Packard Corporation: Feb 16
Packer, Kerry: Nov 1
Paine, Webber & Co.: July 26
Paley, William S.: Jan 2; Sep 19, 26; Dec 23
Palmerston, Henry, Lord: Mar 23
Palmisano, Samuel J.: Jan 23
Pan Am Building: Aug 8
Pan American Airways (Pan Am): June 28; Aug 8;
    Oct 4, 7; Dec 4
Pan American Petroleum Company: Apr 7
Panama Canal: Jan 22
Panics, financial: Mar 27; May 11, 17; July 2. *See
    also* Asian financial panic; Black Friday;
    Black Thursday; Black Tuesday; Great
    Depression; LTCM; Stock market crashes
    of 1837: Jan 8; July 10; Aug 1
    of 1857: Aug 8, 14, 24
    of 1869: Jan 6; Feb 25; Sep 24
    of 1873: Feb 18; Mar 24; Aug 14; Sep 18
    of 1893: Feb 20; Aug 14
    of 1901: Mar 24; May 9
    of 1907: Jan 12; Feb 10, 25; Mar 13; July 3;
        Aug 14, 20; Oct 21, 23, 24, 25, 28;
        Nov 3, 4, 16; Dec 22
    of 1929: Feb 27; Mar 5; Apr 11; May 26, 28;
        Aug 14; Sep 3; Sep 7; Oct 4, 16, 24,
        27, 29; Nov 23
    of 1987: Oct 19, 27.
Paper money, first in America: Feb 3
Paradigm shift defined: Feb 15
Paramount Studios (Pictures): Feb 2; May 8; Sep
    20; Oct 7
Paris sacked: Mar 28
Paris stock exchange: July 19
Parker, Bonnie: Apr 10
Parker, Dan: Apr 7
Parker, George: Dec 19
Parker, John Palmer: Jan 14
Parker, Suzy: Feb 18
Parker Brothers game company: Feb 7; Dec 19
Parker Ranch: Jan 14
Parkes, Alexander: Dec 29

Parkinson, Cyril Northcote: July 30
Parkinson's law: July 30
Parmalee, Du Bois D.: Feb 5
Parnell, Charles: Sep 23
Parsons, Ed: Nov 25
Parton, Dolly: Jan 29
Pascal, Blaise: Mar 16
Pasteur, Louis: Dec 7
Patent law, first U.S.: Apr 10
Paterson, William: Jan 22; July 27; Nov 4
Pathé Brothers (Charles and Emil): Dec 25
Patterson, John Henry: Jan 30
Pawnshop, first: Sep 28
Paycheck, Johnny: Jan 18
Pazzi family of bankers: Apr 26
Pecora, Ferdinand: Apr 11; May 26; June 30
Pecora congressional hearings: Mar 8; Apr 11;
    May 26; June 30
Pedde, Giacomo: Sep 6
Peel, Robert: June 5
Pemberton, John Styth: Jan 31; Mar 29
Pencil-with-eraser patented: Mar 30
Penn Central Railroad: Feb 14; June 15, 21
Penney, J. C.: Apr 14; May 30
Pennsylvania Packet and Daily Advertiser: Sep 21
Pennsylvania Railroad: Feb 14, 18; Mar 28; June
    15; Oct 8; Dec 8
Pennsylvania Rock Oil Company: Dec 30
Pennzoil: Nov 21
Pentagon (the building): Jan 15; Sep 11
People Express airline: Apr 30
Pepperidge Farm baked goods: Aug 17
Pepsi-Cola companies: Feb 28; Mar 11; Apr 22;
    Dec 13
Pepys, Samuel: Mar 21; Aug 14, 15
Perelman, S. J.: Oct 25
Perils of Pauline, The: Dec 25
Perlman, Alfred: June 15; July 3
Perry, Matthew: July 9
Perry, Stephen: Mar 17
Peter the Great: Dec 14
Peterloo Massacre: Aug 16
Pew, Joseph Newton: July 25
Pew Memorial Trust: July 25
Pfennig, E.: July 15
Phelps, Edward John: Jan 24
Philadelphia and Reading Railroad: Feb 20
Philadelphia Athletics: May 18
Philadelphia Saving Fund Society: Feb 25
Philadelphia Star Ledger: Dec 2
Philip II, king of Spain: Apr 11; Nov 29
Philip Morris tobacco company: Apr 2, 14
Philippe II, duc d' Orleans: Jan 5
Philips, Anton Frederick: Mar 14
Philips, Gerard: Mar 14
Philips electric company: Mar 14
Philips Petroleum company: May 22; June 1
Phonograph patented: Feb 19
Physiocrats: May 10; June 4; Dec 16
Pickens, T. Boone: May 22; Dec 1
Pickford, Mary: Apr 9, 20; May 8; June 8
Pilgrims: Nov 15
Pilgrim's Progress (Bunyan): Mar 17

Pillsbury, Charles Alfred: Dec 3
Pillsbury Dough Boy introduced: Mar 18
Pillsbury food company: Dec 3, 8
Pinault, Francois: Dec 5
Pineapples first planted in Hawaii: Jan 11
Pinkerton's Detective Agency: July 6
Pinkham, Lydia Estes: Feb 9
Pirates (privateers): Apr 11
    employment practices of: Jan 26; June 30
Pirelli, Giovanni: Dec 27
Pitman, Benn: Jan 4
Pitman, Isaac: Jan 4
Pitman shorthand system: Jan 4
Pitofsky, Robert: Feb 5
Pittman, Robert: July 18
Pius II, Pope: Aug 1
Pixar Animation Studios: Feb 24; Nov 29
Place, Francis: June 21
Planters Peanuts: Dec 1
Playboy: Dec 10
Plimsoll, Samuel: Feb 10
Plimsoll footwear, origin of term: Feb 10
Plimsoll line: Feb 10
Plunkett, Roy: Feb 4; Apr 6
Plymouth automobile introduced: July 7
Plymouth Colony: Dec 13
Pocahontas: Aug 31
Poincare, Raymond: Aug 27
Polaroid Land Camera: Nov 26
Pollock, Oliver: Apr 1
Polo, Marco: Jan 9; Feb 12
Polyester: Feb 16
Pomeroy, S. C.: Nov 24
Pompadour, Madame de: June 4
Pond, Theron T.: Jan 9
Pontiac automobile: Sep 16
Pony Express: Apr 3, 13
Ponzi, Carlo (Charles): Jan 14
Ponzi scheme: Jan 14
Poor Law Amendment Act, Britain: Aug 14
Pope, Alexander: Sep 23
Porsche, Ferdinand: Jan 17; June 22
Portenar, A. J.: Apr 28
Porter, Sylvia: Nov 5
Post, Charles William (C. W.): Jan 1; May 9;
    Oct 26
Post, Marjorie Merriweather: Oct 26; Dec 9
Post Toasties: Oct 26
Postum (the company and the beverage):
    Jan 1; Mar 6; May 9; Oct 26;
    Dec 9
Potato famine, Irish: Mar 23
Potemkin mutiny: June 27
Power, quotes on: Jan 19; Feb 7; Apr 5
Premier (smokeless cigarette): Aug 21
Premium coupons introduced: Mar 25
Presley, Elvis: July 7; Oct 24
Pressed Car Steel Company: Jan 1
Price, T. Rowe: Nov 9
Price regulation law, first: July 29
Pricing agreement, monopolistic: Jan 8; Sep 17;
    Dec 17
Prime, Nathan: Mar 5

Prince, The (Machiavelli): June 21
Prince Albert Tobacco: July 29
Principles of Economics (Marshall): July 26
Print patent first issued: Mar 7
Printing industry, development of: Jan 23; Apr 17; Sep 12; Nov 18. *See also* Gutenberg, Johann
Private Life of Henry VIII, The: Sep 16
Procter & Gamble: Feb 10; June 30; Sep 15, 22; Oct 10
Prodigy computer service: June 18
Prohibition of alcohol sales in U.S.: Feb 21
Provenzano, Anthony: July 30
Proxmire, William: Oct 31
Proxy fight by shareholders, first significant: June 14
Prudent Man Rule: Oct 23
Prudential Insurance Company of America: Aug 20; Oct 28
Psychic Network: Jan 28
"Public be damned!" origin of the expression: Oct 8
Public Interest Research Group: June 17
Public opinion poll, first: July 24
Public transportation, first practical system of: Mar 16
Publishers' Association of New York: Apr 1
Publishing industry. *See* Newspaper and publishing industry; Printing industry, development of
Pulitzer, Joseph: Apr 29; Dec 9
Pullman, George: May 11; June 26
Pullman (Car) strike: May 11; June 26
Purcell, Philip: Feb 6
Pure Food and Drug Act: June 23; Sep 14; Oct 9
Putnam, Samuel, Justice: Oct 23

QE II (ocean liner): Sep 27
Quaker Oats (the cereal and the company): Jan 27; Sep 4
Quant, Mary: Nov 2
Quantity theory of money: Feb 27
Quayle, Dan: Dec 6
Queen Mary (ocean liner): Sep 27
Queensboro Realty Company: Aug 28
Quesnay, Francois: June 4; Dec 16

R. H. Macy Company: Oct 27; Nov 27; Dec 7, 24
R. J. Reynolds tobacco company: Apr 14; May 5; June 2
Radford, Arthur W.: Feb 25
Radio industry, development of: Feb 27; May 1, 11; June 2, 6; July 1; Aug 28; Sep 15, 19; Dec 16, 23. *See also* Marconi; RCA; Sarnoff; Transistors
Radio Shack: Aug 3, 12
Raguet, Condy: Dec 2
Raikes, Jeff: June 25
Railroad industry: Feb 20, 27, 28; Mar 25; Apr 2; July 4; Aug 10, 18; Sep 15; Nov 18; Dec 11. *See also names of specific railroad lines and historical figures*

Raines, Delno: Jan 14
Raines, Franklin D.: Jan 14
Rainforest Action Network: Aug 26
Raise the Titanic: Dec 22
Raleigh, Walter: Mar 25
Rama IX, Thai king: Aug 11
Randolph, Edmund: Apr 10
Raritan Indians: May 24
Rathbone, Monroe: Aug 9
Ravitch, Diane: June 17
Raymond, Henry J.: Sep 18
RCA (Radio Corporation of America): Feb 27; Apr 4; May 30; Aug 8; Sep 9; Oct 14, 17; Nov 11; Dec 6
RCA-Victor: Feb 10; Apr 25
Reading Railroad: July 17
Reagan, Ronald: June 2; July 9; Oct 15; Dec 11
Real estate first taxed: July 9
Red Hat software company: Mar 24; Nov 5
Red October Candy Factory: Nov 29
Reebok International Ltd.: Feb 17
Reggiani, Patrizia: Mar 27
Reichsbank: Aug 27; Nov 6, 20
Reis, Philipp: Jan 7
Rely tampons withdrawn: Sep 22
Remington Corporation: June 12; Sep 12
Remington Rand company: Feb 27; Mar 30; Apr 9; June 14
Remington & Sons, E.: Apr 12
Renaudot, Theophraste: May 16
Report on a National Bank (Hamilton document): Dec 14
Report on the Public Credit (Hamilton document): Dec 13
Resor, Stanley Burnet: Apr 30
Reuter, Julius: Apr 16; July 21
Reuters news agency: Feb 2; Apr 16
Reuther, Val: Sep 1
Reuther, Walter P.: Feb 9; May 9, 13, 26; Sep 1; Oct 19
Revere, Paul: Mar 14
Revlon, Inc.: June 16; Aug 24; Oct 11
Revolutionary War, U.S.: Mar 18; Aug 4; Oct 3; Dec 13. *See also* Morris, Robert
Revson, Charles: June 16; Aug 24; Oct 11
Reynolds, Milton: Oct 6
Reynolds, Richard Samuel: July 29
Reynolds, Richard Joshua (R. J.): July 20, 29
Reynolds, R. J., tobacco company. *See* R. J. Reynolds tobacco company
Reynolds, William: July 20
Reynolds Metal Company: July 29
Reynolds Wrap: July 29
RFC (Reconstruction Finance Corporation): July 3, 17
Ricardo, Abraham Israel: Apr 19
Ricardo, David: Apr 19
Ricci, Ruggiero: May 25
Riccoboni, Marie Jeanne, Madame: Mar 9
Rich, Frank: Oct 31
Richard III: Sep 16
Richelieu, Cardinal: Apr 25; May 16
Ridder Publications: Feb 5

Risk and chance, quotes on: Jan 15, 20; May 4.
    See also Halley, Edmund
Ritty, James: Jan 30
RJR Nabisco: Aug 21; Nov 30
RKO Pictures Corporation: Mar 18
Roadrunner cartoons: Sep 17
Roaring Twenties: Mar 24, 31; Oct 4
Roberts, Ed: Dec 19
Roberts, Xavier: Nov 12
Robinson, Edna: Nov 1
Robinson, Frank: Jan 31
Robinson, Sugar Ray: Nov 1
Rochdale Society of Equitable Partners: Dec 21
Rock of Gibraltar (advertising symbol): Aug 20;
    Oct 28
Rockefeller, Cettie: Nov 30
Rockefeller, John D.: Jan 2, 29; Feb 2; Mar 25;
    May 15, 19, 23; July 8; Aug 3; Sep 26, 29;
    Oct 25; Nov 30
Rockefeller, William: July 8
Rockefeller Center: May 30; Sep 12
Rockwell, Norman: May 29; Dec 29
Roddick, Anita: Aug 22; Nov 27
Roebling, Mary Gindhart: Oct 28
Roebuck, Alvah C.: Dec 7
Rogers, Francis: Feb 3
Rogers, Henry H.: Jan 29; May 19
Rogers, Will: Apr 7; Oct 29; Nov 10
Rolaids trademarked: June 22
Rolfe, John: Aug 31
Rolling Stones: Jan 30; Aug 24
Rolls, Charles Stewart: June 18; Aug 27; Nov 20
Rolls-Royce (the company and the car): Feb 4, 6;
    Mar 6; June 18; July 3; Aug 27; Nov 20
Rolodex, invention of: Feb 27
Roosevelt, Eleanor: Nov 1
Roosevelt, Franklin D.: Jan 20, 30; Feb 15; June
    3, 5, 6, 12, 30; Oct 12, 17; Nov 9, 23
Roosevelt, Theodore: Mar 17; May 12; June 23;
    July 17; Aug 3, 20; Sep 14; Oct 13, 23;
    Nov 2, 4, 23
Root beer name coined: Aug 19
Rose, Billy: Oct 26
Rose Bowl: June 25
Rose Marie: Dec 26
Rosenbaum, Ruth: Sep 15
Rosie the Riveter (workers' icon): May 29, 31
Rothari, Lombard king: Nov 22
Rothschild, Karl Meyer: Apr 24
Rothschild, Mayer Amschel: Feb 23; Sep 19
Rothschild, Nathan: Feb 23
Rothschild banking dynasty: Feb 23; May 11;
    Dec 8
Rothschild Inc.: Aug 1
Rouhani, Faud: Sep 10
Rowland, Tiny: Mar 4
Royal Society of London: Jan 27
Royce, Frederick Henry: June 18; Aug 27;
    Nov 20
Rubber band patented: Mar 17
Rubinstein, Helena: Mar 12; Apr 1
Rubicam, Raymond: Sep 19
Rubin, Jerry: Aug 24

Rubin, Rick: Oct 4
Rubinstein, Helena: Dec 25
Ruddiman, Edsel: Nov 6
Rudkin, Margaret: Aug 17
Rukeyser, William S.: Apr 14
Run-DMC music group: Oct 4
Rush Communications: Oct 4
Russell, Majors and Waddell company: Apr 3
Russell, William Hepburn: Apr 3
Russia, westernization of its economy: Mar 6; Sep
    25; Nov 29
Russian Revolution: May 30; June 27
Ryan, Claude: Aug 28

Saab airplane/automobile company: June 10;
    Dec 16
Sachs, Paul: Oct 12
Sachs, Samuel: July 28
Sacket-Wilhelms Lithographic and Publishing
    Company: July 17
Safety razor. *See* Gillette, King Camp
Safeway Inc.: Oct 19
Sage, Russell: Aug 4
Sainsbury's supermarket chain: May 26
Sajak, Pat: Nov 10
Salomon Brothers brokerage: Sep 25
Salomon Smith Barney: Jan 13, 29
Salviati, Archbishop: Apr 26
Samuelson, Paul: Jan 13; Aug 16; Sep 19
San Francisco Examiner: Apr 29
Sandelur, Thomas, Jr.: Apr 14
Sanders, Harlan: Sep 9
Sanders, Thomas: July 9; Aug 25
Santa Fe Trail: Nov 24
Santander, Luis de: Apr 17
Santiago al Sur Railroad: Oct 16
Sara Lee food company: Mar 15
Sargon health tablet: June 25
Sarnoff, David: Feb 27; Apr 4; July 1; Sep 9; Oct
    17; Nov 11; Dec 12, 23, 30
Sason, Sixten: June 10
Satcom satellites: Dec 6
Saturday Evening Post: May 29
Saunders, Stuart: June 21
Savage, Royce H., Judge: Feb 1
Savings and loan (S & L) scandals: Oct 15
SBC Communications: Oct 26
Scarlet Pimpernel, The: Sep 16
Schacht, Hjalmar Horace Greeley: Nov 20
Schlaet, Arnold: Apr 7
Schnitzer Steel company: Oct 8
Schoffer, Peter: Aug 22
Scholes, Myron S.: Oct 14
Schon, Hendrik: Nov 8
Schubert Brothers (J. J. and Lee): Dec 25
Schultz, Charles M.: Oct 24
Schumacher, E. F.: May 4; Oct 19
Schumpeter, Joseph: Feb 8
Schwab, Charles M.: Feb 25; Sep 28; Dec 12
"Scientific management": Feb 24; Mar 3, 20; Apr
    28; May 24
Scott, Tom: Mar 25; Dec 8
Scrabble board game: Dec 1

Scribner's Magazine: Oct 9
Sculley, John: June 25
Seabrook, Charles: Dec 9
Sea-Land Service: Aug 15
Searles, Joseph Louis, III: Feb 12
Sears, Richard Warren: Dec 7
Sears Roebuck: Jan 25; May 13; July 28, 29; Aug 2; Oct 12, 26; Dec 7, 28
Seaton, Stuart L.: Feb 17
Seawell, William T.: Aug 8
SEC (Securities and Exchange Commission): Mar 8, 30; May 1, 26; June 6, 13, 30; July 28; Aug 2; Sep 17; Oct 16; Nov 14
Securities Exchange Regulation Bill: May 26
Seiberling, Frank Augustus: Aug 29
Seinfeld, Jerry: Dec 24
Selden, George B.: June 14
"Selden patent": June 14
Selfridge, Harry Gordon: Jan 11; Mar 15
Selfridge, T. E.: Feb 8
Selfridge's department store: Jan 11; Mar 15
Selwyn, Archibald and Edgar: Nov 19
Sen, Amartya: Dec 15
Seven Years War: Sep 25
Severus, Septimus, Emperor: Feb 4
Seward, William H.: Mar 27
Sewing machine industry. *See* Howe, Elias; Singer, Isaac M.
Sex discrimination, cases and quotes on: Mar 22, 28
Shakur, Tupac. *See* Tupac Shakur
Shaw, Henry Wheeler: June 5
Shays, Daniel: Jan 25
Shays's Rebellion: Jan 25
Shehadie, Nicholas: Mar 26
Shell oil company: Sep 17
Shenandoah Corporation: Dec 4
Sherman, John: July 2
Sherman, William Tecumseh: July 2
Sherman Anti-Trust Act: Jan 2; July 2; Oct 15
Shopping malls, development of: Apr 22
Sibley, Hiram: Feb 6
Siebert, Muriel: Dec 28
Siegel, "Bugsy": Dec 26
Siemens, Werner von: Dec 13
Siemens industries: Dec 13
Silhouettes, The (music group): Jan 29
Silliman, Benjamin, Jr.: Dec 30
"Silver Thursday" market collapse: Mar 27
Simmons, Joey: Oct 4
Simmons, Russell: Oct 4
Simon, William: May 19
Simpkin, Thomas: Apr 18
Sinclair, Harry F.: Apr 7; May 31
Sinclair, Upton: Feb 24; June 23
Sindona, Michael: Sep 8
Singer, Isaac M.: Aug 12; Oct 27
Siraj-ud-Daula: June 20
Skadden, Arps, Slate, Meagher & Flom: Apr 1
Skadden, Marshall: Apr 1
Skilling, Jeffrey: Feb 7; Aug 14
Skousen, Mark: Apr 19
Slate, John: Apr 1

Slater, Samuel: June 9; Dec 20
Slavery: Jan 20, 21; July 4, 31; Aug 31
Sloan, Alfred P.: Feb 11, 17; May 16, 18, 23
Smith, Adam: Mar 9; June 4, 5; July 10, 17; Aug 29; Dec 16
Smith, Edward: Mar 19
Smith, Frederick E.: Nov 7
Smith, Patti Grace: Oct 4
Smith, Raymond W.: Aug 1
Smith, Roger: Apr 16
Smith, William: Aug 27, 28
Smithsonian Institution: June 26
Smyrna (Tennessee) automobile factory, Nissan company: July 27
Snow White and the Seven Dwarfs: Aug 9; Dec 21
Snyder, Howard: July 14
Socialism: Nov 8
Sockman, Ralph W.: Nov 17
Soffe, Gloria Ward: Nov 15
Sohne, Julius Adolph von: Jan 15
Sony corporation: Jan 26; Feb 19; Mar 4; May 7; June 7, 15; Sep 27; Oct 4; Nov 25, 26; Dec 3, 19
Sorrell, Martin: June 11
Sotheby, John: Mar 11
Sotheby, Samuel: Mar 11
Sotheby, Samuel Leigh: Mar 11
Sotheby's auction house: Mar 11; May 2; Dec 5
Soup, condensed, invented: Sep 21
South Improvement Company (SIC): Mar 25; Nov 30
South Sea Bubble: Jan 21; Apr 7, 14, 21, 22; Sep 23
South-Carolina Price-Current: July 30
Southeastern railroad: Dec 11
Southern Pacific Railroad: May 31
Southwest Airlines: Feb 20; Nov 27
Space tourism: Oct 4
SpaceShipOne: Oct 4
Spafford, Horatio G.: Mar 17
Spain, bankruptcy of: Nov 29
Spam (the meat): June 26; Aug 30
Spangler, James Murray: Oct 30
Spanish Armada(s): Apr 11; Nov 29
Speculation (financial), origins of term: May 1. *See also* Investment and speculation, quotes and slogans on
Speedwell Iron Works: Jan 6
Sperm whale oil: June 27
Sperry Rand company: Mar 30; Apr 9
Spies, August: May 3
Spindletop oil strike: Jan 10; Apr 7; Dec 31
Spinning jenny: Apr 22
Spinning mule: Dec 3
Spitzer, Eliot: July 28
Sports Illustrated: Aug 16
Sputnik I: Oct 4
Squibb, E. R., Company: Apr 19
SSEC computer: Jan 24
St. Francis of Assisi Foundation: May 15
St. Helen's Intelligencer: Aug 6
St. Louis Dispatch: Dec 9
St. Louis Post-Dispatch: Dec 9

Stamp Tax Act, British: June 29; July 11
Standard Oil Company: Jan 2, 29; May 15, 19;
    Aug 3; Sep 14
Standard Oil of New Jersey: Aug 9
Standard Oil Trust agreement: Jan 2
Standard time introduced: Nov 18
Stanhope, Philip: Feb 5
Stanley, Harold: Oct 2
Stanley, William: Oct 2
Star, origin of term: Mar 11
"Star system" in entertainment industry: June 8
Star Trek: Dec 19
Star Wars: Oct 31
Starbucks coffee company: Apr 30
State Farm insurance companies: June 7
Staten Island Advance: May 24
Staten Island sold: May 24
Statler Hotel chain: Jan 3
Statue of Liberty patented: Feb 18
Stavisky, Serge: Feb 6
Stavisky affair: Feb 6
Steam technology/industries, development of:
    Feb 27; Mar 16; May 17, 22; Sep 25. *See
    also* Watt, James
Steamboat Willie (Disney cartoon): Nov 18
Steel, Helen: June 19
Steel industry: Jan 6; Mar 3; June 2, 11; Oct 8.
    See also Bessemer, Henry; Carnegie,
    Andrew; U.S. Steel
Steinway, Charles Herman: June 3
Steinway & Sons piano corporation: June 3
Stempel, Herb: Nov 26
Stephenson, George: Sep 15, 27
Sternbach, Leo and Herta: June 22
Stevens, Anne: June 7
Stevens, John: Mar 23
Stevenson, Adlai: Mar 22; July 14
Stewart, Martha: Feb 12; June 25; Oct 15
Stillman, James: May 2
Stock analysts, performance of: Aug 8
Stock Exchange Regulation Bill: May 26
Stock market crashes: Mar 27; Apr 18. *See also*
    Panics, financial
Stock options (including their expensing): June 8;
    July 8, 14; Aug 4; Oct 14
Stock ticker, development of: Jan 19; May 20;
    Nov 6, 15; Dec 29
Stockman, David: July 9
Stockton and Darlington Railway: Sep 27
Stokes, Edward S.: Jan 6
Stone, Christopher: July 7
Stone, Oliver: Dec 11
Strahan, William: Mar 9
Strauss, Levi: Feb 26
Strauss-Kahn, Dominique: May 11
Strikes, labor: Jan 29; Feb 14; Mar 19, 21, 28;
    Apr 1, 3, 4, 20; May 1, 3, 4, 12, 18, 25;
    June 2; July 17, 21, 25; Sep 6; Nov 21
    sit-down: Jan 11; Feb 11; Nov 13. *See also*
        Coal strike of 1902; Homestead steel
        strike; Pullman (Car) strike
Strong, Benjamin: Nov 3
Strutt, Jedidiah: June 9

Studebaker, Clement: Feb 16
Studebaker brothers: Feb 16
Studebaker company: Jan 3
Success, quotes on: Jan 10; Mar 10; Apr 19; June
    24; Aug 15, 20; Oct 5, 20; Dec 2, 6
Suez Canal: July 26
Sullivan, Scott: Mar 2
Sun Records: July 7
Sunoco (Sun Oil Company): July 25
Supermarket carts introduced: June 4
Supreme Court, U.S.: Jan 20; Mar 6; May 10,
    15, 16, 29; June 2, 16; July 2; Aug 11;
    Dec 8
Surrey Iron Railway: July 26
Susan B. Anthony dollar: Sep 26
Sutro Bros. & Co.: May 21
Sweet, Robert, Judge: Sep 4
Sweet 'n Low: Dec 17
Swift, Gustavus: May 16; June 24
Swift meat company: Jan 20; June 24
Swift v. United States: Jan 20
Swope, Herbert Bayard: Mar 16
Synergy Myth, The, (Geneen): Jan 22

Taddeo, Joseph: Apr 14
Taft-Hartley Act: Mar 19; June 4
"Take This Job and Shove It" (song): Jan 18
Talley, Lee: May 19
Tamla-Motown Records: Nov 28
Tammany Hall: Oct 21
Tan, C. M.: Oct 23
Tandy company: Aug 3
Tappan, Lewis: May 23; Aug 1
Tarbell, Ida: Jan 29; Nov 5
Tariff Act of 1883: May 10
Tariff commission, first U.S.: June 7
Tariff of Abominations: May 19
Tariki, Abdullah: Aug 9; Sep 10
Taubman, A. Alfred: May 2; Dec 5
Taxes, quotes on: Feb 1; July 11
Taylor, Frederick Winslow: Feb 24; Mar 3, 20;
    Apr 28; May 24
Teagle, Walter: Sep 17
Teamsters union: May 29; July 7
Teapot Dome Scandal: Apr 7; May 31
Technicolor: Dec 23
Teflon: Feb 4; Apr 6
Telecommunication Act of 1996: July 24
Telecommunications industry. *See* FCC;
    Telegraph; Telephone industry; Television
    industry; Radio industry
Telegraph, history of: Feb 6; Apr 3, 8, 16; May
    20; June 2; July 12, 21; Aug 26; Nov 6,
    13; Dec 29. *See also* Morse, Samuel F. B
Telephone industry. *See* AT&T; Bell, Alexander
    Graham; Bell Telephone companies
Teleregister Corporation: May 21
Television industry. *See also* ABC; Baird, John
    Logie; CBS; NBC
    history of: Apr 3; May 3, 9; July 1, 24; Aug
        19; Nov 25, 29; Dec 16, 30
    quotes on: Sep 22; Oct 12
Tellabs company: Sep 18

Tennant, Anthony: May 2; Dec 5
Tennant, Don: Dec 8
Tennessee Coal and Iron Company: Nov 4
Terasawa, Yoshio: June 7
Texaco oil company: Apr 7; Nov 5, 21; Dec 31
Texas Air Commission: Feb 20
Texas Instruments: Sep 12
Texas International airlines: Feb 20; Nov 27
Textile industry: Jan 10, 18; Apr 22; June 9, 20;
    July 7, 25; Nov 25; Dec 3, 8, 20. *See also*
    Whitney, Eli
Thailand
    hyperinflation in: July 28
    license plate auction in: Aug 11
Thalberg, Irving: Nov 28
Thanksgiving holiday: Nov 23
Thanksgiving Day parade: Nov 27
Theft of largest single object: June 5
Theodore, Jean-Francois: Mar 20
"Theory X, Theory Y" (McGregor theory): Sep
    16; Oct 13
Third Man, The: Sep 16
This Land Act (tenant farmer act of Charles
    Parnell): Sep 23
Thomas, Benjamin Franklin: Nov 12
Thomas, Dave: Nov 15
Thomas, Ransom H.: Oct 24
Thompson, J. Walter: Apr 30; Oct 28
Thompson, John (banker): May 2; Sep 12
Thomson-Houston Electric Company: Apr 15;
    June 1, 28; Dec 30
Thoreau, Henry David: Jan 18; Mar 3; Aug 17
Thorne, Oakleigh: Oct 23
Thornton, Charles "Tex": July 22; Oct 1, 20
Three Little Pigs: Jan 13
3M Company: Mar 1
Thyssen, Fritz: Feb 20
Tientsin, Treaty of: Aug 26
Ticker-tape parade, first: Nov 15
Tiffany, Charles Lewis: Sep 18
Tiffany & Co.: Sep 18
Time: Mar 3, 21; Apr 3; Nov 28
Time clock: Sep 24; Oct 30
Time Warner: Jan 6, 12, 30; Apr 24; July 18
Time-and-motion study: Mar 20; May 24;
    Oct 19
Time-Life company (Time, Inc.): Feb 28; Apr 3;
    Aug 16, 21; Nov 22. *See also* Luce, Henry
Tires. *See* Automobile tires
Tisch, Andrew H.: Apr 14
Tisch, Laurence: Apr 18
Titanic (ocean liner): Apr 29
Titusville oil strike: Jan 9; July 25; Aug 27 28;
    Nov 5; Dec 30
Tobacco and cigarette industry: Jan 31; Feb 1;
    Mar 8; Apr 2, 14; May 5; June 28, 29; July
    15, 20, 29; Aug 21, 31; Sep 1; Oct 10;
    Nov 7, 22; Dec 8
Tobacco Trust: Jan 31
Tobias, Andrew: Oct 11
Todd, Mike: Mar 31
Tokunaka, Teruo "Terry": Dec 3
Tokyo Stock Exchange: Apr 30; July 6

Tolfa alum mines: Aug 1
Tolkien, J. R. R.: Oct 24
"Tolpuddle martyrs": Mar 19
Tony the Tiger: Dec 8
Torres, Raquel: July 31
Toshiba company: Aug 4
Toshio, Doko: Aug 4
Totsuko company: Feb 19; May 7
Town, Richard: May 23
Townsend, Charles: Apr 12
Townsend, James: Aug 27
Townsend Acts, 1767: Apr 12
Townsend electrochemical process: Nov 23
Toxic shock syndrome: Sep 22
Toy Story: Nov 29
Toynbee, Arnold: Aug 23
Toyoda, Kiichiro: Aug 18
Toyoda, Sakichi: Aug 18
Toyota Motor Co.: May 28; Aug 18, 28; Oct 12;
    Dec 18
Trademarks, landmark: Oct 25; Dec 17
Trahey, Jane: Sep 18
Transamerica Corporation: June 3
Transistors and chips (semiconductors),
    development of: Feb 19; Mar 28; Apr 25;
    June 1, 30; Sep 12; Oct 10; Nov 8; Dec 19
Trans-Siberian Railroad: July 21
Travel agency industry founded: July 5
Travelers Cheque: July 7; Aug 5
Travelers Group: Apr 6; Sep 25
Travelers Insurance Company: Feb 1
Treasury Department, U.S.: Sep 26
Treneer, Maurice: Feb 21
Trenton Trust Company: Oct 28
Triangle Publications media group: Feb 11
Trimline telephone, design of: Mar 2
Trippe, Juan: Oct 7
Trivial Pursuit board game: Nov 10
TRS-80 computer: Aug 3, 12
Truman, Harry: Mar 19; May 8; June 2, 4
Trump, Donald: June 14
Trust Company of America: Oct 23; Nov 3
Trust-busting, first case in U.S. history: Jan 8
Trusts, economic: Jan 2; Mar 25; Sep 14; Nov 10;
    Dec 4. *See also* Monopolies, economic;
    Pricing agreement; Roosevelt, Theodore;
    Sherman Anti-Trust Act; Standard Oil
    Company; *and specific trusts* (Beef, Ice,
    Money, Tobacco)
Truth in Securities Act of 1933: Apr 11
Ts'ai Lun: Mar 11
Tucker, Preston: Mar 30
Tudor, Frederick and William: Sep 4
"Tulipmania" (Dutch economic bubble): Feb 3
Tupac Shakur: Oct 24
Tupper, Earl S.: July 28
Tupperware: July 28; Sep 13
Turgot, Anne-Robert-Jacques: May 10
Turner, Ted: Apr 18; June 1; Nov 19; Dec 6
Turner Broadcasting: Apr 18
TWA: Jan 3
Twain, Mark: Jan 29; Apr 18; Dec 2
Twentieth Century Fox: Feb 2

Twenty-One: Nov 26
Two-dollar bill: Sep 26
Tyco companies: Jan 16; June 10
Tylenol tablets recalled: Oct 5
Typographical Society: May 31

Underwood, John: Apr 12
Underwood, John Thomas: Apr 12
Underwood Typewriter Manufacturing Company:
    Apr 12
Uneeda Biscuits: Feb 4; Nov 11; Dec 27
Unilever company: June 6
Union Carbide: Oct 26; Dec 2
Unions, labor: Jan 4; Mar 19, 21; May 23, 25,
    26, 31; June 4, 21; Aug 2; Sep 1; Oct 18;
    See also specific unions (AFL, AFL-CIO,
    CIO, ILGWU, Teamsters, United Auto
    Workers, United Mine Workers, United
    Steelworkers)
Union Pacific Railroad: July 26; Aug 4
Union Stock Yard, Chicago: Dec 25
Unisys company: Apr 9
United Airlines: Sep 6
United Artists Corp.: Apr 9
United Auto Workers union (UAW): Feb 11; Apr
    16; May 13, 23; June 18; July 27; Nov 21
United Brands: Feb 3
United Cigar Manufacturers: July 28
United Copper Company: Oct 21
United East India Company, Dutch: Sep 4
United Fruit Company: Feb 3; June 17; Aug 18;
    Oct 17
United Mine Workers of America: Jan 25; May
    12; July 17
United Parcel Service (UPS): Aug 28
United States Tobacco Co.: Apr 14
United Steelworkers union: Apr 11; Aug 13
UNIVAC computer: Mar 30; June 14
Universal Music: Oct 4
Universal Pictures company: June 8
U.S. Post Office: Apr 18; Sep 7; Dec 12
U.S. Steel: Feb 25; Apr 11; May 19; Sep 5, 16;
    Nov 4, 21; Dec 12
USA Today: Sep 15
Used car dealership, first: Oct 22

Valentino, Rudolph: May 8
Valium: June 22
Value
    marginal utility theory of: June 1; Dec 16
    paradox of: June 1
Van Doren, Charles: Nov 26
Van Dyke, W. S.: July 31
Van Heusen shirts: Oct 18
Vanderbilt, Cornelius: Jan 17, 20; May 27; Oct 8
Vanderbilt, Phebe: May 27
Vanderbilt, William (son of Cornelius): Oct 8
Vanderlip, Frank Arthur: Nov 17
Variety: Nov 2
Vaseline: Jan 9; Sep 8
"Vast wasteland," origin of phrase describing
    television: May 9

Veeck, Bill: July 12
Velcro: May 13
Venable, Willis E.: Mar 29
Venter, J. Craig: June 26
Verizon telephone company: Apr 26
Versailles Treaty, World War I: Feb 29
Viacom corporation: May 8
Viagra approved: Mar 27
Victor Talking Machine Company: Apr 25
Victoria, Queen: Jan 4
Vietnam War: Nov 14
Vikings: Mar 28
Villard, Henry: Apr 15
Virginia Company, colonial: June 29
Virginia Railroad: May 19
Visa credit card: Feb 18
Vitaphone: Aug 6
Vogue: Dec 10
Voice of America: Mar 22
Volcker, Paul: Jan 30; June 2
Volkswagen: Jan 17; Feb 17; May 26; June 22;
    July 3, 30; Aug 5; Oct 22
Voltaire: Jan 5
Volvo: Dec 16
Von Braun, Wernher: July 10
Vreeland, Diana: Dec 10
Vulcanized rubber: Dec 29

W. T. Grant stores: Oct 2
W2XBS television station: July 1
Wagner, Franz X.: Apr 12
Waksal, Sam: Feb 12; Oct 15
Waldorf-Astoria hotel: Jan 3
Walgreen, Charles R.: Oct 9
Walgreen's drug stores: Oct 9
Walker, Charles J.: Dec 23
Walker, Felix: Feb 25
Walker, Madame C. J.: May 25; Dec 23
Walker, Maggie Lena: July 15
Wall Street: Dec 11
Wall Street, construction of: May 12
Wall Street Journal, history of: July 8; Nov 6
Wal-Mart: Jan 31; Feb 22; Mar 29; May 9; July 2
Walras, Leon: Dec 16
Walsingham, Francis: Apr 11
Walton, Sam: Mar 29; May 9; July 1
Walpole, Horace: Feb 19; May 1
Walpole, Thomas: Feb 19
Walt Disney Company. *See* Disney Corporation
Walter, John, I: Nov 16
Walters, Alan: July 28
Wanamaker, John: Mar 12; July 11
Wanamaker's department store: Feb 7; July 11
Wang, An: Aug 18
Wang companies: Aug 18
War of 1812: Mar 1; May 27; June 16; Dec 24
Warburg family of bankers and economists:
    June 12
Ward, Aaron Montgomery: Feb 17; Aug 2. *See
    also* Montgomery Ward stores
Ward, Ferdinand: May 6
Warhol, Andy: Mar 1

Warner, Harry: Oct 6
Warner, Sam: Aug 6; Oct 6
Warner Brothers: Aug 6; Oct 6
Warner Corset Company: Nov 13
Warner EMI Music: Jan 30
Warner-Lambert companies: May 15
Warnock, Mary: Nov 25
Washington, George: Feb 22; May 16; June 2; Dec 14
Washington Post: July 17
Washington Post Company: July 14; Dec 13
Waterloo, Battle of: Feb 23
Waters, George: Oct 1
Watson, John B.: Apr 30
Watson, Peter: Nov 30
Watson, Thomas A. (Bell colleague): Jan 18; July 9; Dec 13
Watson, Thomas, Jr.: Jan 8; June 1; Aug 7; Dec 31
Watson, Thomas, Sr.: Jan 8; Feb 14; June 19; Aug 7
Watt, Charles
Watt, James: Jan 19; Mar 8; Aug 17, 25; Sep 3
Waugh, Auberon: Dec 16
WBZ radio station: Sep 15
WEAF radio station: Aug 28
Wealth and money, quotes on: Jan 10; Feb 11, 18, 19, 21, 24; Mar 3, 12, 21, 27, 31; Apr 3, 10, 14, 27; May 15, 16; July 5, 23, 25; Sep 19; Oct 6, 29; Nov 2, 27, 28
Wealth of Nations (Smith): Mar 9; June 4, 5
Webster, Daniel: Jan 13
Weckquaesgeek Indians: May 24
Wedgwood, Josiah: July 12
Wedgwood, R.: Oct 7
Wedgwood pottery: Mar 30; July 12
Weill, Sandy: Jan 13; Sep 25
Weinberg, Sidney James: July 23; Oct 12
Welch, Jack: Apr 1; Sep 22; Nov 19, 22; Dec 24, 30
Welles, Orson: Oct 12
Wellington, Duke of: Sep 15
Wells, Henry: May 20; Dec 12
Wells & Co.: May 20
Wells Fargo: May 20; Dec 12
Wenders, Wim: Apr 25
Wendy's restaurants: Nov 15
Wesley, Edward B.: Sep 18
Western Electric: Jan 14; Feb 6, 19; July 9; Aug 6; Sep 7
Western Federation of Miners: June 27
Western Union: Jan 14; Feb 6; Aug 4; Oct 9
Westervelt, Conrad: June 29; Oct 1
Westinghouse company: Feb 16, 19; Aug 6; Sep 5; Oct 17
Westray investment partnership: May 19
WGY radio station: May 11
Wharton, Joseph: Mar 3
Wharton, Samuel: Mar 3
Wharton School of Finance and Commerce: Mar 3
Wheel of Fortune: Nov 10

Wheeler, E. I.: Sep 27
Wheelwright, William: Mar 16
Whieldon, Thomas: July 12
Whinfield, John Rex: Feb 16
White, Edward, Judge: May 15
White, William: June 14
"White knight" investors: Apr 18; Sep 23
White Shadows in the South Seas: July 31
Whitehead, Joseph Brown: Nov 12
Whitman, Meg: Sep 24
Whitney, Eli: Jan 8; Mar 14; Apr 16; Dec 8
Whitney, George: Apr 11
Whitney, Richard: Mar 8; Apr 11
"Whiz Kids" at Ford Motor Company: July 22; Oct 1
Whyte, William: Jan 12
Wickman, Carl Eric: Aug 13
Wile E. Coyote (cartoon character): Sep 17
Wilhelm II, Kaiser: July 8
Wilkins, Roy: Nov 1
Willard and Frick Manufacturing Company: Oct 30
William III, King of England: Jan 22
William Morris Agency: Nov 2
Williams, John H.: June 2
Willys Motors: May 9
Wilson, Arnold: Apr 19
Wilson, Charles Erwin: Jan 15
Wilson, Harold: Mar 18; Nov 17
Wilson, Jackie: Nov 28
Wilson, Joseph C.: Oct 22
Wilson, Kemmons: Jan 5; Aug 1
Wilson, Woodrow: Feb 3; Apr 24; Dec 22
Wilson meat company: Jan 20
Windsong Allegiance Group: Oct 18
Winthrop, John: Aug 23
Winzeler, Henry Simon: Oct 6
Wise, Bonnie: July 28
WNBC radio station: Aug 28
Wobblies. *See* IWW
Wolfert's Roost (Irving): Dec 2
Wolff news agency: Feb 2
Wolfsburg automobile factory: May 26; July 30; Aug 5
"Wonders will never cease," origin of phrase: Sep 13
Women, business psychology and: Sep 2; Nov 25. *See also* Sex discrimination
Wonder Bread: Aug 2
Wood, Kimba, Judge: Nov 21
Woodbury Vineyards Winery: June 5
Woodhull, Claflin & Co.: Jan 20
Woodhull, Victoria Claflin: Jan 20; May 10
Woodhull and Claflin's Weekly: Jan 20
Wood-pulp paper: Dec 26
Woolworth, Frank Winfield (F. W.): Feb 22; Apr 13; June 21; Aug 8
Woolworth, Jennie: Aug 8
Woolworth Building: Apr 13, 24
Woolworth's five-and-dime stores: Feb 22; Apr 13; June 21

Worcester, Dorothy: Nov 8
Work, quotes on: Jan 9, 24; Feb 5, 12;
    Mar 10, 20; Apr 1, 2, 17, 28; May 4, 15,
    24, 25; June 17, 21, 22, 23; July 16, 21;
    Aug 7, 17; Sep 7, 10; Oct 9, 25, 29;
    Dec 3, 4, 19
Worker's compensation, landmark agreements
    and laws: Jan 26; May 14; Nov 22
Workhouse, British: Aug 14
World Bank: July 3; Dec 27
World Trade Center, New York: Sep 11
World War I: Apr 5; July 31. *See also* German
    war reparations
World War II: Feb 29; May 29, 31. *See also*
    Japanese postwar recovery; Rosie the
    Riveter
World Wide Web: Jan 15; June 18; Nov 12
WorldCom: Feb 7; Mar 2; June 25
World-Wide Shipping: Nov 10
WOW! potato chips: Feb 10
Wozniak, Stephen: Aug 11
WPP Group advertising company: June 11
Wright, Orville and Wilbur: Feb 8
Wrigley, William, Jr.: Jan 26; Sep 30
Wrigley's chewing gum: Jan 26; June 26;
    Dec 9
Wriston, Walter B.: Jan 20
Writing paper first created: Mar 11
Wussler, Bob: Apr 18
WWJ radio station: Aug 20

X Prize: Oct 4
Xerox (the company and its products): Feb 8;
    Mar 1; Apr 27; Oct 22

Yahoo!Japan: Mar 27
Yamani, Ahmed Zaki, Sheik: Dec 20
"Yellow dog contracts": Mar 23
"Yellow journalism": Apr 29
Yippies: Aug 24
"You can fool all the people some of the
    time. . ." saying coined: Sep 8
Young, Brigham: Oct 16
Young, John B.: Sep 18
Young, John Orr: Sep 19, 29
Young, Owen: July 11
Young, Robert R.: Jan 25; June 14, 15
Young and Rubicam, Inc.: Jan 6; Feb 14;
    Sep 19, 29
Yue-kong, Pao: Nov 10
Yutang, Lin: Feb 22

ZCMI (Zion's Co-Operative Mercantile
    Institution) department store: Oct 16
Zen: Jan 14, 26
Zeppelin, Ferdinand: July 2, 8
Zeppelin aircraft: Jan 16; July 2, 8
Zilog company: Aug 3
Zukor, Adolph: May 8; Oct 7; Nov 19
Zuylen, Baron de: June 1
Zyman, Sergio: Aug 6